LGBTQ+ Runaway and Homeless Youth

LGBTQ+ Runaway and Homeless Youth

A Guide to Practice, Policy, and Research

Elaine M. Maccio and
Kristin Ferguson

Columbia University Press
New York

Columbia University Press
Publishers Since 1893
New York   Chichester, West Sussex
cup.columbia.edu

Library of Congress Cataloging-in-Publication Data
Cataloging-in-Publication Data available from the Library of Congress.

ISBN 978-0-231-22070-5 (hardback)
ISBN 978-0-231-22071-2 (trade paperback)
ISBN 978-0-231-22072-9 (ebook)

LCCN 2025028045

Printed in the United States of America

Cover design: Julia Kushnirsky
Cover image: Shutterstock

GPSR Authorized Representative: Easy Access System Europe—Mustamäe tee 50,
10621 Tallinn, Estonia, gpsr.requests@easproject.com

For Bill Cohen of Harrington Park Press, whose unwavering commitment to centering marginalized voices through stories that matter inspired so many. Your legacy continues in every page you envisioned, in every voice you elevated, and in the hope you helped create for LGBTQ+ youth experiencing homelessness through a practice-inspired book. Thank you for believing in them—and in this work.

Contents

Part III. Practice, Programs, Policies, and Advocacy

Part IV. The Future

Acknowledgments

To Bill Cohen, publisher and editor-in-chief, Harrington Park Press, for envisioning that our initial toolkit on this topic could better serve youth and the practice and policy communities as a book. Your extensive network of friends and colleagues, whose minds and hearts touched this project, has been an invaluable gift to us.

To Debra Riegert, executive editor-at-large, Harrington Park Press, who spent countless hours with us reviewing sample chapters, processing reviewer feedback, and narrowing our target audience for the book. Your deep understanding of the social work readership resulted in many enhancements to the contents of this book (e.g., case studies, glossaries, websites as resources), making it more relevant to social work education and practice.

To Steven Rigolosi, senior consulting editor, Harrington Park Press, for your wisdom and insights into readers' appreciation for predictability, which helped us draft chapters with a uniform structure and length.

To Barbara Conover, consulting editor, Harrington Park Press, for helping us establish a chapter submission schedule and coordinating the review process for the book. Your careful "look-sees" of our work regularly resulted in helpful feedback that improved our overall product.

To Patrick Ciano of Ciano Design, for your boundless creativity in cover designs for early drafts of our book. The half-dozen images you created were equally impressive in visualizing our topic in a powerful way.

To Samuel B. Robison, associate director of the LSU Social Research & Evaluation Center and associate professor of research, Louisiana State University, for your careful proofreading of our work and detailed instruction on reporting methodology and statistics to our target audience.

To Christian Winting, associate editor, Columbia University Press, for facilitating the review process of our complete manuscript. Your efforts in coordinating the reviews greatly contributed to the refinement of our work.

To Justine Evans, director of rights and contracts, and Julia Brown Simmons, subsidiary rights assistant, Columbia University Press, for your expert guidance and support in managing the legal and logistical aspects of the publication process. Your responsiveness and attention to detail were instrumental to the completion of our work.

To the Columbia University Press design team, for your time and talent in creating several visual representations for the book cover. The symbolism within your designs captured the resilience and hope of the young people at the center of this work.

To Marielle Poss, director of editing, design, and production, Columbia University Press, Kalie Hyatt, senior project manager, books, KnowledgeWorks Global LTD, and Kara Cowan, copyeditor, for shepherding our final manuscript through production and getting us over the finish line.

And to Stephen Wesley, editor, Columbia University Press, for initially championing our work with your editorial team and supporting us step-by-step through the publication process. Your vision for this book will enrich the training of countless helping professionals who will work with LGBTQ+ youth experiencing homelessness in their careers.

Preface

In 2012, Gary Mallon, the founder of the former National Resource Center for Permanency and Family Connections, invited us to create a resource for practitioners working with lesbian, gay, bisexual, transgender, and queer and/or questioning (LGBTQ+) runaway and homeless youth (RHY). *Toolkit for Practitioners/Researchers Working with Lesbian, Gay, Bisexual, Transgender, and Queer/Questioning (LGBTQ) Runaway and Homeless Youth (RHY)* contains information on promising practices, policies and legislation; service gaps and limitations; and directions for future research with this population.[1] The centerpiece of this work was a qualitative study of twenty-four direct practice professionals, program directors, and administrators from nineteen agencies serving LGBTQ+ RHY, wholly or in part, from around the United States. In it we asked participants about their agency's philosophy, policies, outreach, intake and assessment, programs and services (i.e., physical health, mental health, family, legal and mediation, case management, education and employment, and housing), youth voice and leadership, cultural diversity training for staff, and cultural

---

[1]   This text can be accessed via the Child Welfare Information Gateway: https://cwlibrary .childwelfare.gov/discovery/delivery/01CWIG_INST:01CWIG/1218286110007651.

sensitivity training for youth. The idea for this book was based on that toolkit—a comprehensive review of the literature, informed by our experience as practitioners and researchers with LGBTQ+, runaway, homeless, and other historically excluded youth populations.

The purpose of this book is to provide you with information on practice, research, and policy with LGBTQ+ RHY. This is the only textbook of its kind, rich in data from the extant literature and dedicated exclusively to LGBTQ+ RHY, and one of very few books in general available on the subject. It is also a crucial resource, given the overrepresentation of LGBTQ+ youth among the RHY population, and a timely one, with increasing attention finally being paid to transgender and nonbinary-gender individuals, in particular. Likewise, this book is timely given that the number of people who are chronically homeless is on the rise.[2] Its broad-based coverage of sexual orientation and identity, gender identity and expression, youth and adolescence, homelessness and runaway behavior, and the accompanying risks (e.g., health, mental health, and substance use problems; violence and victimization) makes it a valuable teaching tool across disciplines and curriculum topics. This book is suggested as a resource to prepare practitioners, researchers, and policymakers to address the increasing trend of homelessness and the overrepresentation of LGBTQ+ youth in this population.

To enhance your experience, this book is supported by several key elements. Every chapter begins with learning objectives and an introduction. The learning objectives inform you of what you can expect to take away from each chapter and serve as guideposts while reading. An introduction previews the information contained in the chapter. Supplemental features augment content with external resources, reflection questions, and examples. "Read All About It!" refers you to websites, reports, and other publicly available materials where you can learn more about the topic. "What Do You Think?" poses questions that promote critical thinking and deeper understanding. A case vignette, inspired by youths' lived experiences, is weaved throughout the chapter to illustrate common problems that youth

---

[2.] T. de Sousa et al., *The 2024 Annual Homelessness Assessment Report (AHAR) to Congress: Part 1—Point-in-Time Estimates of Homelessness* (U.S. Department of Housing and Urban Development, 2024), https://www.huduser.gov/portal/sites/default/files/pdf/2024-AHAR-Part-1.pdf.

experience and the types of programs, services, and staff that can assist them. Each chapter ends with a summary, case vignette questions, key concepts, and chapter highlights. The summary reinforces each chapter's overall theme, and the case vignette questions aid in the application of concepts and ideas. The key concepts section serves as a glossary of key terms, which appear in bold throughout the chapter. Chapter highlights reinforce the theme of the chapter, focusing on specific ideas that you are expected to grasp after reading. Because of the ever-changing nature of LGBTQ+ terminology, advances, and threats, we include online resources throughout to keep you abreast of current knowledge, resources, and events.

This book comprises eleven chapters spanning four content areas: "Understanding LGBTQ+ RHY," which lays the groundwork for understanding sexuality, gender identity, and RHY; "The Biopsychosocial Contexts of LGBTQ+ Populations," which explores the LGBTQ+ RHY population in depth; "Practice, Programs, Policies, and Advocacy," which looks at the mezzo- and macro-level environments and institutions affecting this population; and "The Future," which provides recommendations for next steps based on our current understanding of the field.

Part I, "Understanding LGBTQ+ RHY," begins with "Understanding Sexuality and Gender Identity" (chapter 1). This chapter introduces LGBTQ+ terminology, recognizing that acceptable and appropriate language used by and to describe this population changes frequently. It also defines underlying concepts, such as sexual orientation and identity and gender identity and expression. Also covered are theoretical frameworks for the disclosure of one's sexuality or gender identity (i.e., coming out) and the stages of sexual development and transgender emergence. Chapter 2, "The Prevalence of Homelessness Among LGBTQ+ RHY," explores the sampling methods, sample sizes, participant ages, recruitment settings, and LGBTQ+ composition of samples used in research to determine the prevalence of homelessness among LGBTQ+ youth within the larger RHY population. We do so by comparing the chronological periods of pre-2010 and 2010 to the present. Chapter 3, "Who Are LGBTQ+ RHY?," identifies the demographic and related characteristics of LGBTQ+ youth research samples since 2010. We offer a picture of LGBTQ+ RHY in terms of gender, gender identity, sexual orientation, sexual identity, age, race and ethnicity, education, physical and mental health, substance use, family income, citizenship status, and employment.

Part II, "The Biopsychosocial Contexts of LGBTQ+ Populations," delves into the lives and experiences of LGBTQ+ RHY. Part II begins with chapter 4, "Physical and Mental Health Concerns," which addresses mental health problems (e.g., depression, post-traumatic stress disorder, anxiety, self-harm, suicide), sexual health (e.g., pregnancy, sexually transmitted infections including HIV), and substance use (e.g., nicotine, alcohol, marijuana/cannabis, opiates). Chapter 5, "Internal and External Risk and Protective Factors," identifies the most common risk factors among LGBTQ+ RHY, such as violence and victimization, mental health problems, substance use, and high-risk sexual behaviors (e.g., having multiple sex partners, unprotected sex, survival sex). It also presents protective factors, including social networks and social support, resilience, coping, adaptation, and inner strength. Chapter 6, "LGBTQ+ RHY and Their Parents and Families," takes a step back from the micro level to look at the experiences of LGBTQ+ RHY with their families of origin and other caregivers, such as foster families and kinship caregivers. The chapter discusses strategies for keeping the youth in the home, exploring out-of-home care options, promoting reunification, and, when in the best interest of the youth, petitioning for the youth's emancipation.

Part III, "Practice, Programs, Policies, and Advocacy," begins with chapter 7, "Direct Practice." The primary themes of the chapter are LGBTQ+-affirming practice and the phases of work with individuals, families, and groups. Barriers to and facilitators of care are also covered, as is conversion therapy, the largely discredited practice of attempting to curb or eliminate an individual's same-sex sexual attraction or change their LGBTQ+ identity. Chapter 8, "Programs and Services," reviews the findings of our National Study of Integrated and Dedicated Services for LGBTQ+ RHY, which provides a detailed examination of services for this population divided by program target: integrated, serving both LGBTQ+ and non-LGBTQ+ youth, and dedicated, serving LGBTQ+ youth separately. Integrated services are discussed with regard to their primary focuses: physical health, mental health and substance use, case management, family, legal and mediation, education and employment, and housing services. Programs are described by their delivery methods, including street outreach, drop-in centers, shelters, and transitional living programs. In chapter 9, "Policies," we examine federal and state policies that either support or hinder LGBTQ+ RHY. Some, such as the federal Runaway and Homeless Youth Act, speak to all RHY, whereas others, such as executive orders prohibiting discrimination in housing and those prohibiting hiring and employment practices based on sexual orientation and gender identity, address sexual orientation and gender identity specifically. State policies are presented with regard to their focus on schools, housing, family services, and child welfare. Chapter 10, "Advocacy," begins with a definition of this term that sets the stage for a discussion of advocacy strategies in areas such as programs and services, intake interviews, assessment interviews, and legislation. The chapter also includes a list of LGBTQ+ RHY advocacy organizations.

Part IV, "The Future," consists of a single chapter, chapter 11, "Recommendations." Drawing from our immersion in the extant literature, our expertise in the fields of LGBTQ+ issues and RHY, and our previous research in these two areas, we identify practice and program needs to be met, propose new directions for future research, and recommend necessary policy changes.

This book is intended to be accessible to a wide audience, appealing to readers embedded in various settings and across various disciplines. Primary among the intended readership is the student learner. Educators in the fields of social work, psychology, sociology, criminal justice, public health, child welfare, and human development and family science, among others, will find this a useful tool for conveying material on youth who are forced or compelled to leave home, experiencing homelessness, LGBTQ+, involved in the juvenile justice or foster care system, and minoritized or who have otherwise historically been excluded. Its expansive coverage of programs and services, policies and legislation, and advocacy provides a backdrop for courses that focus on these areas, and the specific examples it provides may also be useful in general intervention, public health, and policy courses. For use as a textbook, this work may be most appropriate for upper-level undergraduate and graduate courses that focus on historically excluded youth populations, child and adolescent psychology and development, children and families, counseling and psychotherapy, criminology, education and schools, youthful offenders, LGBTQ+ people, people experiencing homelessness, people with mental health problems, and people with substance use or other behavioral health problems. Secondarily, practitioners such as social workers, counselors, psychologists, and others who work with children and youth, LGBTQ+ people, or people experiencing homelessness will also find this text helpful given its extensive review of best practices and promising programs currently in use. It also provides insight into general behavior patterns, risk and protective factors, and family dynamics that apply across various vulnerable populations. Practitioners will also find LGBTQ+-affirming and culturally competent practice guidelines and resource lists helpful in their work with LGBTQ+ youth.

Understanding LGBTQ+ RHY

1 | Understanding Sexuality and Gender Identity

LEARNING OBJECTIVES

Readers of this chapter will be able to:

1. Define sexual orientation and identity and gender identity and expression,
2. Identify various sexual and gender identities, and
3. Recognize stages of sexual identity development and transgender emergence.

CASE VIGNETTE: BRITTANY

As a young white, cisgender woman aged twenty, Brittany is quick to share her enthusiasm for her upcoming birthday. Turning twenty-one will define her—for herself as much as for everyone around her—as an adult. This distinction is important to her given the lack of clarity she has in other areas of her life, such as college major, career choice, boyfriends, and, perhaps most stressful of all, how she will live independently and support herself if her foster parents force her out of the home once their obligation to care for her ends after her twenty-first birthday. Amid all this, Brittany is struggling with her sexuality.

While her friends have already settled on their sexual identities, Brittany is filled with uncertainty about how she wants to—or whether she even has to—define herself to others.

INTRODUCTION

Before we can delve into the topic of lesbian, gay, bisexual, transgender, and queer and/or questioning (LGBTQ+) runaway and homeless youth (RHY), we must first define and conceptualize the central characteristics of the subpopulation we are discussing: sexuality (i.e., sexual orientation and identity) and gender, especially gender identity and expression. What does "LGBTQ+" mean? What are sexual orientation and gender identity? What does it mean to come out as LGBTQ+, and how does that happen? In this chapter, we explore current understandings of the terminology used and processes referred to throughout this book, in practice, and in contemporary society. We remind you, however, that as with any culture, language and definitions can change quickly and frequently, and what is acceptable now may be unacceptable, or downright offensive, five years, two years, or even just six months from now. At the end of the chapter, we provide online resources to keep you updated on meanings and terminology.

A NOTE ABOUT LANGUAGE

Homosexuality was removed from the *Diagnostic and Statistical Manual of Mental Disorders* (*DSM*), the reference manual of psychiatric disorders and conditions, in 1973 by the American Psychiatric Association (APA) (Bayer 1987). As a result of its historical association with pathology (Gonsiorek et al. 1995), the term *homosexual* has fallen out of favor and has been replaced by more affirming terms that will be explained in this chapter. Thus, throughout this book, the term *homosexual* has been replaced by *lesbian* or *gay*. The term *homosexuality*, however, is still typically used to refer to same-sex sexual orientation. Other omitted terms are *sexual preference*, which suggests that sexual orientation is a choice, and *lifestyle*, which reduces LGBTQ+ identity to a way of life and implies that the lives of LGBTQ+ people are somehow qualitatively different from those of heterosexual and cisgender individuals (Gonsiorek et al. 1995). These and other terms are covered in greater detail by GLAAD (formerly the Gay and Lesbian Alliance Against Defamation) (2022a, 2022b) and the American Psychological Association (2022a, 2022b).

Terms that will be covered include *sexual orientation and identity*, *gender identity and expression*, and specific LGBTQ+ identities, some of which are illustrated in table 1.1. The table is intended to provide a visual

TABLE 1.1 Sexual orientation, sexual identity, and gender identity

Sex at birth was . . .	Gender is . . .	Sexually oriented toward . . .	Gender identity and sexual identity
Male	Male	Women	Cisgender heterosexual man
		Men	Cisgender gay man
		Two genders	Cisgender bisexual man
		Any gender and gender identity	Cisgender pansexual man
		No genders	Cisgender asexual/neutrois man
	Female	Women	Transgender lesbian
		Men	Transgender heterosexual woman
		Two genders	Transgender bisexual woman
		Any gender and gender identity	Transgender pansexual woman
		No genders	Transgender asexual/neutrois woman
	Nonbinary	One or more genders, no genders, or any gender identity	Nonbinary person with self-defined sexual identity
Female	Female	Men	Cisgender heterosexual woman
		Women	Cisgender lesbian
		Two genders	Cisgender bisexual woman
		Any gender and gender identity	Cisgender pansexual woman
		No genders	Cisgender asexual/neutrois woman
	Male	Men	Transgender gay man
		Women	Transgender heterosexual man
		Two genders	Transgender bisexual man
		Any gender and gender identity	Transgender pansexual man
		No genders	Transgender asexual/neutrois man
	Nonbinary	One or more genders, no genders, or any gender identity	Nonbinary person with self-defined sexual identity

conceptualization of these terms; however, doing so may inadvertently convey an oversimplification of sexual and gender identities. It is important to keep in mind that sexuality and gender are complex phenomena with virtually innumerable variations and identities (only a fraction of which are represented in the table) that, at their intersection, produce even more nuanced possibilities.

ORIENTATION, IDENTITY, AND EXPRESSION

The essence of sexuality and gender can be explained by orientation, identity, and expression. Typically, *orientation* refers to sexuality, *expression* to gender, and *identity* to both sexuality and gender. As with its general usage, *orientation* denotes direction and suggests an inherent characteristic over which one has little control, much like a personality trait. *Identity*, on the other hand, is simply a label one adopts to represent oneself to others. Often, one's sexual orientation and identity, for example, are congruent, meaning the individual's identity matches their orientation. That is, a woman who recognizes her sexual orientation as same-sex oriented will likely identify (privately if not also publicly) as lesbian. *Expression*, as one might assume, is the way one presents oneself to others with regard to, for example, appearance and mannerisms. Gender expression, in this case, refers to how one presents oneself as masculine or feminine, neither, or somewhere in between. We further elaborate these terms throughout the chapter.

SEXUAL ORIENTATION AND IDENTITY

Sexual orientation has been defined as sexual attractions or fantasies and behaviors (Gonsiorek et al. 1995) and sexual thoughts, fantasies, feelings, attractions, and behaviors (Gordon and Silva 2015). Combining these definitions, we simplify sexual orientation here as one's sexual thoughts (i.e., fantasies), feelings (i.e., attractions), and behaviors, which can be directed toward members of the same sex (**homosexuality**), the opposite sex (**heterosexuality**), or both sexes (**bisexuality**). More recently, new terms have entered the lexicon that further delineate one's experience of sexuality. Some individuals may have orientations directed toward others regardless of their sex or gender identity (**pansexual**), whereas others have no sexual orientation at all (**asexual** or **neutrois**) or find themselves attracted to others only after they have formed a close bond (**demisexual**). These terms may be more easily understood as existing on continuums of sexuality and asexuality. The sexuality continuum (regarding the direction of one's sexual orientation), introduced by Alfred Kinsey, a biologist who later in his career became known for his research on sexuality (Brown and Fee 2003), and his colleagues, has at one end *exclusive heterosexuality* (0 on the scale) and at the other end *exclusive homosexuality* (6 on the scale), with bisexuality in between to varying degrees (Kinsey et al. 1948). This continuum regards sexual orientation as dichotomous: one is oriented toward males and/or females only. An inclusive continuum might be anchored by unisexuality at one end and pansexuality at the other, with bisexuality in between. (It must be noted, however, that *pansexuality* speaks to attraction to any gender identity as much as it does any gender.) More recent is the asexuality continuum, based loosely on the work of Storms (1980) and Yule et al. (2015), which has asexuality at one end and sexuality on the other. Whereas the sexuality continuum measures the direction of sexuality, the asexuality continuum measures the presence or absence of sexuality itself. On this scale, demisexuality could be considered to exist between the two poles.

The etiology of sexual orientation as a product of biology (i.e., nature or essentialism) or environment (i.e., nurture or social constructionism) is not clear, but research suggests that it may be some combination of the two (i.e., interactionism). In 1991, Bailey and Pillard published one of the most well-known studies on the biology of sexual orientation. Among their sample of pairs of brothers in which one brother was gay, the researchers found that the other brother was gay 52 percent of the time among identical twins, 22 percent among fraternal twins (who are no more alike than any other set of genetic brothers), 11 percent among adopted brothers, and only 9.2 percent among nontwin biological brothers. This research highlights the biological component of sexual orientation. However, equally important is the remaining 48 percent of gay men whose twin brothers were not gay, suggesting that factors other than biology are also at work. That is, if sexual orientation were purely biological, then 100 percent of identical twin pairs would both have been gay given that their DNA is identical. Thus, 48 percent of the variance is explained by nonbiological (e.g., environmental) factors. In another study of twin brothers, Kirk et al. (2000) found statistically significant differences between concordance rates of identical twins and fraternal twins on attractions to and sexual behavior with other men (although not on self-identified sexual orientation). The authors point to their data that show genetic rather than environmental influences at work.

Whereas sexual orientation is the innate experience of sexual thoughts, feelings, and behaviors, *sexual identity* is a label one uses to identify oneself to others (Gordon and Silva 2015; Parks et al. 2009). In some cases, the terms for sexual orientation and for sexual identity are one and the same (Moser 2016). For example, some individuals who recognize their orientation to be heterosexual, homosexual, or bisexual may use those terms to identify themselves. People whose sexual orientation is heterosexual typically identify themselves as heterosexual or straight, and those whose orientation is bisexual typically identify as bisexual. However, given the negative connotation that the term *homosexual* has, an artifact of its twenty-one-year classification as a mental disorder in the *DSM*, many same-sex-oriented people have chosen labels that affirm their identity. Same-sex-oriented men typically prefer the term *gay*, while women may choose *lesbian* or *gay*. Some individuals eschew these traditional terms, which they may see as pigeonholing identities that are actually very complex. Instead, *queer*, for example, has been reclaimed by LGBTQ+ people from its use as an epithet to become an empowering term of identification (Rand 2004). Identifying as queer also reflects a rejection of the discrete—and more traditional—labels of lesbian, gay, and bisexual and what some perceive as **homonormativity**, or the privileging of LGB people who idealize and adhere to **heteronormative** standards. According to Duggan (2003), homonormativity "is a politics that does not contest dominant heteronormative assumptions and institutions, but upholds and sustains them, while promising the possibility of a demobilized gay constituency and a privatized, depoliticized gay culture anchored in domesticity and consumption" (179). Transgender and **nonbinary** people may also identify as queer; indeed, *queer* is an intentionally nebulous term. As Eve Kosofsky Sedgwick has written, "That's one of the things that 'queer' can refer to: the open mesh of possibilities, gaps, overlaps, dissonances and resonances, lapses and excesses of meaning when the constituent elements of anyone's gender, of anyone's sexuality aren't made (or *can't* be made) to signify monolithically" (1993, 8, emphasis in original). Adopting *queer* as a gender identity will be covered more in the next section. The "Q" in "LGBTQ+" can also mean *questioning*, acknowledging that some who are early in their sexual or gender identity development may not have yet determined their identity as LGBT.

GENDER IDENTITY AND EXPRESSION

Unlike sex, which is defined by one's internal and external genitalia and reproductive organs, gender is instead one's internal experience of being male or female (Hoffman 2001). As our understanding of gender has expanded, we also recognize the possibilities of being both male and female, neither, or something else entirely. Gender is typically assigned at birth based on the infant's sex. Most often, one's sex and gender are congruent; that is, one's gender aligns with their sex and thus the gender they were assigned at birth. In some cases, an individual's gender does not match their sex or the gender they were assigned at birth, such that sex and gender are crossed—the *trans* in *transgender*. **Gender identity**, then, is how one identifies themself to others, whether **cisgender** (sex–gender congruent), transgender, or nonbinary gender (Tate et al. 2013).

Transgender used to be, and for some still is, an umbrella term that refers to several variations of binary, and sometimes nonbinary, genders (Chang et al. 2017). Historically, *transgender* included transvestism and cross-dressing (i.e., wearing clothes typical of another gender for sexual gratification or nonsexual fulfillment), drag performing (i.e., wearing clothes typical of another gender for entertainment purposes), androgyny (i.e., appearing both male and female), and transsexualism (i.e., the experience of incongruence between one's gender and sex and the gender they were assigned at birth). Since identity is a form of self-labeling, which is further subject to the individual's interpretation of that label, not all individuals who find themselves described in the list given earlier would adopt the term *transgender*. Indeed, that conceptualization of *transgender* is no longer used. Moreover, the term *transgender* has replaced the older term *transsexual* (GLAAD 2022b), such that *transgender* now most often refers to individuals experiencing incongruence between their gender and the gender they were assigned at birth. *Transgender* itself is evolving into the more informal, less medicalized *trans*. However, cisgender practitioners, researchers, and others are encouraged to default to the more formal *transgender* in oral and written communication and with transgender clients until invited by the transgender individual to do otherwise (Austin and Papciak 2022).

Unlike homosexuality, identifying as transgender is still found in the latest edition of the *DSM*, the *DSM-5-TR* (APA 2022) as gender dysphoria (formerly gender identity disorder). However, not all transgender individuals experience gender dysphoria (Davy 2015), especially if they are able to live as the gender with which they identify, a **gender-affirming**, transformative process referred to as **_transitioning_**. As the name implies, gender dysphoria is primarily characterized by distress stemming from the incongruence between one's gender and the gender they were assigned at birth. This dysphoria is experienced most often in the early stages of transgender emergence (discussed later in the chapter).

Up to this point, we have conceptualized gender as dichotomous: male and female. However, we can also view gender, like sexuality, on a continuum or at least occupying more than the two categories of male and female. Defining heterosexuality as sexual thoughts, feelings, and behaviors directed toward the *opposite* sex, suggesting there are only two genders, invisibilizes genders outside the male–female binary.

Individuals who identify as **genderqueer** might position themselves as somewhere between male and female, a location defined as both male and female to varying degrees. It may also be that a genderqueer individual's gender, and the intensity of that gender, change over time. Thus, *genderqueer* refers to the fluidity of gender (Factor and Rothblum 2008). Much like those who identify as queer as a rejection of the more traditional labels of lesbian, gay, and bisexual, individuals who identify as genderqueer may do so as a rejection of the male–female gender binary and the cisgender-transgender identity binary. Others may adopt a queer identity in reference to their gender identity. In this sense, *queer* can refer to someone's sexual orientation, gender identity, or both. Still others may embody two (**bigender**) or more genders (**pangender**) or possess no gender at all (**agender**).

Disorders of sex development (DSDs) describe a number of conditions involving the presence, absence, ambiguity, or malformation of genital, reproductive, and sex physiology. According to Blackless et al. (2000), DSDs, broadly speaking (i.e., including "chromosomal, genital, gonadal, or hormonal" presentations [161]), occur in approximately seventeen out of every 1,000 live births. The authors estimate that between 1 percent and 16 percent of the general population undergoes surgery for DSDs (Blackless et al. 2000). The most common conditions are late-onset congenital adrenal hyperplasia (15/1,000 live births), hypospadias (1.9/1,000), and Klinefelter syndrome (0.9/1,000) (Blackless et al. 2000). However, the validity of these figures depends on how DSDs are defined. According to Sax (2002), DSDs are "those conditions in which chromosomal sex is inconsistent with phenotypic sex, or in which the phenotype is not classifiable as either male or female" (177). In that case, DSDs are present in fewer than 2 out of every 10,000 live births, the most common conditions being congenital adrenal hyperplasia and complete androgen insensitivity syndrome (Sax 2002). Some people with DSDs, having been marginalized on the basis of their atypical sex or gender presentations, find themselves aligning with the LGBTQ+ community.

Gender expression is the way that one demonstrates their sense of being male or female, regardless of (although typically aligning with) one's sex as male or female, respectively. Gender expression can also be conceptualized on a continuum of masculine to feminine. It is important to note, however, that masculinity and femininity do not necessarily align with one's gender or even one's gender identity. Some individuals who are male both in sex and gender may express some degree of what most would consider femininity, while some who are female may likewise express masculinity (Reddy-Best and Pedersen 2015).

Expressions of gender are typically external manifestations and can be intentional, such as the choice of hairstyle or clothing and the use of cosmetics (or not), or subconscious, such as mannerisms, for example, expressiveness and gait. Also intentional is one's choice of pronouns, whether female (she, her, hers, herself), male (he, him, his, himself), or gender inclusive (they, them, their, themself, themselves). This refers to one's pro-nouns of reference, or the pronouns one identifies with and uses to refer to themself. While many cisgender and transgender people are likely to use singular, binary pronouns, others, including genderqueer and gender-non-binary individuals, might be more inclined to use gender-inclusive plural pronouns. Still others might welcome singular and plural pronouns. Vari-ations of gender-inclusive pronouns exist, such as the **neopronouns** ze/zie /zim/zir/zis/zieself and xe/xem/xyr/xyrs/xemself (HRC n.d.). Some youth eschew pronouns altogether, instead choosing to be referred to only by their name. According to the Advocates for Trans Equality (A4TE n.d.b), "If you're not sure what pronouns someone uses, ask" ("How to Be Respect-ful"). Although doing so "may feel awkward at first, [it is] one of the simplest and most important ways to show respect for someone's identity" ("How to Be Respectful"). GLAAD (2021) also suggests offering one's own pronouns first. For example, one might say, "Hi, I'm Jade. I use 'they'/'them'/'their' pronouns. What pronouns do you use?" Sometimes, even the most well-intentioned person will inadvertently **misgender** someone. GLAAD advises, "If you accidentally use the wrong pronoun, apologize quickly and sincerely, then move on. The bigger deal you make out of the situation, the more uncomfortable it is for everyone" (2021). (See box 1.1, *What Do You Think?*) What should be unequivocally avoided is intentional misgendering by knowingly referring to an individual with names or pronouns they do not use or as a gender with which they do not identify. **Deadnaming** is the intentional or unintentional use of a name that a transgender or nonbinary person no longer uses, such as their birth name. Intentional misgendering and deadnaming is considered highly offensive by many, if not most, trans-gender and nonbinary individuals and their allies.

LGBTQ+ PEOPLE

"LGBTQ" is an initialism created in the early 1990s as a more inclusive term to encompass the diverse groups represented in the community and to replace the more general terms *gay* and *gay and lesbian* (Brown 2016). A great discrepancy continues to exist among the many variations in the initials used to reflect different sexual orientations and gender identities.

BOX 1.1. WHAT DO YOU THINK?
SEXUAL AND GENDER IDENTITIES

- Which terms for sexual orientation and identity and for gender identity and expression had you heard before reading this chapter? Which terms are new for you?
- What other terms have you heard that have not yet been mentioned here? What do those terms mean?
- Anzaldúa (2009) asserted that *queer* as an umbrella term "homogenizes, [and] erases our differences" (164), especially for queer people of color. What did she mean by that? Do you agree or disagree?
- In a qualitative study of transgender inclusion and exclusion, Davidson (2007) interviewed leaders of two intersex advocacy groups who contested the inclusion of intersex people in the transgender movement by transgender organizations. What might be some of the advantages and disadvantages of subsuming intersex people under the transgender umbrella?
- What are some ways, other than those discussed here, that you could broach the subject of personal pronouns, either yours or someone else's?

Perhaps the most often used is "LGBTQ," yet new variations continually emerge. With their numerous letters (and in some cases numbers or symbols), these initialisms have been referred to as the "alphabet soup" of sexual and gender identities (Brown 2016). Newer variants include some combination of the letters in "LGBTQIP2SAA," to represent not only LGBTQ people but also those who identify as intersex ("I"), pansexual ("P"), Two-Spirit ("2S" or "2-S," a term adopted by some North American Indigenous individuals and communities [Estrada 2011]), and asexual ("A"), as well as **allies** ("A," a term for heterosexual and cisgender supporters of LGBTQ people). (See box 1.2, *Read All About It!*) A second "Q" is sometimes added (e.g., "LGBTQQ") to make queer *and* questioning both visible. More recently, "LGBTQ+" has come to stand for all identities under the umbrella of sexual and gender minority. As new identities emerge and as those who adopt them desire greater visibility and inclusion, it is certain that new variations of the initialism will be added to the mix.

BOX 1.2. READ ALL ABOUT IT! RESOURCES FOR ALLIES

- A number of resources are available to those wishing to be heterosexual or cisgender allies to LGBTQ+ people. Here is a partial list of materials available online:

  - *Being an LGBTQ+ Ally* (HRCF 2022): https://reports.hrc.org/being-an-lgbtq-ally
  - *Guide to Being an Ally to Trans and Nonbinary People* (PFLAG 2024): https://pflag.org/wp-content/uploads/2016/04/S4E-Trans-Ally-Guide-FINAL.pdf
  - *Guide to Being an Ally to LGBTQ+ People* (PFLAG 2025): https://pflag.org/wp-content/uploads/2025/06/S4E-LGBTQ-Ally-Guide-FY25.pdf
  - "Solidarity Week" (GLSEN n.d.): https://www.glsen.org/programs/solidarity-week
  - "Supporting Transgender People" (A4TE n.d.a): https://transequality.org/trans-101/supporting-transgender-people

---

Together, LGBTQ+ people represent the sexual and gender minorities. Despite the fact that the groups represent distinct concepts—sexual orientation and gender identity—what unites them is their position on the margins of sexuality and gender. It is important to point out that LGBTQ+ people have both a sexual orientation and a gender identity. A same-sex sexual orientation and a transgender gender identity are not mutually exclusive—not all LGB people are cisgender (some are transgender), and not all transgender and genderqueer people are heterosexual (some are LGB). Perhaps this most of all highlights the complexity of sexuality and gender.

COMING OUT

Brittany would love nothing more than to finally be comfortable with a sexual identity label—at this point, any one of them. But there doesn't seem to be one that fits her, at least not that she's comfortable with. She's only ever had boyfriends, but she has recognized attractions to at least two or three young women over the past few years. "Does that mean I'm bisexual? Is it possible I'm straight and just find other women attractive? Isn't that normal?" At this point, she has no desire to pursue a romantic relationship with another woman, but she has an acquaintance, a young woman who has also only ever had boyfriends but who identifies as bisexual. Brittany has yet to confide in her close friends for fear that they won't understand and will distance themselves from her. She certainly can't see herself telling her foster parents, lest they hasten her departure from the home if her disclosure to them isn't received well.

The process of disclosing one's sexual orientation or gender identity to another person is referred to as **coming out**, a shortened version of the metaphor "coming out of the closet." Likewise, to be "closeted" is to keep one's nonheterosexual or noncisgender identity private by not disclosing it. Some who choose not to disclose may attempt to "pass," that is, live by society's sexual and gender norms so as not to betray their true sexual or gender identity. However, before the step of disclosure is the recognition of oneself as LGBTQ+. With regard to sexuality, the first acknowledgment of same-sex feelings occurs at an average age of 11.3 years, followed by the first self-identification as LGB (16.2 years) and first same-sex intimate relationship (18.4 years) (Martos et al. 2015). Gay men recognize their same-sex feelings earlier than lesbians, who recognize them earlier than bisexuals. Most gay men (78 percent) reported being aware of their feelings before the age of 14 years, compared with lesbians (53 percent) and bisexual women (53 percent) and men (39 percent) (Minkin et al. 2025). With regard to racial and ethnic differences, Latinx individuals had an earlier self-awareness, at age 11 years, compared with white people (11.3 years) and Blacks/African Americans (11.7 years) (Martos et al. 2015). With regard to gender identity, on average, transgender girls recognized themselves as transgender at 13.4 years of age and disclosed their identity for the first time at 14.2 years of age (Grossman et al. 2006). Transgender boys came out later, both to themselves, at age 15.2 years, and to others, at age 17 years (Grossman et al. 2005).

LGB youth are coming out earlier than the cohorts that preceded them (Grov et al. 2006). For example, a 2025 Pew Research Center survey found that those aged 50 years and older came out at a median age of 21 years, those aged

30 to 49 years came out at 20 years of age, and those aged 18 to 29 years came out at 17 years of age (Minkin et al. 2025). With regard to race and ethnicity, whites came out at an average age of 19.2 years, compared with Latinx people (19.8 years) and Blacks/African Americans (20.1 years) (Martos et al. 2015). First intimate relationships were delayed among older versus younger cohorts, as well, with those between the ages of 45 and 59 years reporting a first experience at an average age of 21.2 years, followed by those aged 30 to 44 years at an average age of 19.5 years and those aged 18 to 29 years at an average age of 16.6 years (Martos et al. 2015). (See box 1.3, *Read All About It!*)

Individuals disclose to others whom they trust or with whom they are close, typically LGB peers first, followed by heterosexual peers, and then family (Martos et al. 2015). Despite the lack of consensus on whether mothers (Savin-Williams 2001) or siblings, specifically sisters, (Toomey and Richardson 2009) are told first, one area of agreement is that fathers are usually told last. LGBTQ+ people are sometimes "outed" against their will, such as when others accidentally or intentionally disclose an LGBTQ+ person's sexual orientation or gender identity to unsuspecting others. Risk of disclosure may be situationally widespread, such as when LGBTQ+ people were discharged from the military under the former "Don't Ask, Don't Tell, Don't Pursue" policy barring openly LGBTQ+ individuals from military service, as well as in the early years of the HIV/AIDS pandemic, when gay

---

BOX 1.3. READ ALL ABOUT IT!
THE 2025 PEW RESEARCH CENTER REPORT

- The Pew Research Center data cited here appear in the 2025 report *The Experiences of LGBTQ Americans Today*. The report follows similar Pew studies in 2013 and 2022 of LGBTQ+ people. To read the report and learn more about their earlier work, visit https://www.pewresearch.org/social-trends/2025/05/29/the-experiences-of-lgbtq-americans-today/.

men tested positive for a virus known at the time to have been transmitted only through sex between men.

Coming out can be met with negative responses including abandonment and violence. Approximately 39 to 51 percent of LGBTQ+ youth are kicked out of their homes because of negative reactions to and attitudes toward their sexual orientation or gender identity (Berberet 2006; Rosario et al. 2012b). Another 58.7 percent of LGB youth (Whitbeck et al. 2004) and 27.3 percent of trans youth (Grossman et al. 2005) are physically victimized. In 2019, 1,637 LGBTQ+ people (53.9 percent of them gay men and 13.9 percent transgender or gender nonbinary) were victimized based on their sexual orientation or gender identity (FBI 2020). If the victimization is determined to be a hate crime, perpetrators can be tried under the 2009 Matthew Shepard and James Byrd Jr. Hate Crimes Prevention Act. However, anti-LGBTQ+ crimes may be underreported or determined not to be a hate crime (Marzullo and Libman 2009).

IDENTITY DEVELOPMENT

Brittany wonders whether finally having a relationship with another woman will signify that she is no longer heterosexual and whether her current feelings represent merely a "phase" of identifying as lesbian. She can't imagine never having a boyfriend again, though. There's a young gay man she sometimes sees at parties and other gatherings with friends, and she is thinking about working up the courage to speak with him privately about her feelings. She sees this as a big step because it will be the first time has shared these thoughts aloud, which makes it feel real to her and no longer incidental.

The emergence of a nonheterosexual or noncisgender identity often follows a typical pattern of development that can be conceptualized as occurring in stages. Researchers continue to develop new and refine existing identity development models to reflect nuance and new understandings of sexuality and gender, but classic models have endured over time. We present the three most common models for lesbian/gay, bisexual, and transgender identity development next.

Lesbian and Gay Identity Development

Perhaps the most oft-cited model of lesbian and gay identity development is that of Vivienne Cass. According to Cass (1979), sexual identity development is represented by six stages ranging from first awareness to integration. The first stage, *identity confusion*, is an individual's first inkling that they may not be heterosexual, which results in confusion. Identity confusion is followed by *identity comparison* in which the individual compares themself to LGB people in search of factors that confirm or deny their suspicion. Next is *identity tolerance*, which signals the individual's attempt to minimize isolation by seeking out other LGB people. Stage 4, *identity acceptance*, marks the individual's first disclosure to others, typically LGBTQ+ people first, followed by heterosexual family and friends. Stage 5, *identity pride*, is characterized by intense positive feelings for the LGBTQ+ community and other LGB people and negative feelings for heterosexual people. Finally, stage 6, *identity synthesis*, involves the integration of the individual's sexual orientation into the whole of their identity. Like many developmental processes, sexual identity development is not necessarily linear, with some individuals returning to earlier stages or skipping stages altogether. Other sexual identity development models exist, many of which resemble Cass's model.

Bisexual Identity Development

The disproportionate attention paid to lesbian and gay identities over the years has rendered other sexual and gender identities, including bisexuality, invisible (Davila et al. 2019; Monro et al. 2017). Despite this erasure, bisexual identity is a distinctly different experience from lesbian and gay identities. In our dichotomized world of heterosexuality versus homosexuality, realizing that one has a sexual identity that is neither can be a challenge, especially when it means incurring hostility from both ends of the continuum (Weinberg et al. 1994). In their seminal work involving in-depth interviews in 1983 and 1988 of 139 people using a San Francisco nonprofit center for bisexual individuals, Weinberg et al. (1994) set out to categorize these unique developmental experiences.

The first stage of bisexual identity development is *initial confusion*. This can refer to the unexpected realization of an attraction to both men and women or not knowing that an alternative to heterosexual and homosexual identities exists, among other dilemmas. *Finding and applying the label* is stage 2 and begins, for example, when a turning point (e.g., engaging in sex with someone of a gender with which they had not done previously) or encouragement (e.g., from a friend or intimate partner) leads the individual to acknowledge a bisexual identity. The third stage, *settling into the identity*, is characterized by a relative comfort with labeling oneself as bisexual and being committed more to their own identity than to the gender of their intimate partners. That is, whereas the gender of their partners may change over time, their bisexual identity does not. Despite the fact that some bisexuals feel at ease in this stage, Weinberg et al. (1994) felt compelled to add a fourth stage that appears to belie the previous one. *Continued uncertainty* describes the confusion and doubt that the researchers perceived among some participants with regard to the legitimacy or stability of their bisexual identity. However, this may have as much or more to do with external rather than internal factors. In addition to a lack of bisexual role models, the researchers speculated, "The social reaction [bisexual] people received made it difficult to sustain the identity over the long haul" (Weinberg et al. 1994, 35). For others, doubt stemmed from an imbalance of feelings toward or relationships with one gender or another. For example, bisexual men's long-term relationships with or stronger attractions toward women led them to question whether they might actually be heterosexual. Regardless, a final stage that implied indefinite uncertainty and doubt failed to capture the actual experiences of many bisexual people.

The researchers revisited this apparent lack of closure with a follow-up study in 1996 involving fifty-six individuals from the original samples (Weinberg et al. 2001). They found that all those years later, many participants had, in fact, realized certainty and closure. However, the researchers did not suggest changing the name of the fourth stage or adding a fifth one. Tom Brown (2002) relabeled Weinberg et al.'s (1994) fourth stage *identity maintenance*, although there are several other possibilities for conceptualizing these later stages: continued uncertainty and identity maintenance may be two paths that an individual could take following the third stage, settling into the identity; continued uncertainty may be part of the third stage or part of a new fourth stage, identity maintenance; or continued uncertainty may simply represent a reversion back to stage 1, initial confusion. The history of the bisexual identity development model illustrates the continuing evolution of our understanding of human sexuality.

Transgender Emergence

Transgender emergence speaks to the developmental process associated with gender identity. Models of transgender emergence do for transgender identity what models of sexual identity development do for sexual identity (Lev 2004). They consist of stages that an individual passes through on the way to identifying as transgender. Lev (2004) posited a six-stage model of transgender emergence as a twenty-first-century update of previous models. The first stage is *awareness*, when transgender individuals first realize that they are different from others and experience distress as a result of the disconnect between their gender and their sex. Next is *seeking information/reaching out*, which refers to learning more about gender identity and connecting with others like themselves. *Disclosure to significant others*, stage 3, involves coming out to their family of origin (e.g., parents, siblings, extended family), family of procreation (e.g., partners, spouses, children), and family of choice (e.g., close friends). Stage 4, *exploration: identity and self-labeling*, is the time during which transgender people determine the identity that fits them best and begin living openly, for example, by wearing clothing and accessories typical of another gender. Following this stage is *exploration: transition issues/possible body modification*, when transgender individuals consider whether and when transitioning to their identified gender would be right for them. Gender-affirming care (i.e., health care that assists individuals in their gender transition) can range from least invasive (e.g., little to no body modification, such as a change in name, attire, or hairstyle) to most invasive (e.g., partial or full gender-affirming surgery) (WPATH 2016). In between are treatments such as hormone therapy, which induces the secondary sex characteristics of the identified gender. Finally, in stage 6, transgender people reach *integration: acceptance and post-transition issues.* At this point, individuals have integrated their transgender identity as just one part of the self. They may choose to stay connected to the transgender community or not to identify as transgender at all, living and identifying as simply a man or a woman (Lev 2004). (See box 1.4, *What Do You Think?*)

Table 1.2 illustrates patterns of identity development for lesbian/gay, bisexual, and transgender people. Although the stages do not completely align across identities, a side-by-side comparison highlights similarities between the models. These models can be useful for educating and training practitioners and other supports, such as family and friends, to assist with and bear witness to the coming-out process of LGBTQ+ individuals. Remember that these models speak to general experiences and do not account for variations among subpopulations, including LGBTQ+ people

TABLE 1.2 Stages of sexual identity development and transgender emergence

Stage	Lesbian and gay identity development (Cass 1979)	Bisexual identity development (Brown 2002; Weinberg et al. 1994)	Transgender emergence (Lev 2004)
First awareness	Identity confusion	Initial confusion	Awareness
Alienation	Identity comparison		Seeking information, reaching out
Reaching out	Identity tolerance	Finding and applying the label	
Labeling			
Disclosing	Identity acceptance	Settling into the identity	Disclosure to significant others
Articulation			Exploration: identity and self-labeling
Commitment	Identity pride	Continued uncertainty	Exploration: transition issues, possible body modification
Integration	Identity synthesis	Identity maintenance	Integration: acceptance and post-transition issues

---

BOX 1.4. WHAT DO YOU THINK?
LGBTQ+ IDENTITY DEVELOPMENT

- What are possible developmental processes for heterosexual identity, asexual identity, cisgender identity, and agender identity?
- According to a survey by the Pew Research Center (Minkin et al. 2025), gay men realize their same-sex feelings earliest, followed by lesbians, bisexual women, and bisexual men. What might account for those differences?
- Martos et al. (2015) reported that whites come out younger (19.2 years) than Latinx people (19.8 years) and Blacks/African Americans (20.1 years). What might explain that?
- Table 1.2 describes the similarities of lesbian/gay, bisexual, and transgender identity development. How are they different? What sets bisexual identity development apart from lesbian/gay identity development? What differentiates the stages of transgender emergence from those of lesbian/gay and bisexual identity development?

---

of color, LGBTQ+ immigrants, LGBTQ+ people with disabilities, and LGBTQ+ people living in rural areas, among other intersectionalities.

SUMMARY

Lesbian, gay, and bisexual are *sexual* identities that reflect one's sexual orientation, whereas transgender is a *gender* identity that reflects an inner experience of gender that does not align with the gender one was assigned at birth. Other sexual and gender identities, such as queer, pansexual, asexual, demisexual, agender, and genderqueer, to name just a few, speak to the many ways of being with regard to sexuality and gender. The developmental pathways that individuals take on the way to adopting an LGBTQ+ identity, usually culminating in coming out, are as varied as the identities themselves, although developmental models do share much in common. As people come to better understand the nuances of sexuality and gender, new terms and developmental theories may be added, and existing ones may fall away. What is important is that each individual is allowed to define, and be accepted as, their own identity.

REVISITING BRITTANY

- If you were to apply the model of bisexual identity development to Brittany, which stage would you say she is in? Why?
- What evidence would demonstrate that she has moved to the next stage?
- Let us imagine that Brittany goes on to adopt a bisexual identity one year from now, shortly before she enters her first same-sex relationship and two years before she comes out to her family. How do her developmental milestones (e.g., first recognition of same-sex feelings, first self-labeling, first disclosure, and first same-sex relationship) compare with those reported by Martos et al. (2015) and the Pew Research Center (Minkin et al. 2025)?
- What might be some of the pros and cons of disclosing Brittany's bisexual identity to her foster parents now? How might those pros and cons change if she were to come out two years from now?
- Describe some ways that you could be an ally to Brittany in her coming-out process and beyond.

KEY CONCEPTS

- *Agender*: having no gender and experiencing no distress as a result (see also *neutrois*)
- *Allies*: members of a majority population who support members of a minority counterpart population (e.g., heterosexuals, cisgender people, whites, and men who support LGB people, transgender people, people of color, and women, respectively)
- *Asexual*: experiencing no sexual attraction toward any gender
- *Bigender*: having two genders
- *Bisexuality*: a sexual orientation directed toward more than one gender

- *Cisgender*: a gender identity congruent with gender assigned at birth
- *Coming out*: the disclosure of one's sexual orientation or identity or gender identity to others
- *Deadnaming*: the intentional or unintentional use of a name that a transgender or nonbinary person no longer uses, such as their birth name
- *Demisexual*: experiencing sexual attraction toward an individual only after developing an emotional bond with that person
- *Disorders of sex development*: any number of conditions involving the presence, absence, malformation, or ambiguity of genitalia or reproductive physiology
- *Gay*: a sexual identity, usually among men, indicating a sexual orientation directed toward the same gender
- *Gender-affirming*: broadly speaking, a perspective of transgender and nonbinary gender identities as valid and a natural part of human gender diversity
- *Gender expression*: the outward demonstration of one's gender
- *Gender identity*: the experience of one's gender, whether congruent or incongruent with gender assigned at birth
- *Genderqueer*: a gender or gender identity that defies conventional categorizations that are dichotomous (male/female), discrete (cisgender, transgender), or fixed
- *Heteronormative*: a privileged standard associated with heterosexuality that is thus preferred over standards of other sexualities
- *Heterosexuality*: a sexual orientation of women directed toward men and of men directed toward women
- *Homonormativity*: the privileging of LGB people who idealize and adhere to heteronormative standards
- *Homosexuality*: a sexual orientation toward others of the same gender
- *Lesbian*: a sexual identity among women indicating a sexual orientation toward women
- *Misgender*: to intentionally or unintentionally refer to someone (through the use of pronouns or direct reference) as a gender with which they do not identify

- *Neopronouns*: gender-neutral alternatives (e.g., ze/hir/hirs, fae/faer) to gendered (he/him/his, she/her/hers) and plural (they/them/their/theirs) pronouns
- *Neutrois*: having no gender and experiencing distress as a result (see also *agender*)
- *Nonbinary*: a gender or gender identity that falls outside the male/female dichotomy
- *Pangender*: having multiple genders
- *Pansexual*: experiencing sexual attraction to others regardless of their sex, gender, or gender identity
- *Queer*: a sexual or gender identity that defies the traditional categories of LGBT
- *Sexual identity*: a label used to represent one's sexual orientation toward others
- *Sexual orientation*: the direction of one's sexual thoughts, feelings, and behaviors
- *Transgender*: a gender identity in which one's gender is not congruent with their gender assigned at birth
- *Transitioning*: relinquishing the characteristics of the gender assigned at birth and assuming those of the gender with which one identifies

CHAPTER HIGHLIGHTS

- Terminology changes frequently given the subjective nature of sexual and gender identities.
- Homosexuality was removed from the *DSM* in 1973.
- Sexual orientation is believed to be influenced by biology and environment.
- Gender identity disorder was renamed gender dysphoria in the fifth edition of the *DSM*.
- LGBTQ+ youth are coming out at younger ages, and those ages vary by gender, sexual and gender identity, and race and ethnicity.
- As many as half of LGBTQ+ RHY are kicked out of their homes, and between one-third and one-half are victimized.

- Lesbian/gay, bisexual, and transgender identities each follow their own developmental pathway.
- Models of sexual and gender identity development share a number of key similarities, including initial awareness, self-labeling, coming out, and integration.

ONLINE RESOURCES

- Accord Alliance: http://www.accordalliance.org/
- Advocates for Trans Equality: https://transequality.org/
- Bystander Intervention Training: https://righttobe.org/bystander-intervention-training/
- GLAAD: http://www.glaad.org/
- GLSEN: http://www.glsen.org/
- Human Rights Campaign: http://www.hrc.org/
- Learning for Justice, "How to be an Ally": https://www.learningforjustice.org/magazine/spring-2018/how-to-be-an-ally
- National LGBTQ Task Force: http://www.thetaskforce.org/
- PFLAG: https://pflag.org/
- Safe Zone Ally Training: https://thesafezoneproject.com/about/what-is-safe-zone/

2 | The Prevalence of Homelessness Among LGBTQ+ RHY

LEARNING OBJECTIVES

Readers of this chapter will be able to:

1. Identify changes in LGBTQ+ RHY prevalence over time,
2. Explain the sampling methodology used with LGBTQ+ and homeless populations, and
3. Use LGBTQ+ RHY prevalence data to guide decisions in practice, research, and policymaking.

CASE VIGNETTE: BEN

Standing around a barrel fire behind an abandoned warehouse on a bitterly cold January night, Ben, a cisgender gay man twenty-one years of age, was approached by a member of the outreach staff of a local Midwestern RHY shelter. The agency was conducting its annual point-in-time (PIT) census count of RHY in their county. The worker was part of a large team of staff and volunteers canvassing informal living quarters (e.g., abandoned buildings) and outdoor locations (e.g., parks and bridges) where RHY are known to congregate. Ben wasn't feeling very cooperative, given how cold it was, but the outreach worker offered Ben and his friends small bags of snacks, juice boxes, and travel-size toiletries in exchange for their time.

INTRODUCTION

Building on the comprehensive understanding of sexuality and gender identity presented in chapter 1, let us next look at the prevalence of homelessness among LGBTQ+ RHY. Estimating the scope of a public health problem such as homelessness is necessary for several reasons. First, prevalence rates alert interested parties to a potential problem and give them an opportunity to address it, such as by developing programs, services, and accommodations. Second, service providers can adequately provide those programs, services, and accommodations only when they know how many people are affected. Third, prevalence rates allow funders to prepare their budgets with an allocation of resources in mind. For instance, does a state raise and set aside enough money to serve one thousand people or ten thousand? This chapter provides a broad picture of prevalence rates over time. To accurately examine the scope of the problem of unstable housing and homelessness among LGBTQ+ RHY, it is important first to understand a few key statistical terms such as *prevalence, sampling frame, sampling methods*, and *statistical trends*.

PREVALENCE

The census that Ben and his friends were participating in provides valuable information on the number and characteristics of RHY within that county. Ben informed the worker of sites where a few other RHY hung out that the worker hadn't known about. Although the agency knows they will not be able to find all the RHY in their county, or get those they do find to participate in the census, its staff are confident that they are reaching most of them. Ben had heard about the agency but, given his age, he figured he was "too old" for services, and, identifying as gay, he wasn't sure if the agency would be welcoming. He also felt responsible for some of the younger members of his group and couldn't see himself "abandoning" them to seek shelter himself. The worker let Ben know that he was eligible for services, that agency employees were LGBTQ+-affirming, and that he was welcome to come by to get warm, take a shower, and get some food.

Prevalence is the rate at which a phenomenon exists within a population. A common term in epidemiology, *prevalence* typically refers to the presence of a disorder or condition in a given population. For example, 22.8 percent of U.S. adults had a mental disorder in 2023 (SAMHSA 2024). From an anthropological perspective, *prevalence* can also refer to a sociocultural aspect, such as race, ethnic traditions, religious practices, migration patterns, or place of birth. In this case, an example is that 6.6 percent of the population of New York City identified as Puerto Rican in 2023 (U.S. Census Bureau, n.d.a).

Another aspect of prevalence is its type, identified as the time period during which the phenomenon is observed. **Point prevalence** is a measurement of a phenomenon at a certain point in time. For example, on a single night each January, the U.S. Department of Housing and Urban Development conducts a **point-in-time (PIT) count** of sheltered and unsheltered individuals experiencing homelessness. The purpose is to account for as many people as can be located and record their demographic information, such as age, ethnicity, gender, gender identity, race, sexual orientation, and other relevant characteristics. PIT workers coordinate their efforts to ensure thorough coverage of each county and get as representative a sample as possible, though the degree of representativeness cannot be known with certainty. Previous count data and peer information from those they speak with during the PIT count is used to estimate the number of people experiencing homelessness in a county. These data help inform practice, policy, and funding decisions regarding the number of sheltered and unsheltered individuals in a given county each year, and they enable the tracking of changes in these populations from year to year. In 2023, the PIT count revealed 653,104 homeless children and adults living unsheltered (i.e., on the streets), in emergency shelters, and in transitional housing (USDHUD 2023b). (See box 2.1, *What Do You Think?*)

Period prevalence is the presence of a phenomenon within a set period of time. For instance, the twelve-month prevalence rate of homelessness among thirteen- to seventeen-year-olds between 2016 and 2017 was an

---

BOX 2.1. WHAT DO YOU THINK? ENGAGING HARD-TO-FIND POPULATIONS IN RESEARCH

- Where would you look for research participants from hard-to-find populations such as people experiencing homelessness and LGBTQ+ people?
- Create a brief oral introduction that you could use to approach sheltered or unsheltered LGBTQ+ RHY to invite them to participate in research.
- What might be their reasons for participating and not participating in research?
- What kinds of confidentiality assurances would you provide to potential participants?
- What sorts of incentives would you offer to those who choose to participate (keeping in mind that incentives are not to be so generous as to be coercive)?

---

estimated 4.3 percent (Morton, Dworsky et al. 2018). (In this study, data were collected once in 2016 and once in 2017 and then combined.) That is, 4.3 percent of households reported a family member in that age range having been homeless in the last twelve months. Last is **lifetime prevalence**, or the presence of a phenomenon at any point in one's lifetime. For example, nearly one in five youth (19.4 percent) reported having run away from the home of a parent or caregiver at some point in their life (Pergamit 2010). However, prevalence cannot be interpreted outside the sampling frame on which it is based. As such, identifying the sampling frame is a crucial step in determining the prevalence of a particular condition in a given population.

Sampling Frame

Statistics based on samples are estimates and are thus susceptible to error, whereas statistics based on populations are, in theory, accurate and thus less prone to error. Therefore, estimates are bound by the limits of the **sampling**

frame, a subset of the specific units of a population. A key reason that we use samples, not populations, in research is that for many groups, such as LGBTQ+ RHY, we do not know the total number of youth in the population. Ideally, a sampling frame includes all units of the target population—no more and no fewer. But realistically, sampling frames may inadvertently include units outside the desired frame and exclude others. The more or less representative the sample, the more or less **generalizable** the results, respectively. **Representativeness** is possible when the sampling frame from which a sample is drawn is representative of the target population. Large samples whose **random sampling** methods were uninfluenced by bias are also likely to be representative. As easy to achieve as that may sound, however, a number of factors confound the process. For example, not everyone chosen at random will agree to participate in a survey, let alone have their responses included. In some cases, the demographics of the final sample can be compared with those of the population (when the population is known and population estimates are free from bias) to determine the sample's representativeness, or the degree of sameness between the sample and the population from which it was drawn. Researchers can also compare those who ended up in the sample with those who did not, such as those on a wait list or those who started but did not complete a survey. In the absence of statistically significant differences between the sample and the population on key variables, we would say that the sample is representative (of the population). Another problem is that not every population is known, or determinate. Some populations, LGBTQ+ and homeless included, are impossible to count with certainty because some of their members are not easily, if ever, identified. Thus, samples derived from these populations can be representative only of the populations as they are found, not as they may actually be. This makes precise representativeness of the actual populations unknowable.

This latter point speaks to a key challenge to conducting research on LGBTQ+ and homeless people—invisibility—which occurs in a number of ways. First, by virtue of their housing instability (i.e., a lack of a permanent address or use of sleeping arrangements that remove them from the streets and shelters but that are nonetheless unstable, such as sleeping on a friend's couch) and, in some cases, migration or transience (i.e., frequent travel to new geographic locations or back to those where they previously resided), homeless individuals can sometimes be a difficult population simply to find. Thus, although homeless individuals within a known group can be randomly selected, homeless populations cannot be randomly sampled (Wright et al. 1995).

Similar challenges emerge when attempting to determine the prevalence of sexual orientation or gender identity in a population. There is no **biomarker** or **sociocultural signifier** identifying who is and who is not LGBTQ+. Unlike race, ethnicity, age, gender, class or socioeconomic status, physical ability, mental ability, and citizenship status, each of which has at least some degree of tangible classification (e.g., phenotype, proof of birthplace and year of birth), sexual orientation and gender identity are based solely on one's personal experience of sexuality and gender. One might say that this is similar to religion; however, religious affiliation or identity is a choice, whereas it is now widely accepted that sexual orientation and gender identity are not choices but rather the result of complex interactions between biology and environment, nature and nurture (see, e.g., Bailey et al. 2016; Martin 2008). There is no proof of one's sexual orientation or gender identity, only evidence, and even then, the evidence is far from definitive. For example, we might say that evidence of a same-sex orientation is same-sex sexual behavior, acknowledging the physical attractiveness of a person of the same sex, and participation in LGBTQ+-affirming community events. However, none of these behaviors, taken alone or together, is indicative of one's true sexual orientation. Kuperberg and Walker (2018) found that among heterosexual college students, 11.8 percent of men and 24.7 percent of women reported that their most recent sexual encounter was with a person of the same sex. However, among heterosexual adults aged eighteen to forty-four years, only 2.8 percent of men and 12.6 percent of women reported having engaged in same-sex sexual behavior (Copen et al. 2016). These findings suggest that early same-sex sexual encounters may have less to do with sexual orientation and more to do with sexual experimentation and other aspects of human sexual development.

Second, in the absence of biomarkers, it is up to each LGBTQ+ individual to decide whether to publicly disclose their sexual orientation or gender identity, and there are at least two reasons why an individual might choose not to. One is obviously the desire to protect their privacy by deflecting the question, refusing to answer, or presenting oneself as heterosexual (i.e., passing). The other is that the individual may not yet be aware of their non-heterosexual orientation or noncisgender identity. In terms of Vivienne Cass's (1979) stages of (lesbian and gay) sexual identity development, for example, we might say that the individual is in stage 1, identity confusion, when they are only starting to recognize themself as different from heterosexual others.

In sum, the LGBTQ+ community is a population of unknown parameters (e.g., size, demographic characteristics), which makes it impossible to know whether a sample drawn from it is representative of the whole. Nevertheless, several practitioners and researchers have attempted to capture prevalence to the extent possible.

Sampling Methods

Finally, a word on the means by which researchers identify and select participants for their studies. Though what we provide here is far from an exhaustive list, our focus is those sampling methods most common and feasible to use with people experiencing homelessness in light of the limits posed by the sampling frame of this population. Ideally, sampling provides researchers with a group of people that is exactly representative of the population from which that group was drawn. A perfectly representative sample is rare, and the population–sample difference, referred to as *error*, must be accounted for. Deviation of the sample from the population is reflected in the sampling error, a statistical value that indicates the amount of variation that is unaccounted for in the statistical model.

Sampling methods can first be categorized as either probability or nonprobability (table 2.1). **Probability sampling** involves methods that allow each unit of the sampling frame an equal chance of being chosen for a sample. All random sampling methods fall into the probability sampling category. Examples of random sampling include simple random sampling, systematic sampling, stratified sampling, cluster sampling, and multistage sampling (Kalton 1983). Because the parameters of the homeless population are unknowable, random sampling is not possible. Instead, researchers may choose to look at target subpopulations or sampling frames, such as people

TABLE 2.1 Probability and nonprobability sampling methods

Probability sampling	Nonprobability sampling
• Simple random sampling • Systematic sampling • Stratified sampling • Cluster sampling • Multistage sampling	• Convenience (or accidental) sampling • Purposive (or judgment) sampling • Snowball sampling • Quota sampling

experiencing homelessness who use a particular shelter or set of shelters; shelters themselves can also be a target population. The U.S. Department of Housing and Urban Development's annual PIT count of homeless individuals could be considered a target population, from which a sample could be drawn for further investigation.

Nonprobability sampling, on the other hand, occurs when units are selected from a population with an imperfect sampling frame, such as the LGBTQ+ and homeless populations. Convenience (or accidental) sampling, purposive (or judgment) sampling, snowball sampling, and quota sampling are common forms of nonprobability sampling (Rubin and Babbie 2017). A common example of convenience sampling is interviewing people on a street corner or in a shopping mall. As the name implies, finding participants for a study using this method is a matter of convenience. Purposive sampling might involve approaching program directors of area homeless agencies and drop-in centers. Researchers using this method deliberately identify and approach people known to fit their study's inclusion criteria, especially those who have specific knowledge in an area of interest to the researcher (Schutt 2012). Asking participants to invite others like them to participate in a study is an example of snowball sampling; like a snowball that increases in size as it rolls downhill, the sample size has the potential to grow exponentially if each person told about the study then tells others, who in turn tell others, and so on. (See box 2.2, *What Do You Think?*) Quota sampling fulfills a researcher's sampling requirement through a nonrandom selection of a group of individuals (or a quota) based on characteristics of interest. For example, let us say that the youth residing in a

---

BOX 2.2. WHAT DO YOU THINK?
NONPROBABILITY SAMPLING IN RESEARCH

- Can you identify the purposive and snowball sampling techniques used in the 2013 study by Ford et al. on intimate partner violence prevention for LGBT people? The authors described their sampling approach as follows: "An e-mail request was distributed to all persons affiliated with the city and county domestic violence prevention and intervention networks, and the county's network of mental health providers. Network members could forward the email to other professionals not affiliated with these formal networks" (843).

---

three-story building that houses a transitional living program are a population for a study of health outcomes. To increase the representativeness of the sample, the researcher sets a quota of ten participants from each floor, rather than risking a sample of thirty participants from two floors and no participants from the third. All youth are invited to participate, and the samples may even be proportional to the number of youth living on the floor from which the sample was drawn. However, participants were not randomly selected from each floor. The researcher was simply looking for a certain number (i.e., a quota) of youth from each floor. Stratified random sampling, on the other hand, divides a known population into groups and selects a proportional number of participants from each group, and it does so randomly. Using our example of the transitional living program, youth from each floor would be selected at random, and the sizes of the three samples, one from each floor, would be proportional to the number of people living on the floor from which each sample was drawn. Thus, stratified random sampling is a probability sampling method because it is based on a known sampling frame (the program staff know how many youth live on each floor) and nonbiased randomization (each youth has an equal chance of being selected for their floor's sample). Thus, quota sampling and stratified random sampling are similar except that quota sampling relies on nonprobability sampling methods and stratified random sampling relies on probability sampling methods. In sum, nonprobability sampling is more common in research with LGBTQ+ and homeless populations, whose total populations are unknown and hard to find, often leading to small, unrepresentative sampling frames.

LGBTQ+ RHY Prevalence

Several estimates of the prevalence of LGBTQ+ youth in the RHY population exist, perhaps none more common than the figure of 20 to 40 percent. Although sometimes attributed to Nicholas Ray (2006), the author of *Lesbian, Gay, Bisexual and Transgender Youth: An Epidemic of Homelessness*, a report of the National LGBTQ Task Force (formerly the National Gay and Lesbian Task Force), Ray cites the original source as a piece written by Dylan Nicole de Kervor (2004) for *Nation's Cities Weekly*. In it, de Kervor states, "The National Network of Runaway and Youth Services has estimated that 20–40 percent of youths who become homeless each year are lesbian, gay, or bisexual" (para. 4).

This estimate is not far from the prevalence rates reported by practitioners and researchers over the last thirty years. Since 2010, prevalence estimates of LGBTQ+ youth in the RHY population have ranged from 18 to 50.6 percent, with a **weighted mean** (i.e., average prevalence across all samples, factoring in each study's sample size) of 25.2 percent and a **median** (i.e., the midpoint of all prevalence values across samples) of 24.8 percent (Freeman and Hamilton 2013; Gattis and Larson 2017; Hein 2010; Kattari et al. 2017; Martin and Howe 2016; Rabinovitz et al. 2010; Rew et al. 2019; Santa Maria et al. 2018; Tyler and Schmitz 2018a; Walls and Bell 2011). Subsamples of LGBQ youth only (i.e., excluding transgender RHY) range in prevalence from 20 to 50.6 percent (weighted mean [M] = 25.2 percent, median = 25.5 percent) (Gattis and Larson 2017; Hein 2010; Martin and Howe 2016; Rabinovitz et al. 2010; Rew et al. 2019; Santa Maria et al. 2018; Tyler and Schmitz 2018a; Walls and Bell 2011). Transgender prevalence rates of just 3.8 to 5.7 percent (weighted M = 4.2 percent, median = 4.2 percent) (Hein 2010; Rew et al. 2019) may reflect the smaller size of the transgender population overall, or they may be the result of researcher definitions

---

BOX 2.3. READ ALL ABOUT IT! REPORTS ON LGBTQ+ RHY

- Representatives from nearly two dozen federal agencies came together to form the Interagency Working Group on Youth Programs, which created the Youth.gov website (Youth.gov n.d.a). Among the many topics Youth.gov addresses is sexual orientation and gender identity; its page on the topic includes information on homelessness and housing, child welfare, behavioral health, families, and schools. LGBTQ+ youth, families, and service providers may find this information helpful. Although the website was removed in early 2025, it can be accessed through the Internet Archive's Wayback Machine at https://web.archive.org/web/20250131055035/https://youth.gov/youth-topics/lgbt.

---

of transgender and nonbinary identities that exclude these youth (e.g., transgender youth must, at a minimum, have been on gender-affirming or puberty-blocking hormones for at least the previous six months), researcher categorization of transgender and nonbinary participants as sexual-minority (i.e., LGBQ) youth, or transgender and nonbinary youth identifying as LGBQ or otherwise not disclosing their gender identity.

These data mirror those presented by Durso and Gates (2012), who conducted a survey of 381 RHY service providers from 354 agencies across the United States. Respondents reported that approximately 30 percent of the youth they served identified as gay or lesbian and that another 9 percent identified as bisexual. Estimates of transgender RHY served ranged between 3 and 5 percent. Based on estimates of LGBTQ+ youth prevalence in the general population ranging from 3 to 5 percent (Quintana et al. 2010) and up to 9.5 percent (Conron 2020), LGBTQ+ youth are indeed overrepresented in the RHY population. (See box 2.3, *Read All About It!*)

TRENDS

A few days after the PIT count, Ben talked some of his friends into going with him to the shelter to see what it had to offer. While there, Ben ran into the outreach worker he had spoken with a few nights before and asked if the worker had gotten what he needed. The worker said that the information Ben provided was helpful and will be used when the agency applies for public (e.g., state and federal) and private (e.g., foundation) funding to maintain existing services and develop new ones. As they were talking, Ben noticed that a couple of his younger friends seemed interested in the pool table and video games the agency had for the youth to use.

Identifying **trends** (i.e., increases or decreases in a behavior or condition over time) requires an examination of longitudinal data. To that end, this section reviews prevalence data from before 2010, which was the starting point for the data presented up to this point and which will serve as a point of reference for comparison.

Prevalence rates from before 2010 are somewhat similar to those during and after 2010 (figure 2.1). Since at least the early 1990s, LGBTQ+ youth have composed 7 to 39 percent (weighted M = 23.5 percent, median = 20.4 percent) of the RHY population. Nontransgender RHY represented

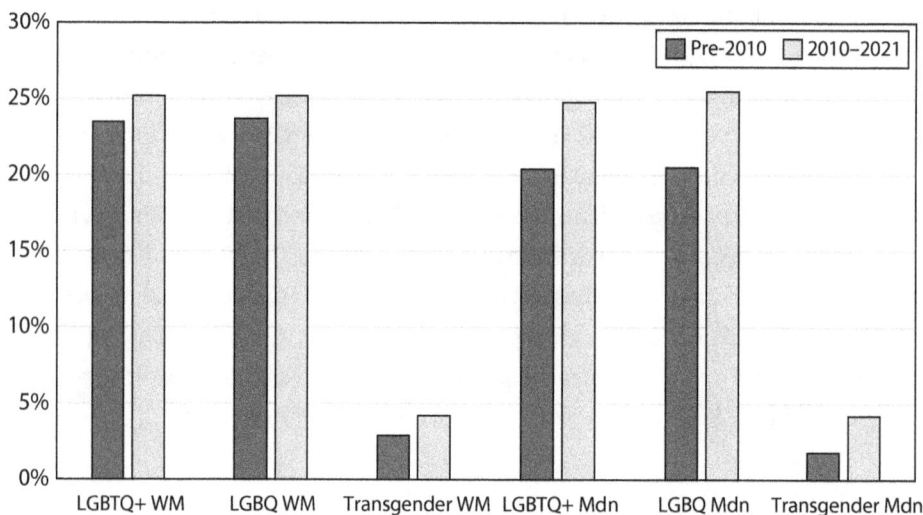

FIGURE 2.1 Comparison of LGBTQ+, LGBQ-only, and transgender-only prevalence per time period, pre-2010 and 2010–2021.

Abbreviations: Mdn, median; WM, weighted mean.

7 to 36.4 percent of the population (weighted M = 23.7 percent, median = 20.5 percent) (Cauce et al. 2000; Clatts et al. 1998; Cochran et al. 2002; Freeman and Hamilton 2008; Gangamma et al. 2008; Kennedy 1991; Milburn et al. 2006; Moon et al. 2000; Noell and Ochs 2001; Rew et al. 2001; Rew et al. 2005; Solorio et al. 2006; Tyler 2008; Unger et al. 1997; Van Leeuwen et al. 2006; Wagner et al. 2001; Walls et al. 2009; Whitbeck et al. 2004; Wilder Research 2005; Yates et al. 1988), and transgender RHY represented 0.3 to 5.3 percent (weighted M = 2.9 percent, median = 1.8 percent). (See box 2.4, *What Do You Think?*) The increase in prevalence revealed in the ranges and weighted means from the earlier period (1991–2009) and the period that followed is reflected in the findings of Durso and Gates (2012), who also reported an increase over the ten-year period before their 2011–2012 data collection in the number of RHY service providers working with LGBTQ+ RHY. This increase may be a function of more RHY identifying as LGBTQ+, more LGBTQ+ youth becoming homeless, more services becoming available to identify LGBTQ+ RHY, or some combination of these. This increase translates to a need for additional LGBTQ+-affirming RHY programs and services and practitioners trained to staff them.

BOX 2.4. WHAT DO YOU THINK?
TRENDS IN LGBTQ+ RHY PREVALENCE

- What do you make of the difference between pre-2020 prevalence rates and rates since then? Is the difference between them more or less than what you expected?
- Why are the recent medians so much higher than the earlier ones?
- What are some of the reasons that the means and medians for transgender participants are lower than those for LGBQ and LGBTQ+ participants?
- Given the trend in prevalence rates over the past thirty years, what would you expect future prevalence rates to look like if they were represented in the graph in figure 2.1?

SUMMARY

Prevalence rates are key to understanding the scope of a problem, in this case, homelessness among LGBTQ+ RHY in the United States. Prevalence rates for this population have been relatively stable, though there has been a modest increase over time. The oft-cited figure of 20 to 40 percent of the RHY population being LGBTQ+ is supported here, with two-thirds (65.6 percent) of studies reporting LGBTQ+ prevalence rates within or above that range (weighted $M = 24.1$ percent). Compared with the estimate of 3 to 9.5 percent of the general population being LGBTQ+ youth (Conron 2020; Quintana et al. 2010), LGBTQ+ youth are most certainly overrepresented in the RHY population.

These statistics remind practitioners, researchers, and policymakers to be aware of the likelihood that the LGBTQ+ youth with whom they come into contact and on whose behalf they advocate have had experiences with running away from or being kicked out of their home and becoming homeless. Professionals must be intentional in including LGBTQ+ RHY in their program development, study recruitment, and policymaking. This is especially true for subpopulations of LGBTQ+ RHY, such as transgender and nonbinary gender youth and youth of color, who are disproportionately affected by homelessness.

REVISITING BEN

- Does the census that Ben participated in capture point prevalence, period prevalence, or lifetime prevalence?
- What kinds of **magnet events** could the agency develop that might encourage Ben and other RHY to participate in the PIT count?
- In what ways is the PIT count limited? What could increase the representativeness of the PIT count data?
- How many RHY would you expect a PIT count team to find in your county? Where might the team locate them?
- Being the oldest of his close-knit group of friends, some of whom are under eighteen and look up to him, Ben feels a sense of responsibility

for their welfare. Is Ben legally, ethically, or morally responsible for the minors in the group, a street family for many of them?

- Imagine that you are the director of a program for LGBTQ+ RHY. One day, you read that, despite your program's best efforts, the prevalence of LGBTQ+ youth in the RHY population has increased. What kinds of appeals could you make with these data? Whom would you approach? What kinds of services or policies would you request or advocate for?

KEY CONCEPTS

- *Biomarker*: an organic identifier (e.g., gene, chromosome) that signifies the presence of a characteristic, *or* a characteristic (e.g., gene, chromosome) of an organism that indicates the presence of a trait
- *Generalizability*: the degree to which findings based on a sample can be applied to a population
- *Magnet events*: events that attract members of a population (here, youth experiencing homelessness), especially for the purpose of increasing the visibility of that population during census counts
- *Median*: the midpoint; the value halfway between all values placed in numerical order
- *Nonprobability sampling*: sampling methods in which some units of the target population have zero chance of being selected into the sample; examples include convenience (or accidental) sampling, purposive (or judgment) sampling, snowball sampling, and quota sampling
- *Point-in-time (PIT) count*: census data collected within a narrow window of time, such as within a single day
- *Prevalence (point, period, and lifetime)*: the rate of the presence of a phenomenon in a population; point, period, and lifetime prevalence, respectively, are the rates of presence of a phenomenon in a population at a specific point in time (point prevalence), over a given period of time (period prevalence), and over one's lifetime (lifetime prevalence)

- *Probability sampling*: sampling methods in which each unit of the target population has an equal nonzero chance of being selected into the sample; examples include simple random sampling, systematic sampling, stratified sampling, cluster sampling, and multistage sampling
- *Random sampling*: a process whereby each unit in a population has an equal chance of being selected for a sample
- *Representativeness*: the degree to which a sample reflects the traits of the population from which it was drawn
- *Sampling frame*: a list of units or members of a population from which a sample is drawn
- *Sociocultural signifier*: a social or cultural indicator (e.g., country of origin, religious ritual) that signifies membership in a group
- *Trends*: patterns that can be noticed over time that indicate changes in a condition or behavior
- *Weighted mean*: an average in which some values contribute more (i.e., carry more weight) than others because, for example, they are more representative of the population or they are more important than other factors

CHAPTER HIGHLIGHTS

- It is impossible to randomly sample homeless and LGBTQ+ populations.
- 3 to 9.5 percent of youth in the United States identify as LGBTQ+ (Conron 2020; Quintana et al. 2010).
- The prevalence of LGBTQ+ youth in the RHY population is often cited as ranging from 20 to 40 percent (de Kervor 2004).
- 59.4 percent of studies in our review had samples comprising 20 to 40 percent LGBTQ+ youth; 65.6 percent had samples of 20 percent or higher.
- The weighted means of samples before 2010 (23.5 percent) and from 2010 to 2021 (25.2 percent) are similar.

3 | Who Are LGBTQ+ RHY?

LEARNING OBJECTIVES

Readers of this chapter will be able to:

1. Describe the LGBTQ+ RHY population according to demographic trends,
2. Identify gaps in LGBTQ+ RHY demographic data, and
3. Critique the ways demographic data are measured across studies.

CASE VIGNETTE: CHENICE

Just shy of her nineteenth birthday, Chenice, an African American transgender, heterosexual young woman known as Nee-Nee to her close friends, is presenting at an emergency shelter for youth in hopes of landing a coveted spot in their transitional living program. She's found herself staying in emergency shelters before, either relegated to the boys' side of a facility or isolated in a room usually reserved for overnight staff. This time, she wants something more stable. The well-intentioned intake worker attempts to reassure Chenice, saying, "You know, you're not alone. We see a lot of young people just like you." Indignant, Chenice huffs, "I know! I'm livin' it!"

INTRODUCTION

Runaway and **homeless youth** (RHY) are a diverse group. Young people from all backgrounds run away from home, get kicked out, or otherwise find themselves without stable housing. It must be noted, however, that youth with particular **demographic** characteristics, such as a same-sex sexual orientation or identity or a transgender or nonbinary gender identity, find themselves overrepresented among the RHY population. Knowing exactly who these youth are, where they come from, and the backgrounds they represent assists practitioners, program developers, and policymakers in tailoring services, programs, and policies that best meet this population's needs.

This chapter presents the demographic characteristics of LGBTQ+ RHY, specifically their gender, gender identity, sexual orientation and identity, race and ethnicity, age, education, employment, family socioeconomic status (SES), and national origin. Demographic data were collected primarily from research participants **recruited** from **emergency shelters, drop-in centers, transitional living programs**, youth agencies and organizations, and outreach and street locations, also referred to as **street outreach**. LGBTQ+ RHY are defined here as currently or recently (within the past eighteen months) unstably housed or homeless **unaccompanied minors** and young adults twenty-six years of age or younger.

To put these demographic data in context, let us first discuss how information on LGBTQ+ RHY is collected and reported. Some studies clearly capture the gender, gender identity, and sexual orientation or identity of the participants in their **samples**. Others, however, are beset by limitations in categorization, definition, and language. For instance, some studies have reported sexual and gender minority participants as one group (e.g., LGBT), whereas others have reported sexual orientation and gender identity separately, although sometimes without reporting the overlap, which is an important factor to consider since some LGBTQ+ people identify as both a sexual minority and a gender minority (e.g., a transgender lesbian) (Begun et al. 2019; Forge, Hartinger-Saunders et al. 2018; Freeman and Hamilton 2013; Samuels et al. 2018; Shelton, DeChants et al. 2018; Walls and Bell 2011). In other cases, gender identity is conflated with sexuality, and gender with sex. Some note the gender but not always the gender identity of their participants, and even when gender identity is captured, the specific gender of transgender participants (e.g., transgender man) sometimes is not. Still others do not specify the gender of their heterosexual-cisgender and LGBTQ+ subgroups. The inconsistencies in categorization and definition make summarizing demographic data challenging at best. Like bisexual people, transgender people are often presented as a monolith, with transmen and transwomen lumped together into the single category of transgender (e.g., Begun et al. 2019; Forge, Hartinger-Saunders et al. 2018), whereas cisgender people are recognized by their individual genders. To be sure, transgender participants are often few in number, warranting collapsing transmen and transwomen into one subcategory for analytic purposes. However, the risk in doing so may be a distorted picture of how transgender (and nonbinary) people view the world as male or female (or both or neither). Eliminating transgender participants altogether is an even bigger concern. One possible solution to remedying both problems is **oversampling**, when appropriate (Vaughan 2017). Reporting practices such as those described here can sometimes make comparisons difficult if not impossible, although such inconsistencies in the literature are not uncommon. Therefore, it is important to keep these practices in mind when reading and interpreting research involving LGBTQ+ RHY.

GENDER, GENDER IDENTITY, SEXUAL ORIENTATION, AND SEXUAL IDENTITY

Chenice has been out of the house since just after turning seventeen. She vacillates between defiantly stating that she left an untenable situation at home and blaming her parents for kicking her out because of her "feminine mannerisms," although Chenice wasn't yet identifying as transgender. Her father was especially verbally abusive, once yelling, "No son of mine is gonna act like that! Not in my house!" Chenice laments being homeless but adds that it has given her the freedom to be who she truly is. She finds herself attracted to heterosexual-cisgender men and transgender women, although she explains away her limited relationship history by saying she's "too busy for people's drama."

Categorization

Although more researchers are now aware of the difference between sexual orientation or identity and gender identity, some still refer to transgender individuals as a sexual minority instead of a gender minority or offer transgender identity as a response option among a mutually exclusive list of sexualities, which forces transgender individuals who identify as LGB to choose between their gender identity and their sexual orientation or identity. Moreover, some studies that do acknowledge transgender participants in their samples fail to capture or report their specific gender. The mutually exclusive *male/man*, *female/woman*, and *transgender* options again force transgender individuals to choose, this time between identifying as a man or a woman and identifying as a gender minority; the former makes invisible their gender minority status, while the latter makes invisible their gender as male or female, unless participants are given the option to choose the more specific *transgender man* or *transgender woman*, or else *male/man* or *female/woman*, as well as *transgender* or *cisgender*. Also lost are the many other nonbinary identities such as genderqueer, **transmasculine or transfeminine**, and agender, for example, which are often relegated to a category of *other*, if acknowledged at all.

Definition

Definitions of participant gender also vary in research, with gender (i.e., one's internal sense of being a man or a woman) sometimes being conflated with sex (i.e., one's identification as male or female based on biological signifiers, such as sex chromosomes and reproductive organs). For example, a study that recruits men who have sex with men may intend a sample of men who were assigned male at birth but may also include gay transmen and gay cisgender men. Here, "men," which refers to gender, was assumed to be defined by sex assigned at birth (birth sex). Notorious examples of conflating sex and gender are some states' "bathroom bills," which require people, when faced with a choice between a men's restroom or a women's restroom, to use the restroom that aligns with their gender assigned at birth. This wrongly presumes that sex and gender are—or should be perceived as—one and the same.

Language

Also consequential is the language used to refer to participants who might identify as transgender or nonbinary gender. In some studies, participants are eligible if they identify as "biologically male" or "biologically female." This language is imprecise because every human is "biological"; what the researcher is asking about is the participant's anatomical sex. However, even then, one's anatomical sex is not an indicator of their birth sex since some transgender people undergo **gender-affirming surgery**, which changes their genitals and some secondary sex characteristics (e.g., male vs. female breasts) from those of one sex to those of another. To capture a participant's birth sex, it is currently preferable to instead ask, "What sex were you assigned at birth, meaning on your original birth certificate?," followed by the choices of *male* and *female* (Clark and Kosciw 2022, 9), and to capture gender identity with the question, "Which best describes your current gender identity?," followed by the choices of *male, female, "indigenous or other cultural gender minority identity (e.g., two-spirit),"* and *"something else (e.g., gender fluid, non-binary"* (Bauer et al. 2017, 23). If the responses to both questions do not match, then ask, "What gender do you currently live as in your day-to-day life?," followed by the choices of *male, female, "sometimes male, sometimes female,"* and *"something other than male or female"* (Bauer et al. 2017, 23). (See box 3.1, *Read All About It!*)

Gender and Gender Identity Prevalence

The prevalence of cisgender male RHY (regardless of sexual orientation) ranges from 32.7 to 71.9 percent, with a weighted mean of 55.3 percent, while the prevalence of cisgender female RHY ranges from 16 to 55 percent, with a weighted mean of 41.1 percent. These figures align with point-in-time (PIT) research on RHY youth (de Sousa et al. 2024), which finds a

---

BOX 3.1. READ ALL ABOUT IT! TRANSGENDER AND NONBINARY GENDER RESOURCES

- Several resources exist to help health professionals, researchers, and policymakers serve transgender and nonbinary-gender individuals with dignity and sensitivity, including the following:
  - Advocates for Trans Equality: https://transequality.org/
  - Center of Excellence for Transgender Health: https://prevention.ucsf.edu/transhealth
  - Lambda Legal: https://www.lambdalegal.org/publications/fs_transgender-affirming-hospital-policies
  - National LGBTQIA+ Health Education Center: https://www.lgbtqiahealtheducation.org/
  - Trans Student Educational Resources: http://www.transstudent.org/about/
    - The Gender Unicorn: http://www.transstudent.org/gender/
  - University of California, San Francisco, Transgender Care: https://transcare.ucsf.edu/guidelines
  - World Professional Association for Transgender Health: https://www.wpath.org/

---

higher prevalence of males (57.7 percent) than females (38.9 percent) in this population.

With regard to gender identity, 0.7 to 27.5 percent (weighted $M = 3.2$ percent) of RHY identify as transgender, genderqueer, or other related identity (Begun et al. 2019; Forge, Hartinger-Saunders et al. 2018; Freeman and Hamilton 2013; Gattis and Larson 2017; Ream et al. 2012; Rew et al. 2019; Robinson 2018a; Samuels et al. 2018; Shelton, DeChants et al. 2018; Walls and Bell 2011). This figure is higher than prevalence rates found in PIT research (de Sousa et al. 2024) for this subpopulation of RHY and may result from studies that oversampled transgender participants for analytic purposes. Transgender males compose 0.8 to 3 percent (weighted $M = 1.7$ percent) of the RHY population, and transgender females compose 2.5 to 21 percent (weighted $M = 7.5$ percent) (Freeman and Hamilton 2013; Ream et al. 2012; Robinson 2018a; Samuels et al. 2018).

Sexual Orientation and Identity Prevalence

LGBQ RHY comprise 6.8 to 50.6 percent (weighted M = 17.7 percent) of the RHY population (Begun et al. 2019; Cutuli et al. 2020; Forge, Hartinger-Saunders et al. 2018; Freeman and Hamilton 2013; Gattis and Larson 2017; Hein 2010; Martin and Howe 2016; Rew et al. 2019; Rice et al. 2015; Samuels et al. 2018; Santa Maria et al. 2018; Shpiegel and Simmel 2016; Tyler 2013; Tyler and Schmitz 2018b; Walls and Bell 2011). Lower prevalence rates reflect samples of middle- and high-school students (Cutuli et al. 2020; Rice et al. 2015), who may feel more dependent on their parents or guardians for their survival and thus be less likely to leave home or be kicked out. Excluding those samples, the weighted mean prevalence of LGBQ youth among RHY samples rises to 25.1 percent. This finding supports the commonly cited statistic of 20 to 40 percent of RHY identifying as LGBTQ+ (see chapter 2).

It is not uncommon for lesbian and gay people, and sometimes lesbian, gay, and bisexual people, to be grouped together in research outcome data, making it difficult, if not impossible, to discern prevalence rates for each subgroup. Among the research that does make that distinction, lesbians (3.8–6.7 percent, weighted M = 4.1 percent) and gay men (1.7–6.7 percent, weighted M = 2.3 percent) together make up 5.5 to 13.8 percent (weighted M = 10.6 percent) of RHY (Begun et al. 2019; Forge, Hartinger-Saunders et al. 2018; Freeman and Hamilton 2013; Hein 2010; Rew et al. 2019; Samuels et al. 2018; Santa Maria et al. 2018). When bisexuals (6.7–22.3 percent, weighted M = 13.5 percent) are included, LGB people account for 18.1 to 50.6 percent (weighted M = 21.2 percent) of the RHY population (Cutuli et al. 2020; Gattis and Larson 2017; Martin and Howe 2016; Rice et al. 2015; Shpiegel and Simmel 2016; Tyler 2013; Tyler and Schmitz 2018b; Walls and Bell 2011).

Gender Comparisons by Sexual Orientation and Identity

Most studies provide at least broad details about their sample (e.g., sample size; participant age, gender, race), but the more specific our inquiry into prevalence, the fewer studies there are on which to draw. When examining the intersection of gender identity and sexual orientation and identity, for instance, we must use caution given that few studies offer this level of detail. That said, heterosexual RHY samples tend to skew male, whereas LGBTQ+ RHY samples vary with regard to gender, with about half skewing male and half female. Little research with nonbinary participants exists, although such studies are increasing in number. LGBTQ+ males make up 22.2 to 71.9 percent (weighted $M = 42.1$ percent) of the sexual- and gender-minority RHY subpopulation, and LGBTQ+ females make up 28.1 to 68.9 percent (weighted $M = 44.5$ percent) (Bidell 2014; Freeman and Hamilton 2013; Gattis and Larson 2017; Ream et al. 2012; Robinson 2018a; Shelton, DeChants et al. 2018). This is atypical of the general population of RHY, which has a higher prevalence of males (de Sousa et al. 2024). It is likely that the combination of cisgender LGBQ females and transgender females (who outnumber transgender males) accounts for the higher prevalence compared with LGBTQ+ males.

Gender, gender identity, sexual orientation, and sexual identity are the focus of this section, but problems, especially with regard to categorization and definition, make summarizing and interpreting findings difficult and sometimes impossible. This serves as a reminder to consider research results with caution. Many studies report participants' gender and sexual orientation but not their gender identity. Transgender youth have been completely unaccounted for in nearly half the research on RHY. Also problematic is overlooking transgender participants' gender identity and referring to them only by the gender they were assigned at birth. Research (Sterzing et al. 2017) has shown that transgender youth are particularly vulnerable to street violence, which makes documenting their prevalence and experiences while homeless all the more important.

Similarly, some research relies solely on participants who were assigned male at birth. With females composing more than one-third (de Sousa et al. 2024) to one-half (Hammer et al. 2002) of the RHY population and three-quarters of those who seek help (Pergamit et al. 2010), young women cannot afford to be omitted from research. This shortcoming can be solved with all-female samples or by **quota sampling** methods that ensure female representation equal to that of other genders in a sample.

That LGBTQ+ participants aged sixteen years and older compose 25.1 percent of the overall population of homeless youth supports claims in the extant literature that LGBTQ+ youth are overrepresented in the RHY population (Benoit-Bryan 2011; Corliss et al. 2011; Keuroghlian et al. 2014; Quintana et al. 2010). This means that practitioners working with LGBTQ+ youth are likely to encounter those who have experienced **unstable housing** or homelessness at some point in their young lives. It also points to the need for continued research with and advocacy on behalf of this vulnerable population.

AGE

RHY generally range in age from ten to twenty-six years, averaging between 12.2 and 21.5 years (weighted $M = 19.3$) (Begun et al. 2019; Bidell 2014; Forge, Hartinger-Saunders et al. 2018; Freeman and Hamilton 2013; Gattis and Larson 2017; Hein 2010; Rew et al. 2019; Rice et al. 2015; Santa Maria et al. 2018; Schmitz and Tyler 2018b; Shelton, DeChants et al. 2018; Tucker et al. 2012; Tyler 2013; Tyler and Schmitz 2018b; Walls and Bell 2011). Most RHY are aged fifteen years and older, particularly eighteen years and older (Cutuli et al. 2020; Martin and Howe 2016; Samuels et al. 2018; Shelton 2015); those aged eighteen years and older have a weighted mean age of 20.9 years. Male RHY are generally older than their female counterparts (e.g., 20.9 years vs. 20.7 years, respectively [Freeman and Hamilton 2013; Johnson et al. 2006]). According to Tompsett et al. (2009), gender prevalence is more nuanced and depends on age: adolescents aged thirteen to seventeen years are overwhelmingly female (67.5 percent), whereas young adults aged eighteen to thirty-four years are mostly male (63.1 percent).

LGBTQ+ RHY tend to be slightly older than the general RHY population. Average ages of the former range from 20.1 to 21.2 years (weighted $M = 20.9$) (Bidell 2014; Gattis and Larson 2017; Schmitz and Tyler 2018b; Shelton, DeChants et al. 2018; Tucker et al. 2012), compared with 12.2 to 21.5 years (weighted $M = 19.3$) among the latter (Forge, Hartinger-Saunders et al. 2018; Rice et al. 2015; Santa Maria et al. 2018; Tyler 2013; Walls and Bell 2011). These findings contradict other reports that have identified LGBTQ+ RHY as younger (Corliss et al. 2011); however, some general-population studies include younger participants (aged ten to sixteen years) more often than LGBTQ+-only studies.

Although most studies provide the age range of their participants, only some report means and **standard deviations**, and fewer than half provide all three. Moreover, gaps and inconsistencies in reporting across studies make it difficult to compare outcomes according to age, gender, sexual orientation, sexual identity, and gender identity. However, what the data here do show is a slightly older group of LGBTQ+ RHY compared with the general RHY population, perhaps because of the varying age ranges in the studies. Given the developmental differences between adolescence and young adulthood, having more complete age data would assist in fine-tuning the services offered to LGBTQ+ RHY.

RACE AND ETHNICITY

RHY are a racially and ethnically diverse group. Most RHY are youth of color (21.8–94.7 percent, weighted M = 66.6 percent), highlighting their overrepresentation in the RHY population compared with their white counterparts (5.3–78.2 percent, weighted M = 33.3 percent) (Begun et al. 2019; Bidell 2014; Cutuli et al. 2020; Forge, Hartinger-Saunders et al. 2018; Freeman and Hamilton 2013; Hein 2010; Krause et al. 2016; Martin and Howe 2016; Ream et al. 2012; Rew et al. 2019; Rice et al. 2015; Robinson 2018a; Samuels et al. 2018; Santa Maria et al. 2018; Schmitz and Tyler 2018b; Shelton 2015; Shelton, DeChants et al. 2018; Tucker et al. 2012; Tyler 2013; Tyler and Schmitz 2018b; Walls and Bell 2011). Blacks/African Americans are the largest subgroup (17.9–71 percent, weighted M = 26.9 percent), followed by biracial/multiracial individuals (1.1–33 percent, weighted M = 15.4 percent), Hispanic/Latinx individuals (6.2–61.6 percent, weighted M = 12.6 percent), other (1.1–13.3 percent, weighted M = 7.1 percent), American Indians/Alaska Natives (0.7–5.6 percent, weighted M = 3.9 percent), Asians/Asian Americans (0.5–4 percent, weighted M = 1.3 percent), and Native Hawaiians/Pacific Islanders (0.3–3.3 percent, weighted M = 0.42 percent). Studies of the prevalence of Indigenous youth among the RHY population, however, have found much higher rates. American Indian/Alaska Native

(AI/AN) youth aged thirteen to seventeen years have a rate more than triple (12.2 percent) and young adults aged eighteen to twenty-five years a rate more than double (10.2 percent) that of non–AI/AN youth (3.1 percent) and young adults (5.4 percent) (Morton, Chavez et al. 2019). In Canadian studies of RHY prevalence, a disproportionate percentage (32.6 percent) of Indigenous youth have been found to use shelters compared with non-Indigenous youth (Jadidzadeh and Kneebone 2022).

As with the general RHY population figures cited earlier, people of color also represent a majority of LGBTQ+ RHY (50–90.9 percent, weighted M = 81.8 percent) compared with white LGBTQ+ RHY (9–50 percent, weighted M = 17.8 percent) (Bidell 2014; Krause et al. 2016; Ream et al. 2012; Robinson 2018a; Shelton 2015; Shelton, DeChants et al. 2018; Tucker et al. 2012). Black/African American youth (19.7–52 percent, weighted M = 32.5 percent), biracial/multiracial youth (5–33 percent, weighted M = 21.3 percent), Hispanic/Latinx youth (15–38.2 percent, weighted M = 21 percent), youth from other races/ethnicities (1.1–13.3 percent, weighted M = 11.3), Asian/Asian American youth (2.6–4 percent, weighted M = 2.9 percent), and AI/AN youth (2.2–3 percent, weighted M = 2.6 percent) disproportionately contribute to the LGBTQ+ RHY population. Native Hawaiian/Pacific Islander RHY are virtually invisible in the LGBTQ+ RHY literature, meaning we know little about them and how best to meet their needs.

Thus, youth of color, both LGBTQ+ and heterosexual-cisgender, are considerably overrepresented among the RHY youth population. This is particularly true for Black/African American youth, who represent 13.5 percent (ages fourteen to seventeen years) and 14.1 percent (ages eighteen to twenty-four years) of same-aged youth in the general U.S. population, and for Hispanic/Latinx youth, who represent 24.5 percent (ages fourteen to seventeen years) and 22.7 percent (ages eighteen to twenty-four years) (U.S. Census Bureau 2020). It is possible that these majorities are partially explained by the higher concentration of homeless youth of color in certain geographic locations (e.g., New York City, Los Angeles) or recruitment settings (e.g., urban shelters and drop-in centers) where RHY research is often conducted. Yet these figures also point to the fact that youth of color, like LGBTQ+ youth, are simply overrepresented in the RHY population (Hammer et al. 2002). The vulnerability experienced by LGBTQ+ RHY of color, then, is compounded by the intersectionality of their race and ethnicity and their sexual orientation and identity and gender identity. These data indicate that youth of color, including those who are LGBTQ+, are disproportionately affected by homelessness and the risks associated with it.

Asian/Asian American/Pacific Islander (AAPI) and AI/AN youth are often missing from studies on RHY. Like transgender youth, AAPI and AI/AN youth are also overrepresented in the RHY population but to a lesser degree. There are several possible explanations for this finding. First, cultural factors may make these youth less likely to experience homelessness as unaccompanied minors, thus keeping their rates lower than those of their Black/African American and Latinx peers but still higher than those of their white peers. Second, AAPI and AI/AN youth may have limited access to typical temporary housing solutions (e.g., **couch surfing**, RHY services), or they may use these options at lower rates than their peers of other races and ethnicities. Third, it is also possible, if not likely, that strategies to recruit AAPI and AI/AN youth into RHY research or programs and services may not be reaching them successfully (Morton, Chavez et al. 2019). In these latter two cases, they are not available to participate in research, census counts, or RHY programs and services, meaning their (over)representation may actually be higher than reported. Indeed, more Indigenous LGBTQ+ youth experience homelessness (44 percent) than multiracial (36 percent), white (27 percent), Latinx (27 percent), Black (26 percent), and AAPI (16 percent) LGBTQ+ youth (DeChants et al. 2021). In Canada, for example, Indigenous youth compose a greater percentage of the RHY population than in the RHY population in the United States (Jadidzadeh and Kneebone 2022), as do LGBTQ+ RHY among them (28.6 percent) (Kidd, Thistle et al. 2019). Regardless of the reason, the low numbers of AAPI and AI/AN youth in study samples make it difficult to analyze data in a meaningful way, leading researchers to omit them or combine them with other racial or ethnic groups into an "other" category, which still renders them invisible. Racial- and ethnic-minority youth who, like transgender youth, are at the margins of an already marginalized population are particularly

---

BOX 3.2. WHAT DO YOU THINK?
REPRESENTATION OF RHY OF COLOR

- What might explain the overrepresentation of youth of color among the RHY population compared with their white counterparts?
- Why might youth of color be overrepresented among RHY? Why might Black/African American youth be the largest subgroup among them?
- Using U.S. Census Bureau data, find the sizes of the general AAPI and AI/AN youth populations. How do those figures compare with the prevalence rates of these and other RHY groups presented in this section?

---

vulnerable—even more so when those identities intersect, as in transgender youth of color. A greater effort must be made to recruit RHY of color who have historically been underrepresented in research and overlooked as consumers in need of programs and services. Program directors and researchers may also consider focusing their efforts on these understudied populations to better understand their unique needs and experiences. (See box 3.2, *What Do You Think?*)

EDUCATION

The intake worker confirmed Chenice's nagging worry: that people see her only as a stereotype and not for the ways that she is anything but. She comes from a middle-class family. She used to love school. Although she was shunned by most of her male classmates, she was very close with several of her female classmates, who knew her as Lewis before she transitioned. Before she left home, she didn't have a formal job, but she liked to spend time at a nearby hair salon where the owner would tip her for helping out. She doesn't have HIV or any other sexually transmitted infections (STIs), which she believes people wouldn't expect. Although she has engaged in sex with strangers a couple times in exchange for a place to sleep or money for food, she regrets it but realizes she had no choice. She is health conscious and has sought testing at a free clinic, which confirmed her HIV- and STI-negative health status. Chenice is confident that the transitional living program will provide her enough stability to finish her education and get herself on the path to financial independence and self-sufficiency.

Few studies survey the educational status of their participants, and the level of detail they gather about participants' educational attainment varies. What we do know is that many RHY have earned a high school diploma or certificate of high school equivalency (by passing the four General Educational Development [GED] tests) (7.9–71 percent, weighted M = 42.5 percent) (Bidell 2014; Tucker et al. 2012) or are currently enrolled in high school (0–65.8 percent, weighted M = 19.1 percent). However, a significant percentage drop out of school (14.3–45.1 percent, weighted M = 43.6 percent) (Castellanos 2016; Forge, Hartinger-Saunders et al. 2018).

High school and GED completion rates among LGBTQ+ RHY vary from 17.4 to 71 percent (Hein 2010; Tucker et al. 2012). Moreover, not only do some youth earn their high school diploma or GED, but more than a third (35.7 percent) also go on to college, with 7.1 percent earning an associate's degree (Castellanos 2016). Dropout rates also vary, from 14.3 to 52.2 percent (Castellanos 2016; Hein 2010), and of those who drop out, most do so in the eleventh and twelfth grades (Bidell 2014; Hein 2010). Practitioners working with LGBTQ+ RHY in their later years of high school, then, should assess their dropout risk and identify prevention strategies to minimize that risk.

According to a report of RHY service providers (Choi et al. 2015), transgender youth generally fare worse than LGBQ youth on educational factors. For example, fewer transgender youth were currently enrolled in high school or had a high school diploma or GED compared with LGBQ youth, and more transgender youth were high school dropouts. However, more transgender youth were enrolled in GED programs than were LGBQ youth, indicating that although they may drop out more, some do return to finish. Studies that asked transgender RHY directly about their education had slightly opposite findings: more transgender youth reported having a high school diploma or GED (Freeman and Hamilton 2013) and reported

dropping out less often (Hein 2010) compared with their LGB counterparts. However, Freeman and Hamilton (2013) found that more LGB
than transgender youth had some college exposure, suggesting that once
transgender youth finish high school, they are less likely to continue on to
postsecondary education. Given their experience in high school, transgender youth may have little appetite for going on to college, where they risk
encountering the same prejudice and discrimination. Online postsecondary opportunities may provide safer alternatives to in-person schooling, but
they deny transgender youth the face-to-face and classroom experiences
they may prefer and to which they have a right to access free of harassment
and hostility. This points to the need for transgender-affirming spaces in
education and training, inclusive postsecondary policies that prohibit discrimination on the basis of gender identity and sexual orientation and identity, and accountability for those who interfere with others' ability to access
these opportunities.

That a number of youth have been reported as currently enrolled in
school or a GED program reminds us that RHY have academic needs and
goals that must be met despite their **housing instability** or homelessness.
In fact, the McKinney–Vento Homeless Assistance Act requires accommodations for these youth (U.S. Department of Education 2016). These education data also indicate that RHY have histories or aspirations of attending
college, which must be fostered, yet little is known about LGBTQ+ RHY
enrolled in higher education (Maccio and Ferguson 2016). With so little
data on educational status, our understanding of the academic needs of
LGBTQ+ RHY is incomplete. If a lack of formal education is a pathway
to homelessness and if educational attainment offers a way out, then it is
incumbent upon practitioners, researchers, and policymakers to address
the academic barriers facing LGBTQ+ RHY.

EMPLOYMENT

Despite unemployment being a considerable factor in homelessness,
employment status among RHY is rarely discussed. Rates of employment
among RHY (17–33 percent) are lower than among youth aged sixteen to

twenty-four years in the general population (51.7 percent) (U.S. Bureau of Labor Statistics 2023). Lower rates of employment are also found among LGBTQ+ youth (17 percent) than among heterosexual youth (26 percent) (Freeman and Hamilton 2013). The possible explanations for these findings are varied. For example, these youth may become homeless before receiving parental guidance on job-seeking and job-retention skills or before becoming old enough to be formally employed. Or their actual or perceived sexual- or gender-minority status may make potential employers view them as undesirable employees.

Employment discrimination is a reality for LGBTQ+ people and for individuals experiencing homelessness, and when those identities intersect, job prospects are further reduced. Researchers have chronicled the extensive employment discrimination experienced by transgender individuals (e.g., Koch and Bales 2008; Spicer 2010), which has resulted in staggering unemployment rates for this population (Spicer 2010). Although the hiring, firing, and promotion of LGBTQ+ youth in the workplace is beyond the control of RHY service providers, LGBTQ+ RHY can benefit from interview preparation and vocational training, which providers can offer or refer youth to.

FAMILY SOCIOECONOMIC STATUS

Most LGBTQ+ RHY come from families of low or medium SES. Approximately half of LGBTQ+ RHY (42.1–50 percent) described their families as economically lower class to middle-lower class, though some (7.1–22.4 percent) described their families as upper class (Castellanos 2016; Krause et al. 2016). These findings demonstrate that LGBTQ+ youth homelessness cuts across economic and class strata, as middle SES and upper SES (50–57.9 percent) are more than marginally accounted for. A better understanding of the socioeconomic backgrounds of these youth can help challenge common stereotypes and the myth of a singular LGBTQ+ RHY experience or worldview. A family's SES may matter little to an LGBTQ+ youth whose family rejected them.

NATIONAL ORIGIN

Few studies report the national origin of participants in their demographic data. In two that did, nearly all (71.4–88.9 percent) participants were born in the United States (Castellanos 2016; Shelton 2015). It is unclear where outside the United States the other participants were born or whether they were U.S. citizens, but both studies were conducted in New York City, where more than a third (36.4 percent) of residents are born outside the country (U.S. Census Bureau n.d.b), primarily in the Caribbean, China, Mexico, and South America (NYC Mayor's Office of Immigrant Affairs 2023). Thus, international-born youth, at least those in New York City, are underrepresented in the RHY population. Either there truly are fewer international youth in the RHY population of New York City, or they are undercounted in research, possibly because of their underuse of RHY services.

These studies categorized participants as born in or outside the United States but did not specify participants' citizenship status. Yet, regardless of whether those born outside the United States are citizens, their path to homelessness may be evident. Language barriers (if originating from non-English-speaking countries), separation from family or other social supports, employment discrimination, a lack of immigrant documentation, an inability to access services, and other challenges may lead to housing instability and homelessness for immigrants to the United States. Culturally affirming programs offer bilingual or multilingual staff, interpreter services, and culturally sensitive and appropriate services and referrals. (See box 3.3, *Read All About It!*)

SUMMARY

The terminology and conceptualizations of gender, gender identity, sexual orientation, and sexual identity change frequently. Even for practitioners and researchers who work closely with LGBTQ+ RHY, keeping up with the changes can be a challenge. Researchers use the terminology that is current when they conduct their research, but by the time the findings are

---

BOX 3.3. READ ALL ABOUT IT!
UNDOCUMENTED LGBTQ+ RHY

- Despite their virtual absence from the literature, undocumented LGBTQ+ RHY are not uncommon. Experiencing homelessness makes these youth particularly vulnerable to deportation. Read more about their plight and the resources available to help them:

  o "Rethink Immigration: A Homeless, Undocumented & Detained LGBT Teen's Struggle for Due Process" (Georgevich 2013): https://www.immigrantjustice.org/staff/blog/rethink-immigration-home less-undocumented-detained-lgbt-teens-struggle-due-process
  o *Stronger Together: Supporting LGBT Asylum Seekers in the United States* (McGuirk et al. 2015): http://assets2.hrc.org/files/assets /resources/LGBT_Asylum_Seekers_FINAL.pdf
  o "This Young Advocate Is Helping Providers Serve Undocumented LGBTQ Youth" (Desgarennes 2017): https://truecolorsunited.org /young-advocate-developing-tool-help-providers-serve-undoc- umented-lgbtq-youth/
  o "Why Trans Youth Are More at Risk for Deportation" (Anspach 2017): https://www.teenvogue.com/story/why-transgender-youth -more-likely-to-be-deported

---

disseminated, that terminology may be obsolete. Moreover, because identity is innately subjective, pinning a definition to any term may seem like a fruitless endeavor. LGBTQ+ RHY and those who work with them have a general understanding of what a particular term means but also understand that it may mean something very different to any given individual who identifies with that term. Policymakers, whose work often requires the precise use of language, face the delicate task of having to define the terms spelled out in the policies and legislation they propose, definitions that may inadvertently include some and exclude others. Thus, terminology and definitions are moving targets.

With that caveat, we can describe the LGBTQ+ RHY population by their demographic characteristics but with a great deal of caution. What is certain is that LGBTQ+ youth are overrepresented in the RHY population.

Among them, LGBTQ+ youth of color, especially Black/African American youth, are particularly vulnerable given the intersection of their multiple minority identities. LGBTQ+ RHY experience high rates of school-based bullying and harassment, which interfere with their ability to complete their education successfully. Finding and keeping a job can be complicated by employment discrimination, making it difficult to exit homelessness. Parents and caregivers who reject their LGBTQ+ children may provide little financial support even if they have the means to do so.

LGBTQ+ RHY who are AAPI, AI/AN, or immigrants to the United States are seldom represented in the literature, leaving gaps in our understanding of their unique experiences. Their absence in the literature could be the result of program and research recruitment strategies that do not reach them, resulting in lower rates of service use and research participation among these groups.

Of course, it is unrealistic, and in some cases impossible, for all studies to gather and report all relevant demographic characteristics, but there may be ways to close the gaps. (See box 3.4, *What Do You Think?*) Given their overrepresentation in the RHY population and the discrimination and

---

BOX 3.4. WHAT DO YOU THINK? GATHERING DEMOGRAPHIC DATA

- Design the demographic portion of a research survey with LGBTQ+ RHY. Here are some points to consider:
  - How would you word survey items to gather the information you are seeking?
  - Which items, if any, would be open-ended (e.g., allowing for written or typed answers)? Which, if any, would be closed-ended (e.g., check boxes)? What are some of the benefits and drawbacks of each?
  - For closed-ended questions, what response options would you provide?
  - Would you include an "other" category anywhere? Why or why not?

prejudice they are subjected to in educational and employment settings, in addition to the intersectionality that makes many of them minorities in terms of age, race and ethnicity, and socioeconomic status, LGBTQ+ youth are a particularly vulnerable population. Having as much information about them as possible is thus crucial to better understanding their experiences and developing services and advocating for policies that better meet their needs.

REVISITING CHENICE

- How do Chenice's demographic characteristics compare with the demographic trends presented in this chapter?
- Which of Chenice's demographic characteristics make her more marginalized than RHY with different characteristics?
- If you were Chenice's intake worker, what words of reassurance could you offer her that would be sensitive and appropriate?
- If you were the supervisor of the emergency shelter at which Chenice presented, and none of the transitional living program apartments were vacant, would you admit Chenice to the shelter? If so, would you house her on a floor or wing with boys, a floor or wing with girls, or somewhere else in the shelter? Why?
- Would you attempt to reunify Chenice with her parents? Why or why not?

KEY CONCEPTS

- *Couch surfing*: staying with friends or acquaintances as an informal, temporary housing solution
- *Demographic*: relating to a population, such as with regard to descriptive characteristics
- *Drop-in center*: a nonresidential agency or location that provides immediate services or programs on a walk-in basis

- *Emergency shelter*: housing that provides basic needs on a short-term basis (i.e., a few days to three weeks) to homeless or unstably housed individuals
- *Gender-affirming surgery*: surgery that changes physical features, usually the genitals and reproductive organs, associated with one gender to those of another to align with the individual's gender identity
- *Homeless youth* (or youth experiencing homelessness): multiple federal definitions of *homeless youth* exist; for example, the Runaway and Homeless Youth Act (1974) defines a youth experiencing homelessness as "an individual—(A) who is—(i) less than 21 years of age, or, in the case of a youth seeking shelter in a center under part A [basic centers for RHY and their families], less than 18 years of age . . . and (ii) for the purposes of part B [transitional living programs] not less than 16 years of age . . . (B) for whom it is not possible to live in a safe environment with a relative; and (C) who has no other safe alternative living arrangement ([3] Homeless Youth)"
- *Housing instability*: conditions that contribute to a risk of homelessness, including high rent or mortgage and utilities payments relative to income, missed payments, threats of eviction, poor or no alternative housing options, and frequent moves (Solari et al. 2017)
- *Oversampling*: purposely drawing members of a particular population to ensure adequate representation, usually for analytic purposes
- *Quota sampling*: a nonprobability sampling method that captures a sample with demographic or other characteristic proportions that mirror the population from which the sample was drawn
- *Recruit*: to invite individuals to participate in a research study; in the case of RHY, recruitment settings typically include emergency shelters, drop-in centers, outreach neighborhoods, and squatting sites
- *Runaway youth*: according to the Runaway and Homeless Youth Act (1974), a runaway youth is "an individual who is less than 18 years of age and who absents himself or herself from home or a place of legal residence without the permission of a parent or legal guardian" (56)
- *Sample*: the units (e.g., people) being studied, drawn from a population

- *Standard deviation*: a measure of dispersion that indicates the distance of a data point from the overall mean, with one standard deviation representing approximately 68.3 percent of data points, two standard deviations representing 95.5 percent, and three standard deviations representing 99.7 percent
- *Street outreach*: approaching individuals experiencing homelessness in nontraditional settings (e.g., the streets, train and bus stations, parks and other public spaces) where they congregate and reside to provide them with basic necessities and referrals to agency-based services
- *Transitional living program*: a program that provides basic needs to homeless and unstably housed older adolescents and young adults with a goal of fostering independence and self-sufficiency
- *Transmasculine or transfeminine*: describes a transgender person whose identity is more masculine or more feminine but who does not identify as a trans man or trans woman
- *Unaccompanied minor* (or youth): "a homeless child or youth not in the physical custody of a parent or guardian" (McKinney–Vento Homeless Assistance Act 1987)
- *Unstable housing*: according to Krause et al. (2016), *housing instability* is a broad term better understood by its constituent parts: unstable living circumstances (e.g., "temporary/transnational housing, jail, drug treatment facility, halfway house, and/or temporarily living with friends/family" [513]) and unstable sleeping circumstances (e.g., "in/on the street, park, abandoned building/automobile, public place [subway/bus station], shelter, limited stay/single room occupancy, and/or a welfare motel/hotel" [513])

CHAPTER HIGHLIGHTS

- Transgender youth are particularly vulnerable to street violence, yet they were unaccounted for in more than a third (36 percent) of the studies reviewed here and were referred to by some as the gender they were assigned at birth instead of the gender with which they identify.

- Similarly, nearly one in six studies (16 percent) in this review excluded females from their samples despite females composing more than one-third (de Sousa et al. 2024) to one-half of the RHY population (Hammer et al. 2002) and three-quarters of those seeking help (Pergamit et al. 2010).
- Among the samples reported here, LGBTQ+ RHY were slightly older than heterosexual-cisgender RHY. This may be the result of two mixed-sexuality studies with age criteria that allowed children as young as ten years of age to participate.
- LGBTQ+ RHY of color are overrepresented in the literature, although Asian/Asian American and AI/AN LGBTQ+ RHY are often missing from samples.
- The McKinney–Vento Homelessness Assistance Act requires educational accommodations for RHY, such as the provision of transportation to school (U.S. Department of Education 2016).
- LGBTQ+ RHY are represented in all categories of SES and class.
- Little is known about the national origin and citizenship status of LGBTQ+ RHY. Nonetheless, the discrimination and oppression they experience as immigrants may contribute to their homelessness.
- Identifying as LGBTQ+ and homeless compounds the problem of employment discrimination for LGBTQ+ RHY.

II
The Biopsychosocial Contexts of LGBTQ+ Populations

4 | Physical and Mental Health Concerns

LEARNING OBJECTIVES

Readers of this chapter will be able to:

1. Identify the most common negative physical and mental health outcomes among LGBTQ+ RHY according to the extant literature,
2. Connect LGBTQ+ RHY risk factors with their resulting negative health outcomes, and
3. Articulate gaps in knowledge of negative health outcomes among LGBTQ+ RHY.

CASE VIGNETTE: TY

Ty, a fifteen-year-old white heterosexual youth, uses the gender-neutral abbreviation of their birth middle name and plural pronouns as part of their identification as transgender. Ty's sex was assigned female at birth, and they were subsequently raised as a girl by their mother and, a few years later, their stepfather. However, sometime after the onset of puberty, Ty began to shun gendered references to themself and asked family and friends to use

"Ty" and the pronouns "they," "them," and "their" to refer to them. Given Ty's history of running away—at ages eleven, thirteen, and fourteen—their parents eventually relented and switched from using their birth name to using "Ty" to appease Ty and avoid another runaway episode. However, Ty's parents refuse to refer to Ty's gender as anything but female, which Ty considers offensive.

INTRODUCTION

RHY are susceptible to a number of risks and perils, many affecting their physical and mental health. From violence and victimization to survival sex to lack of access to health care, youth living on their own, whether in unstable housing or on the streets, are exposed to conditions that put their physical and mental health at risk. Castro et al. (2014) found that the longer a youth stayed on the street, the more psychiatric problems they exhibited, and that longer homeless periods were associated with **major depressive episodes**, **social phobia**, and substance abuse.

Because of the stigma, prejudice, discrimination, and violence they experience regarding their sexual orientation and identity and gender identity and expression, LGBTQ+ RHY are at greater risk of poor physical and mental health outcomes. Health risks are compounded by the additional vulnerabilities that many LGBTQ+ RHY experience based on the intersectionality of their identities as youth of color; youth with physical, learning, or developmental disabilities; non-Christian youth; and immigrant and undocumented youth.

Chapter 4 identifies four primary risk factors among LGBTQ+ RHY—violence and victimization, mental health problems, substance use, and high-risk sexual behaviors—and discusses the physical and mental health consequences they face because of these risks. Practitioners, researchers, and policymakers who encounter LGBTQ+ RHY will undoubtedly meet youth with one or more physical and mental health concerns, which must be considered when planning assessments, interventions, and data collection; interpreting findings; and making policy decisions.

PHYSICAL HEALTH

Ty is routinely bullied and physically assaulted by the kids at school, and not just by those Ty's age and older but also by younger kids—those in ninth grade—which only adds to Ty's humiliation. Ty feels vulnerable around both their male and female peers, having been shoved into walls and lockers, knocked to the ground, and punched in the arms by boys who find Ty's gender identity threatening, and being ostracized, stared at, name-called, and threatened with physical harm by girls who see Ty as an easy target for gender-based ridicule. Having a learning disability doesn't help matters. When Ty tries to engage their mother with their complaints, she dismisses Ty, blaming Ty for giving the kids a "reason" with Ty's masculine appearance. As an only child with an estranged father and a stepfather they never bonded with, Ty feels alone, in both their experience as a transgender youth and having no sympathetic adult to turn to for support.

LGBTQ+ and heterosexual-cisgender RHY alike are often forced into behaviors and situations that put their health and safety at risk (e.g., exposure to the elements, living in close quarters, trading sex). The most commonly reported physical health consequences stemming from the four primary risk factors (violence and victimization, mental health problems, substance use, and high-risk sexual behaviors) are infectious diseases, particularly those that spread through sexual contact and injection drug use, and injuries resulting from violence and victimization (self-injury is discussed later in the chapter) (Edidin et al. 2012; Kulik et al. 2011; Youth.gov n.d.b). This section describes the nature and scope of these consequences.

Infectious Diseases

By virtue of their precarious living situations, RHY are susceptible to a number of bacterial and viral infections affecting the skin, teeth and gums, respiratory system, reproductive organs, urinary system, and digestive system (including the mouth, liver, and rectum) (see, e.g., Edidin et al. 2012;

Kulik et al. 2011). Bacteria and viruses are present in bodily fluids, such as saliva, mucus, and blood, and transmitted from person to person through the air (e.g., when droplets from an infected person's cough or sneeze are inhaled by an uninfected person) and through direct contact (e.g., when the skin or bodily fluids of an infected person come into contact with points of entry of an uninfected person, such as mucous membranes in the mouth, vagina, or urethra or the bloodstream via needle injections or cuts in the skin). Infectious diseases are the manifestations of bacteria and viruses in a previously uninfected person (Institute of Medicine 2011).

Sexual contact involving vaginal, anal, or oral penetration and injection drug use involving needle sharing are common routes of transmission among RHY. In 2018, **chlamydia, genital herpes, gonorrhea, human papillomavirus (HPV), syphilis,** and **trichomoniasis** were the most common sexually transmitted infections (STIs) (CDC n.d., 2024h); **human immunodeficiency virus (HIV)** and **hepatitis B** are often considered STIs but can also be spread via injection drug use, which is the primary route of transmission of **hepatitis C** (CDC 2024f). Table 4.1 lists the infectious diseases discussed here, along with their categorization as a bacterium or virus (or parasite), whether they are transmitted via sex, injection drug use, or both, and where the infection appears in or on the body. To put the exposure of LGBTQ+ RHY into context, we will first examine the broader scope of these diseases.

According to estimates from the Centers for Disease Control and Prevention (CDC) (n.d., 2022b, 2024h), HPV was the most common of the new cases of STIs in 2018 (13 million), followed by trichomoniasis (6.9 million), chlamydia (4 million), gonorrhea (1.6 million), herpes simplex virus type 2 (often referred to as genital herpes; 572,000), syphilis (146,000), hepatitis C (50,300), HIV (32,600), and hepatitis B (8,300).

Approximately 1.2 million people in the United States had HIV as of 2022 (CDC 2024d). Two-thirds (67 percent) of the estimated 31,800 new cases in 2022 were among men who have sex with men versus 22 percent among individuals exposed through heterosexual contact and 7 percent among injection drug users (CDC 2024d). Blacks/African Americans are disproportionately represented among both men who have sex with men and those who become infected through heterosexual contact (CDC

TABLE 4.1 Infectious diseases transmitted via sexual contact and/or injection drug use

	Bacterium, virus, or parasite	Route of transmission	Site of infection
Chlamydia (CDC 2021)	Bacterium	Vaginal, anal, and oral sex	Urogenital (urinary tract, genitals), rectum, oropharyngeal (mouth, throat)
Genital Herpes (CDC 2024a)	Virus	Vaginal, anal, and oral sex	Mouth, vagina, genitals, rectum
Gonorrhea (CDC 2023c)	Bacterium	Vaginal, anal, and oral sex	Urogenital, rectum, throat
Hepatitis B (CDC 2024e)	Virus	Sexual contact involving an exchange of bodily fluids, needle sharing	Liver
Hepatitis C (CDC 2024f)	Virus	Needle sharing (rarely, sexual contact)	Liver
HIV (CDC 2024b)	Virus	Vaginal and anal sex, needle sharing	Various
HPV (CDC 2024c)	Virus	Vaginal, anal, and oral sex, skin-to-skin contact	Genitals, anus, throat
Syphilis (CDC 2023a, 2024i)	Bacterium	Vaginal, anal, and oral sex	Genitals, vagina, mouth, rectum, anus
Trichomoniasis (CDC 2023b)	Parasite	Vaginal, anal, and oral sex	Urogenital, mouth, anus

2024d). More than half (60 percent) of new cases in 2022 appeared in individuals thirteen to twenty-four years of age, 75 percent of whom were men who have sex with men and disproportionately men of color (CDC 2024d). (See box 4.1, *What Do You Think?*) Despite the prevalence of these diseases and the public health risk they pose, very little is known about their impact on RHY, particularly LGBTQ+ RHY.

A review by Caccamo et al. (2017) of ten articles published between 2000 and 2015 on the subject of STIs (excluding HIV) among RHY revealed

---

BOX 4.1. WHAT DO YOU THINK? STI TRENDS

- How has the prevalence of STIs changed over the past fifty years?
- How do you expect the prevalence of STIs to change in the next ten, twenty-five, and fifty years?
- What might account for these changes?
- Why do STIs affect some populations (e.g., men who have sex with men, Black/African American people, people ages thirteen to twenty-four) more than others?

---

overall prevalence rates ranging from 6.4 to 32 percent, with a median of 13.2 percent. Hepatitis C (3.8–12 percent), chlamydia (2.8–18.3 percent), hepatitis B (1.4–17 percent), HPV/genital warts (a symptom of HPV; 1.3–3.5 percent), herpes (1.1–11.8 percent), gonorrhea (0.4–24.9 percent), and syphilis (0.2–3.5 percent) were all represented in the RHY samples in the review, although HPV appeared at rates far lower than in the general population, perhaps because of the push to vaccinate adolescents and the limited benefit in vaccinating adults (Meites et al. 2019).

Transgender women and men who have sex with men, including those who are young and homeless, are disproportionately affected by chlamydia, gonorrhea, and syphilis, especially if they are also infected with HIV, which is easier to contract in the presence of other STIs (CDC 2024g; Shannon et al. 2019). LGB RHY have a higher risk than heterosexual RHY of contracting HIV (Gangamma et al. 2008; Tyler 2013). Available reports estimate HIV infection among LGBTQ+ RHY as ranging between 16 percent (Ream et al. 2012) and 20 percent (Ali Forney Center n.d.). Among several independent variables assessing HIV risk, survival sex, which is more common among LGB RHY than heterosexual RHY (Walls and Bell 2011), has been identified as the strongest predictor (Gangamma et al. 2008; Tyler 2013). Far too little is known about the presence of HIV among LGBTQ+ RHY relative to the attention paid to the population's disproportionate risk and the dire warnings about its spread.

Injury and Death

Life on the streets offers little to no protection from physical and sexual violence and victimization and too often results in injury or death. As vulnerable as RHY are because of their age, LGBTQ+ RHY are even more so because of their sexual orientation and identity and gender identity and expression. Housed LGBTQ+ youth are more vulnerable to bullying and abuse than are their heterosexual peers; this disparity is no different for LGBTQ+ youth who run away, are thrown away (i.e., kicked out), or are otherwise unstably housed or homeless, and the results are devastating.

The literature is rife with reports of violence and victimization of LGBTQ+ RHY. Research has shown that significantly more LGBTQ+ RHY than heterosexual-cisgender RHY are victimized while homeless (Forge, Hartinger-Saunders et al. 2018; Morton, Samuels et al. 2018). One Southern California study (Rabinovitz et al. 2010) found that 28 percent of LGBT RHY had been physically assaulted compared with 18 percent of their heterosexual-cisgender counterparts. Moreover, LGBTQ+ RHY are vulnerable even in places where they should expect to be safe, such as shelters. In fact, some LGBTQ+ RHY are willing to risk their health, such as by taking sleeping pills to be able to sleep in the cold, just to avoid shelters. As one youth put it, "'Safer for me to be popping pills and sleeping outside in minus zero degree weather than being in the shelter system [because of] transphobia and homophobia'" (Abramovich 2017, 1491). Violence is not always perpetrated by strangers and acquaintances. Indeed, rates of having experienced intimate partner violence are higher among LGBTQ+ youth who report having been homeless within the past twelve months than LGBTQ+ youth who report not having been homeless during the same period (Langenderfer-Magruder et al. 2016). Neither is victimization limited to the streets. Unstably housed LGBTQ+ youth are victimized (i.e., "pushed, shoved, slapped, hit, or kicked") at school significantly more than their stably housed LGBTQ+ and unstably housed heterosexual peers (Baams et al. 2019, 3).

Sexual victimization, too, is reported at alarming rates. Compared with heterosexual RHY, LGBQ RHY experience higher rates of sexual assault (i.e., unwanted touching of one's genitals or another's genitals) and forced sex (i.e., attempted or completed rape), and transgender and nonbinary-gender RHY experience higher rates of forced sex than do cisgender RHY (Morton, Samuels et al. 2018; Santa Maria, Breeden et al. 2020; Tyler and Schmitz 2018b). These types of victimization lead to poorer physical and mental health outcomes in adulthood (Pearson et al. 2017), making premature death more likely among LGBTQ+ RHY than among their heterosexual-cisgender counterparts (Morton, Samuels et al. 2018). (See box 4.2, *Read All About It!*, for an excerpt of the research brief of the 2018 study by Morton, Samuels et al.) More data are needed on mortality among LGBTQ+ RHY.

BOX 4.2. READ ALL ABOUT IT! EXPOSURE TO VIOLENCE AND VICTIMIZATION AMONG LGBTQ+ RHY

- Research by the University of Chicago's Chapin Hall (Morton, Samuels et al. 2018) paints a grim picture of the realities faced by LGBTQ+ RHY regarding their physical well-being, especially compared with their heterosexual-cisgender RHY peers. According to their report *Missed Opportunities: LGBTQ Youth Homelessness in America*,

  LGBTQ youth had over twice the rate of early death among youth experiencing homelessness. Similarly, while virtually all youth facing homelessness experience adversity, LGBTQ youth describe particularly pervasive exposure to trauma both before and during their periods of homelessness. In the in-depth interviews, individuals who identified as LGBTQ reported more physical harm from others versus their non-LGBTQ peers (62 percent vs. 47 percent) and . . . [were more likely to report] having been forced to have sex (38 percent vs. 15 percent). These findings illustrate why it is critical that new efforts emerge to integrate safe spaces, rapid and sustained exits from homelessness, positive adult connections, and culturally attuned mental and physical health supports into service plans for LGBTQ young people. (8–9)

- To download the *Missed Opportunities* report, visit https://www.chapin hall.org/wp-content/uploads/VoYC-LGBTQ-Brief-FINAL.pdf.

MENTAL HEALTH

Ty has never thought of themself as having a mental disorder, which just sounds scary to them. Still, they couldn't deny the fallout of the bullying and physical assault: dreading the thought of going to school, skipping certain classes or school altogether for fear of more victimization, having trouble paying attention in class, not having much of an appetite at school or at home, and feeling sad and lonely much of the time. At times, Ty secretly wishes it "would all just go away."

Mental health refers to the status of one's cognitive, affective, and behavioral well-being. Dysfunction in one or more of those areas that causes the individual distress or impairment in functioning can typically be attributed to a mental disorder identified by the American Psychiatric Association (APA), the professional organization for psychiatrists in the United States. The APA has been responsible for categorizing and defining mental disorders since 1952, when it published its first set of diagnostic guidelines, the *Diagnostic and Statistical Manual of Mental Disorders* (*DSM*) (APA n.d.). Since then, the *DSM* has undergone several revisions, with disorders being added, eliminated, renamed, redefined, and recategorized. For example, homosexuality was removed in 1973, and gender identity disorder was renamed gender dysphoria (and its criteria modified) in 2013. Nevertheless, LGBTQ+ RHY remain disproportionately affected by mental health problems.

LGBTQ+ RHY are routinely found to experience mental disorders at higher rates than their heterosexual-cisgender counterparts. In 2012, RHY service providers reported that a median of 65 percent of LGBTQ+ RHY demonstrated mental health problems (Durso and Gates 2012), a figure that was teased apart three years later, revealing that 65 percent of LGBQ RHY and 75 percent of transgender RHY exhibited mental health problems (Choi et al. 2015). Nearly two-thirds (64.3 percent) of a sample of LGBTQ+ RHY reported a mean Global Severity Index score on the Brief Symptom Inventory that indicated overall mental health problems (Bidell 2014). These broad findings warrant a closer look at the mental health challenges facing LGBTQ+ RHY.

Among RHY, identifying as LGBTQ+ is significantly associated with emotional distress (Moskowitz et al. 2013). Rates of internalizing symptoms (e.g., depression, anxiety) and externalizing symptoms (e.g., conduct problems, substance use) among LGBTQ+ RHY surpass not only those of heterosexual-cisgender RHY but also those of LGBTQ+ youth who are housed (Rhoades et al. 2018; Rosario et al. 2012a). This is also true for self-harm, such as cutting and burning oneself (Walls et al. 2010). According to Rosario et al. (2012a), the negative psychological effects experienced by LGBTQ+ RHY are mediated by the stress they experience as youth experiencing homelessness and by social factors such as mistreatment and having minimal social support. (See box 4.3, *What Do You Think?*) Depression (Bidell 2014; Gattis and Larson 2017; Grafsky et al. 2011; Narendorf et al. 2017; Rhoades et al. 2018), suicidality (i.e., suicidal ideation, having suicidal thoughts, or making suicide attempts) (Moskowitz et al. 2013; Rhoades et al. 2018), self-harm (Moskowitz et al. 2013), anxiety (Bidell 2014), and **post-traumatic stress disorder** (**PTSD**) (Rhoades et al. 2018) are the psychiatric symptoms and disorders most often seen in this population.

Depression

Significantly more unstably housed LGBTQ+ youth exhibit depression than their heterosexual-cisgender counterparts (Baams et al. 2019). Moreover, depression affects subpopulations of LGBTQ+ RHY differently and for

---

BOX 4.3. WHAT DO YOU THINK?
MEDIATORS AND MODERATORS

- What do Rosario et al. (2012) mean when they say that the negative psychological effects faced by LGBTQ+ RHY are *mediated* by the stress they experience as homeless youth and by social factors such as mistreatment and minimal social support?
- What is an example of a **mediating variable**? What is an example of a **moderating variable**? How are they different?
- In the context of the mental health of LGBTQ+ RHY, are negative psychological effects, stress, and social factors dependent variables, independent variables, or some combination of the two?

different reasons. For example, Gattis and Larson (2017) found significantly higher depressive scores among Black LGB RHY compared with their heterosexual counterparts, which the authors attributed to the LGB participants' experiences of LGBT racial **microaggressions** (those that contain elements of heterosexism, cissexism, white supremacy, and structural racism). (See box 4.4, *What Do You Think?*) Depressive symptoms were, in turn, found to be related to suicidality. Gay men are particularly affected by major depressive episodes (i.e., two-week periods of sustained symptoms that form the foundation of a diagnosis of **major depressive disorder**) (APA 2022) compared with their heterosexual male peers (Tucker et al. 2012). A contributing factor may be sexual orientation stigma—whether external (i.e., coming from others) or internal (i.e., coming from the self)—which contributes to depression in

BOX 4.4. WHAT DO YOU THINK? MICROAGGRESSIONS

- In 1970, the psychiatrist Chester M. Pierce coined the term *microaggressions*, which he and his colleagues later defined as "subtle, stunning, often automatic, and nonverbal exchanges which are 'put downs' of blacks by offenders" (Pierce et al. 1977, 65).
- The definition of *microaggressions* has broadened to include other vulnerable populations (Sue 2010).
- What are some examples of microaggressions in relation to the following identities or "others"?

  o People of color
  o People of non-European ethnicities
  o Lesbian, gay, bisexual, pansexual, asexual, and queer people
  o Transgender, genderqueer, intersex, agender, and nonbinary people
  o Women
  o People who are poor
  o People with a physical disability or chronic illness
  o Children and older adults
  o People who do not practice Christian religions or who practice no religion at all
  o People who were not born in the United States or who are not U.S. citizens

homeless young men who have sex with men (Bruce et al. 2014). Bisexual RHY demonstrate a greater likelihood of probable depression than their lesbian and gay peers (Siconolfi et al. 2019), perhaps because of the marginalization they experience as bisexual individuals even within the LGBTQ+ community. Questioning youth (i.e., those who are unsure of their sexual orientation or gender identity), as well as those outside the heterosexual-cisgender–LGBT binary, have significantly less confidence than their LGBT-identified peers that "the future has structure and is manageable" (Rew et al. 2019, 3). Perhaps feeling uncertain about one's identity or experiencing prejudice and discrimination as a person with a nonbinary identity dampens their optimism about the future, possibly leading to depression or depressive symptoms.

The consequences of depression extend beyond its challenging and sometimes debilitating symptoms. For example, when LGB RHY are depressed, they are more likely than their heterosexual counterparts to consume alcohol (Tyler et al. 2019). In gay males, a greater number of depressive symptoms is associated with trading sex for resources (Tucker et al. 2012), which carries its own set of risks. A complete understanding of depression includes an awareness of consequences such as these, as well as others, not least of which is suicidality.

Suicidality

Suicidal ideation and attempts as consequences of severe depression are also more common among LGBTQ+ RHY than among their unhoused heterosexual-cisgender and housed LGBTQ+ peers (Baams et al. 2019; Moskowitz et al. 2013; Rhoades et al. 2018). Between one-third (34.7 percent) (Walls et al. 2009) and one-half (54.5 percent) (Rhoades et al. 2018) of LGBTQ+ RHY have attempted suicide in their lifetime; one in five (22.3 percent) have attempted suicide in the past year (Walls et al. 2010); 15 percent plan to attempt suicide in the future (Rhoades et al. 2018); and 43.3 percent have seriously considered suicide (Baams et al. 2019). Among a sample of 524 LGBTQ+ youth using crisis services, compared with those who had never been homeless, those who had were more likely to feel hopeless and burdensome (Rhoades et al. 2018), each of which is a predictor of suicide (Roeder and Cole 2019). Suicide attempts are more common among transgender youth (Eisenberg et al. 2017) and LGBTQ+ RHY with histories of engaging in survival sex and being in the custody of social services (Walls et al. 2009).

Anxiety and Post-Traumatic Stress Disorder

Given the high levels of stress and victimization to which they are exposed, LGBTQ+ RHY are also susceptible to anxiety and PTSD (formerly considered an anxiety disorder but now considered a trauma- and stressor-related disorder) (APA 2022). Indeed, LGB RHY are more anxious than their housed counterparts (Rosario et al. 2012a) and are more likely to have PTSD than are heterosexual RHY (Tyler et al. 2010) and housed LGBTQ+ youth (Rhoades et al. 2018). Since PTSD is the result of exposure to trauma, mental health care, especially trauma-focused therapy, should be a component of the basic services provided to LGBTQ+ RHY.

Related Concerns

Although less common, other psychosocial problems have been reported and deserve additional investigation and monitoring. For instance, LGBTQ+ RHY exhibit significantly higher rates of somatic (i.e., physical) complaints, social problems, delinquency, and aggression (Grafsky et al. 2011; Rhoades et al. 2018). They also have high scores on the paranoid ideation (i.e., paranoia) and **psychoticism** dimensions of the Brief Symptom Inventory (Bidell 2014), suggesting problems in these areas as well. Somatic complaints may manifest as headaches, gastrointestinal problems, and muscle and joint pain for which there may or may not be an identifiable cause. Delinquency, aggression, and paranoia can interfere with a youth's ability to form healthy relationships and receive the social support they so desperately need. All these concerns can be addressed by practitioners who recognize these presentations in RHY and have the skills to address them using an LGBTQ+-affirming approach.

SUMMARY

The extant literature makes clear that LGBTQ+ RHY experience negative physical and mental health outcomes, worse so compared with their heterosexual-cisgender RHY and housed LGBTQ+ peers. Their worse health may result from the high-risk behaviors in which they engage, the injuries and diseases to which they are susceptible, the harsh social and environmental conditions to which they are exposed, the lack of access to health care for LGBTQ+ youth, and their concerns about seeking services from those whom they perceive to be unknowledgeable, unfriendly, or downright hostile. Some youth, fearing shelter violence, opt to sleep in abandoned houses instead (Coolhart and Brown 2017). Youth service providers must ensure that the health care specialists to whom they refer youth are LGBTQ+-affirming, culturally competent on issues of sexual orientation and identity and gender identity and expression, and sensitive to the unique needs of this population.

Although there is no shortage of literature on the violence and victimization, mental health problems, substance use, and high-risk sexual behaviors that lead to negative health outcomes among LGBTQ+ RHY, we know little about the impact of those health outcomes on this population. According to the research that exists, most common among these outcomes are infectious diseases including HIV, injury, depression, anxiety, PTSD, suicide, and death. However, the knowledge base is shallow. A better understanding of these problems is needed to understand how best to address them through intervention and policy at the micro, mezzo, and macro levels.

Despite what may seem like insurmountable obstacles to their good health and well-being, LGBTQ+ RHY survive owing to their resilience, which is no doubt bolstered by life on the streets. They have coping skills they can rely on and strengths they can call on to meet the challenges they face while navigating their way toward stable housing. Practitioners can capitalize on these reserves and empower LGBTQ+ RHY to transform their lives. These protective factors and others are discussed at length in chapter 5.

REVISITING TY

- What possible diagnoses do Ty's emotional symptoms suggest (assuming that other diagnostic criteria are met)?
- If you were employed as a social worker at Ty's high school, how might you intervene with Ty? With Ty's aggressors? With the school's principal and other administrators?
- In a one-on-one session with Ty, what questions would you ask? What would you want to know first? What factors would you want to assess?
- Would you reach out to Ty's parents? If so, what would be your rationale for doing so, and how might you approach them?
- What antibullying policies and laws are in place in your school district, city or town, and state?

KEY CONCEPTS

- *Chlamydia*: an STI that can lead to chronic arthritis and pregnancy problems including infertility (CDC 2021; NIAMSD 2024)
- *Genital herpes*: caused by the herpes simplex virus type 2; can cause pregnancy complications; poses a greater threat to newborns and people with compromised immune systems (CDC 2024a)
- *Gonorrhea*: infected people may be asymptomatic or have only mild symptoms; treated with antibiotics (CDC 2023c)
- *Hepatitis B*: a short- or long-term liver infection that can cause cirrhosis of the liver or liver cancer; preventable through vaccination (CDC 2024e)
- *Hepatitis C*: a short- or long-term liver infection that can cause cirrhosis of the liver or liver cancer; a chronic condition in approximately half of those infected; no vaccine available (CDC 2024f)
- *Human immunodeficiency virus (HIV)*: a virus that compromises the immune system and, if left untreated, can lead to opportunistic infections, an indication that an individual has developed acquired immunodeficiency syndrome (AIDS) (CDC 2024b)

- *Human papillomavirus (HPV)*: the most common STI; usually resolves on its own but, depending on type, can cause cancer at the site of infection (CDC 2024c)
- *Major depressive disorder*: a depressive disorder characterized by the presence of at least one major depressive episode, the absence of manic and hypomanic (i.e., bipolar) episodes, and not better explained by other disorders
- *Major depressive episode*: the presence of five characteristic depressive symptoms, including feeling sad or depressed and/or loss of interest or pleasure in activities formerly enjoyed, for a minimum of two weeks
- *Mediating variable*: "accounts for the relation between the predictor [i.e., independent variable] and criterion [i.e., dependent variable]; whereas moderator variables specify when certain effects will hold, mediators speak to how or why such effects occur" (Baron and Kenny 1986, 1176)
- *Moderating variable*: "[affects] the direction and/or strength of the relation between an independent or predictor variable and a dependent or criterion variable" (Baron and Kenny 1986, 1174)
- *Microaggressions*: "subtle, stunning, often automatic, and nonverbal exchanges which are 'put downs' of blacks by offenders" (Pierce et al. 1977, 65); the definition has now been broadened to include other populations (Sue 2010)
- *Post-traumatic stress disorder (PTSD)*: a response to a traumatic event
- *Psychoticism*: a personality dimension characterized as aggressive, cold, egocentric, impersonal, impulsive, antisocial, unempathetic, creative, and tough-minded (Eysenck 1996)
- *Social phobia*: an anxiety disorder involving a fear of social situations in which there is the potential to be judged, scrutinized, or embarrassed (APA 2022)
- *Syphilis*: an STI whose symptoms appear in stages; treated with antibiotics (CDC 2023a)
- *Trichomoniasis*: the second most common STI, especially among women; 70 percent of those who have it do not exhibit symptoms (CDC 2023b).

CHAPTER HIGHLIGHTS

- The most commonly reported physical health consequences among LGBTQ+ RHY are infectious diseases, particularly STIs, injury, and death, resulting primarily from abuse, assault, and other forms of violence and victimization.
- Survival sex, which is more common among LGB RHY than heterosexual RHY, is the strongest predictor of HIV risk.
- The actual or perceived threat of shelter violence leads some youth to risk sleeping in less safe environments such as abandoned buildings or outside.
- PTSD, depression, suicidal ideation, and self-harm are the most commonly reported mental health problems among LGBTQ+ RHY.
- LGBT racial microaggressions might account for higher depressive scores among Black LGB RHY compared with their heterosexual counterparts.
- LGBTQ+ RHY, especially transgender RHY, experience higher rates of suicidal ideation and suicide attempts.
- Negative health outcomes among LGBTQ+ RHY may result from or be compounded by the lack of access to health care for LGBTQ+ youth or their concerns about seeking care.

5 | Internal and External Risk and Protective Factors

LEARNING OBJECTIVES

Readers of this chapter will be able to:

1. Define internal and external risk and protective factors,
2. Explain reasons that LGBTQ+ and heterosexual-cisgender youth leave home, and
3. Identify risk and protective factors among LGBTQ+ RHY.

CASE VIGNETTE: JULIANA

Juliana, a seventeen-year-old cisgender, bisexual adolescent of Puerto Rican, Cuban, and Irish descent, recently left home because of intense family stress following her father's discovery of her intimate relationship with another girl. Juliana lived at home with her parents and two younger siblings until last year, when her father began berating her, yelling at her, and using anti-LGBTQ+ slurs to refer to her and her girlfriend.

INTRODUCTION

Estimates of youth experiencing homelessness vary widely depending in part on how homelessness among youth is defined and on the methodology used to study this population. A commonly cited statistic is Hammer et al.'s 2002 finding that more than 1.68 million youth run away from or are kicked out of their homes each year. More recent estimates suggest that seven hundred thousand thirteen- to seventeen-year-olds and 3.5 million eighteen- to twenty-four-year-olds experience homelessness annually (Morton et al. 2017). Intersectionality is an important aspect of RHY prevalence since youth who are Black, Hispanic/Latinx, pregnant or parenting, LGBTQ+, or without a high school diploma are disproportionately represented among this population (Morton et al. 2017). The good news is that 99.6 percent of youth return home (Hammer et al. 2002), usually in short order, 30 percent within six months (Milburn et al. 2007). However, for the time that those youth are away from home, and for the youth who do not return at all, life on the streets carries several significant, troubling, and often tragic risks, including death. Among 1,871 Montreal street youth (Roy et al. 2010), 1.7 percent died between initial data collection and semiannual follow-ups, and in a sample of 218 San Francisco youth experiencing homelessness (Auerswald et al. 2016), 5.1 percent died between 2004 and 2010. In both studies, most deaths were attributed to suicide or alcohol and drug use or overdose. The deceased were disproportionately white and to a lesser degree biracial or multiracial.

The outcomes of LGBTQ+ RHY can vary based on a number of risk and protective factors, both internal and external, which are discussed in depth in this chapter. An understanding of these factors is helpful for the practitioners, researchers, and policymakers who work with these vulnerable youth because it allows them to intervene to reduce risk or strengthen protective factors through effective social welfare policies and programs. The World Health Organization and the youth programs and services arm of the U.S. government rely on the definitions of risk and protective factors discussed next. (See box 5.1, *Read All About It!*)

BOX 5.1. READ ALL ABOUT IT!
RISK AND PROTECTIVE FACTORS IN YOUNG PEOPLE

- *Preventing Mental, Emotional, and Behavioral Disorders Among Young People: Progress and Possibilities* (O'Connor et al. 2009), a report from the National Research Council and the Institute of Medicine, describes the prevention of and early intervention for mental disorders and substance abuse in young people. Visit https://nap .nationalacademies.org/to download the free report.

DEFINING RISK AND PROTECTIVE FACTORS

According to O'Connor et al. (2009), a **risk factor** is "a characteristic at the biological, psychological, family, community, or cultural level that precedes and is associated with a higher likelihood of problem outcomes" (xxviii). Said another way, risk factors "are conditions or variables associated with a lower likelihood of socially desirable or positive outcomes and a higher likelihood of negative or socially undesirable outcomes in a variety of life areas from health and well-being to social role performance" (Jessor et al. 1998, 195). No definitive ranking of risk factors among LGBTQ+ RHY exists. However, violence and victimization, mental health problems, substance use, and high-risk sexual behaviors are common risk factors in this population (Keuroghlian et al. 2014; Rosario et al. 2012b; Tyler and Schmitz 2018b; Van Leeuwen et al. 2006).

Likewise, a **protective factor** is "a characteristic at the biological, psychological, family, or community (including peers and culture) level that is associated with a lower likelihood of problem outcomes or that reduces the negative impact of a risk factor on problem outcomes" (O'Connor et al. 2009, xxvii). Similarly, protective factors "enhance the likelihood of positive outcomes and lessen the likelihood of negative consequences from exposure to risk" (Jessor et al. 1998, 195). In the context of LGBTQ+ RHY, more is known about risk factors than protective factors, including **resilience**: the ability to employ protective factors in the face of adversity.

BOX 5.2. WHAT DO YOU THINK?
RESILIENCE AMONG LGBTQ+ RHY

- Why might there be little research on resilience in LGBTQ+ RHY?
- Why would resiliency be difficult to define for this population?
- What might resilience look like in this population?
- How many protective factors might be present in some of these youth, and what are they?

According to Tyler (2013), "There is a dearth of literature on resiliency (protective factors) among runaway and homeless adolescents because *resiliency* is difficult to define for this population" (1584, emphasis in original). (See box 5.2, *What Do You Think?*) Nonetheless, we know much about the protective factors in the general RHY population. Parent and family connections and support, peer connections and support, self-esteem, natural mentors, and resilience and perceived resilience are the most common. Among LGBTQ+ RHY, social networks and social support are a predominant protective factor but certainly not the only one. Resilience, coping, **adaptability**, and strengths are also evident in this population, all of which we explore in this chapter.

INTERNAL AND EXTERNAL FACTORS

Simply put, **internal risk and protective factors** are those that originate inside a person, whereas external factors originate outside. That is not to say that an individual has control over internal factors and no control over external ones. Rather, internal risk and protective factors are those that reside in an individual mentally (i.e., cognitively or emotionally) or physically. For example, a mental disorder, such as depression, might be an internal risk factor, whereas adaptive coping skills, such as a willingness to seek help, might be an internal protective factor. Remember that everyone

TABLE 5.1 Common risk and protective factors among LGBTQ+ RHY

Risk factors	Protective factors
• Violence and victimization • Mental health problems • Substance use • High-risk sexual behaviors	• Social networks and social support • Resiliency • Coping and adaptability • Strengths

is different, so how depression, for example, affects one person might be different from how it affects another in terms of symptoms and severity. **External risk and protective factors**, on the other hand, are those that exist outside an individual; that is, they exist in others or in the environment. Having parents who rejected them might be an external risk factor for an LGBTQ+ youth, whereas having a street family (i.e., a group of individuals who are unstably housed or experiencing homelessness and who share resources and serve as one another's social support) might be an external protective factor. Again, risk and protective factors affect each individual to varying degrees, which can make generalizing research findings to all members of a group difficult. People are predisposed, susceptible, or vulnerable to risk factors, whereas they are able to call up, employ, or rely on protective factors.

What follows is a closer examination of common risk and protective factors (table 5.1). We begin with a brief overview of the circumstances leading LGBTQ+ youth to become homeless.

SEXUAL ORIENTATION AND IDENTITY AND GENDER IDENTITY AND EXPRESSION

What is it that leads some LGBTQ+ youth to exit the home and others not? Researchers suggest that sexual development may play a role. Rosario et al. (2012b) found that LGB youth experiencing homelessness became aware of their same-sex or bisexual orientation and acted on that sexuality earlier than their housed LGB peers. Given their stage of brain development,

LGB youth who realize their sexuality in early adolescence may blurt out their identity at inopportune moments or act out their identity in not-so-inconspicuous ways. It is possible that such indiscretion can lead to the discovery of a youth's sexuality by their parents or guardians, which may then result in the youth leaving, being pushed out of (e.g., leaving to avoid verbal, emotional, physical, or sexual abuse), or getting kicked out of their home. Once homeless, these youth succumb to substance use at rates higher than those of their housed LGB (Rosario et al. 2012b) and unhoused heterosexual peers (Santa Maria et al. 2018).

Although LGBTQ+ youth are kicked out of their homes at significantly higher rates than are heterosexual youth (Forge, Hartinger-Saunders et al. 2018), the reasons for leaving home are often the same for both groups: "family conflict (59.9 percent), desire for freedom (51.5 percent), and difficulties with a family member (48.5 percent)" (Cochran et al. 2002, 774). However, LGBTQ+ RHY also possess a minority sexual orientation or gender identity, a factor that does not contribute to heterosexual-cisgender youth running away or getting pushed or thrown out of the home and subsequently becoming homelessness. As such, sexual-minority youth leave home because of their sexuality more often than do heterosexual youth (Rosario et al. 2012b), as much as five times more often for gay males compared with heterosexual males (Whitbeck et al. 2004). According to Durso and Gates (2012), RHY service providers cited family rejection (46 percent) as the number one factor leading LGBTQ+ youth to leave home, followed by being kicked out because of their sexual orientation or gender identity (43 percent). In a follow-up study three years later (Choi et al. 2015), providers cited running away or being forced out of the home because of their sexual orientation or gender identity as the primary pathway to LGBTQ+ youth homelessness. This is especially true for transgender and gender-expansive youth (Brown et al. 2020), whose rates tend to be much higher than those of cisgender LGBQ+ youth (66.7 percent) (Shelton and Bond 2017). According to one transgender and gender-expansive youth, "'I remember coming home from work and my stuff was packed, the locks were changed, and there was a note. There was 200 dollars in an envelope, and [my mother] told me to find somewhere to go'" (Shelton and Bond 2017, 287). According to at least one account (Durso and Gates

2012), 68 percent of LGBTQ+ youth experience family rejection, and more than half (54 percent) are exposed to abuse. Exposure in the home to physical, sexual, and emotional abuse, as well as to alcohol use, also contributes to an LGBTQ+ youth's decision to leave (Durso and Gates 2012; Rosario et al. 2012b). Less common reasons are aging out of foster care (17 percent), emotional or financial neglect (14 percent), and the youth's substance use (12 percent) (Durso and Gates 2012).

LGBTQ+ RHY are also overrepresented among clients and consumers of state agencies. Nearly half these youth have been involved with child welfare and juvenile justice systems, more so than heterosexual RHY (Castellanos 2016; Forge, Hartinger-Saunders et al. 2018). This finding reflects a pattern of disproportionate family rejection, homelessness, and state custody, causing LGBTQ+ RHY to face even more rejection. Shelton and Bond (2017) reported the experience of one transgender youth being ejected from two foster group homes for dressing as her authentic self. For some LGBTQ+ RHY, then, the child welfare system is not always the haven it is intended to be.

With home and family life as common denominators for the many pathways to homelessness (table 5.2), practitioners, researchers, and policymakers would do well to use these as starting points for prevention efforts. Intervening early—when youth first recognize same-sex sexual thoughts or feelings or before or soon after they disclose them to critical caregivers, such as parents or foster parents—is key to preventing the departure of youth from their homes and any consequences of that disclosure. Practitioners,

TABLE 5.2 Reasons RHY leave home

General RHY population	LGBTQ+ RHY population
• Family conflict • Desire for freedom • Difficulties with a family member	• Family rejection • Sexual orientation or gender identity • Exposure to physical, sexual, or emotional abuse • Exposure to substance use • Aging out of foster care • Emotional or financial neglect • The youth's substance use

in particular, can assist youth as they decide whether, when, how, and to whom to disclose.

RISK FACTORS

Juliana's father's behavior toward her lasted several months until Juliana could no longer tolerate the constant verbal abuse. She first went to the home of her paternal aunt, Alejandra, where she stayed only a few days because of her aunt's concern that letting Juliana stay would upset her father, who would see Alejandra as siding with Juliana and going against his beliefs that same-sex relationships were "against God and against the family." Since then, Juliana has been couch surfing, sometimes staying with her girlfriend and her parents and other times staying at the homes of classmates. Juliana's grades started slipping a few weeks before she left home, but she still attends high school fairly regularly.

Violence and Victimization

Violence and victimization can refer to physical (e.g., assault, mugging), psychological or emotional (e.g., intimidation, harassment), or sexual (e.g., rape, molestation) crimes against an individual, and LGBTQ+ RHY are more often subjected to violence and victimization than heterosexual-cisgender RHY (Forge, Hartinger-Saunders et al. 2018). LGB RHY, especially lesbian youth (Whitbeck et al. 2004), are more likely than heterosexual RHY to experience physical victimization (Baams et al. 2019; Tyler and Ray 2019; Whitbeck et al. 2004). When they do, it is most often at the hands of strangers, followed by family members and intimate partners (Marsiglia et al. 2009). Sexual violence, however, appears to dominate the RHY literature. According to the Centers for Disease Control and Prevention and the National Center for Injury Prevention and Control (Basile et al. 2014), the uniform definition of **sexual violence** is

a sexual act that is committed or attempted by another person without freely given consent of the victim or against someone who is unable to consent or refuse. It includes: forced or alcohol/drug facilitated penetration of a victim; forced or alcohol/drug facilitated incidents in which the victim was made to penetrate a perpetrator or someone else; nonphysically pressured unwanted penetration; intentional sexual touching; or non-contact acts of a sexual nature. Sexual violence can also occur when a perpetrator forces or coerces a victim to engage in sexual acts with a third party. (11)

Sexual violence terminology varies throughout the literature, and rarely do studies provide definitions; however, sexual violence includes sexual assault (Durso and Gates 2012; LaLota et al. 2005), sexual victimization (Tyler 2008; Tyler et al. 2004), sexual exploitation (Durso and Gates 2012; Rice et al. 2013), and sexual abuse (Rew et al. 2005; Whitbeck et al. 2004). We use these terms here as they appear in the literature.

RHY service providers estimate that 40 percent of LGBTQ+ RHY are subjected to sexual assault and sexual exploitation (Durso and Gates 2012), including **sex trafficking** (i.e., sex work "induced by force, fraud, or coercion, or in which the person induced to perform such act has not attained 18 years of age") (National Institute of Justice 2022). Compared with heterosexual-cisgender RHY, LGBTQ+ RHY are more likely to experience sex trafficking (Forge, Hartinger-Saunders et al. 2018), especially if they identify as bisexual or transgender (Greeson et al. 2019), and sexual victimization (Tyler 2008; Tyler and Ray 2019; Whitbeck et al. 2004), including by people they know (Alessi et al. 2021). Sexual victimization by a friend or acquaintance is more common among young gay and bisexual males than among heterosexual males (Tyler et al. 2004). In fact, Tyler et al. (2004) found that the more often a young male had run away, the greater his chances of being sexually victimized by someone known to him. It may be that the increase in victimization is the result of the increased exposure to a street lifestyle or to the need to survive homelessness created by the greater number of runaway episodes. LGBTQ+ RHY are no safer with strangers, though, as avoiding shelters and staying with someone unknown to them, which LGBTQ+ and Black/African American RHY are more likely to do than other RHY subpopulations, puts these youth at risk of sexual exploitation (Rice et al. 2013). Deciding to stay with strangers as opposed to in a shelter may result from a perception of shelters as unsafe or that staying with a stranger is safer than staying on the streets. LGBTQ+ RHY are, however, more likely than heterosexual RHY to use drop-in centers (Pedersen et al. 2016) and street outreach programs (Tyler et al. 2012). These short-term, nonresidential services likely pose less of a risk than shelters to LGBTQ+ RHY, who find themselves vulnerable to discrimination and victimization in shelters (Abramovich 2017; Alessi et al. 2021).

Sexual victimization can also mean being coerced or forced into having sex (Santa Maria et al. 2015), which LaLota et al. (2005) found to be the case for young men who have sex with men (YMSM) and who have a history of running away, more so than for their YMSM nonrunaway peers. Men are most often the perpetrators of rape against both women and men (Basile et al. 2022), making gay men, like heterosexual women, targets of sexual violence, perhaps more so than lesbians. Protecting LGBTQ+ RHY from violence, including sexual violence, may involve educating them on the lower risk associated with shelter stays relative to living on the streets or staying with strangers.

Mental Health Problems

That mental health problems are more prevalent among LGBTQ+ RHY than among their heterosexual-cisgender peers is well documented (Mallory et al. 2025; Prock and Kennedy 2020; Whitbeck et al. 2004) and may be explained by factors unique to this population. LGBTQ+ RHY not only face the vulnerability of being homeless, but they also experience more stress than their heterosexual-cisgender counterparts (Moskowitz et al. 2013), especially Latino males (Rosario et al. 2012b). They must also manage the stigma of identifying as a sexual or gender minority. Such stigma is associated with higher rates of depression, suicide, anxiety, and other mental health problems (Hatchel et al. 2018; Kelleher 2009), as is family rejection (Mereish and Poteat 2015; Ryan et al. 2009), which many LGBTQ+ youth experience. Low social support and negative social interactions only compound the problem (Rosario et al. 2012b), as do racial discrimination (Gattis and Larson 2016) and microaggressions (Gattis and Larson 2017) among Black RHY.

These factors increase the risk of suicide and other self-injurious behaviors, to which LGBTQ+ RHY are particularly vulnerable (Moskowitz et al. 2013). Identifying as an LGBTQ+ RHY increases one's odds of suicidal ideation (Fulginiti et al. 2016) and suicide attempts (Rhoades et al. 2018; Walls et al. 2009). LGB RHY, especially lesbian youth, think about and attempt suicide significantly more often than do their heterosexual and housed LGB counterparts (Rhoades et al. 2018; Van Leeuwen et al. 2006; Whitbeck et al. 2004). In some cases, suicidality is compounded by other risk factors, such as family rejection and substance use. In Robinson's (2018b) ethnography, a young Hispanic transgender woman stated, "'The only reason I started doing dope was because I felt unwanted from my family. Gay was a big issue. Me liking boys was a big issue. I tried to kill myself by doing the dope—to hurt my family'" (389).

Nonsuicidal self-injury (NSSI), that is, self-injurious behavior without suicidal intent, includes types of self-mutilation such as cutting, scratching, burning, biting, and hitting (Tyler et al. 2010), and is more common among LGB RHY than among heterosexual RHY (Moskowitz et al. 2013; Tyler et al. 2003). LGB RHY are more likely to engage in self-mutilation, and to do so more than once, than are heterosexual RHY (Tyler et al. 2010). Methods of self-mutilation vary; whereas LGB RHY most often employ cutting, scratching, and headbanging, heterosexual RHY most often cut themselves, burn themselves with a lighter or match, and carve words into their skin (figure 5.1).

Self-mutilation is associated with depression, victimization, and subsistence strategies and may be a way for RHY to manage stress or emotions (Tyler et al. 2003). NSSI serves various functions, including affect regulation (i.e., modifying one's emotional reactions) (Berking and Whitley 2014), self-punishment, interpersonal influence (e.g., to manipulate others), and antidissociation (i.e., to remain in the present). It also is a visible demonstration of an individual's inner pain—a nonverbal signal to others that help is needed (Klonsky and Muehlenkamp 2007). Assessing whether a youth has engaged in NSSI is as important as assessing whether they have engaged in suicidal ideation or made suicide attempts. Although internalizing behaviors such as these are more common among LGBTQ+ RHY than among heterosexual-cisgender RHY (Budescu et al. 2022), externalizing

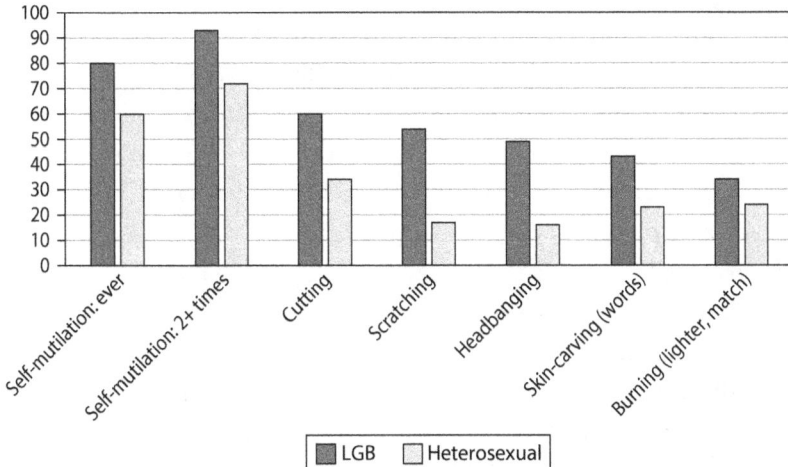

FIGURE 5.1 Percentage of frequency and type of self-mutilation among LGB and heterosexual RHY.

Source: Tyler et al. 2010.

behaviors, such as those exhibited in conduct disorder and its concomitant violence toward and victimization of others, are less common (Crawford et al. 2011; Whitbeck et al. 2004).

Despite the alarming rates of mental health problems among LGBTQ+ RHY, or perhaps because of them, LGBTQ+ RHY are more likely to use counseling and therapy than are heterosexual RHY (Narendorf et al. 2017; Tyler et al. 2012). Narendorf et al. (2017) found that identifying as LGBTQ+ was significantly correlated with using outpatient therapy in the past year and with having taken psychotropic medications in the past year, but it was also correlated with mental health needs remaining unmet. This may be because of youths' reporting mental health problems, perhaps based on previous diagnoses, or the severity of those problems, such that treatment seeking is more likely among youth whose symptoms are worse. It may also be that, despite seeking treatment, their mental health problems went either unresolved or unaddressed altogether. (See chapter 8 for an in-depth discussion of programs and services for this population.)

Substance Use

Substance use among RHY is common (Lim et al. 2016), more so for LGBTQ+ RHY, who, compared with heterosexual RHY, have higher rates of recent and lifetime substance use (Rosario et al. 2012b; Salomonsen-Sautel et al. 2008; Van Leeuwen et al. 2006). A median 35 percent of LGBQ RHY, a median 40 percent of transgender RHY (Choi et al. 2015), and a median 53 percent of LGBT RHY (Durso and Gates 2012) have reported using alcohol and drugs. Moreover, this use runs the gamut of illicit, prescription, and over-the-counter (OTC) drugs, as well as alcohol and tobacco.

Studies have found greater use, and in some cases significantly greater use, of cocaine or crack, ecstasy, gamma-hydroxybutyrate (GHB), hallucinogens (e.g., ketamine, lysergic acid diethylamide [LSD], mushrooms, phencyclidine [PCP]), inhalants, marijuana, opiates (e.g., heroin, morphine, codeine, oxycodone), sedatives (e.g., tranquilizers, Quaaludes, valium), stimulants (e.g., speed, methamphetamine, crystal meth, crank), injection drugs, and OTC drugs among LGBTQ+ RHY compared with their heterosexual-cisgender counterparts (Santa Maria et al. 2018; Van Leeuwen et al. 2006). Among those who acknowledged using injection drugs, LGB RHY took more precautions than heterosexual RHY, for example, by sharing needles and works (e.g., cotton balls, spoons, pipes) less often and using disinfecting bleach kits more often (Van Leeuwen et al. 2006). LGB RHY initiate substance use on or shortly after becoming homeless (Rosario et al. 2012b), suggesting that substance use may be a coping mechanism for homelessness, not the cause of it.

Drug use may be more problematic for sexual-minority female RHY than for heterosexual RHY. Whitbeck et al. (2004) found drug abuse (a disorder renamed "substance use disorder" in the fifth edition of the *Diagnostic and Statistical Manual of Mental Disorders*) to be more common among lesbian RHY (47.7 percent) than among heterosexual female RHY (32.5 percent). Use of amphetamines and injection drugs, however, was more likely among both gay and bisexual males and lesbian and bisexual females compared with heterosexual RHY (Whitbeck et al. 2004). Tobacco use is also more common among LGB RHY than among heterosexual RHY, with more LGB RHY having tried cigarettes (Van Leeuwen et al. 2006) and using alternative smokeless tobacco products (e.g., tobacco sticks and snus) (Tucker et al. 2014).

There is less consensus among researchers regarding alcohol use, however. Some studies indicate that LGBTQ+ RHY are more likely to use (Forge, Hartinger-Saunders et al. 2018; Santa Maria et al. 2018; Van Leeuwen et al. 2006) or abuse (Chen et al. 2006) alcohol than heterosexual-cisgender RHY, whereas other studies have found that to be only partially true. For example, lesbian RHY exhibited alcohol abuse at higher rates than heterosexual female RHY (Whitbeck et al. 2004) and gay and bisexual male RHY (Noell and Ochs 2001; Whitbeck et al. 2004), while gay male RHY exhibited lower rates than heterosexual male RHY. Still other studies (Tyler and Ray 2019) have found no significant difference in rates of binge drinking between LGB RHY and non-LGB RHY and even that LGB RHY consumed significantly fewer drinks per day on average than heterosexual RHY (Wenzel et al. 2010). Wenzel et al. (2010) attributed lower alcohol use to the increased presence of adult authority figures, which may be the result of help-seeking. In addition to being more likely to seek mental health counseling than heterosexual RHY, LGBTQ+ RHY are also more likely to participate in a substance use treatment program (Van Leeuwen et al. 2006). Both settings put LGBTQ+ youth in contact with adult authority figures in the form of practitioners and other service providers.

Although LGBTQ+ RHY are at significantly greater risk of substance use and related problems, in part because of their status as sexual and gender minorities, they are somewhat protected by their higher propensity to seek treatment for substance use problems and by the presence of positive adults in their lives. Improving services, then, would involve increasing the availability and accessibility of mental health services and substance use treatment programs that are LGBTQ+-inclusive or wholly dedicated to treating this population.

High-Risk Sexual Behaviors

High-risk sexual behaviors include having multiple sex partners, having unprotected sex (i.e., sex without a condom), and engaging in **sex work** (e.g., trading sex for money, food, or shelter), a form of which is referred to as "survival sex." Such behaviors, discussed in detail next, put RHY at risk for sexually transmitted infections (STIs), including HIV. Moreover, in those with a history of exposure to violence, HIV risk is heightened (Marsiglia et al. 2009).

Multiple Sex Partners

LGBTQ+ RHY are often found to have had more sexual partners than heterosexual RHY have had. In one study (Tyler 2013), 41 percent of LGBTQ+ RHY, as opposed to 23 percent of heterosexual RHY, reported having had more than ten sexual partners in their lifetime. In particular, YMSM who had run away were more likely to have had both male and female sexual partners and more sexual partners overall compared with their nonrunaway YMSM (LaLota et al. 2005).

While LGBQ youth experiencing homelessness are more likely than their heterosexual counterparts to have multiple sex partners (Kattari et al. 2017; Tyler 2013), having someone in their social circle who discussed safe sex with them made LGBQ youth experiencing homelessness less likely to have had multiple sex partners (Kattari et al. 2017). YMSM also had fewer sex partners if at least three individuals in their social network attended school regularly (Tucker et al. 2012). They had more sex partners if their social networks consisted of those who drank heavily, engaged in high-risk sexual behaviors, and used hard drugs (Tucker et al. 2012). Thus, LGBQ RHY fare better when surrounded by conscientious, prosocial peers. Asking a youth about their friends and other peers can be an opportunity for a practitioner to steer the youth toward healthy, supportive relationships and away from those that jeopardize the youth's safety and well-being.

Unprotected Sex

LGBTQ+ RHY are generally more likely than their heterosexual counterparts to have **unprotected sex** (Rice et al. 2013; Tyler 2013). For example, one study found that 69.2 percent of lesbian and gay youth had engaged in the practice within the past thirty days, followed by pansexual youth, bisexual youth, and heterosexual youth (Logan et al. 2013). Yet commensurate with their higher exposure to risk is their likelihood to seek testing for STIs, including HIV (Tyler et al. 2012). Further, more LGB RHY than heterosexual RHY report having been tested for HIV and hepatitis C (Van Leeuwen et al. 2006).

LGBTQ+ RHY are more likely to engage in unprotected sex than are their heterosexual-cisgender peers (Kattari et al. 2017; Tyler 2013) and their housed LGBTQ+ peers (Halkitis et al. 2013). More than a quarter (27 percent) of YMSM (aged thirteen to twenty-four years) experiencing homelessness have unprotected sex some of the time, while another quarter (23 percent) have unprotected sex every time (Tucker et al. 2012). Unprotected sex is associated with being older, being of Hispanic origin, having a history of child abuse, having lower educational attainment, having less positive beliefs about condom use, and having more relatives in one's social network. Having individuals in one's network who attend school, however, reduces the likelihood of having unprotected sex. LGB youth experiencing homelessness are not, however, significantly more likely to engage in unprotected sex than members of other street subcultures (Kipke, Montgomery et al. 1997).

Survival Sex

Various terms, such as *survival sex, sex work,* and *prostitution,* refer to exchanging sex for a commodity or resource, although *survival sex* is most often used to represent this subsistence practice among RHY. Along with panhandling, stealing, shoplifting, drug dealing, and scavenging, **survival sex** is considered by some a "deviant" subsistence strategy (Chen et al. 2006, 389) and is associated with the physical (Whitbeck et al. 2004) and sexual (Tyler and Schmitz 2018b) victimization of LGBTQ+ RHY. However, these strategies reflect the limited means upon which many LGBTQ+ youth must rely for survival. LGBTQ+ RHY have reported discrimination in landing a job, leaving them without safe, stable employment (Alessi et al. 2021). Transgender youth, in particular, have difficulty joining the formal workforce, leading to disproportionately high rates of unemployment among them (Alessi et al. 2021; Koch and Bales 2008; Spicer 2010).

LGB RHY are more likely than their heterosexual peers to be approached for (Van Leeuwen et al. 2006), to engage in (Tyler and Schmitz 2018b), and to have friends who engage in (Tyler 2008) such high-risk sexual behaviors (Kattari et al. 2017). For example, LGB RHY are more than 2.5 times as likely to engage in survival sex as are heterosexual RHY—even when controlling for substance use, mental health, and other health-related variables—and transgender youth more so than cisgender males (Marshall et al. 2010; Walls and Bell 2011).

Sex work is more common among currently and previously homeless YMSM than among YMSM who have never been homeless (Clatts et al. 2005). YMSM begin engaging in sex work at an average age of seventeen to eighteen years following negative life events, such as housing instability, suicide attempts, and involvement with the criminal justice system, and contemporaneously with substance use (Clatts et al. 2005). Such negative experiences are not uncommon and have been documented by Alessi et al. (2021) in their qualitative study of survival sex among LGBTQ+ RHY. Participants described growing up in impoverished homes where their parents were abusive, used substances, and were unsupportive of their child's LGBTQ+ identity; experiencing child abuse increases one's odds of later trading sex for food (Tyler and Schmitz 2018b). After becoming homeless and engaging in survival sex, LGBTQ+ RHY experience violence at the hands of their customers, their pimps, and even other sex workers, and, in the case of LGBTQ+ RHY of color, are the targets of racial slurs from police officers (Alessi et al. 2021).

Perhaps unsurprisingly, then, survival sex is also associated with mental health problems. For YMSM (Tucker et al. 2012), trading sex is more common among those who exhibit depressive symptoms and sleep outside (as opposed to in a shelter). Complicating this risky behavior, survival sex predicts suicide attempts (Walls et al. 2009). Survival sex is also associated with conduct disorder, many behaviors of which could also be considered risky; however, gay male RHY are at less risk of this disorder than are heterosexual male RHY (Whitbeck et al. 2004).

These sexual risk-taking behaviors are less a function of LGBTQ+ RHY's sexual orientation and identity and of their gender identity and expression than they are of the vulnerability that their sexual- and gender-minority status creates. (See box 5.3, *What Do You Think?*) LGBTQ+ RHY more

BOX 5.3. WHAT DO YOU THINK?
HIGH-RISK SEXUAL BEHAVIORS AMONG LGBTQ+ RHY

- Why might YMSM who have run away be more likely than those who have not to have had both male and female sexual partners?
- Why might more lesbian and gay RHY (69.2 percent) than bisexual RHY (55.3 percent) have unprotected sex (Logan et al. 2013)?
- Why do you think survival sex is considered by some to be a "deviant" subsistence strategy (Chen et al. 2006, 389)?
- Why do transgender youth experience higher rates of unemployment than LGB youth?
- Why do you think that gay males (27.8 percent) are so much more likely, according to Whitbeck et al. (2004), to engage in survival sex compared with females, both lesbian (11.4 percent) and heterosexual (11.7 percent)?

often have histories of child sexual abuse and subsequent street victimization than heterosexual-cisgender RHY (Tyler and Schmitz 2018b). Compared with their heterosexual-cisgender peers, LGBTQ+ people are more often the victims of rape and other forms of sexual violence (Rothman et al. 2011), which may occur without the perpetrator's use of a protective barrier against STIs. LGBTQ+ RHY who are victims of sex trafficking may be forced by their pimps or traffickers to take on multiple sex partners. When relying on survival sex as a subsistence strategy, having multiple sex partners may be economically necessary. In either case, their sex partners may require or force youth to engage in oral, vaginal, or anal sex without the use of condoms.

Rather than a passive approach of simply offering services geared toward LGBTQ+ RHY, intervention with this population may warrant proactive steps that identify and interrupt high-risk sexual behaviors and sexually exploitative operations (e.g., sex trafficking) involving these youth, as well as assessing when they were last tested (if ever) for STIs, including HIV.

PROTECTIVE FACTORS

Juliana is currently a junior in high school and is well liked by her peers, who find her bubbly, kind, and optimistic. Juliana wants to stay in school because she is planning to enroll in cosmetology classes offered during her senior year. What little spending money she has comes from babysitting jobs, which have become more infrequent since she lacks reliable transportation to and from families' homes. Juliana would like to return home; her mother and siblings, with whom she has good relationships, miss her and would like to have her home. Her mother is sympathetic but unable to convince her husband to relent and accept Juliana's sexuality.

Social Networks and Social Support

Summarizing from their own and others' research on the subject, Lazarus and Cheavens (2017) define **social networks** as "the individuals with whom the participant has a specific type of relationship, with that relationship defined by the researcher" (340). Social networks can exert both positive and negative influences on an individual; here, we focus on those that provide positive social support.

RHY cite the importance of the support that their street families and friends provide, especially when first becoming homeless. These peers offer emotional and financial support, safety, mentorship with regard to the norms and expectations of street life, and support while youth acclimate to living on the streets, and they serve as a buffer to loneliness and isolation (Kidd 2003). These factors may be particularly salient for LGBTQ+ RHY, who must manage the added vulnerability of identifying as a sexual and gender minority. Intimate partners, too, are important to many RHY, adding another layer of support, inspiring them to be accountable to someone other than themselves, and giving them a reason to fight to survive (Kidd 2003).

Despite the isolation that can accompany homelessness (Wright et al. 2017), LGBTQ+ RHY are resourceful in developing their networks, demonstrating an ability to establish social support within very narrow confines, such as treatment facilities and juvenile detention centers (Schmitz and

Tyler 2018b). This suggests to practitioners and researchers that there are opportunities to assist LGBTQ+ RHY in developing prosocial, supportive networks even within agencies and institutions not necessarily designed for social purposes. Doing so may increase their post-discharge social support or at least their self-efficacy to develop such supports outside those institutions.

While LGBTQ+ RHY typically experience more rejection than do heterosexual-cisgender RHY from their families of origin, especially their parents, some youth do receive support from family members, particularly siblings. Positive family connections inspire RHY to keep going and remind them that there are others who care about them (Kidd 2003). Level of support, however, may be related to racial and ethnic background, with a pattern of greater support having been found among Latino gay and bisexual male RHY (Rosario et al. 2012b), who report economic support from (69.2 percent), connections with (76.9 percent), and reunification with their families (76.9 percent) (Castellanos 2016). Moreover, ethnic identification and linguistic acculturation among Latinx LGBTQ+ homeless and other minoritized youth populations act as protective factors against HIV risk (Marsiglia et al. 2009).

However, LGBTQ+ RHY generally receive less support from their families than from other sources. Similar-aged friends, significant others, street family, and professionals provide slightly more support than families of origin (Forge, Hartinger-Saunders et al. 2018; Martin and Howe 2016); professional service providers (Barman-Adhikari et al. 2016) and adult friends (Forge, Hartinger-Saunders et al. 2018) afford the greatest support. These findings are thus an important reminder to practitioners not to underestimate the support that the youth in their care derive from the professional relationship, which also serves as a model for future healthy relationships with potential social supports.

Like support from families, peer support has a number of benefits. Social support from friends serves to buffer LGBTQ+ RHY from conduct problems. LGBTQ+ RHY with high levels of support from friends have conduct problems on par with their housed peers, whereas LGBTQ+ RHY with low levels of such support exhibit considerably more conduct problems (Rosario et al. 2012b). LGBQ RHY who discuss safe-sex behaviors with peers in their social network are less likely to have multiple sex partners compared with heterosexual RHY (Kattari et al. 2017). Helping LGBTQ+ RHY to establish peer supports should be a part of services provided, along with addressing mental or behavioral health concerns that interfere with youths' ability to form these important connections.

Despite the positive effects that peer support can have, LGBTQ+ RHY unfortunately have too little of it, or at least too little of the right kind. For example, compared with their heterosexual counterparts, sexual-minority youth experiencing homelessness have significantly more relationships with peers who exhibit negative behaviors (e.g., unemployment, not being enrolled or failing grades in school, running away from home) (Gattis 2013). But even when LGBTQ+ RHY do have emotional support, it may not be enough in some circumstances. Emotional support, and even tangible support, make little difference in the high-risk sexual behaviors of YMSM experiencing homelessness (Tucker et al. 2012). These findings emphasize that helping LGBTQ+ RHY establish peer support should involve helping them develop sound judgment and interpersonal boundaries and educating them about what healthy peer relationships look like.

Resilience

The adversity that LGBTQ+ RHY face makes them resilient, and they know it (DeChants et al. 2022; Forge, Lewinson et al. 2018). These youth find resilience in supporting themselves and being able to express their sexual and gender identities, which many of them could not do at home (Alessi et al. 2021; Shelton, Wagaman et al. 2018). In a qualitative study of resilience among transgender youth and young adults experiencing homelessness, Shelton, Wagaman et al. (2018) found two emergent themes: "personal agency and future orientation" (149). Personal agency manifested in the youth as defining themselves and making their own decisions, including the decision to leave home (DeChants et al. 2022). Attaching positive meaning to the experience of being homeless and imagining a future home spoke to future orientation. Youth who identify as questioning or unsure about their sexual orientation or gender identity are less optimistic about the future (Rew et al. 2019), perhaps because the uncertainty about their identity makes it difficult to imagine what their future might look like and whether it will be positive. Resilience also exists in LGBTQ+ RHY who have engaged in survival sex, which, although risky, affords them a certain amount of independence. These youth are finally able to live as their authentic selves, have families of choice on whom they can rely (i.e., social support), and stand up for themselves in the face of authority (Alessi et al. 2021). It may be these circumstances that give LGBTQ+ RHY the strength to persevere through the hardships of street life in general and survival sex in particular.

Resilience can also be fostered through supportive relationships (Warf et al. 2020), including those with health and mental health care providers, teachers, faith leaders, and mentors. Researchers and service providers can also foster resilience in LGBTQ+ RHY by engaging them in creative endeavors. Photovoice, for example, is a qualitative data collection method for research or assessment in which participants are asked to take photos around particular topics or themes, typically those found in their everyday life. A similar method, photo elicitation, is an interviewing technique in which the interviewer shows or the interviewee chooses photos that the interviewee then explains using criteria and prompts supplied by the interviewer. Both are particularly relevant approaches to capturing and fostering resilience in LGBTQ+ youth. With these methods, youth are able to express themselves, their lived experience, and their perceptions of self, others, and the world around them with a nuance that might otherwise be hidden or omitted in other, more traditional forms of assessment or research interviews. Photovoice in particular affords youth an opportunity to be creative and to remain in complete control of the way they capture their perspective and whether and how they choose to share it.

Studies using photovoice and photo elicitation have revealed remarkable resilience among LGBTQ+ youth, including those who have run away from home, been kicked out, or who are otherwise homeless or unstably housed. Findings from photovoice projects have evidenced themes of self-sufficiency, self-reflection, insight, confidence, future orientation, and having a positive outlook (Craig et al. 2021; Forge, Lewinson et al. 2018). In one example, a nineteen-year-old youth who identified as transgender/gender diverse and lesbian explained the symbolism in one of their photos: "I don't know, [the photo with pigeons] just reminds me of how my relatives, my extended family, treated me. Like they just threw me out, they didn't care, they didn't want anything to do with me. . . . But I'm still here, still living my best life" (Craig et al. 2021, 7).

Telling one's own story in a manner that affords them control and autonomy, such as through their own photographs, is an empowering experience that in itself promotes resilience.

Coping and Adaptability

Some youth and young adults use substances to cope with mental health problems, previous trauma, and homelessness (DeHart et al. 2021; Glasser et al. 2022; Harrington-Motley et al. 2017). This avoidant coping method is associated with engaging in high-risk sexual behaviors and consequently an increased risk of HIV infection (Hotton et al. 2013). Thus, this form of coping, which may contribute to homelessness, interferes with the ability of unhoused youth to realize protective factors that will get them off the streets and into stable housing (DeHart et al. 2021; Harrington-Motley et al. 2017; Robinson 2021). Maladaptive though it may be, substance use nonetheless helps LGBTQ+ RHY cope with their circumstances. That is not to say that the use of substances is justified in helping youth manage negative emotions, trauma histories, and the harsh realities of homelessness; rather, it is an acknowledgment that without it, these youth may succumb to the very pressures from which they are trying to escape. In fact, RHY themselves recognize the harm in using substances to cope: " 'Smoking weed was a problem. Smoking weed for me is a medication, 'cause it helps me eat. And it also numbed the pain from going to school. Numb the pain of people looking at me. People calling me fa**ot' " (Robinson 2021, 8). Another youth stated, " 'People think it's like we think it's cool, [but] we know it's not. It's just the life we live right now that does it to us' " (Kidd 2003, 251).

RHY also turn to their friends to help them cope. Being with peers who are living the same experience serves as a distraction from their environment, especially when substance use is involved. Smoking marijuana and drinking alcohol are social activities, making it typical for these two common coping strategies to intersect (Kidd 2003). Yet RHY also engage in solitary coping activities, such as sleeping, praying, listening to music, pursuing hobbies, taking time to be alone with their thoughts (Kidd 2003; Robinson 2021), expressing their creativity (DeChants et al. 2022), and thinking about the future (Forge, Lewinson et al. 2018).

Future orientation is evidenced in the goals that LGBTQ+ RHY set for themselves, which speak to the hope these youth maintain. Moving out of the house and away from family members who have rejected them is an immediate goal and can be very empowering. In this way, youth exert control over themselves and their situation. Short-term goals include finding another place to live or preparing to live on the streets. Continuing their education and finding a job are long-term goals that will hopefully lead them back to stable housing. Some LGBTQ+ RHY are motivated by strong connections with siblings or their own children, whereas others simply want to get out of shelters and off the streets. Their ability to enact this plan demonstrates their resilience (DeChants et al. 2022).

Adapting, that is, modifying one's behavior or expectations, is another form of coping. LGBTQ+ RHY wishing to use homelessness services adapt to heteronormative and cisnormative shelter environments, for example, by resigning themselves to the fact that the alternative is spending another night on the street (Côté and Blais 2019). Some may go one step further by concealing their sexual orientation or gender identity if revealing it would pose a risk to their safety (Schmitz and Tyler 2018a). At other times, LGBTQ+ RHY assert themselves and challenge such prejudice and discrimination, which is a sign of their inner strength and resolve (Côté and Blais 2019).

Inner Strength

RHY draw on their inner strength to navigate dangerous situations and fend off negative messages they endure as youth who are homeless and, disproportionately, sexual and gender minorities. Their ability to see themselves as having value and worth is a strength that allows them to steel themselves against what others think about them (Kidd 2003). The ability to do so protects their self-esteem and self-image, which may then mitigate unhealthy coping strategies and make positive outcomes more likely. In some cases, it is the very circumstance of experiencing homelessness and managing the concomitant hardships that make them feel stronger (Kidd 2003). The knowledge, skills, and motivation that RHY possess contribute to their ability to survive in a harsh environment, which in turn strengthens their self-efficacy and their belief that a better, brighter future is within their reach.

In one photovoice project, some LGBTQ+ RHY used images of trees to represent their strength: the ability to withstand storms and grow back after being burned down. Adversity makes them stronger, but sometimes they need to rely on others for support to "bloom" (Forge, Lewinson et al. 2018, 815).

Notwithstanding organized religion's history of rejecting sexual and gender minorities and those in same-sex relationships, some LGBTQ+ RHY find strength in establishing or growing their relationship with God. In some cases, such a relationship is tied to important people or times in their lives, such as family or happy memories, or to faith-based organizations that served as resources after becoming homeless (Forge, Lewinson et al. 2018). For others, it is religion itself that gives them strength and comfort, even while acknowledging that religion has also been a source of pain and trauma for some LGBTQ+ people (Forge, Lewinson et al. 2018).

Other Protective Factors

While social support and social networks, resilience, coping, adaptability, and inner strength are some of the more universal protective factors for LGBTQ+ RHY, other less common yet nonrandom sources of protection exist. Schools (Krause et al. 2016), community youth organizations (Damian et al. 2022), violence prevention, and health care (Greenfield et al. 2020) can also play protective roles in the lives of these youth. For example, in a sample of sexual-minority young men, being enrolled in school lowered the odds of experiencing housing instability, defined as living on the streets or elsewhere outside their own home (e.g., prison, an inpatient facility, with friends or family) (Krause et al. 2016). It might be that school offered these youth access to supportive peers and adults or to other resources to combat their housing instability.

SUMMARY

LGBTQ+ RHY face some of the same risk factors as heterosexual-cisgender RHY, but they face additional risks associated with prejudice, discrimination, and stigma regarding their sexual orientation and identity and gender identity and expression, making them more vulnerable to the dangers associated with living on the streets. For example, all RHY are susceptible to mental health problems resulting from or exacerbated by homelessness, such as depression stemming from isolation, and post-traumatic stress disorder (PTSD) from violence and victimization. However, LGBTQ+ RHY must also contend with rejection related to their sexual- and gender-minority status, which leaves them estranged from family and peers back home and experiencing stigma and prejudice, which makes accessing housing and services difficult. Their sexual and gender identities also leave them open to hate-based violence, which can lead to or worsen existing PTSD. As a result, LGBTQ+ RHY may use substances to self-medicate mental health problems, which they experience at higher rates than their heterosexual-cisgender peers (Mallory et al. 2025; Prock and Kennedy 2020), numb themselves from their everyday realities (which may include having to engage in survival sex) (Cochran et al. 2002), or cope with traumatic experiences, both past and present (Saewyc et al. 2006). Screening for mental health and substance use problems must be a requisite part of intake and assessment with LGBTQ+ RHY, followed by culturally competent and affirming services to subsequently address these issues.

In the face of extreme vulnerability, LGBTQ+ RHY exhibit remarkable resolve and tenacity. They develop networks of social support and join street families, and some maintain connections with members of their families of origin. Many of these youth recognize the resilience that living on the streets has fostered in them and, with it, the confidence to persevere.

LGBTQ+ RHY find ways to cope, albeit sometimes harmful ones if it means getting them through the day, the hour, or the moment. When they can, they assert themselves by advocating for themselves, and when they cannot, they adapt to the situation. Their inner strength, and for some, their religion and spirituality, sustains them during acute crises, such as sexual assault, and chronic hardships, not least of which are food insecurity and housing instability. The risk and protective factors discussed in this chapter point to several implications for practice, research, and policy. Practitioners working with this population can mitigate risk by, for example, addressing family tension and estrangement, treating youth mental and behavioral health problems, and educating youth about healthy relationships and safe-sex practices. Enhancing protective factors might involve helping youth identify healthy coping mechanisms, nurturing their creative instincts and recreational interests, and fostering their self-esteem and self-confidence by highlighting the strengths and resilience they possess. Photovoice and photo elicitation are tools that practitioners and researchers can use to help youth process their experiences, feel heard and understood, and recognize their own inner resources. Researchers are also in a position to close the gap in our formal understanding of protective factors, which is far outweighed by research on risk factors. Last, with LGBTQ+ RHY being at particular risk of sexual exploitation, anti–human trafficking legislation must be sensitive and responsive to the role that sexual orientation and gender identity play in this form of victimization. Further, the recent wave of state-level anti-LGBTQ+ bills proposed in the United States makes it more difficult for sexual- and gender-minority RHY to access, without harassment and discrimination, the resources and services (e.g., education, employment) they need to exit homelessness. This is a legislative trend that must be reversed.

REVISITING JULIANA

- What risk and protective factors does Juliana exhibit?
- What strengths does she possess?
- As a practitioner, what would be your primary focus of attention in helping Juliana?

- As a researcher, which of Juliana's circumstances would you target for further investigation?
- At the macro level, what existing or potential policies could ensure Juliana's success—whether that be reunification with her parents, placement in an emergency shelter or transitional living program, or a transition to independence—given her current circumstances?

KEY CONCEPTS

- *Adaptability*: the ability to conform to new situations or surroundings
- *External risk and protective factors*: factors that exist outside the individual, for example, in others or in the environment
- *High-risk sexual behaviors*: sexual behaviors that put individuals at risk of injury, illness, or death (e.g., multiple sex partners, unprotected sex, and survival sex or sex work)
- *Internal risk and protective factors*: factors that an individual has within themself mentally (i.e., cognitively or emotionally) or physically
- *Protective factor*: "a characteristic . . . associated with a lower likelihood of problem outcomes or that reduces the negative impact of a risk factor on problem outcomes" (O'Connor et al. 2009, xxvii)
- *Resilience*: the ability to employ protective factors in the face of adversity
- *Risk factor*: "a characteristic . . . that precedes and is associated with a higher likelihood of problem outcomes" (O'Connor et al. 2009, xxviii)
- *Sex trafficking*: sex work "induced by force, fraud, or coercion, or in which the person induced to perform such act has not attained 18 years of age" (National Institute of Justice 2022)
- *Sex work*: the exchange of sex for money or goods and services (Sawicki et al. 2019)
- *Sexual violence*: "a sexual act that is committed or attempted by another person without freely given consent of the victim or against someone who is unable to consent or refuse" (Basile et al. 2014, 11)

- *Social networks*: "individuals with whom the participant has a spe-cific type of relationship" (Lazarus and Cheavens 2017, 340)
- *Survival sex*: exchanging sex for a commodity or resource (e.g., food, shelter, money, physical protection), generally to fulfill an immediate need; a form of sex work
- *Unprotected sex*: sexual behaviors that put an individual at risk of transmitting or acquiring STIs resulting from the failure to employ behaviors or devices (e.g., condoms) that prevent or reduce the risk of transmission or acquisition
- *Violence and victimization*: physical, psychological or emotional, or sexual crimes against an individual

CHAPTER HIGHLIGHTS

- 99.6 percent of runaway youth return home, 30 percent within six months.
- Violence and victimization, mental health problems, substance use, and high-risk sexual behaviors are common risk factors for LGBTQ+ RHY, whereas social networks and social support, resilience, coping, adaptability, and inner strength are common protective factors.
- LGBTQ+ RHY leave home for some of the same reasons as heterosexual-cisgender RHY (e.g., family conflict, independence), as well as reasons unique to their sexual orientation or gender identity (e.g., being kicked out of the home because of family rejection).
- RHY service providers estimate that 40 percent of LGBTQ+ RHY experience sexual assault and sexual exploitation.
- LGBTQ+ RHY are more likely than heterosexual-cisgender RHY to use substances, including tobacco, cocaine or crack, ecstasy, GHB, hallucinogens, inhalants, marijuana, opiates, sedatives, stimulants, injection drugs, and OTC drugs.
- Compared with their heterosexual-cisgender counterparts, LGBTQ+ RHY exhibit higher rates of risky sexual behaviors, such as having multiple sex partners and engaging in unprotected sex and survival sex.

- LGBTQ+ RHY generally find the most support from service providers, followed by peers and friends, and then family.
- LGBTQ+ RHY demonstrate resilience in their ability to manage the experience of homelessness and in their experiences of prejudice and discrimination as sexual and gender minorities. This adversity strengthens their resilience, which they recognize as a positive aspect of who they are.
- Photovoice and photo elicitation afford RHY an opportunity to process their experiences creatively and in a way that gives them control over what they capture and whether and how they choose to share it.
- LGBTQ+ RHY employ a variety of coping strategies, some healthier than others, but all with the goal of alleviating distress, anxiety, depression, and boredom, among other negative emotions and experiences.
- Experiencing homelessness requires a certain amount of adaptability, more so for LGBTQ+ youth who must sometimes make a choice between hiding their LGBTQ+ identity to access services and disclosing their identity and being denied those services. Such a choice can mean the difference between sleeping in a shelter bed and sleeping outside.
- Inner strength is a pool of internal resources (e.g., knowledge, street smarts, motivation, problem-solving skills, good judgment) on which LGBTQ+ RHY can draw to sustain themselves in dangerous situations and during times of desperation and uncertainty.

6 | LGBTQ+ RHY and Their Parents and Families

LEARNING OBJECTIVES

Readers of this chapter will be able to:

1. Describe the primary prevention and intervention options available to RHY and their families,
2. Identify the resources, systems, and institutions involved in each of these options, and
3. Explain the circumstances under which each option might be most appropriate.

CASE VIGNETTE: ZACH

Zach, a sixteen-year-old white, cisgender gay youth experiencing homelessness, is a world away from where he ever imagined he'd be, especially at such an early age. His lower-middle-class upbringing in what he thought was a "typical" family should have, in his mind, led to at least the same outcome his small-town high school friends were enjoying: getting a part-time job and thinking about going to trade school or the community college in the neighboring small city. Now he finds himself couch surfing, unable to reconnect with his family, and unsure of what his next move should be.

INTRODUCTION

LGBTQ+ youth leave home for many reasons. Whether they are kicked out (thrown away) or leave on their own (run away), their departure is rarely voluntary. Before leaving home, RHY find themselves in inhospitable conditions that make staying an untenable option. The term *runaway* ostensibly implies a choice on the part of the youth to leave, but this is often not the case. We use the term throughout this book not to suggest that running away or experiencing homelessness is a choice but to speak the language used by many scholars and most, if not all, government entities, all of which share a common understanding of the pathways to youth homelessness.

This chapter explores the role that parents—whether birth, adoptive, or foster parents; grandparents or other kinship parents (e.g., aunts and uncles, siblings); or legal guardians or nonlegal custodians (e.g., godparents, family friends)—and families play in the risks and reality faced by youth who leave home and their subsequent experiences of housing instability and homelessness. While not all LGBTQ+ RHY are expelled from the home because of their sexual orientation and identity and their gender identity and expression, these often play a role—and do so in a way that they do not for heterosexual-cisgender youth. The common themes in the literature regarding LGBTQ+ RHY and their parents and families are the factors leading LGBTQ+ youth to leave home, runaway and homelessness prevention, foster care, permanency solutions (i.e., reunification and adoption) when possible, and emancipation when permanency solutions are not possible. Chapter 5 addressed the factors leading LGBTQ+ youth to leave home; we cover the remaining themes here.

RUNAWAY AND HOMELESSNESS PREVENTION

The most ideal solution to the problem of youth homelessness is prevention, namely keeping youth in the home (provided the parents' or other caregivers' home environment is not a source of physical, sexual, verbal, or emotional abuse or neglect). All RHY are at risk of harm or worse while living on the streets, LGBTQ+ RHY even more so (Forge, Hartinger-Saunders et al. 2018; Morton, Samuels et al. 2018); thus, preventing youth homelessness in the first place is of paramount importance.

The best-case scenario for LGBTQ+ youth living at home is having at least one parent or guardian who supports the youth as they are, including accepting their sexual orientation and identity and their gender identity and expression. However, it is not uncommon for parents and families of LGBTQ+ youth to struggle with doing so, especially upon first learning of their LGBTQ+ identity. Negative reactions from family members to a youth's disclosure (or the inadvertent or intentional disclosure by a third party) can lead to depression and low self-esteem in the youth (Ryan et al. 2015). In anticipation of negative reactions, youth may first disclose to family members whom they believe will receive the information best. Mothers or siblings, especially sisters, are typically the first to know (Ryan et al. 2015; Savin-Williams 2001; Toomey and Richardson 2009), while fathers are rarely the first to know (Ryan et al. 2015; Savin-Williams and Ream 2003). When family members, especially parents, do not—or are expected not to—take the news well, intervention by trained professionals is key, especially since disclosing to parents is associated with homelessness (Semborski et al. 2021). Such intervention minimizes the likelihood of youth finding themselves on the wrong side of their front door.

With disproportionate numbers of LGBTQ+ youth getting kicked out of their homes compared with heterosexual youth (McLaughlin et al. 2012), there is a need not only for focused attention on prevention in this vulnerable subpopulation but also "for putting them at the center of efforts to prevent and address youth homelessness in order to end youth homelessness overall" (Morton, Samuels et al. 2018, 7). Yet despite the importance of keeping LGBTQ+ youth in the home, few programs and even fewer studies and reports exist on the topic. Most of what does exist is a recognition of the problem, a call to do something about it, and vague plans for doing so. The LGBTQ+ RHY researcher and professor Jama Shelton (2018) acknowledged, "To reference the 'upstream/prevention parable,' we are pulling young people out of the river and saving their lives—critical work, yes—but we haven't yet figured out how to stop them from falling into the river in the first place" (542–43).

The problem of LGBTQ+ youth homelessness is a worldwide phenomenon, drawing attention from national and international bodies alike.
United Nations (UN) experts have called for an end to youth homelessness,
noting the impact of homelessness on LGBTQ+ youth and its likely causes,
including intolerance and criminalization (Madrigal-Borloz and Farha
2019). (See box 6.1, *Read All About It!*) The UN calls on nations to provide
shelters for LGBTQ+ youth experiencing homelessness, affordable housing
for LGBTQ+ individuals, and not only an end to anti-LGBTQ+ laws but
also the implementation of nondiscrimination policies that protect individuals on the basis of sexual orientation and gender identity. Closer to home,
in its 2020 vision for eliminating youth homelessness, the U.S. Interagency
Council on Homelessness acknowledged a need to address "family conflict
and rejection around sexual orientation and gender identity" (2015, 3),
citing family conflict as a primary cause of homelessness among all youth

BOX 6.1. READ ALL ABOUT IT!
INTERNATIONAL ADVOCACY FOR LGBTQ+ YOUTH

- In 2015, the United Nations rolled out its 2030 Agenda for Sustainable Development, of which goal 11 is to "make cities and human
  settlements inclusive, safe, resilient and sustainable" (UN 2015).
  Two independent experts for the UN have asserted, "As a result of
  religious and cultural intolerance that may include sexual and other
  forms of violence, lesbian, gay, bisexual, trans and gender diverse
  (LGBT) youth around the world face socio-economic exclusion,
  including from within their own homes and communities, and family disapproval and punishment can force them to leave home, which
  renders them more vulnerable to yet more violence and discrimination" (Madrigal-Borloz and Farha 2019, para. 1).
- This progressive statement is a bold stance for advisers working
  on behalf of the UN, an entity composed of and representing 193
  diverse nations, including those with strict views and laws regarding
  sexual orientation and identity and gender identity and expression.
  To learn more, visit https://www.ohchr.org/en/statements/2019/08
  /right-housing-lgbt-youth-urgent-task-sdg-agenda-setting.

(Centrepoint 2016; Landers 2019). The plan for doing so, however, is left up to communities, the criteria and benchmarks for which make no mention of LGBTQ+ youth or their unique challenges and needs (USICH 2018). Without such specific guidance, communities may easily overlook this and other RHY subpopulations.

Much of LGBTQ+ youth homelessness prevention focuses on keeping youth who are already living outside the home, whether **couch surfing**, in foster care, or in the juvenile justice system, from winding up on the streets. The purpose of the present discussion, however, is preventing youths' eviction from the home altogether—"falling into the river," as it were. This is where knowledge and strategies are lacking, especially with regard to LGBTQ+ youth. As recently as within the last few years (Brown et al. 2020; Toro et al. 2007), authors have lamented a lack of understanding of the pathways by which youth subpopulations, including LGBTQ+ youth, find themselves at risk of homelessness and have called for more research on the subject.

We do know that youth typically leave home because of conflict with their parents (Centrepoint 2016; DeHart et al. 2021; Landers 2019), which may have its roots in aspects of early development such as parent–child attachment. Youth who enjoy secure attachment with parents or caregivers may be less likely to experience negative consequences of disclosure that can lead to feeling compelled to run away from home or being kicked out (Katz-Wise et al. 2016). Their parents value them irrespective of their identities, even if the disclosure is unexpected or difficult to hear. Insecurely attached youth, on the other hand, may face intolerable abuse and rejection that leave them with no other apparent options to leaving home. Yet even once supportive parents can struggle with feelings of shock, fear, anxiety, anger, and grief and loss as they face the reality that they and their children may not have the futures they imagined or expected (Ashley 2019; Harvey and Stone Fish 2015; Malpas 2011). These feelings often interfere with parents' ability to support their LGBTQ+ children, support that these youth want and need. One youth articulated what it would have meant to have his family's support: " '[Friends] won't always be there; family will always be there, so I think, like a stronger foundation of family support would've been like amazing' " (Roe 2017, 58).

One possible solution, then, is to address fragile and frayed parent–child relationships through family therapy. Successful approaches involve supporting parents as they learn to support their LGBTQ+ children. Strategies for practitioners working with parents include providing psychoeducation, fostering empowerment, probing meaning-making (by using reflection and exploring coping narratives), addressing marital and parenting conflicts, and, where relevant, processing decisions regarding a transgender youth's gender-affirming transition (Malpas 2011). Harvey and Stone Fish (2015) developed a three-stage approach grounded in queer theory to assist parents and their LGBTQ+ children achieve healthier relationships. Creating refuge (stage 1) allows family members to share their beliefs and concerns openly in a supportive environment. Difficult dialogs (stage 2) are honest conversations about family dynamics and how they have impaired relationships between family members. Nurturing queerness (stage 3) is possible when parents come to accept their child's LGBTQ+ identity and acknowledge their child's resilience in the face of societal and even family opposition as a strength.

One standout program is the Family Acceptance Project. (See box 6.2, *Read All About It!*) The Family Acceptance Project is the "first evidence-informed family support model to help racially, ethnically, and religiously diverse families learn to support their LGBTQ children to reduce mental health risks and to promote well-being in the context of their family, cultures, and faith communities" (Ryan 2019, S58). The program was born out of the realization that little research existed on LGBTQ+ youth disclosure, parental reactions to disclosure, and the consequences of parental reactions, including youth running away from home or being thrown out. One purpose of the program, then, is to prevent youth homelessness by keeping youth in their homes (Ryan 2010). Findings from research on the program indicate that educating parents about the effect of their reactions reduces the likelihood of youth separating from the home (Wilbur et al. 2006). Founded on her and her colleagues' research, Ryan (2014) outlines several approaches to working with LGBTQ+ youth and their families. (See box 6.3, *What Do You Think?*)

In the meantime, LGBTQ+ youth may find a preventive safety net in school. According to Krause et al. (2016), "Having access to counselors,

BOX 6.2. READ ALL ABOUT IT!
THE FAMILY ACCEPTANCE PROJECT

- Visit the Family Acceptance Project online (https://familyproject .sfsu.edu/) for these and other resources:
  - Assessment resources
  - Videos to help families learn how to support their LGBTQ children
  - Evidence-based posters to educate people about the critical role of family support in building healthy futures for LGBTQ children and youth
  - Educational materials for families
  - *A Practitioner's Resource Guide: Helping Families to Support Their LGBT Children*
  - Information about training, consultation, and program development

BOX 6.3. WHAT DO YOU THINK?
WORKING WITH PARENTS AND FAMILIES

- The following is an excerpt from the Family Acceptance Project's *A Practitioner's Resource Guide: Helping Families to Support their LGBT Children* (Ryan 2014), which outlines approaches for professionals working with LGBTQ+ youth and their families:

Approach to Working with Families

  - Engage, approach, and connect with families and caregivers by meeting them "where they are," and view each family as an ally.
  - Let parents and caregivers tell their story.
  - Give families respectful language to talk about sexual orientation and gender identity.
  - Educate families on how family rejecting behaviors affect their LGBT child.
  - Educate families on how supportive and accepting behaviors affect their LGBT child. (8–10)

- Role-play one or more of these approaches with your classmates. How would you, as a social worker, therapist, or counselor, engage parents and other family members? What would each approach look like? How would you tailor your responses to accommodate various family forms and characteristics (e.g., families of color, religious families, single-parent families, blended families)?

social workers, teachers, or other trusted adults and an overall positive school climate might help prevent potentially adverse housing circumstances" (522).

Preventing youth homelessness is not only the most desirable outcome but also the most cost-effective. Keeping youth in the home—when it is safe to do so—saves money that would otherwise be spent on conducting street outreach, providing temporary shelter, and addressing crisis and emergency needs (e.g., hospitalization). In a comprehensive investigation into the total cost of youth homelessness, Centrepoint (2023), a nonprofit organization dedicated to youth homelessness in the United Kingdom, found that the primary expense associated with homelessness is unemployment and economic inactivity, especially among older youth and young adults who are not always engaged in—nor always able to engage in—the formal labor force. This "lost output" has both short-term ("lost gross value added [GVA] contributions, which include the tax revenue loss for the government"), and long-term impacts ("the effect of being jobless on productivity over time" [13]). Rounding out the top three costs are those associated with the criminal justice system (when youth are offenders) and housing services (including assessment and home-finding) (Centrepoint 2023) (table 6.1). With an estimated 312,504 unhoused young people (ages sixteen to twenty-four) in the United Kingdom, the approximate cost of youth homelessness is £27,347 (US$34,014) per person and £8.5 billion (US$10.6 billion) per year (Centrepoint 2023; Pleace 2015). Thus, for physical, psychological, and economic well-being, prevention remains the first line of defense against youth homelessness.

FOSTER CARE

Zach has been staying with friends and their families for periods lasting anywhere from a few days to almost six months but usually around four to six weeks. Most of his friends' parents have taken him in reluctantly, worried that they're going against his parents' wishes but relenting because of their own children's pleading. None of the parents know that Zach is gay; his friends simply tell them that Zach is having a hard time at home and that his parents

TABLE 6.1 Costs associated with homelessness among youth aged sixteen to twenty-four years, 2021/2022 GPB

Cost type	Total cost per year, to nearest £1,000	Per-head cost per year, to nearest £1	Share, %
Output loss due to inactivity or unemployment	5,534,844,000	17,711	64.8
Criminal justice	845,956,000	2,707	9.9
Homelessness services	492,648,000	1,576	5.8
Lower productivity	478,094,000	1,530	5.6
Social security	472,744,000	1,513	5.5
National Health Service (NHS) health services	456,179,000	1,460	5.3
Mental health services	140,886,000	451	1.7
Substance misuse services	124,540,000	399	1.5
Total*	**8,545,891,000**	**27,347**	**100**

*Difference due to rounding.
Note: See the 2023 Centrepoint report for more information.
Source: Centrepoint 2023, 5. Reprinted with permission.

"need some space to cool off." Zach isn't sure how child protective services work, but he knows he doesn't want his friends' parents to report him. Based on the (exaggerated) stories he's heard, the idea of foster care terrifies him.

The child welfare system is a collection of services and programs that includes **child protective services, out-of-home care** (e.g., kinship or foster care, residential or group homes), and adoption. These formal arrangements are institutionalized and effectuated by state governments. In 2022, some 3.1 million children were the subject of child protection investigations (with some the subject of more than one investigation), and 558,899 of those children were found to be victims of **maltreatment** (Children's Bureau 2024). Nearly 200,000 children also entered foster care in 2022. In the United States as of September 30, 2022, 368,530 youth were in foster care (Children's Bureau 2023).

According to data from the second National Survey on Child and Adolescent Well-Being, approximately 15.5 percent of youth (aged 11 to 17.5 years) involved in the child welfare system, specifically those referred to child protective services, identify as LGB (Dettlaff et al. 2018). This figure represents a disproportionate number of LGB youth, especially the sexual-minority girls and youth of color among them. This overrepresentation may stem from families' negative reactions to their children's sexual orientation or gender identity and the consequent relationship strain and family disintegration, leading to parental rejection, abandonment, or maltreatment. As a result, youth run away from, are kicked out of, or are removed from their homes. Foster care often provides these youth a stable home environment while they await **reunification** or other permanency placement, though some youth stay in foster care until they **age out** (i.e., reach the age at which they are no longer eligible for services), when they may again face homelessness (Mountz and Capous-Desyllas 2020; Robinson 2021). For some LGBTQ+ youth, however, the child welfare system is no more welcoming than the homes they left, leaving them little choice but to live on the streets (Robinson 2021).

Despite their overrepresentation in the child welfare system (Dettlaff et al. 2018; Fish et al. 2019), LGB youth (20.7 percent) are no more likely than their non-LGB peers (20.5 percent) to report having been placed in out-of-home care. That is, although LGB and heterosexual youth wind up in foster care at the same rate, more LGB youth remain in care. This may be because fewer LGB youth exit care through reunification or adoption, leaving more LGB youth in the system (Fish et al. 2019). For example, LGBTQ+ youth, especially LGBTQ+ youth of color, experience a greater number of foster care placements and group home placements than do non-LGBTQ+ youth (Poirier et al. 2018). The similar rates of out-of-home placement between LGB and non-LGB youth may also result from the absence of transgender youth in the sample (Martin et al. 2016), youth who would otherwise add to the percentage of LGBTQ+ youth in care. Data regarding the percentage of transgender and gender-diverse youth in the child welfare system are lacking (Dettlaff et al. 2018), although we know that they are also overrepresented in foster care, perhaps at a greater rate than LGB youth (Wilson et al. 2014). Wilson et al. (2014) estimate that 5.6 percent of youth in foster care in Los Angeles identify as transgender, compared with just 2.3 percent of youth not in foster care who identify as transgender. While not representative of the LGBTQ+ RHY population, comparisons such as these based on samples drawn from large cities cannot be dismissed out of hand. Although LGB youth in care are more likely than their non-LGB counterparts to live in urban areas, the groups do not differ with regard to rates of family poverty (high), family stress (high), or parental education (low) (Dettlaff et al. 2018).

With a lower likelihood of reunification and adoption among LGB youth in out-of-home care compared with their non-LGB peers (Fish et al. 2019), seeking out another important adult may be a feasible and more successful alternative for LGBTQ+ youth. Extended family members are a logical choice, but others, such as adults known from a school or church setting, should also be considered (Jacobs and Freundlich 2006). What is important for a successful placement is an adult who is supportive and can provide a stable home environment. When adults known to the youth are not available, others willing to foster or adopt the youth should be considered. LGBTQ+ adults should be among those considered as temporary or permanent caregivers for LGBTQ+ youth (Jacobs and Freundlich 2006; Mountz and Capous-Desyllas 2020).

PERMANENCY SOLUTIONS

Even though Zach realized early on that his parents would likely never come to terms with his sexuality, he didn't anticipate the mounting challenges he would face. What he thought would be better than having to stifle his feelings and stay away from the small group of other LGBTQ+ youth in town—that is, living with his friends and their families—is wearing thin on him and on the families with whom he is staying. He couldn't imagine moving back in with his parents and whatever it would take to even make that happen, but he didn't see a way to make it on his own, either. What landlord would rent an apartment to a sixteen-year-old, and how would Zach pay for it anyway?

When prevention measures fail or are overlooked, youth may find themselves unstably housed or homeless. The next step, then, is intervening early in the experience to reestablish stable housing by identifying a safe, feasible, long-term solution to youth homelessness; reunification and adoption are two such remedies. These **permanency solutions** must be prioritized

(Jacobs and Freundlich 2006), and first among them is reunification with the youth's family of origin.

Reunification

The reunification process prepares families to welcome the youth back into the home. This can occur only when the initial reasons for homelessness or out-of-home placement are addressed. One or more family members, parents especially, may have a difficult time coping with the reality that their child or sibling is LGBTQ+ and may react poorly, resulting in a traumatic experience for all involved (Jacobs and Freundlich 2006). Such challenges require intervention, which often falls to child welfare professionals. The child welfare system acts as a safety net for children and adolescents whose well-being is in jeopardy by interceding when parents or other caregivers are unable—or unwilling—to provide adequate care and support. Far from the stereotype of tearing children away from their parents, child welfare workers aim to keep or reunite children with their families. Indeed, it is often their number-one goal, followed by adoption, another permanency solution (CWIG 2021) (figure 6.1).

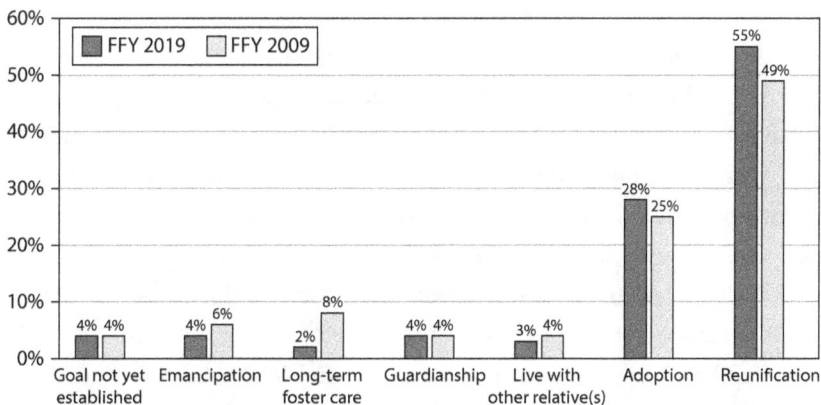

FIGURE 6.1 Comparison of foster care permanency goals, 2009 and 2019.

Source: CWIG 2021, 5.

Before youth return home, child welfare workers should assess the family's ability to support the youth, assess the safety of the environment, and intervene in repairing family relationships (Wilbur et al. 2006). According to Ream and Peters (2021), "It is rarely as simple as bringing everyone together to facilitate the repair of past wrongs" (47), because that can sometimes make things worse. Moreover, not all parents are willing participants (Ream and Peters 2021). Promising strategies for the successful reunification of youth from the general population include parent–child visits, family-centered practice, and intensive family reunification services (e.g., Pine et al. 2014); however, it is unknown how LGBTQ+ youth and their families fare with these practices. Nevertheless, family therapy is an important strategy in making the home environment safe and supportive before the youth return.

To that end, in 2011, Senator John Kerry introduced the Reconnecting Youth to Prevent Homelessness Act, a bill that in part directed the establishment of programs focused on strengthening relationships in families of LGBTQ+ youth. It was also one that, for the first time in history, mentioned LGBTQ+ youth by name (Gordon and Krehely 2011). However, the bill never made it out of the Senate (RYPHA 2011), leaving youth homelessness prevention up to individual communities and agencies.

Families may benefit from LGBTQ+-affirming community resources, faith communities, and support groups, such as PFLAG, a national network of families helping families with LGBTQ+ loved ones. Founded in 1973, PFLAG chapters exist in cities and towns across the United States to support parents and caregivers struggling to understand, accept, and support their LGBTQ+ children (PFLAG n.d.). New members are typically welcomed by parents and family members who have evolved in their understanding of sexual orientation and gender identity and are able to support others who are where they themselves once were.

LGBTQ+ youth who are separated from their families must be allowed continued contact with them—if it is desired by the youth and safe to do so—until they are reunited, if ever (Erney and Weber 2018; Wilbur et al. 2006). As rejecting as some parents can be toward their LGBTQ+ children, they can also be a source of support, motivation, and coping. It would be a disservice to these youth to expect them to cut ties with their family of origin (Gallardo et al. 2023). Based on their extensive experience with LGBTQ+

youth in the child welfare system, the foster care and adoption experts Jill Jacobs and Madelyn Freundlich (2006) reassure us that "families often experience changes in their feelings and perceptions about their children's sexual orientation and gender identity . . . and, with continuing support and assistance to the family and youth, the youth can safely return home" (311–12).

Adoption

To the best of our knowledge, no research exists on the experience of LGBTQ+ as adoptees following the **termination of parental rights**. There are reports of the need for families to foster and adopt LGBTQ+ youth (Associated Press 2016; Larson 2008) but no account of youths' experiences once adopted. This clearly represents a gap in our understanding of LGBTQ+ youth permanency outcomes. The dearth of information may be evidence that few LGBTQ+ youth exit foster care via adoption. This passive form of rejection is yet another obstacle to finding a permanent solution. Indeed, rejection seems to be the common denominator in the endless cycle of out-of-home care: rejection by families of origin is repeated by foster and **kinship families** (Mountz and Capous-Desyllas 2020; Woronoff et al. 2006), leaving youth to languish in institutions until they age out of the system (McCormick et al. 2016). In their qualitative study of LGBTQ+ youth formerly in foster care, Mountz and Capous-Desyllas (2020) found that rejection "often resulted in interrupted placements, failed reunification, and/or limited permanency opportunities upon aging out of foster care" (7). Repeated failed placements can leave youth with little appetite for further attempts. As Woronoff et al. (2006) state, "Many of these youth do not want to return to a family setting under any circumstances" (20). In such cases, **emancipation** may be the best option, albeit an imperfect one, and certainly one of last resort.

EMANCIPATION

Parents are legally responsible for their children until the child is emancipated. Most youth are emancipated when they reach the **age of majority** (i.e., when they become a legal adult); in other cases, youth are emancipated when they marry or join the military or when they or their parents or legal guardians petition the court for the youth's emancipation. In most states, the age of majority is eighteen, and the age to become an emancipated minor is sixteen (Legal Information Institute 2022). (To find laws regarding the ages of majority and emancipation in your state, visit https://minors.uslegal.com/age-of-majority/.) Here, we are referring to minor youth who choose **judicial emancipation** (i.e., emancipation via petition) to sever ties with their legal guardians, whether their family of origin or the child welfare system.

Although there is little formal literature on youth experiencing or at risk of experiencing homelessness and their desire to emancipate before reaching the age of majority, one well-publicized case received media attention for its atypical outcome. First, it is important to remember that emancipation in any form relieves the legal guardian of financial responsibility for the child. For Jhette Diamond, however, the courts ultimately granted the unusual arrangement of simultaneous emancipation and child support from her mother. Jhette left home at the age of thirteen because of the presence of domestic violence and substance abuse in her mother's home (Justia n.d.):

> She moved from place to place, crashing on friends' sofas and supporting herself through a variety of jobs in her hometown of Espanola, New Mexico. Diamond remained in school and continued to excel scholastically throughout this unsettled period in her life, and because she was such a good student and never got into any type of trouble, she stayed under the radar and avoided being placed in foster care. For Diamond, winning emancipation would mean she could have her own bank account, get a driver's license, and obtain medical and dental care without parental consent. It would also mean she would avoid ever being placed in foster care. (USD 2015, paras. 1 and 5)

Upon turning sixteen, Jhette successfully petitioned the court to be emancipated from her mother but still receive child support from her. Again, this legal decision is not typical, but the case highlights the resilience of homeless and unstably housed youth. (See box 6.4, *Read All About It!*)

BOX 6.4. READ ALL ABOUT IT!
JHETTE DIAMOND, ATTORNEY AT LAW

- Jhette went on to graduate from the University of San Diego School of Law and pass the California bar exam. To learn more about Jhette's experience, visit https://www.sandiego.edu/news/law/detail .php?_focus=52607.

When considering emancipation, youth must weigh the advantages against the disadvantages. What they may gain by leaving dysfunctional families and chaotic and abusive households, they typically lose in financial support. However unpredictable and minimal that support might have been, it was mandated by law. Having traded their financial dependence for financial independence, these youth, still considered minors by law, may find it difficult to support themselves (Cataldo 2014). If they were not homeless already, they may become so. Emancipation is thus an option of last resort after all other options have been exhausted or deemed infeasible.

SUMMARY

LGBTQ+ youth and their families can be helped through prevention services or, if the youth is already out of the home, through interventions that support the youth and their families. Ideally, youth at risk of running away or being kicked out of the home are brought to the attention of social workers, therapists, and counselors who can assist the entire family before they reach their breaking point. Nevertheless, families of RHY with a goal of reunification can benefit from a similar approach: to repair relationships and help parents commit to supporting their LGBTQ+ children. Family therapy may afford one such opportunity, if not to the point of reunification, then to at least increase the level of support that caregivers provide. Kinship care and foster care can provide temporary but stable housing while the youth, their families, and their child welfare workers determine next steps.

The most common permanency solutions are reunification, when returning home is feasible and safe for the youth, and adoption, when finding a new permanent home for the youth is the better alternative. In some cases, when prevention, foster care, reunification, and adoption are not possible or not desired by or in the best interest of the youth, judicial emancipation may be the youth's best (albeit not ideal) option. Although emancipation means surrendering all claims to financial support from the family, it frees the youth to speak and act on their own behalf without the need for parental consent. However, emancipation comes with many serious disadvantages and should not be entered into without first having considered all other alternatives or without serious consideration and planning.

REVISITING ZACH

- Based on this chapter's case vignette, make a list of all of Zach's known needs and challenges. How might you prioritize the items on this list? Which need or challenge should be addressed first? Which ones are least pressing?
- How would you approach reunification and informal kinship care (i.e., without the child welfare system's involvement) with Zach? What information do you still need to determine whether either option would be appropriate?
- If you were Zach's school social worker, would you contact his parents to notify them that you were working with him? If not, why? If so, which details would you share with them? Would you invite his parents to your sessions with Zach? Would you make a referral for family therapy? Why or why not?
- Zach has considerable fear about being placed in foster care. What stereotypes and misinformation surround foster care and the child welfare system? How might you discuss these with Zach in a way that is reassuring yet honest?

- Zach has not ruled out the possibility of becoming independent before he turns eighteen (through judicial emancipation). What thoughts and feelings do you have about this? How would you process this option with him without introducing your own thoughts and feelings? How would you help him develop safety or harm-reduction measures should he decide to pursue emancipation?

KEY CONCEPTS

- *Age of majority*: the age at which an individual is considered an adult; this is eighteen years in almost all states and the District of Columbia
- *Age out*: to exit the child welfare system by reaching the age of majority
- *Child protective services*: a function of the child welfare system that investigates reports of suspected child maltreatment
- *Couch surfing*: usually informal and short-term living arrangements with extended family, friends, acquaintances, or strangers
- *Emancipation*: gaining independence by reaching the age of majority or, as a minor, through legal means (e.g., marrying, enlisting in the military, petitioning a court)
- *Judicial emancipation*: independence granted to a minor by decree in response to a court petition
- *Kinship families*: extended family members who act as a substitute for a child or youth's family of origin
- *Maltreatment*: child abuse and neglect; "at a minimum, any recent act or failure to act on the part of a parent or caretaker, which results in death, serious physical or emotional harm, sexual abuse or exploitation . . . or an act or failure to act which presents an imminent risk of serious harm" (CAPTA 1974, sec. 3)
- *Out-of-home care*: court-ordered living arrangements in environments outside the home of the child or youth's family of origin (e.g., kinship care, foster care, group home)
- *Permanency solutions*: permanent alternatives to out-of-home placement and homelessness such as reunification and adoption

- *Reunification*: the return of a child or youth who has been placed in out-of-home care or been homeless to their family of origin
- *Termination of parental rights*: a voluntary or involuntary court action that ends a parent's custodial rights to their child or children

CHAPTER HIGHLIGHTS

- Research suggests that LGBTQ+ youth disclose first to those whom they believe will respond best, usually their mothers and siblings (sisters more often than brothers); rarely are fathers the first to know of their children's LGBTQ+ identity.
- National and international organizations alike have called for the elimination of LGBTQ+ youth homelessness, speaking in part to the rejection that some LGBTQ+ youth face at home and the discrimination that LGBTQ+ individuals face regarding their sexual orientation and gender identity.
- Parents and families struggling to support their LGBTQ+ children and siblings may benefit from family therapy. The Family Acceptance Project seeks to prevent the rupture of fractious relationships that can lead to LGBTQ+ youth becoming homeless. Organizations such as PFLAG support family, friends, and other loved ones of LGBTQ+ youth and adults.
- It is estimated that a disproportionate 15.5 percent of youth referred to the child welfare system identify as LGBTQ+, many of whom are girls and youth of color.
- Despite foster care placement rates being similar for LGBTQ+ and heterosexual-cisgender youth, more LGBTQ+ youth are in care, possibly because of the lower rates of reunification and adoption among LGBTQ+ youth. These lower rates—which can be interpreted as representing passive forms of rejection—leave many LGBTQ+ youth in foster care until they age out of the system (usually at eighteen).
- Extended family, mentors, and other trusted adults—those who can provide a safe, stable, supportive home environment—can serve as viable out-of-home alternatives to formal foster care. In any

out-of-home care situation, LGBTQ+ youth should remain connected with their families of origin—if that is in the best interest of the youth.

- With few exceptions (e.g., unsafe home environments), reunification is often the primary goal of intervention with LGBTQ+ RHY and their families of origin.
- Little has been reported about the adoption or judicial emancipation experiences of LGBTQ+ RHY. Second only to reunification, adoption is a permanency solution prioritized by the child welfare system over judicial emancipation, which should be considered only as a last resort.

Practice, Programs, Policies, and Advocacy

7 | Direct Practice

LEARNING OBJECTIVES

Readers of this chapter will be able to:

1. Explain the history of research and therapy with LGBTQ+ people, beginning with the nineteenth century,
2. Describe the functions and tasks of the phases of clinical practice (intake, engagement, assessment, planning, intervention, evaluation, termination, and follow-up), and
3. Appraise the various individual, family, and group interventions that have been tested with RHY populations.

CASE VIGNETTE: JACE

Jace, fifteen, nonbinary, and Indigenous, sat across from the intake worker feeling defeated. They weren't exactly coerced into counseling, but their case-worker made it clear that Jace was expected to follow through with the referral she made for them. "Do you belong to a tribe?" the intake worker asked indifferently. Jace rolled their eyes, thinking, "Ugh. Try 'nation.'" Jace instead stifled their annoyance. "Yes." "Do you live on the reservation or off?" the worker asked, still staring at her computer. "Off," Jace replied, hoping that the answer would discourage the worker's stereotypes. Jace was, after all, sitting in a substance abuse clinic because of their alcohol and marijuana use. The questions got even more personal. "Do you identify as straight, lesbian, gay, or bisexual?" Jace wanted to say, "It's complicated," but instead replied, "Bisexual." "If someone's available, they'll see you today, but you might have to wait." "Great," Jace thought. "I'd rather be anywhere but here." The intake worker handed Jace a pen and a clipboard stuffed with forms. "That should keep you busy for a while," she said, amused.

INTRODUCTION

Practice with LGBTQ+ RHY is enacted by a variety of human and social services workers from volunteers to salaried staff, laypeople to licensed professionals, and it occurs in a variety of settings and spaces, both indoor and outdoor, public and private. Often, these youth come into contact with mental health professionals who assist them with cognitive, emotional, or behavioral challenges; peer and intimate relationship problems; parental and family discord; school or academic struggles; and a host of other personal, interpersonal, and environmental issues. This chapter will discuss the roles that these practitioners assume with LGBTQ+ RHY and the type of work in which they engage. Specifically, we examine the nature of the working relationship, the phases of work, the levels of interaction, and barriers to engagement with this population. We discuss interventions appropriate for use with RHY, but we also direct you to practice manuals and other resources for detailed guidance on employing these approaches in treatment. Programs and services, both integrated (open to all RHY regardless of sexual orientation and gender identity) and separate (dedicated to LGBTQ+ RHY), are the subject of chapter 8. Macro-level practice, involving policy and advocacy, is covered in chapters 9 and 10, respectively. Here, we present the nuances of direct practice with LGBTQ+ RHY from the beginning of the working relationship to beyond the final session, as well as factors that hinder or facilitate treatment-seeking and access to services.

DEFINING PRACTICE

Individuals who provide mental health services to LGBTQ+ RHY work in a variety of practice settings, such as mental health, health care, education, substance abuse treatment, child welfare, and juvenile justice, among many others. Psychotherapy and other supportive services for individuals, couples, families, and groups are just some of the services these mental health professionals provide, as are psychotropic medications by those licensed to prescribe them. A few examples of these services are one-on-one therapy, professionally facilitated support groups, intensive outpatient treatment, inpatient substance abuse treatment, and medication management. We refer to those who provide services primarily as *practitioners*, *therapists*, and *providers*, and we use these terms interchangeably.

Practice is defined here as the act of providing services to clients or consumers directly or indirectly. Direct practice sees the worker and the youth interact as part of the exchange of information or the delivery of treatments, services, or resources by the provider to the youth. Examples of direct practice include processing intakes (i.e., new-client registration and paperwork) and referrals (i.e., for clients coming to the agency or being referred to another provider, program, service, or resource), conducting assessments, administering questionnaires, monitoring safety and well-being, supervising custody and accountability, providing basic needs, facilitating access to resources, and inviting and introducing youth to programs and services. For our purposes, clinical practice is a type of direct practice that implies the assessment, diagnosis, or treatment of physical, mental, emotional, or behavioral conditions, illnesses, or injuries. Social workers, mental health counselors, substance abuse counselors, marriage and family therapists, psychologists, psychiatric nurses, and psychiatrists are examples of professionals who engage in clinical mental health practice. In contrast, in macro practice, the practitioner performs activities with and on behalf of the youth that ultimately benefit the youth, although interactions between macro practitioners and youth often look different from direct practice interactions. Program administration and evaluation, agency and organization management, fundraising, grant-writing, advocacy, lobbying, and policy development and analysis are just a few examples of macro practice.

Our focus here is direct practice, particularly clinical practice. First, we turn briefly to adolescent development to better understand this time in a youth's life.

ADOLESCENT DEVELOPMENT

For many, adolescence is a tumultuous time that affects and is affected by a number of developmental domains. At this stage of life, youth undergo biological (e.g., neurological, sexual), psychological (e.g., cognitive, emotional), and social (e.g., family, peer) changes that they must navigate, ultimately emerging as young adults. Adolescence coincides with, or is defined by, the onset of puberty (Herting and Sowell 2017; NASEM 2019). Puberty is as much a cultural marker of the transition from childhood to adulthood as it is a physical one. Some of the tasks associated with this developmental period include individuating from parents, forming deeper peer relationships, exploring one's identity, and developing a sense of personal responsibility (Havighurst 1953; NASEM 2019).

With people identifying as sexual and gender minorities at increasingly younger ages (Meyer 2018; Trevor Project 2023), realizing an LGBTQ+ identity adds another layer to an adolescent's developmental experience. Identifying as heterosexual or cisgender is, in most cases, still presumed to be the default developmental outcome, making the assumption of a nonheterosexual, noncisgender identity unique to the sexual and gender minorities. Vivienne Cass (1979) authored a seminal model of sexual identity development: the six stages of identity confusion, identity comparison, identity tolerance, identity acceptance, identity pride, and identity synthesis. However, this model was designed to address lesbian and gay development only and gives little consideration to intersectional differences (e.g., race, ethnicity, disability); other models specific to distinct LGBTQ+ identities propose more inclusive and culturally sensitive identity development trajectories. Weinberg et al.'s (1994) bisexual identity development model, for example, explains the unique formative process for bisexual individuals, while Lev's (2004) transgender emergence model describes the experience of assuming one's true gender. Appreciating and validating the path these youth must take to become their authentic selves requires the practitioners who work with them to be LGBTQ+-affirming. (See chapter 1 for a broader discussion of these identity development models.)

LGBTQ+-AFFIRMING PRACTICE

A Brief History

Our contemporary understanding of practice with LGBTQ+ people stems most recently from the work of European physicians and psychiatrists two centuries ago. By the 1800s, interest in the study of human sexuality was being influenced by urbanization, the evolution of sexual behavior, and a demand for the exploration of sexuality through a scientific lens (Fuechtner et al. 2018). The field of sexual science, which would later become known as **sexology**, grew rapidly in the mid- to late nineteenth century and was initially characterized by a focus on what were then considered immodest, indiscriminate, and atypical gender and sexual interests and behaviors (e.g., prostitution, same-sex desire, cross-gender presentations, hypersexuality in women). The late French philosopher Michel Foucault (1990), himself a noted scholar of sexuality, cited Heinrich Kaan's 1844 *Psychopathia Sexualis* (*Sexual Psychopathy*) as the emergence of the pathologization of homosexuality and other "perversions" previously discussed in moral terms as "debauchery and excess" (118). This was followed by Karl Westphal's 1870 paper on "*die conträre Sexualempfindung,*" which translates to "contrary sexual feeling" but was often referred to as "sexual inversion," and Richard von Krafft-Ebing's own *Psychopathia Sexualis* in 1886 (Fuechtner et al. 2018; Tobin 2015).

Not all sexologists and their learned contemporaries were from the medical field. At the same time that Kaan, Westphal, and Krafft-Ebing were positing same-sex desire and gender-atypical presentations as mental illnesses, others were challenging this assertion and proposing alternative—including normative—conceptualizations of sexual and gender attractions and behavior. The lawyer and jurist Karl Heinrich Ulrichs postulated a theory of same-sex attraction, which he believed represented a third sex. Men who desired other men were referred to as "urnings" (and same-sex-attracted women "urningins"), a term he adapted from Plato's *Symposium* with the intention of reframing the negative terminology of the day (Tobin 2015). In 1867, during an address to an assembly of fellow jurists, Ulrichs protested the criminalization of sexual behavior between men. In doing so, he became the first (presumably) gay man (by today's standards since the term *gay* had not yet been used in this way) to speak publicly against the discriminatory treatment of men with same-sex attractions and desires (Kennedy 1997). The next year, in a letter to his friend Ulrichs, the journalist Karl Maria Kertbeny coined the term *homosexual* to refer to those who had heretofore been referred to as "inverts." The new term went public in 1869 and eventually took hold in society's lexicon.

The British physician Havelock Ellis also contributed to a more accepting view of homosexuality in his 1896 work, *Sexual Inversion*, a collaboration with the poet, literary critic, and cultural historian John Addington Symonds (Weeks 1977). Ellis, who as a physician had a credible, public platform from which to share his ideas with the medical community, could influence the field in a way that Ulrichs, a relative outsider as a lawyer and jurist, could not. Although at times seemingly at odds with itself, variously seeing inversion (as congenital) as "normal" and homosexuality (as a chosen behavior) as a perversion, *Sexual Inversion* nevertheless "set the tone for liberal attitudes to homosexuality for generations to come" (Weeks 1977, 61). Such were his sympathies that Ellis agreed (somewhat reluctantly) to write a publicity review, solicited by Radclyffe Hall, of Hall's 1928 novel, *The Well of Loneliness* (Souhami 1999). Considered to be the first lesbian novel, *The Well* is most often interpreted as a tale of love between women, although some perceive the protagonist to be transgender, not lesbian (Prosser 1998).

Modern Approaches

Fast-forward to the late twentieth century and the first significant introduction of a queer-positive approach to psychotherapy with LGBTQ+ people. In his article on treating internalized homophobia, Alan K. Malyon (1982) proposed a therapeutic strategy contrary to the prevailing approaches of the day (i.e., conversion therapy, discussed later in this chapter). In **gay-affirmative psychotherapy**, "fixed homoerotic predilections" are viewed as "sexual and affectional capacities which are to be valued and facilitated" through an approach designed to "provide corrective experiences to ameliorate the consequences of biased socialization" (62). Dominic Davies (1998), in his humanistic, particularly person-centered take on Malyon's psychodynamic approach, asserted that gay-affirmative therapy "represents a special range of psychological knowledge which challenges the traditional view that homosexual desire and fixed homosexual orientations are pathological" (111), beginning with the therapist's "retraining," which requires them to examine their own values and biases and learn about LGB people and the heterosexism and homophobia they experience (Davies 1996).

Since then, gay-affirmative psychotherapy has evolved into what we now refer to as LGBTQ+-affirmative psychotherapy or practice. The intent of Malyon's (1982) conceptualization has changed little in forty years, although the language has become more inclusive. According to Perez (2007), LGBTQ+-affirmative practice is "the integration of knowledge and awareness by the therapist of the unique developmental cultural aspects of LGBT individuals, the therapist's own self-knowledge, and the translation of this knowledge and awareness into effective and helpful therapy skills at all stages of the therapeutic process" (408). Focusing on transgender and gender-diverse clients, Singh and Dickey (2017) stated that gender-affirmative practice is "culturally relevant and responsive to TGNC [transgender and gender-nonconforming] clients and their multiple social identities, addresses the influence of social inequities on the lives of TGNC clients, enhances TGNC client resilience and coping, advocates to reduce systemic barriers to TGNC mental and physical health, and leverages TGNC clients' strengths" (4). Dickey and Puckett (2023) later revised this definition by replacing "TGNC" with "trans," acknowledging the cisnormativity of "nonconforming."

All these definitions can be distilled into several shared core principles of affirmative practice across three locus domains: therapist, client, and environment. The *therapist* is responsible for preparing themselves to work with LGBTQ+ people and then employing the skills necessary to do so ethically, competently, and compassionately. Part of that work involves challenging the *client's* internalized heterosexism and cissexism and empowering them to achieve self-actualization. Last, a comprehensive approach to practice with LGBTQ+ people includes addressing macro-level (i.e., *environmental*) injustices that negatively affect the LGBTQ+ individual's well-being and quality of life. The essential principles of LGBTQ+-affirmative practice, categorized by domain, are described next.

The Therapist

- Possesses knowledge of LGBTQ+ people and their culture,
- Demonstrates skill in working with LGBTQ+ people and is responsive to their needs,
- Is culturally sensitive to and aware of each client's intersectionality,
- Is aware of their own biases regarding sexual orientation and identity and gender identity and expression,
- Values LGBTQ+ people and culture, and
- Believes that same-sex orientations and gender-diverse identities are healthy and valid.

The Client

- Possesses strengths that can be drawn upon to help them achieve their goals,
- Demonstrates resilience to overcome hardships and an ability to cope with prejudice and discrimination,
- Has personal agency and the capacity for self-efficacy, and
- May exhibit the negative effects of prejudice and discrimination.

The Environment

- Imposes inequities that impinge on the LGBTQ+ individual's ability to access resources and opportunities and
- Is a target for change by both the client, using their voice and lived experience as personal testimony, and the therapist, who can leverage

their power and privilege to effect change and remove obstacles that prevent LGBTQ+ people from reaching their potential.

Box 7.1, *Read All About It!,* provides a list of commonly used assessments of practitioner competence, affirmation, and attitudes in practice.

BOX 7.1. READ ALL ABOUT IT! ASSESSING COMPETENCE, AFFIRMATION, AND ATTITUDES IN PRACTICE

- Cultural Competence Gender Identity Scale (CCGIS) (Simons et al. 2022)
  - Includes twenty-five items across four subscales: self-awareness of bias, gaining knowledge and skills to counsel gender-diverse individuals, awareness of barriers to gender-diverse practice, professional exposure to gender-diverse individuals
- Lesbian, Gay, and Bisexual Affirmative Counseling Self-Efficacy Inventory–Short Form (LGB-CSI-SF) (Dillon et al. 2015)
  - Includes fifteen items across five domains: application of knowledge, advocacy skills, self-awareness, relationship, and assessment
- Lesbian, Gay, Bisexual, and Transgender Competency Assessment Tool (LGBT-CAT) (Leitch et al. 2021)
  - Includes twelve open-ended questions pertaining to hypothetical micro, mezzo, and macro practice situations and behaviors
- Lesbian, Gay, Bisexual, and Transgender Development of Clinical Skills Scale (LGBT-DOCSS) (Bidell 2017)
  - Includes eighteen items across three domains: clinical preparedness, attitudinal awareness, and basic knowledge
- Lesbian, Gay, and Bisexual Working Alliance Self-Efficacy Scales (LGB-WASES) (Burkard et al. 2009)
  - Includes thirty-two items across three dimensions: emotional bond, tasks, and setting goals

CLINICAL PRACTICE WITH LGBTQ+ RHY

Individuals, Families, and Groups

Clinical practice occurs most commonly with smaller client units, such as individuals, families, and groups. Practice with individuals brings the practitioner and client together in a one-on-one interaction in which no information is shared with others outside the dyad without the client's consent (unless the client expresses an intent to harm themselves or others). Work with youth and their families can proceed in a variety of constellations, whether with birth, adoptive, step-, or foster parents; siblings; grandparents, aunts, uncles, cousins, or other extended family members; godparents, family friends, or other guardians; families of choice; or some combination therein. Groups for youth clients are typically composed of similar-aged peers with a shared lived experience (e.g., homelessness, foster care, trauma histories, substance use problems). A group can be defined according to a theme (e.g., bereavement, substance abuse recovery), with each session's topics relating to the theme, or a group can be defined more broadly, with topics varying from session to session. Although the delivery of services looks different for each client level, the essential elements are the same or similar across all. What follows is a description of practice with LGBTQ+ RHY according to the phases of work typically seen in clinical mental health practice: intake and engagement, assessment and planning, intervention and evaluation, and termination and follow-up.

Intake and Engagement

The intake-and-engagement phase is the youth's introduction to clinical mental health services, the practitioner who will provide those services, and often the setting in which the services will take place. Intake and engagement are sometimes discussed as separate phases or activities, but even if they are performed at different times by different people, they both contribute to fostering a professional relationship with the youth. Research has shown that half of RHY clients who complete the intake process do not return (Winiarski et al. 2020), making it critical to form a positive relationship during that first interaction.

Intake

It is likely that LGBTQ+ youth experiencing homelessness have previously received services that warranted an intake or the initial processing of an individual as a client or consumer at an agency or practice. During a brief interview, an agency staff member or the practitioner, using paper or electronic forms completed by the youth, a staff member, or the practitioner, collects demographic information and a summary of the situation that led the youth to seek or be referred for services. The youth may also be asked to provide documentation, such as their birth certificate, driver's license, Medicaid or private insurance card, or school identification. The intake forms become part of the client's record at the agency. If the intake occurs in advance of the first meeting with a practitioner, this might also be when an appointment is scheduled for that initial session. At this point, or during the first session, the youth may be offered a copy of some of the intake documents, such as a list of client rights and responsibilities, a fee schedule and payment options and expectations, a copy of the agency's or practice's policies, emergency phone numbers for clients in crisis, and agency or practice brochures, among other resources.

Engagement

Jace sat in the waiting room, feeling uncomfortable among a handful of strangers, most of whom were old enough to be Jace's parents or grandparents. The waiting room door opened, and a white man in his twenties scanned the room. "Johnson?" he asked. Jace stood up and thought, "At least he didn't call me 'mister.'" "Hi, I'm Mr. Jacobs," the worker said, extending his hand to Jace. As they walked back to his office, Mr. Jacobs asked Jace casually, "How would you like me to address you?" "'Jace.' It's what I was born with," Jace answered. Once inside Mr. Jacobs's office, and after engaging in what Jace perceived as annoying small talk, the questions Jace was expecting began. "What brings you here?" Mr. Jacobs asked. "Here we go," Jace thought. Jace responded,

"I'm staying at [a nearby youth shelter], and they said I have a problem and needed to be here." "And you'd probably rather be anywhere but here," Mr. Jacobs replied. Jace's eyes widened slightly. "This guy's reading my mind," they thought. After only about thirty minutes of questions, the session ended and Jace left. "So far, so good," they said to themself.

The task during the engagement phase is for the practitioner to build rapport with the youth and develop a therapeutic alliance. Mutual respect, trust, authenticity (genuineness), and honesty form the foundation of a beneficial working relationship. Inherent in these qualities are expressing interest in the youth, showing compassion, being open and accepting, having a nonjudgmental attitude, demonstrating cultural humility, and engaging in active listening (Darbyshire et al. 2006; French et al. 2003; Garrett et al. 2008; Hishida 2016). Trust is especially important to RHY, who have a high rate of exposure to trauma, in turn making trust difficult to establish (Aykanian 2018; Darbyshire et al. 2006). A practitioner–client relationship high in trust fosters youth engagement and retention; a youth's lack of trust in their provider may contribute to attrition (i.e., dropout) (Aykanian 2018). Indeed, for some RHY, the relationships they form with staff are just as important as the services themselves (Garrett et al. 2008). Trust is further enhanced by the setting of healthy boundaries around behavior and expectations, which fosters the client's feelings of safety and security. This protection promotes deeper sharing and allows meaningful change to occur (Hishida 2016).

The engagement phase typically lasts one to two sessions but can be shorter or longer depending on the youth's needs, the agency's or facility's expectations or policies, or the circumstances warranting the help-seeking (e.g., a sudden loss of housing versus long-standing relationship difficulties). In reality, RHY attend an average of three to eight sessions, depending on treatment modality (Slesnick et al. 2011; Winiarski et al. 2020), so engaging with the youth early is crucial. If the rapport-building is successful and the relationship is strong, the youth will be more likely to return (Hishida 2016; Rice et al. 2023). (See box 7.2, *Read All About It!*) According to Rice and his colleagues' RHY-provider coauthors (2023), this positive relationship dynamic "is often unacknowledged outside of youth serving organizations" (367), illustrating that practice knowledge exists but is

---

BOX 7.2. READ ALL ABOUT IT!
ASSESSING THE PRACTITIONER–CLIENT RELATIONSHIP

- Two commonly used measures to assess the practitioner–client relationship are the Working Alliance Inventory (Horvath and Greenberg 1986) and the Working Alliance Inventory–Short Form (Tracey and Kokotovic 1989), both of which can be found at https://wai.profhorvath.com/downloads.

---

not always reflected in the literature. Digging deeper into this finding, it is youth empowerment specifically that promotes service use. Educating RHY about services and how to use them increases the youths' self-efficacy, which makes them more likely to use those services (Rice et al. 2023). Part of the intake and engagement process, then, should involve informing the youth of the services and resources available to them, how they can benefit the youth, and how the youth can access them.

Assessment and Planning

Assessment

Following the engagement phase, or sometimes during it, the practitioner will conduct an assessment interview, an extensive question-and-answer period that aims to provide the practitioner with an understanding of the youth's history and current reality and how both might be contributing to the presenting problem or problems. This qualitative assessment provides a wide-ranging and detailed account of various aspects of the youth's background: childhood, family, education, physical and mental health, substance use and addiction, religion and spirituality, and legal and criminal involvement, among others. The practitioner may also ask about other aspects of the youth's life, such as their interests and hobbies, strategies they use to cope with difficult situations, and experiences of trauma (e.g., verbal, physical, or sexual abuse or other types of violence and victimization). Such a comprehensive interview is often referred to as a **biopsychosocial assessment** and addresses the three primary domains of one's being: physical, mental and emotional, and social functioning. The practitioner usually follows an outline of predetermined questions, interjecting with follow-up questions for clarification and to gather additional details when necessary; they may take notes on paper or electronically.

Some assessments are part of the intervention process itself. For example, the Functional Assessment Interview for Runaways (FAIR) captures the youth's runaway history, the circumstances surrounding their running away, and changes that would prevent further runaway episodes and ends with an intervention plan developed jointly by the youth and the practitioner (Crosland et al. 2020). During the assessment, the practitioner asks the youth about their reasons (i.e., antecedents) for running away (i.e., the behavior)—what the youth was running away from (negative reinforcers such as restrictive rules at home) or running to (positive reinforcers such as an intimate partner)—and the resulting fallout (i.e., the consequences). The youth and the practitioner then identify changes that could keep the youth from running away again (e.g., negotiating agreeable rules and expectations with parents or caregivers, facilitating visits with the youth's partner). Together, the practitioner and the youth devise and plan short-term, achievable goals that align with the youth's preferences, desires, and interests and that keep the youth safe and hold them accountable if they do not follow through. The FAIR consists of seven assessment domains (e.g., school, placement, run experience) and two planning domains: action plan and intervention (e.g., "What are some things that we might consider to make things better so you won't choose to run away again?") and initial plan (i.e., goal, activity, responsible person, follow-up) (Crosland et al. 2020, 81). The FAIR appears in an appendix in Crosland and colleagues' 2020 publication.

During the assessment, the practitioner may also administer paper-and-pencil or electronic questionnaires to the client to gather additional information. Responses to these questionnaires can add depth to the information already gathered, provide new insights, tap into specific areas that may be a focus of work, and provide baseline data for monitoring change over time. **Screening tools** and **measurement instruments** are some of the more common types of questionnaires that clients are asked to complete. These largely quantitative tools and instruments typically assess a client's emotional and behavioral symptoms; substance use; personality traits; intellectual ability; educational, occupational, relational, and social functioning; coping mechanisms; and quality of life.

Screening tools are usually brief, can be easily administered, and can be quickly scored by the practitioner or another staff member. Given the limited number of sessions a practitioner will have with a youth, brevity in administration and scoring is key. The primary purpose of a screening tool is to signal the presence of mental or behavioral health symptoms or a disorder that should be investigated further. Some tools, such as the Patient Health Questionnaire (PHQ-9) (Kroenke et al. 2001), correspond with criteria in the *Diagnostic and Statistical Manual of Mental Disorders* (*DSM*), making the presence or absence of a mental disorder much more certain. Others are less specific but nonetheless helpful in identifying red flags needing clinical attention. For example, the CAGE questionnaire ("CAGE" being an acronym for "Cutting down, Annoyed by criticism, feeling Guilty, and needing an Eye-opener") (Ewing 1984), screens for possible alcohol use problems by tapping into some of the symptoms associated with heavy and sustained drinking. Whereas screening tools suggest the presence of a phenomenon, measurement instruments indicate the quantity or frequency of the phenomenon using a predetermined scale. Many are easy to administer and score, but some take longer to complete, warrant assistance from the practitioner, or require the practitioner to conduct an interview or administer the testing protocol (e.g., displaying images, timing a performance task). Most measurement instruments are standardized, making it possible to position a respondent's score in relation to those of a representative sample of a population. **Standardized instruments** are consistent in their structure and administration and have been evaluated for their reliability (their ability to capture consistent results across administrations) and validity (their ability to measure what was intended). A client's score is a relative indication of the size or amount of the variable being measured. The Adolescent Coping Scale (Frydenberg and Lewis 1996), for example, measures strategies employed by a youth to handle stressful situations, and the Child Behavior Checklist (Achenbach 1978), completed by a parent or guardian, measures a child's social competence and behavior problems. A comprehensive review of screening tools and measurement instruments is beyond the scope of this chapter, so we refer you to Lo et al. (2019) and Moss and Moss-Racusin (2021) for detailed descriptions of the use of assessment instruments with adolescents.

A substantial number of assessments have been identified as intended for or appropriate with RHY. The Runaway and Homeless Youth Training, Technical Assistance, and Capacity Building Center (n.d.a) offers an online database of more than 150 screening and assessment instruments relevant to the RHY population. Users can search for tools by keyword and filter their search by subject area, price range, and respondent age range. Many are free, and several are offered in languages other than English. (See box 7.3, *What Do You Think?*) Other tools help providers prioritize available housing resources based on a youth's level of vulnerability. The youth version

---

BOX 7.3. WHAT DO YOU THINK?
SELECTING MEASUREMENT INSTRUMENTS FOR USE
WITH LGBTQ+ RHY

- Read Jace's case vignette and then visit the Runaway and Homeless Youth Training, Technical Assistance, and Capacity Building Center's (n.d.a) online database of screening and assessment tools: https://resources.rhyttac.org/resources/screening-tool. Consider the following:

  ○ Which tools might be most appropriate for use with Jace?
  ○ What keywords might you use to search for relevant measurement instruments?
  ○ If you were to search by subject area, which area or areas would you choose?
  ○ Would the cost or a requirement for the tool to be administered by a staff member or trained professional factor into your decision to use the tool?

of the Service Prioritization Decision Assistance Tool (Y-SPDAT) (Org-Code Consulting, Inc. 2015b) consists of fifteen domains (e.g., physical and mental health, substance use, legal involvement), each of which is scored according to the youth's responses to several questions. A shorter version of the Y-SPDAT, the Transition Age Youth–Vulnerability Index–SPDAT (TAY-VI-SPDAT) (OrgCode Consulting, Inc. 2015a), measures general levels of vulnerability, indicating which youth require an assessment with the full Y-SPDAT. The Transition Age Youth (TAY) Triage Tool (Rice 2013) is a validated instrument that also assesses RHY with an eye toward prioritizing available housing. With just six items (e.g., "Have you ever become homeless because there was violence at home between family members?"), it can be administered in considerably less time than the twenty-eight-item TAY-VI-SPDAT (Rice 2013, 2). The TAY Triage Tool is available in a manual published online by the Corporation for Supportive Housing. The SPDAT assessments are also available online but require the practitioner to be trained before use. The Downtown Emergency Service Center (DESC) Vulnerability Assessment Tool (DESC n.d.), which also requires user training, and the U.S. Department of Housing and Urban Development's (2015) Determining Homeless Status of Youth tool, available online (https://www.hudexchange.info/resource/4783/determining-homeless-status-of-youth/), are two additional options for assessing vulnerability among RHY.

Planning

This phase culminates in a plan for work, which sets the stage for the intervention in the next phase. Qualitative and quantitative data gathered during the assessment are used to develop what is essentially a contract for the work the clinician and the youth will do together: intervention or treatment goals and objectives; the frequency, duration, and number of sessions; topics to be covered; problems to be targeted; treatments or other interventions to be used; possible referrals to be made; and collaterals (i.e., third-party sources) to be contacted for additional information (e.g., family members, school personnel, health care providers). The plan, sometimes referred to as a **treatment plan**, in whole or in part, can be reviewed with the youth, who may be asked to provide their signature on a document to indicate their understanding of and commitment to the work. The plan, along with the completed assessment, including any screening tools or measurement instruments, are added to the client's record. This phase presupposes that the youth will return to enact the plan. However, with such high attrition among this population (Winiarski et al. 2020), the intake, engagement, assessment, and planning phases, and perhaps even the start of an intervention, may need to be truncated into one session.

Intervention and Evaluation

Three weeks into their individual sessions together, with Jace's permission, Mr. Jacobs enrolled Jace in an ongoing weekly group for adolescents that he has been facilitating for about seven months. He reassured Jace that there were other LGBTQ+ youth in the group, although he wasn't able to reveal their names. The intervention consisted of cognitive-behavioral techniques (to help the youth identify when they're most likely to use substances, their emotions before and after using, and the consequences of their use), motivational enhancement techniques (to help the youth understand how their substance use keeps them from achieving their goals, with Mr. Jacobs providing insights about their use patterns), psychoeducation (about the physiological, psychological, and social risks of the substances each group member uses), and support (to validate the youths' experiences and encourage them to keep coming back to the group). Jace was anxious at their first group session, worried that the other members would figure out they were living at a shelter. Afterward, one youth approached Jace to introduce themself, and then a second youth joined and welcomed Jace to the group.

Intervention

The intervention phase is the point in the working relationship when the focus turns to addressing the presenting problems that led the client to seek services. In most cases, RHY present with complaints of depression, adjustment disorder, anger, and trauma (Winiarski et al. 2020). An intervention is an activity aimed at ameliorating thoughts, feelings, or behaviors that are negatively affecting the youth's quality of life. While the intervention phase marks the official commencement of a change-oriented activity, with RHY, half of whom do not make it past the first session, the initial visit is the "primary intervention point" (Winiarski et al. 2020, 7). The most common type of intervention is treatment, usually psychotherapy, which is sometimes accompanied by psychotropic medication, prescribed to support the client until they begin to experience the benefits of psychotherapy, to alleviate severe symptoms quickly, or to maintain improvements over time.

Psychotherapy, or more informally "talk therapy," involves the practitioner engaging the client in purposeful conversations aimed at alleviating the client's distress and improving their ability to function in everyday life. The practitioner does this by identifying the client's thoughts, feelings, or behaviors that may be contributing to the distress or impairment in functioning and employing therapeutic strategies that move the client toward improved health and well-being. There are countless psychotherapy models (i.e., prescribed practices within frameworks), techniques (i.e., specific words, behaviors, or activities, perhaps from a model, used in isolation), and approaches (i.e., guiding principles, values, and beliefs) to choose from, depending on the client's needs and capacities, the practitioner's skills, and the resources available to both of them. Here, we discuss some models commonly used with RHY, beginning with a brief introduction to comprehensive reviews published by experts in the field of RHY.

In their "Voices of Youth Count" Missed Opportunities series, the University of Chicago's Chapin Hall published a research brief on interventions targeting youth homelessness (Morton, Kugley et al. 2019). This systematic review of published and unpublished literature yielded sixty-two studies, twenty-six of which focused on individual and group counseling and treatment. Twelve focused on brief interventions, with motivation-based approaches being the most common. The rest focused on more intensive treatments targeting mental health problems (e.g., cognitive-behavioral therapy [CBT], dialectical behavior therapy [DBT], mindfulness practice) or health risk behaviors (e.g., the community reinforcement approach).

Similarly, Pergamit and colleagues (2016) reviewed forty-nine interventions appropriate for use with youth experiencing homelessness and their families. Interventions were categorized according to their purpose: prevention, reunification, or reconnection (i.e., repairing relationships regardless of reunification). Two were considered evidence based (i.e., practice based solely on research findings), four were considered evidence informed (i.e., practice that infuses research findings and practice knowledge), and the rest were considered promising, emerging, or of interest. Ecologically based family therapy (EBFT) and functional family therapy (FFT) are evidence-based reconnection interventions; the four evidence-informed models are multidimensional family therapy (MDFT) and multisystemic therapy (MST), both prevention models, and Treatment Foster Care Oregon (TFCO) (formerly known as multidimensional treatment foster care) and Support to Reunite, Involve, and Value Each Other (STRIVE), both reconnection models (Pergamit et al. 2016).

Individual, family, and group interventions that have been well studied with RHY are briefly described next. It should be noted that more than half (55.6 percent) of the illustrative studies presented here reported neither the sexual orientation nor the gender identity of their participants. Given the overrepresentation of LGBTQ+ youth in the RHY population, it is likely that LGBTQ+ RHY were exposed to the interventions; however, the differential impact that those interventions may have had on this population is unknown. It is possible that modifications may need to be made to make the interventions LGBTQ+-inclusive and -affirming.

Motivational Enhancement Therapy Motivational enhancement therapy (MET) derives from Miller and Rollnick's (1991) **motivational interviewing** (MI) technique for people with addictive behaviors. The premise of MI is that change lies within the individual, who may be ambivalent about giving up their drinking or drug use. MI uses an empathetic, rather than authoritative, approach to move the individual along the stages of change from precontemplation (no awareness of problem behaviors) to maintenance (free of problem behaviors for at least six months) and termination (no temptation to engage in problem behaviors) (Prochaska and DiClemente 1983).

MET is conducted over four sessions, the first two of which involve the practitioner providing feedback on the individual's pattern of substance use and associated risks. In the latter two sessions, the practitioner offers reinforcement and encouragement regarding the individual's progress (Miller et al. 1999). Since youth are not likely to seek treatment for substance use, a motivational enhancement approach may be one of opportunity or invitation and may last only one to three sessions (Howard 2020). In motivational enhancement with RHY, practitioners provide feedback in an effort to move the youth toward contemplating a decrease in their substance use. Peterson and colleagues (2006) found motivational enhancement to be successful in reducing illicit drug use in RHY but less so with reducing alcohol or marijuana use in RHY.

Cognitive Therapy for Suicide Prevention Cognitive therapy for suicide prevention (CTSP) is a manualized approach that addresses risk factors for suicide such as feelings of hopelessness and worthlessness and social isolation. According to **cognitive theory**, briefly, an individual's negative perception or interpretation of an internal (e.g., thought, memory) or external (e.g., event) stimulus induces a negative feeling (e.g., sadness, despair) that can lead to maladaptive behaviors (e.g., suicide attempts) (Wenzel et al. 2009). Unlike other suicide interventions, CTSP targets suicidality itself, not a disorder of which suicidality is a symptom (Wenzel and Jager-Hyman 2012). In a study comparing a combination of CTSP and treatment as usual (TAU) (i.e., standard treatment) with TAU alone, youth in both groups experienced a significant reduction in suicidality. However, youth receiving the combination of CTSP and TAU demonstrated a more rapid decline in suicidal ideation, a timeliness that is particularly salient in this case (Slesnick et al. 2020).

Dialectical Behavior Therapy DBT was designed to treat borderline personality disorder, particularly its parasuicidal aspect (i.e., suicidal gestures, suicide attempts, and nonsuicidal self-injury) (Linehan 1987). Therapists use validation, direct communication, problem-solving, and reinforcement with clients and teach them "emotion regulation, interpersonal effectiveness, distress tolerance, and self-management skills (capability enhancement strategies)" (Linehan 1987, 272). In their study with street-involved youth, McCay and colleagues (2015) administered DBT in weekly individual and group sessions over twelve weeks. At post-treatment and at four- and ten-week follow-ups, participants exhibited significant decreases in depression, hopelessness, and mental health symptoms and increases in self-esteem, social connectedness, and resilience. However, decreases in suicidal ideation and alcohol use were not significant. Qualitative feedback from the youth indicated their satisfaction with the intervention and its results.

The Community Reinforcement Approach The community reinforcement approach (CRA) is based on **operant conditioning**, which posits that behavior can be reinforced with rewards and extinguished with punishments. When applied to substance use, CRA identifies positive and negative consequences that influence one's drinking or drug use and replaces pleasurable experiences related to use with those unrelated to use. Behavioral skills training, social and recreational counseling, **relapse prevention**, and relationship counseling are other elements of the approach that aid in changing substance use behavior (Meyers et al. 2011). CRA with RHY has been studied extensively by Slesnick and her colleagues (2013, 2015), who found that CRA is equally as effective as MET, EBFT, and **case management** in reducing substance use, internalizing (e.g., depression, anxiety) and externalizing (e.g., conduct disorder) behaviors, and perceived family conflict, as well as improving perceived family cohesion. CRA is significantly better, however, at reducing substance use and stabilizing a youth's life (i.e., more time spent employed, in school, and housed) (Zhang and Slesnick 2018).

Family Interventions EBFT is a fifteen-session in-home intervention designed specifically for RHY and their families (Slesnick and Prestopnik 2005). In the early sessions, the therapist meets with the youth alone and with the parents or other caregivers alone to prepare all for the subsequent family sessions. HIV prevention is discussed with the youth individually, and parent or caregiver sessions are an opportunity to provide parenting strategies and support. Together, family members are taught communication and problem-solving skills to improve interactions that had heretofore led to problem behaviors in the youth. Substance use is addressed directly, and other family members, such as siblings or extended relatives, are invited to participate as sessions progress (Slesnick and Prestopnik 2005).

FFT is an office-based treatment (with the flexibility to also be delivered in clients' homes) initially designed for youth offenders and their families (Alexander and Robbins 2010). It incorporates **cognitive-behavioral** and communication principles and techniques across five phases, each with its own assessment focus and set of goals: engagement (encouraging attendance), motivation (interrupting dysfunction and fostering alliances), relational assessment (identifying the function of the behaviors being addressed), behavior change (teaching and reinforcing relational skills), and generalization (applying and maintaining new skills in the home) (Alexander and Robbins 2010; Robbins et al. 2016). The intervention is delivered in twelve to fourteen sessions over three months, with fewer sessions necessary for less intensive cases and thirty hours of direct contact warranted for those that are more intensive (Sexton and Alexander 2000).

In studies with RHY, EBFT and FFT performed no better than services as usual (SAU) on measures of psychological and family functioning; however, they were significantly better at reducing alcohol use. FFT elicited reductions soonest, while EBFT had the highest engagement and retention rates, likely owing to the intervention being delivered in the home (Slesnick and Prestopnik 2009). Compared with SAU, EBFT is better at reducing the number of drugs used and use-related consequences, especially among youth with physical or sexual abuse histories (Slesnick and Prestopnik 2005).

STRIVE is an interactive cognitive-behavioral model delivered at a location of the family's choosing, most often the home (Milburn et al. 2012). Designed specifically for newly homeless youth (i.e., those who have been homeless for less than six months), STRIVE is based on the premise that youth run away to resolve conflict with family members. The goal, then, is to reconnect RHY with their families and improve family functioning. The intervention teaches problem-solving, conflict resolution, and emotion regulation skills, among others, over five 1.5- to two-hour family sessions. Family members practice new skills through interactive tasks and materials and receive feedback from the therapist. For the youth, the intervention has been found to result in significantly fewer sex partners and a significant reduction in delinquent behaviors and alcohol and illicit drug use, with the exception of marijuana, which actually increased, perhaps to compensate for decreased alcohol and other drug use (Milburn et al. 2012).

Group Interventions Interventions delivered in a group modality provide the added benefit of social support, a substantial protective factor for RHY. Support-oriented groups that promote social connection via positive peer and mentoring relationships have demonstrated an ability to improve mental health outcomes, such as decreased hopelessness and loneliness (McCay et al. 2011; Stewart et al. 2009).

Mindfulness practice has been used alone and in combination with other treatments and approaches in group settings with RHY. Mindfulness meditation and related techniques have been applied to common problems that RHY experience, such as substance use, high-risk sexual behaviors, interpersonal violence, and mental health problems. Mindfulness skills (.b ["dot b"]) (Santa Maria, Cuccaro et al. 2020), mindfulness meditation (Spiritual Self-Schema) (Grabbe et al. 2012), and mindfulness practice with yoga (Petering et al. 2021) have targeted interpersonal violence and negative thoughts and feelings, resulting in significantly fewer physical and intense verbal fights and decreased stress, anxiety, depression, frustration, and boredom.

Combining several evidence-based interventions for RHY, Kidd and colleagues (Kidd, Vitopoulos et al. 2019; Vitopoulos et al. 2017) implemented an open-ended group intervention with recently homeless youth transitioning to stable housing. Housing Outreach Program–Collaboration (HOP-C) comprised an eclectic mix of CBT and DBT principles and techniques, mindfulness practice, and psychoeducation. Participants showed improvements in mental health outcomes, perceived housing stability, and engagement in education and employment. This intervention has also been adapted for use with Indigenous youth (Toombs et al. 2021).

Groups may be difficult for youth with social anxiety or trauma-related sequelae, which make social interaction and being present difficult (Kidd, Vitopoulos et al. 2019), but for those who are amenable to this format, participants can benefit from the social aspects that group interventions offer.

Most of these models require several sessions, a luxury that many practitioners working with RHY are not afforded because of the high rate of attrition among RHY (Winiarski et al. 2020). Thus, practitioners might do better using an **eclectic approach** since "a non-empirically based intervention is better than no treatment at all" (Winiarski et al. 2020, 7).

Strengths-Based Approaches Up to this point, this discussion of interventions has focused primarily on a deficit model: the client has a problem that they must overcome. However, a **strengths-based approach**, rooted in the social work profession, focuses on a client's capacity for self-determination and growth (Saleebey 2012; Weick et al. 1989). Strengths can be viewed as human capital, that is, inner resources that practitioners can draw on to empower their clients to enact their own change. According to Weick et al. (1989), "All people possess a wide range of talents, abilities, capacities, skills, resources, and aspirations. No matter how little or how much may be expressed at one time, a belief in human potential is tied to the notion that people have untapped, undetermined reservoirs of mental, physical, emotional, social, and spiritual abilities that can be expressed" (352). With strengths-based approaches, practitioners help clients identify and use their strengths to achieve their goals.

Two approaches that harness the strengths of RHY have recently come to the fore. Strengths-based outreach and advocacy is a means of connecting previously disengaged RHY, a particularly vulnerable population, with drop-in and shelter services. The strengths aspect of the approach lies in a focus on the youth's strengths rather than their deficiencies, their self-determination (i.e., they decide which services to accept and how and whether to accept them at all), and a nonhierarchical relationship with the outreach worker or advocate (Slesnick et al. 2016). My Strengths Training for Life (MST4Life) is a two-phase group intervention for youth already engaged in services. Phase 1 consists of ten two-hour workshops delivered in the classroom and in the community as experiential learning. During the classroom workshops, youth are guided through a strengths-identifying exercise. In the community, youth participate in activities that require planning, organizing, and problem-solving and are then guided through a reflection exercise to uncover strengths. Phase 2 consists of a "4-day outdoor adventure residential" stay (Cooley et al. 2019, 5) where youth can apply what they learned in the classroom and community workshops in an outdoor environment (e.g., through team-building exercises, an adventure course) (Parry et al. 2021). Following participation, youth have reported an increased sense of "resilience, self-worth, and well-being" (Cooley et al. 2019, 12).

Evaluation

A component of ethical practice is evaluation: is the client reaching pre-determined milestones (i.e., objectives) on the way to achieving their (treatment) goals? The measurement instruments discussed in this chapter can be administered before treatment begins to determine a client's base-line (i.e., their pre-treatment level of distress, functioning, or other tar-get variable). Those instruments can then be readministered periodically throughout the intervention phase to monitor the client's progress by com-paring baseline scores to subsequent ones. Scores showing improvement can demonstrate to a client that the treatment, and the effort they are put-ting into it, are working and that they are on their way to achieving their goals. Scores showing no improvement—or worse, a decline—although undesirable, are nevertheless informative. The treatment may not be a good fit for the client or appropriate for the problem; the client may not be ready to change or may not understand what is being asked of them; or the practitioner may not have established adequate trust or may lack the skills necessary to implement the intervention effectively. Any of these pose a therapeutic opportunity for deeper exploration of the sticking point. Instruments can continue to be administered at periodic intervals (e.g., three months, six months) after the client's final session to measure the gains sustained following treatment.

Termination and Follow-Up

After six weeks in the group, Jace was feeling at ease and could tell that they were drinking and smoking considerably less often than before meeting Mr. Jacobs. Jace could recall recent high-stress situations when he abstained, situations that, in the past, would have caused him to use. In their biweekly individual sessions, Mr. Jacobs reminded Jace that, although they were encour-aged to continue attending the group sessions, their individual sessions would be winding down soon. Even though Jace knew the sessions were time limited, they still felt a pang of disappointment at hearing the words. Perhaps noticing the look on Jace's face, Mr. Jacobs let them know that an individual session now and then to check in and see how Jace was doing was possible. Jace appreciated that Mr. Jacobs was keeping the door open, and knowing Mr. Jacobs would still be there made Jace feel more independent and self-sufficient. Jace knew they were going to be OK.

Termination

Termination, nihilistic though it may sound, simply marks the end of the practitioner and client's work together. Practitioners prepare clients for termination by broaching the subject in the first session. This reminds the client that the work will come to an end and that the client will have learned skills to be able to function independently of the therapist. It also promotes a smooth transition for the client from having the regular support of the practitioner to functioning without it. It is normal for clients to experience some anxiety as the planned termination date approaches, but this is an opportunity for the practitioner to remind the client that they have it within themself to face challenges, cope with difficulties, and continue to grow in spite of or even because of those difficulties. Preparing for termination includes having a conversation about what comes next, whether that means transferring the client to a new practitioner or unit within the agency, referring the client to other services outside the agency (e.g., intensive outpatient treatment, substance use treatment, medical care), or engaging the client's support networks (Brakenhoff and Slesnick 2018).

It is also common for some clients to attempt to sabotage the planned termination to extend the working relationship, whether because of a lack of confidence and efficacy to manage without the therapist or to avoid the negative feelings that come with having to say goodbye. This phenomenon is sometimes referred to as the "doorknob confession": a disclosure made as the client walks out the door after (what was to be) the last session intended to arouse concern in the therapist and delay discharge. Such a tactic may be more common among youth than among adults since youth sometimes find it easier to express their feelings through demonstrative behaviors than through verbal processing. Some may avoid termination altogether by simply not showing up for one or more of the last sessions. In contrast, many youth welcome the end of therapy and may wish to mark the occasion with a termination ritual such as receiving a certificate of completion, celebrating with a cake, giving their practitioner a greeting card or a small gift, playing a computer or board game with the practitioner, or, for those in groups, holding a graduation ceremony (Young et al. 2016). For youth who do not terminate prematurely, the practitioner must determine when the time is right to end treatment. According to Palmiter (2016), "Many kids who are ready for termination will speak with confidence about how well they are doing and why" (253). Attending to such cues avoids the risk of ending too soon or continuing longer than necessary.

However, as mentioned, many RHY do not return after the third session (Winiarski et al. 2020). Those who complete treatment exhibit decreases in symptoms sooner and function better at follow-up compared with those who drop out (Steinberg et al. 2019). However, the good news is that youth who terminate early can benefit from even some treatment. Moreover, even if a youth decides not to return, a positive engagement experience may make a future return more likely (French et al. 2003). While establishing a positive working relationship early on is key to increasing the likelihood that youth will continue with treatment (Aykanian 2018; Hishida 2016; Rice et al. 2023), a youth's decision to terminate therapy prematurely may have little to do with service quality and more to do with scheduling conflicts, leaving the city or shelter where services are provided (Lynk et al. 2015), being transferred to a new worker or agency (Steinberg et al. 2019), being incarcerated (Garvey et al. 2018), or believing that they do not have a problem or that their problem has resolved, even if the practitioner disagrees (French et al. 2003).

Remaining in treatment versus terminating prematurely may also be influenced by a youth's psychosocial factors. In the simplest of terms, youth with internalizing (e.g., mood, anxiety) symptoms tend to stay, whereas those with externalizing (e.g., conduct) symptoms tend to leave (Holm and Minton 2016; Sunseri 2003). Specifically, age (i.e., being older); having higher anxiety and depression scores; and exhibiting anxiety about sexual behavior, sexual functioning, and sexual partner choice are predictors of treatment completion. By comparison, conduct problems, moderate or severe attention deficit hyperactivity disorder and, most notably, homelessness are predictors of premature termination (Baruch et al. 2009). Youth experiencing homelessness are already less likely to complete treatment than their housed peers. RHY practitioners, then, must work that much harder to keep youth engaged. In intervention research, youth are typically offered an incentive (e.g., cash, a gift card, food) to attend sessions, but this is not a viable option for under-resourced agencies. Reminder cards and reaching out to youth through third-party contacts (e.g., family and friends) may be more realistic strategies for keeping youth engaged in treatment (Garvey et al. 2018).

As with treatment noncompleters, a profile of treatment completers also exists for parents of RHY. Among individuals engaged in family therapy, the level of first-session engagement by adolescents and their parents and the direction of interaction among adolescents, parents, and therapists predict premature dropout (Marchionda and Slesnick 2013). Marchionda and Slesnick (2013) found that parents who were talkative in session, whether that talk was positive or negative, completed treatment or dropped out later than parents who talked less. Parents were also more likely to complete treatment (or drop out later) if the therapist spent more time talking to them than to the adolescent. This finding has implications for therapists, who may be able to promote retention by encouraging parents to be active participants in conversations and engaging with parents as much as with the youth.

Follow-Up

Depending on the client's vulnerability, the presenting problem, the treatment outcome, or other factors, a practitioner may request follow-up contact with young clients. This contact could be as simple as a check-in email, phone call, or text or as formal as an in-person session. Follow-up sessions are a check-up of sorts intended to monitor post-treatment well-being. They can be planned ahead of time, whether built into the contract or required of the intervention, or they might be requested at some point after the fact if the practitioner finds it necessary. Follow-up sessions, sometimes referred to as **booster sessions**, can be an opportunity for the youth to reflect on their progress and achievements and identify new goals to work on to continue their growth. The therapist can also reinforce the skills learned in treatment and remind the client how those skills can be generalized to other situations, with the goal of maintaining gains over time (Young et al. 2016). For example, adolescent CBT with booster sessions was found to be more effective and the gains to be longer-lasting than in adolescent CBT without such sessions (Gearing et al. 2013). However, it is unclear how many booster sessions are needed and how long or how frequent they should be for optimal effectiveness. In reality, these variables may be driven more by youth, practitioner, and agency factors than by treatment guidelines.

BARRIERS TO AND FACILITATORS OF CARE

That RHY attend so few treatment sessions on average warrants a closer look at the reasons why. Increasing the likelihood that they will avail themselves of the services they need means removing obstacles that keep them from attending and promoting factors that make them more likely to participate.

Barriers

Barriers to engaging in therapy lie both within and outside the youth. Young people, who place considerable weight on others', especially their peers', perceptions of them, may see help-seeking as stigmatizing or as a sign of weakness and thus eschew mental health treatment (Chaturvedi 2016; Garrett et al. 2008). Perceived invincibility may also lead them to believe they do not need treatment (Chaturvedi 2016). For those who have not participated in therapy before, their lack of familiarity may make them wary of the unknown. And those who have been in therapy before but had a bad experience are typically reluctant to give it another chance (Chaturvedi 2016; Hishida 2016). Other external barriers include long waiting lists, program or agency rules and restrictions (e.g., age requirements, hours of operation, prohibiting current substance use) (Brands et al. 2005; Garrett et al.

2008; Hudson et al. 2010), peer pressure (Brands et al. 2005), financial costs (Hadland et al. 2009), lack of transportation (DeHart et al. 2021), parental consent requirements, and lack of availability in rural locations (Hishida 2016). Technology-based interventions might be one solution to several of these barriers. Services delivered via text or smartphone application, for example, are confidential and easily accessible (provided the youth has or has access to a phone). They also help agencies and practitioners recruit and engage a traditionally hard-to-find population. Thus far, such interventions have been applied to case management (Bender et al. 2015), smoking cessation programs (Tucker et al. 2021), mental health care (Schueller et al. 2019), substance use and sexual risk reduction (when supplemented with three brief motivational interventions) (Thompson et al. 2020), and identifying and locating services (Greeson et al. 2020).

Facilitators

Factors that facilitate treatment-seeking center on internal and interpersonal themes. Primarily, youth recognize the need to be motivated to seek help, especially regarding substance use treatment (Kozloff et al. 2013). They resist coercion, but some may need gentle prodding before being ready to engage in treatment (Chaturvedi 2016; Kozloff et al. 2013). Youth value the support they receive from family, friends, and significant others who encourage them to seek treatment (Hudson et al. 2010; Kozloff et al. 2013). For youth who are new to therapy, simple explanations about what is entailed and how it can benefit them may help normalize this form of help-seeking and destigmatize what it means to see a mental health practitioner or substance use counselor (Chaturvedi 2016). Experienced peers, such as those in twelve-step programs, are able to be good listeners, model treatment-seeking behaviors, and provide information, which youth have reported to be helpful (Hudson et al. 2010; Kozloff et al. 2013). Youth also endorse recreational opportunities and vocational assistance, as well as multiple services provided under one roof, including basic needs, health care, and integrated care for co-occurring disorders (Kozloff et al. 2013).

CONVERSION THERAPY

Conversion therapy, also known as ex-gay, reparative, and sexual reorientation therapy, is an attempt to change an individual's sexual thoughts, feelings, or behaviors from same-sex to opposite-sex oriented. Although some sexologists of the nineteenth and early twentieth centuries explored the possibility of "curing" homosexuality, the scientific research and practice of such change efforts peaked in the mid-twentieth century. To put this into historical context, Alfred Kinsey and colleagues' landmark work on sexuality, *Sexual Behavior in the Human Male*, published in 1948, reported that 10 percent of males in the general population had engaged in same-sex sexual behavior within the previous three years. This finding led to the widely cited, although misinterpreted, "10 percent rule" of homosexuality prevalence (Kinsey et al. 1948). This seminal monograph was followed by the publication of their 1953 volume, *Sexual Behavior in the Human Female*. The year before, the American Psychiatric Association (APA) published the first *DSM*, which depicted homosexuality as a form of "sociopathic personality disturbance"; in the second edition of the *DSM*, published in 1968, homosexuality was described as a "sexual orientation disturbance" and was categorized under "sexual deviations" (APA 1973; Drescher 2015).

Interest in changing one's sexual orientation coincided with the rise in popularity of behavioral therapy in the 1950s and 1960s. Gay men wishing to rid themselves of their same-sex sexual desires, or, in some cases, those being forced to do so involuntarily, were subjected to heterosexual skills training, orgasmic reconditioning, systematic desensitization (imaginal exposure with relaxation) (Phillips et al. 1976), and aversion therapy, the latter of which was particularly popular. In aversion therapy, a noxious stimulus (e.g., electric shock, a nausea-inducing drug) is paired with homoerotic images or physiological responses to them (i.e., erections in males) to extinguish same-sex desire, and the removal of a noxious stimulus is paired with heteroerotic images to promote opposite-sex desires and physiological responses. Forced intimacy, arranged marriages, chemical and surgical castrations, and lobotomies were also fair game in the name of science and eradicating people's same-sex desires (Murphy 1992).

The 1970s and 1980s saw the next wave of interest in attempting to "cure" homosexuality, this time through religion. Known as **ex-gay ministries**, these informal and largely unregulated attempts to "cleanse" people of their homosexuality primarily took the form of groups for adults and camps for youth, all with the aim of "helping" people "overcome" their homosexuality through prayer, celibacy, and adherence to religious beliefs that condemned homosexuality as "sinful." The first of them, Love in Action, was founded in 1973 (coincidentally the same year that the APA voted to remove homosexuality from the *DSM*) by Kent Philpott, a counselor and the pastor of a nondenominational church in the San Francisco Bay Area (Babits 2019; Besen 2003), and Frank Worthen, a gay businessperson who described an experience of being called by God to renounce his homosexuality and reach out to others who wanted to do the same (Erzen 2006). Other such groups also began to form around the country. In 1976, Michael Bussee and Gary Cooper, cofounders of a Los Angeles group called EXIT ("Ex-Gay Intervention Team"), brought several group leaders together to create Exodus, an umbrella organization of Christian ex-gay ministries (Bussee n.d.). Exodus would later become Exodus International, a global network of 260 affiliates around the world (Trotta and Trianni 2013). In an interview years later, Bussee explained, " 'It was the early seventies and the height of the Jesus movement. . . . There were all sorts of people coming forward and telling all sorts of testimonies about how they used to be a heroin addict or they used to be a prostitute . . . there were exes everywhere . . . so I thought, "Well, maybe the same kind of thing would be possible when it comes to your orientation" ' " (Besen 2003, 84).

By the 1990s, most mainstream religions were represented by (even if they did not officially sponsor) a national ex-gay organization—some of which still exist—usually with affiliates or chapters in cities throughout the United States. The largest among them and the religions they represent or represented include Courage International (also known as Courage Apostolate; Catholic), Transforming Congregations (United Methodist), OneByOne (Presbyterian), Evergreen International (Church of Jesus Christ of Latter-Day Saints), and the Jewish Institute for Global Awareness (formerly Jews Offering New Alternatives to Homosexuality [*Michael Ferguson v. JONAH* 2015]; Judaism). Some of these organizations joined

Exodus International (Banks 2009), while others remained free-standing organizations.

In the wake of the ministries' declining popularity and the steady rise in support for LGBTQ+ people and their rights, the National Association of Research & Therapy of Homosexuality (NARTH) formed to offer a "scientific" (and thus purportedly credible) approach to "treating" homosexuality. Founded by the psychiatrists Benjamin Kaufman and Charles Socarides and the psychologist Joseph Nicolosi in 1992, NARTH was a professional organization for like-minded professionals and laypeople to discuss, promote, and disseminate pathologizing opinions and statements disguised as research. In 2014, NARTH changed its name to the Alliance for Therapeutic Choice and Scientific Integrity (Besen 2014), seemingly suggesting that conversion therapy is both a valid treatment option and supported by science.

Although some of these organizations have rebranded, transferred ownership, or faded away, the practice of attempting to convert people's sexual orientation—or at least to get them to commit to celibacy—continues across the United States. Yet no scientifically sound research has shown conversion therapy to be effective (Przeworski et al. 2021). Of the studies reporting conversions, the methodology (i.e., the methods used to carry out a study) is flawed, the findings are misinterpreted, or success rates are low (Haldeman 1994; Przeworski et al. 2021; Sandfort 2003; Serovich et al. 2008; Shidlo and Schroeder 2002). Perhaps the most well known of these studies was conducted by the psychiatrist Robert Spitzer, renowned for his role in the classification of mental disorders and, coincidentally, in getting homosexuality removed from the *DSM*. Spitzer (2003) studied two hundred former conversion therapy participants and concluded that "change in sexual orientation following some kind of therapy does occur in some gay men and lesbians" (413). The response following a pre-publication leak to the media was swift: proponents touted his findings as evidence that conversion therapy works and that homosexuals could change if they wanted to, whereas LGBTQ+ advocates and researchers criticized the study's methods and the questionable ethics and effectiveness of conversion therapy (Herek 2003; Lund and Renna 2003; Sandfort 2003).

Reports of success have been far outweighed—if not in number, then certainly in gravity—by treatment failure (Rosik et al. 2023), the consequences of which are all too often devastating. Former participants have reported decreased self-esteem and increased anxiety, depression, and suicidality during or following conversion therapy (Flentje et al. 2014; Rosik et al. 2023; Shidlo and Schroeder 2002), and those who underwent conversion therapy as minors were found to be significantly more likely to later exhibit a serious mental health problem compared with individuals who did not undergo conversion therapy (Higbee et al. 2022). Every major health and mental health organization (e.g., the National Association of Social Workers, the American Counseling Association, the American Psychological Association, the APA, American Academy of Pediatrics) has denounced conversion therapy and discouraged the practice by their constituents. Since 2012, twenty-one states (mostly in the western and northeastern United States) and the District of Columbia have enacted statewide legislation prohibiting licensed professionals from practicing conversion therapy with minors. By some estimates, nearly 750,000 adults (aged eighteen to fifty-nine years) have undergone conversion therapy, more than half before the age of eighteen. Another 73,000 youth (aged thirteen to seventeen years) will go through it as a minor, either with a religious adviser or with a licensed mental health professional in states where it is still legal (Mallory et al. 2019).

Nine years after his study appeared in the *Archives of Sexual Behavior*, Spitzer (2012) published a retraction in the same journal—and ended with an apology: "I believe I owe the gay community an apology for my study making unproven claims of the efficacy of reparative therapy. I also apologize to any gay person who wasted time and energy undergoing some form of reparative therapy because they believed that I had proven that reparative therapy works with some 'highly motivated' individuals" (757).

SUMMARY

Direct practice with LGBTQ+ people has come a long way in a relatively short time. Two hundred years ago, same-sex desire was considered a form of sexual deviance of unknown origin. We still do not know the etiology of human sexuality, but we no longer consider LGBTQ+ people sexual deviants or refer to them as "sexual inverts." Just seventy-five years ago, LGBTQ+ people were being exposed to aversive techniques and other inhumane treatments to rid them of sexual attractions considered undesirable, either by the individuals themselves or, more likely, by societal and religious beliefs that compelled them to seek treatment. Enter the era of affirmative practice in 1982, less than two years after the emergence of a mysterious disease that was rapidly claiming the lives of sexually active gay men. Perhaps because of HIV-induced hysteria or the gains being made by the LGBTQ+ community, or both, conversion therapy was taking hold and becoming a fixture of conservative religions in the form of ex-gay ministries. Today a move is afoot to ban conversion therapy, at least with minors, and LGBTQ+-affirming practice is becoming the norm. Research, especially within the past ten to fifteen years, is informing practitioners of the best sexuality- and gender-affirming methods, models, and approaches to implement with LGBTQ+ people, including RHY.

Cognitive therapy for suicide prevention; dialectical behavior therapy; the community reinforcement approach; ecologically based family therapy; functional family therapy; Support to Reunite, Involve, and Value Each Other; mindfulness practices; and eclectic approaches that combine evidence-based techniques have demonstrated positive outcomes with RHY. Motivational enhancement therapy has shown promise but needs further exploration with this population. Central to all work with RHY is a strengths-based approach that capitalizes on the resources these youth already have within them. Strengths-based interventions that incorporate experiential learning, community engagement, and outreach and advocacy, for example, are already being used and successfully so.

The challenge in working with RHY is getting them in the door and engaging them long enough to make a difference. Some barriers lie within the youth themselves, but many other variables are well within the control of practitioners and their agencies and organizations. Adjusting service hours to accommodate youths' school, work, and sleeping schedules; relaxing restrictive policies that exclude some youth; offering transportation to youth living outside the immediate area; and combining services under one roof are just some changes that agencies can consider to make services more accessible to RHY. Practitioners can keep youth coming back by building a strong professional alliance early on, engaging youth in nonhierarchical and nonauthoritative ways, and empowering them by explaining what resources and services are available and how to access them. When youth are listened to, validated, and supported, they can make a difference in their own lives.

REVISITING JACE

- What might Jace have been feeling during the intake session, given the worker's demeanor? What could the intake worker have done or said differently to have left a more favorable impression on Jace?
- If you were the clinic director, how could you encourage staff to be more responsive to the youth? What could you tell them about the relationship between a youth's first experience with clinic staff and their future with the clinic?
- Which of Mr. Jacobs's words and behaviors might have helped him develop rapport with Jace?
- How did Mr. Jacobs demonstrate respect for Jace? What did Mr. Jacobs do that was gender-affirming?
- Knowing there were other LGBTQ+ youth in the group Jace attended put them somewhat at ease. Was it ethical for Mr. Jacobs to have told Jace that? If Jace knew which group members identified as LGBTQ+, Jace could have sought them out for support. Should Mr. Jacobs have shared that information as well?
- If you were Mr. Jacobs, what would you need to see in Jace's thinking and behavior to make you feel comfortable with ending their individual sessions?

KEY CONCEPTS

- *Biopsychosocial assessment*: a comprehensive assessment across the broad domains of an individual's physical, mental and emotional, and social functioning

- *Booster sessions*: sessions that occur at periodic intervals following the termination of treatment for the purpose of assessing the client's well-being and reinforcing and generalizing skills learned during treatment
- *Case management*: comprehensive services brokered by a case manager that help a client identify and access resources (e.g., food, shelter, employment, health care, legal services)
- *Cognitive-behavioral*: a model of practice that targets problematic thoughts and maladaptive behaviors based on the relationship between them
- *Cognitive theory*: a theory stating that an individual's perception or interpretation of a stimulus induces feelings that can influence behaviors
- *Conversion therapy*: a practice that attempts to change people's sexual orientation that has been deemed unethical, ineffective, and potentially harmful
- *Eclectic approach*: an approach to practice that allows the therapist to meet the unique needs of each client by selecting techniques from various theories and models of psychotherapy
- *Ex-gay ministries*: religion-based efforts to change people's sexual orientation or to promote heterosexual functioning or celibacy
- *Gay-affirmative psychotherapy*: introduced in the early 1980s as an alternative to the homosexuality-as-pathology approaches common at that time; a precursor to LGBTQ+-affirming practice
- *Measurement instruments*: questionnaires designed to gather information from clients to assist the practitioner in better understanding the client and their internal, interpersonal, and social perceptions and experiences
- *Mindfulness practice*: techniques based on Eastern philosophy that focus one's attention on the present moment by inner observation achieved through meditation or guided imagery
- *Motivational interviewing*: a strategy to promote change in individuals exhibiting problem behaviors, particularly addictive behaviors, by pointing out discrepancies between the individual's goals and their current behavior

- *Operant conditioning*: a method of modifying behavior by using rewards to reinforce a behavior or punishments to extinguish it
- *Relapse prevention*: efforts aimed at reducing the likelihood of a person's return to problem behavior, usually substance use
- *Screening tools*: questionnaires designed to identify the presence of symptoms or disorders, usually related to mental health
- *Sexology*: during the nineteenth and early twentieth centuries, the scientific study of human sexuality
- *Standardized instruments*: reliable and valid measurement instruments that can provide perspective and context for a client's responses and scores when compared to those of a population
- *Strengths-based approach*: an approach for working with people that focuses on an individual's assets rather than deficits, prioritizes their self-determination, and believes that they have the capacity to enact change on their own behalf and achieve their goals
- *Treatment plan*: an outline of the work that a therapist and client will do together; may include the timing and frequency of sessions, the focus of treatment, the outcome goals and objectives, and the intervention that will be implemented

CHAPTER HIGHLIGHTS

- Direct practice is conducted in a variety of settings by people in various roles. Clinical practice, a form of direct practice, typically occurs in health and mental health care settings. Psychotherapy is practiced by social workers, counselors, marriage and family therapists, psychologists, psychiatrists, and others who are trained and licensed to do so.
- Adolescence is marked by the onset of puberty, during which time a young person experiences marked changes in their development, namely the emergence of secondary sex characteristics and shifts in their social focus away from their parents and toward their peers, among other developmental milestones.

- The nineteenth and early twentieth centuries marked a turning point in the scientific study of human sexuality, a field that would later become known as sexology. Psychologists, psychiatrists, and others within and outside the medical fields developed theories of sexual behavior, with particular interest in "sexual inverts," those attracted to others of the same sex or who took on characteristics of the opposite sex.

- After the mid-twentieth century, a new approach to therapy with gay and lesbian people emerged that deviated from the traditional perspective of homosexuality as a pathology. Gay-affirmative psychotherapy instead focused on homosexuality as a normal variation in human sexuality and one that should be affirmed, not "cured." Today we refer to this approach as LGBTQ+-affirming practice.

- Clinical mental health practice is a goal-directed process involving distinct yet sometimes overlapping phases. During intake and engagement, a youth is formally registered as a client and begins working with a practitioner, whose goal is to establish a strong working relationship. Assessment is an information-gathering phase that leads to a plan for work, or a treatment plan. The intervention phase addresses the youth's concerns through treatment; the youth's progress is evaluated over the course of the intervention, with results being compared with data collected during the assessment. Termination marks the end of the youth and practitioner's work together; follow-up contact via booster sessions may be made to monitor the youth's progress and well-being.

- Motivational enhancement therapy, cognitive therapy for suicide prevention, dialectical behavior therapy, and the community reinforcement approach are well-documented individual or group approaches to working with RHY. Ecologically based family therapy; functional family therapy; and Support to Reunite, Involve, and Value Each Other are evidence-based or evidence-informed models designed to reconnect youth with their families. Group approaches can be treatment focused or supportive and are often eclectic in nature, such as the Housing Outreach Program–Collaboration model. With RHY, a strengths-based approach, which some of these models incorporate, can help foster their resilience, self-efficacy, and self-esteem.

- Many youth terminate services prematurely on their own, either because they perceive that the services are not benefiting them or because they feel their situation has improved. Others will complete treatment but skip the last session to avoid having to say good-bye, or they may relish the opportunity to attend out of a sense of accomplishment.

- Following up with a youth following treatment can be as simple as a quick check-in via phone call, email, or text. If the youth needs additional support, one or more booster sessions, usually in person or via telehealth, can be scheduled at monthly (or longer) intervals to assess the youth's well-being and reinforce the skills they gained during the intervention.

- Internal barriers (e.g., pride, unfamiliarity with services) and external barriers (e.g., transportation, agency policies or operations) keep youth from accessing the care and services they need. Support, encouragement, and "one-stop-shop" services make help-seeking and service use more likely.

- Conversion therapy is the attempt, through a variety of means, to change a person's same-sex sexual orientation (or at least their behavior) to an opposite-sex orientation. Since a same-sex orientation is neither a problem nor a disorder that needs to be fixed or treated, conversion therapy is unnecessary—and it is also unethical. Research on the practice has been discredited as methodologically flawed, or it has shown the practice to be ineffective and, in too many cases, harmful. Although conversion therapy was common during the latter part of the twentieth century, especially in the form of ex-gay ministries, the past ten years have seen the enactment of bans on licensed professionals practicing conversion therapy with minors in twenty-one states, the District of Columbia, and several municipalities.

8 | Programs and Services

LEARNING OBJECTIVES

Readers of this chapter will be able to:

1. Define integrated and dedicated programs and services for LGBTQ+ RHY,
2. Differentiate four common service environments available to this population, and
3. Compare best practices and promising programs currently in use by LGBTQ+ RHY-serving agencies.

CASE VIGNETTE: ARIA

Aria is a white transgender RHY, age seventeen, who has been homeless for thirteen months in a large city. She identifies as pansexual, finding herself attracted to "just people" rather than a particular gender or gender identity. She has been sleeping alongside other young people experiencing homelessness in abandoned buildings or outside in parks when the weather is nice. Aria has begun her transition from male to female by attending pumping parties and using street hormones, which she pays for by working odd jobs (e.g., distributing *flyers, asking for money in the streets, walking dogs). She considers the small, tight-knit group of RHY she shelters and parties with her **street family**.*

INTRODUCTION

As discussed in chapter 5, LGBTQ+ youth face numerous risk factors associated with their sexual orientation and identity and their gender identity and expression that contribute to parental rejection, abuse, abandonment, and ultimately homelessness (Bregman et al. 2013; D'Augelli et al. 2005; Ream and Peters 2021; Rosario et al. 2012b; Whitbeck et al. 2004). Given the growing problem of homelessness among LGBTQ+ RHY and the homelessness risk factors specific to this population, it is important to identify programs and services that integrate the best research evidence available with clinical expertise and **LGBTQ+-affirming** values (Altena et al. 2010; Sackett et al. 2000). By using the best evidence available to develop and implement programs and services, practitioners are more likely to offer effective interventions for LGBTQ+ RHY. This chapter begins with an overview of the two general types of programs and services for LGBTQ+ RHY: **integrated** and **dedicated (or separate)**. Next, we detail the four main service environments for the general population of RHY: street outreach, drop-in centers, shelters, and transitional living programs (TLPs). We then highlight best practices for LGBTQ+ RHY in each of these service environments. Finally, the chapter concludes with proposed future directions for programs and services for LGBTQ+ RHY.

NATIONAL STUDY OF INTEGRATED AND DEDICATED SERVICES FOR LGBTQ+ RHY

In 2012, we conducted a national research study to identify promising integrated and dedicated programs and services for LGBTQ+ RHY. We used telephone interviews with twenty-four staff from nineteen organizations around the United States that provide services to RHY in general and to LGBTQ+ RHY in particular. Among the nineteen organizations, six were mission-specific to serving LGBTQ+ and allied RHY (i.e., LGBTQ+ mission-specific organizations). The remaining organizations offered programs for LGBTQ+ RHY as part of their broader mission to serve all RHY (i.e., general RHY organizations). With respect to the staff who participated in phone interviews, fourteen were in central administrative positions (e.g., executive directors, presidents or chief operating officers), and ten were in direct service positions at the program level (e.g., street outreach workers, clinicians). We have described elsewhere the sampling procedure, data collection methods, and findings from this study (Ferguson-Colvin and Maccio 2012; Ferguson and Maccio 2015; Maccio and Ferguson 2016). (See box 8.1, *Read All About It!*)

Summary of Promising Programs and Services for LGBTQ+ RHY

All organizations participating in our 2012 study—whether LGBTQ+ mission-specific or general—offered two types of programs: *integrated*

BOX 8.1. READ ALL ABOUT IT! TOOLKIT FOR LGBTQ+ RHY-SERVING PRACTITIONERS AND RESEARCHERS

- All the data from our 2012 study appear in the *Toolkit for Practitioners/Researchers Working with Lesbian, Gay, Bisexual, Transgender, and Queer/Questioning (LGBTQ) Runaway and Homeless Youth (RHY)*, which can be found at https://cwlibrary.childwelfare.gov /discovery/delivery/01CWIG_INST:01CWIG/1218286110007651.
- Two follow-up articles summarize promising programs (K. M. Ferguson and E. M. Maccio, "Promising Programs for Lesbian, Gay, Bisexual, Transgender, and Queer/Questioning Runaway and Homeless Youth," *Journal of Social Service Research* 41, no. 5 [2015]: 659–83, https://doi.org/10.1080/01488376.2015.1058879) and service gaps and recommendations (E. M. Maccio and K. M. Ferguson, "Services to LGBTQ Runaway and Homeless Youth: Gaps and Recommendations," *Children and Youth Services Review* 63 [2016]: 47–57, https:// doi.org/10.1016/j.childyouth.2016.02.008).

programs that included services for all subgroups of LGBTQ+ RHY, as well as for heterosexual and cisgender youth, and *dedicated (or separate)* programs that included services for specific subgroups of LGBTQ+ RHY, such as psychoeducational groups for transgender youth, lesbian youth, and men who have sex with men. Despite the marketing of these services to specific subgroups, all LGBTQ+, heterosexual, and cisgender youth were encouraged to attend.

Table 8.1 provides an overview of the promising *integrated* programs and services offered by participating organizations in seven key areas: health, mental health and substance use, case management, family, legal and mediation concerns, education and employment, and housing. Table 8.2 lists resources referenced by participating organizations for specific subpopulations of LGBTQ+ RHY, namely, transgender and nonbinary-gender (NBG) youth. In the following sections, we describe these programs and services, and others supported by recent literature, in detail.

Integrated Services for All Subgroups of LGBTQ+ RHY

Health Services

Participating organizations provided several health care interventions based on clinical evidence. Be Proud! Be Responsible! (ETR n.d.) is one evidence-based sexual health intervention used in multiple organizations. Other promising approaches to health care consisted of using partnerships with LGBTQ+-affirming physicians or health centers in the community to provide youth with health care free of or at very low cost. Several organizations also had peer-led health educator programs in which educators visited schools and juvenile halls and presented workshops on myths and stereotypes regarding the LGBTQ+ community. All participating organizations also provided health information workshops on topics such as HIV/AIDS, sexually transmitted infections (STIs), healthy relationships, and dating violence.

Queer Sex Ed is a sexual health program geared toward LGBTQ+ youth that is delivered online and capable of assessing youths' learning (Mustanski

TABLE 8.1 Promising integrated programs and services (Ferguson-Colvin and Maccio 2012)

Intervention	Source	Description	Website
Health services			
Be Proud! Be Responsible!	ETR (n.d.)	"The curriculum was designed to be used with small groups ranging from 6 to 12 participants. The curriculum has 6 hours of content divided into six 50-minute modules. An optional LGBTQ Supplement is also available. The goals of the program are to: help young people change behaviors that place them at risk for HIV, delay the initiation of sex among sexually inexperienced youth, reduce unprotected sex among sexually active youth, help young people make proud and responsible decisions about their sexual behaviors."	https://www.etr.org/ebi /programs/be-proud-be -responsible/
Mental health and substance use services			
1. Trauma interventions			
Structured Psychotherapy for Adolescents Responding to Chronic Stress (SPARCS)	NCTSN (2012)	SPARCS is a sixteen-session group intervention designed to address the needs of chronically traumatized adolescents "who may still be living with ongoing stress and may be experiencing problems in several areas of functioning including difficulties with affect regulation and impulsivity, self-perception, relationships, somatization, dissociation, numbing and avoidance, and struggles with their own purpose and meaning in life." The program goals include "helping teens cope more effectively in the moment, enhancing self-efficacy, connecting with others and establishing supportive relationships, cultivating awareness, & creating meaning in their lives."	https://www .nctsn .org/sites/default/files /interventions/sparcs _fact_sheet.pdf
Sanctuary Model	Sanctuary Institute (n.d.); Bloom (1997)	The Sanctuary Model "is comprised of three primary components: 1. Theoretical philosophies which form the underpinnings of the model 2. The trauma-informed shared language represented by the acronym S.E.L.F. 3. A set of practical tools, known as the Sanctuary Tool Kit"	https://www .thesanctuaryinstitute.org /about-us/the-sanctuary -model/
Bridges Transition Model	William Bridges Associates (n.d.)	"The Bridges Transition Model helps organizations and individuals understand and more effectively manage and work through the personal and human side of change. The model identifies the three stages an individual experiences during change: Ending What Currently Is, The Neutral Zone and The New Beginning."	https://wmbridges.com /about/what-is-transition/

Additional effective treatments for youth trauma	National Child Traumatic Stress Network (n.d.a)	A repository of more than one hundred resources, including interventions, that can be searched by resource type, trauma type, language, and audience (e.g., families, providers).	https://www.nctsn.org/resources/all-nctsn-resources
Additional effective treatments for youth trauma	Interagency Task Force on Trauma-Informed Care (SAMHSA 2022b)	The Interagency Task Force on Trauma-Informed Care "identifies, evaluates, and make recommendations about: • Best practices for supporting children, youth, and families affected by trauma • How federal agencies can better respond to trauma, like substance use disorders, in families."	https://www.samhsa.gov/mental-health/trauma-violence/trauma-informed-care

2. Interventions for substance use and high-risk sexual behavior

Street Smart: Reducing HIV Risk Among Runaway and Homeless Youth	Centers for Disease Control and Prevention (2020); Rotheram-Borus et al. (1991)	"Street Smart is a multisession skills-building program designed to help groups of runaway youth reduce unprotected sex, number of sex partners, and substance use. The program is based on social learning theory, which describes the relationship between behavior change and a person's beliefs that [they have] the ability to change a behavior and that changing that behavior will produce a specific result."	https://web.archive.org/web/20241106054202/https://www.cdc.gov/hiv/research/interventionresearch/rep/packages/streetsmart.html
Seeking Safety	Treatment Innovations (n.d.); Najavits (2002)	"Seeking Safety is an evidence-based, present-focused counseling model to help people attain safety from trauma and/or addiction. The Seeking Safety book describes how to conduct it in groups of any size as well as individual modality, for all genders. The model has been used with adults and adolescents (and some elements can be used with younger ages)."	https://www.treatment-innovations.org/seeking-safety.html
Motivational interviewing	Motivational Interviewing Network of Trainers (n.d.); Miller and Rollnick (2023)	Motivational interviewing "is a collaborative, goal-oriented style of communication with particular attention to the language of change. It is designed to strengthen motivation for and commitment to a specific goal by eliciting and exploring the person's own reasons for change within an atmosphere of acceptance and change."	https://motivational-interviewing.org/understanding-motivational-interviewing

(continued)

TABLE 8.1 (*continued*)

Intervention	Source	Description	Website
Case management services			
Comprehensive case management for substance abuse treatment	Center for Substance Abuse Treatment (2015)	*Comprehensive Case Management for Substance Abuse Treatment* presents an overview of case management models for substance abuse treatment providers, including the strengths-based, brokerage/generalist, assertive community treatment, and clinical/rehabilitation models.	https://library.samhsa.gov /sites/default/files/sma15 -4215.pdf
Living Room	RI International (n.d.)	A peer-operated crisis alternative named the "Living Room" offers a comfortable, natural setting for clients entering an agency. For example, the space may include couches and a TV, a refrigerator with snacks, and small individual rooms around the perimeter with futons for comfortable sleeping (if desired). Peer support specialists are hired to staff the Living Room and to meet with new clients upon their entry. The peer support specialists assess the clients' presenting needs and initiate referrals to the appropriate agency staff (e.g., psychiatrists, mental health counselors, physicians).	https://riinternational .com/services/
LGBTQ+-affirming comprehensive services model	Various LGBTQ+ RHY drop-in centers around the country	This model entails bringing in a comprehensive array of LGBTQ+-affirming service providers to a drop-in center. In the drop-in center, youth can obtain basic needs services (e.g., food, showers, clothing). They have case managers (or transitional advocates), who use a strengths-based case management model in which staff and youth coauthor a "life road map" (i.e., treatment plan). On this map, youth state their goal(s) and completion date(s), barriers, and action steps. There are ten domains on the life road map (e.g., housing, education, future goals). The youth also indicate on the road map what staff support they need for each goal. Other providers who are present in the drop-in centers include LGBTQ+-affirming Medicaid enrollment specialists, physicians, medical teams, and veterinarians (for youth who care for pets). Attorneys from local legal clinics also provide the youth each week with legal services. Youth can access on-site mental health services with affirming psychiatrists, clinicians, and substance-use counselors as well. Staff and peers also offer psychoeducational groups to the youth.	https://acf.gov/opre /report/reducing -homelessness-among -youth-child-welfare -involvement-phase -ii-implementation

Family services

Family Acceptance Project	Family Acceptance Project (n.d.); Ryan (2010)	"The Family Acceptance Project is a research, intervention, education and policy initiative to prevent health and mental health risks and to promote well-being for lesbian, gay, bisexual, transgender and queer-identified (LGBTQ) children and youth, including suicide, homelessness, drug use and HIV—in the context of their families, cultures and faith communities."	http://familyproject.sfsu.edu
Family Preservation Program	Family Support Services of the Bay Area (n.d.)	The Family Preservation Program supports families to improve parenting and to address their life challenges. The goal of the program is to improve family functioning so children will receive appropriate care and the family will be able to remain intact.	http://fssba.org/family-preservation-program/

Legal and mediation services

1. Legal Services

"Know Your Rights" trainings	True Colors United, National Homelessness Law Center (n.d.)	"Know Your Rights" trainings aim to support LGBTQ+ RHY's self-advocacy and self-efficacy. Legal services and a variety of civil rights trainings are provided to help LGBTQ+ RHY meet their survival needs by knowing and advocating for their civil rights. To create each curriculum module, legal staff use a grassroots approach to develop and test the curriculum in the community by surveying staff and youth at LGBTQ+ RHY partner agencies. Legal staff inquire regarding the specific legal issues with which the youth most struggle and in what areas the youth would like to have training. From these inquiries, legal staff develop the training modules.	https://truecolorsunited.org/wp-content/uploads/2020/04/LGBTQ-Youth_-4-Ways-You-Can-Prepare-to-Safely-Access-Housing-Services.pdf

(continued)

TABLE 8.1 (*continued*)

Intervention	Source	Description	Website
2. Conflict mediation services			
Conflict mediation based on the transformative justice model	Fisher (2006, 2007)	Drawing on principles of the transformative justice model, staff adopting conflict mediation services use the following steps to deescalate conflict in which LGBTQ+ youth are involved. The youth state the following: 1. *This is the story:* youth tell what happened and what the situation was about. 2. *This is what I tell myself about my story:* youth share feelings, thoughts, and personal issues. 3. *This is where I know myself to be:* youth articulate their own personal image (e.g., "I am a strong, articulate young lesbian woman"). 4. *This is what I need from you:* youth make a clear statement of their needs to the system, adult, or peer. 5. *This is what I am willing to compromise:* youth state what they are willing to do or give up to meet this need.	https://librarysearch .bond.edu.au/discovery /fulldisplay?vid=61BOND _INST:BOND&docid =alma993045495860238l &lang=en&context =L&offset=0&from FeaturedResult =true&prevPersonId =n85093791
Educational and employment services			
Supported education	University of Kansas School of Social Welfare (Manthey et al. 2012)	Supported education aims "to provide opportunities, resources and support to people with psychiatric disabilities in order to gain admittance to and succeed in the pursuit of education. Education is an activity that enables individuals to gain access to meaningful employment, a new identity, and the fulfillment of life goals."	https://socwel.ku.edu /university-kansas -supported-education -toolkit-30-0
Supported employment: individual placement and support (IPS)	IPS Employment Center (n.d.); Ferguson et al. (2012)	"IPS supported employment helps people living with behavioral health conditions work at regular jobs of their choosing. Although variations of supported employment exist, IPS (Individual Placement and Support) refers to the evidence-based practice of supported employment. Characteristics of IPS supported employment: It is an evidence-based practice; Practitioners focus on each person's strengths; Work promotes recovery and wellness; Practitioners work in collaboration with state vocational rehabilitation counselors; IPS uses a multidisciplinary team approach; Services are individualized and last as long as the person needs and wants them; The IPS approach changes the way mental health services are delivered."	https://ipsworks.org/

Program	Source	Description	URL
Agency-based social enterprises	Various LGBTQ+ RHY agencies; Social Enterprise Alliance (n.d.); Teasdale (2012)	In agencies that operate social enterprises, LGBTQ+ RHY receive training from career professionals in vocational and technical, business, and life skills required to start agency-run businesses. Agency businesses create opportunities for LGBTQ+ RHY to acquire job skills and employment. These businesses can also serve as a pipeline into select careers for the youth.	https://socialenterprise.us/
YouthBuild	YouthBuild (n.d.)	YouthBuild is a full-time, ten-month workforce development and General Education Development (GED) program that serves low-income young people ages eighteen to twenty-four. Young people enrolled in the program work toward their GED or high school diploma while learning job skills by building affordable housing for homeless and low-income people. A strong emphasis is placed on leadership development and community service.	https://youthbuild.org/
Job Corps	Job Corps (n.d.)	"Job Corps provides free career training and education for low-income 16- through 24-year-olds. Here, students get the experiences they need to begin a career or apprenticeship, go on to college, or join the military."	https://www.jobcorps.gov/
Housing services			
Host Home program	Avenues for Youth (n.d.), ConneQT (Minnesota)	The LGBTQ+ Host Home program is an innovative housing model providing an alternative to the shelter system for LGBTQ+ youth experiencing homelessness. The program trains Host Home volunteers who invite homeless LGBTQ+ youth aged eighteen to twenty-four into their homes for one to two years. The goal of the program is to ease youth into adulthood and toward a path of independent living by providing a safe home and the stability necessary for the youth to focus on pursuing educational and vocational opportunities.	https://avenuesforyouth.org/host-home-landing-page/

TABLE 8.2 Resources for programs and services for transgender and nonbinary-gender RHY (Ferguson-Colvin and Maccio 2012)

Intervention	Source	Description	Website
Eli Coleman Institute for Sexual and Gender Health	University of Minnesota Medical School (n.d.)	"The Eli Coleman Institute for Sexual and Gender Health (ISGH) is one of the largest clinical, teaching, and research institutions in the world specializing in human sexuality and gender. [The institute has] a strong research agenda in sexual aggression and compulsive sexual behavior, transgender and gender-diverse health, relationship and sex therapy, and sexual health that has been supported by millions of dollars in state and federal funding."	https://med.umn .edu/sexualhealth
Trans Advisory & Action Team	University of Minnesota Gender and Sexuality Center for Queer and Trans Life (n.d.)	"The University of Minnesota's Trans Advisory & Action Team, TAAT, . . . is a coalition of students, faculty, staff, alumni and community members organizing across disciplines and departments for access and liberation for transgender and gender nonconforming people. TAAT is led by trans and gender nonconforming people and open to persons of all gender identities and expressions."	https://gsc.umn.edu /programs/trans -advisory-action -team-taat
HIV and transgender people: What CDC is Doing	Centers for Disease Control and Prevention (2022a)	"CDC is pursuing a high-impact HIV prevention approach to maximize the effectiveness of HIV prevention interventions and strategies for transgender people. Funding state, territorial, and local health departments and community-based organizations (CBOs) to develop and implement tailored programs is CDC's largest investment in HIV prevention."	https://web .archive.org /web/20230315112741/ https://www.cdc.gov /hiv/group/gender /transgender/what -cdc-is-doing.html

et al. 2015). Online education provides the privacy that some youth might require when learning about sexual health, and it has the potential to reach youth not connected to formal services or agencies through which they could otherwise access this information. Importantly, virtual delivery should however, go beyond HIV prevention education, for example. Steinke and colleagues (2017) state that "any digital health intervention for [sexual- and gender-minority youth] should include opportunities for interpersonal connection, community development, and comprehensive health information," especially "mental health and well-being" (546).

Mental Health and Substance Use Services

We identified promising mental health and substance use interventions to address challenges experienced by LGBTQ+ RHY in two areas: (1) trauma and (2) substance use and high-risk sexual behaviors. First, given the high rates of trauma and post-traumatic stress disorder among LGBTQ+ RHY, organizational staff collectively aimed to ensure that their interactions with youth were **trauma informed**. Following this approach, staff incorporated trauma-related information into their conversations with youth and when devising behavioral consequences for youths' actions (e.g., if a youth violated house rules, staff would approach consequences from a trauma-informed perspective). Common trauma interventions used across organizations included Structured Psychotherapy for Adolescents Responding to Chronic Stress (SPARCS) (NCTSN 2012), the Sanctuary Model (Bloom 1997), and the Bridges Transition Model (William Bridges Associates n.d.). Staff also commonly relied on the National Child Traumatic Stress Network and the Substance Abuse and Mental Health Services Administration's National Center for Trauma-Informed Care for trauma interventions and resources for LGBTQ+ RHY.

Regarding substance use and sexual risk behaviors, all organizations adopted a **harm-reduction approach** to addressing youths' high-risk behaviors. Harm-reduction strategies (e.g., safe-sex practices, STI prevention, HIV testing and counseling, and substance abuse counseling) are used to help young people reduce or eliminate harmful behaviors associated with substance use and high-risk sexual activity through small achievable steps

(Denning 2001). Three additional commonly cited harm-reduction interventions used in various organizations were Street Smart (Rotheram-Borus et al. 1991), Seeking Safety (Najavits 2002), and motivational interviewing (Miller and Rollnick 2023).

An innovative system-of-care approach to serving LGBTQ+ RHY is iTEAM ("My Treatment Empowerment for Teens on the Move"), developed around 2009 through a collaboration between the University of Arizona's Southwest Institute for Research on Women and several community agencies (Powell et al. 2016). The program's primary focus is providing mental health and substance use services, but it also boasts a "one-stop shop" that includes case management services, housing referrals, education and employment support, and HIV education (Powell et al. 2016, 187).

Case Management Services

Three commonly used case management models identified across participating organizations were strengths-based case management (SBCM), the "Living Room" Program (Ashcraft and Anthony 2006), and the LGBTQ+-affirming comprehensive services model. Each model served as a complement to organizations' mental health programs.

Strengths First is an example of the SBCM framework adapted for multiethnic sexual-minority youth (Craig 2012). SBCM appeared in the 1980s as an approach to working with people with chronic mental health problems (Rapp and Chamberlain 1985) and was later adapted for use with high-risk youth (Arnold et al. 2007). The purpose of SBCM is to help clients identify their own strengths to "reinforce clients' control over their lives and build feelings of competence" (Rapp and Chamberlain 1985, 419). The approach adapted for vulnerable youth is designed to foster a close relationship between client and case manager, promote client retention, and, with its community-based approach, make it accessible to youth.

Family Services

Many organizations incorporated family reunification services into their programming, particularly for younger LGBTQ+ RHY who might still be reunited with their families of origin. For young people still connected to their families, staff commonly offered family therapy, individual and group counseling, and preservation services. A number of participating organizations provided or referred youth to family reunification services, such as the Family Acceptance Project (Ryan 2010) and the Family Preservation Program of Family Support Services of the San Francisco Bay Area. These programs and services aimed to address the risk factors that contribute to youth leaving home (e.g., rejection, abuse, neglect) and to educate caregivers in how to better support their LGBTQ+ children.

The Los Angeles LGBT Center is home to the RISE (Recognize Intervene Support Empower) program, an initiative funded by the Children's Bureau of the federal Administration for Children and Families (PIIET 2016). RISE promotes permanency by addressing problems that lead to housing instability and homelessness among LGBTQ+ youth, namely family rejection and anti-LGBTQ+ bias in the child welfare system (PII n.d.). The program offers a comprehensive, four-phase series of strategies via two primary interventions: (1) care and coordination and (2) outreach and relationship building. (See box 8.2, *Read All About It*)

BOX 8.2. READ ALL ABOUT IT! RISE: RECOGNIZE INTERVENE SUPPORT EMPOWER

- Manuals for RISE's two primary interventions, care coordination and outreach and relationship building, can be found on the Los Angeles LGBT Center website: https://rise.lalgbtcenter.org/publications/.
- "Strengthening the workforce to support youth in foster care who identify as LGBTQ+ through increasing LGBTQ+ competency: Trainers' experience with bias, a preliminary evaluation" (Weeks et al. 2018) appears in the journal *Child Welfare*. The article describes a study examining trainer fidelity, trainee bias, and the effect of participant bias on LGBTQ+-competence training for child welfare workers.

Legal and Mediation Services

Staff across cities reported that the four most common legal services for LGBTQ+ RHY were name changes and document replacements, street encounters with the police, engagement in sex-work services (e.g., training youth on safety with regard to police involvement, how to interact with the police based on their rights, and how to deal with police who discriminate based on sexual orientation or gender identity), and "quality-of-life" offenses (e.g., the criminalization of the behaviors of people experiencing homelessness, such as sleeping in public spaces [though this is sometimes done only because no shelter beds are available] and jumping turnstiles at subway stations [though this is sometimes done to get to important appointments, such as with probation officers]). To address the legal needs of LGBTQ+ RHY, organizational staff frequently collaborated with LGBTQ+-affirming legal clinics, law schools, and lawyers who took pro bono cases. Two commonly used legal services across participating organizations were "Know Your Rights" trainings and workshops conducted by the organization Streetwise and Safe.

Several organizations around the country provide LGBTQ+-specific "Know Your Rights" trainings, workshops, and resources. The Los Angeles LGBT Center (n.d.) refers to itself as "the nation's largest community-based provider of LGBTQ+-related legal services," including those targeting LGBTQ+ youth. The New York Civil Liberties Union (2008) offers "Know Your Rights" training for LGBTQ+ youth in schools, and Lambda Legal (n.d.) offers a variety of online resources for LGBTQ+ youth and young adults, as well as their families and allies. Others can be found through an internet search using, for example, the phrase "LGBTQ youth know your rights." Providers who serve historically excluded populations, including LGBTQ+ youth, should know both their clients' rights and their own. In a 2016 article, Brendan Conner, an attorney for Streetwise and Safe at the time of the article's publication, explains search and arrest warrants, warrantless searches and arrests, and professional liability associated with breaking confidentiality, involuntary commitment, and false reporting.

Conflict mediation services also were noted by staff as necessary to confront, process, and overcome conflicts encountered by LGBTQ+ RHY with surrounding systems, adults, and peers. The most frequently cited conflict mediation service used by participating organizations was based on the **transformative justice model**. Transformative justice adopts a systems approach to viewing crime from the perspective of its underlying causes and its impact on victims, offenders, and surrounding communities and systems. It advocates for an examination of systems that perpetuate and reinforce domination and oppression, such as white supremacy, structural racism, sexism, homophobia, ableism, and classism. Through a critical examination of these systems and a focus on healing, accountability, and forgiveness, it promotes a transformative relational and educational experience for those involved in an offense (Gready and Robins 2014). The field would benefit from additional research on the use of the transformative justice model with LGBTQ+ RHY, similar to that done with housed LGBTQ+ youth on related models of transformative leadership (Zook 2017) and transformative organizing (Wernick et al. 2014).

Educational and Employment Services

Organizations with educational or employment services combined a variety of models, including **supported education**, **supported employment** (i.e., the Individual Placement and Support model), **social enterprises**, and referrals to existing job placement programs such as YouthBuild and Job Corps. Given that many LGBTQ+ RHY have a low level of educational attainment and limited employment histories, most participating organizations offered combined educational and employment services. Further, because mental health challenges often affected their educational and employment outcomes, organizations commonly offered integrated clinical, case management, and life skills services, the latter of which included educational and employment programming.

The SF LGBT Center's Transgender Employment Program (SF LGBT Center n.d.) helps transgender and NBG individuals find, keep, and protect their jobs. Although this publicly funded Transgender Employment Program is available only to those who live locally, it can serve as a model to other communities for how to help transgender, NBG, and other LGBTQ+ individuals enter, remain in, and be successful in the workforce. (See box 8.3, *Read All About It!*)

BOX 8.3. READ ALL ABOUT IT! LGBTQ+ YOUTH EMPLOYMENT CHALLENGES AND RECOMMENDATIONS

- *Left Behind: How LGBT Young People Are Excluded from Economic Prosperity* (Pérez 2014) paints a picture of today's LGBTQ+ millennials, the risks that complicate their entry into the workforce, the discrimination they face once they are in it, and policy recommendations to give them a fair chance at what the author calls the "American bargain of hard work begetting upward economic mobility" (19). The report can be found online at https://cdn.americanprogress.org /wp-content/uploads/2014/07/LGBTyouthJobs-report.pdf

---

Housing Services

Participating organizations that provided housing services offered combinations of short-term emergency and crisis shelters, long-term TLPs, and other supportive housing options, such as scattered apartments (housing units dispersed throughout the community) and **host homes**. The Host Home program is an innovative housing model providing an alternative to the shelter system for LGBTQ+ RHY. Host Home volunteers are trained and supported in housing homeless LGBTQ+ youth in their homes for several years. The goal is to facilitate the transition to adulthood for LGBTQ+ RHY and to help them develop the skills needed to live independently by providing a safe home and the stability needed to focus on pursuing educational and vocational opportunities.

Staff across participating organizations agreed that funding sources often dictated whether and how organizations housed LGBTQ+ RHY. For that reason, some organizations refused to accept federal or state funding for housing. In these cases, staff had more flexibility to house youth as they desired, giving preference to the youths' preferred sleeping arrangements, particularly for transgender and NBG youth, who are often placed with others of a gender with which they do not identify or isolated from their peers. In organizations not bound by federal or state guidelines, staff prioritized the youths' safety above all else in making housing decisions with them. One such organization is currently experimenting with housing three youth from the same street family together, with adult supervision, as a way to honor the young people's existing natural supports.

In contrast, for organizations that accepted federal or state funding, staff employed various strategies to ensure the youths' safety and meet their individual housing needs. One approach involved organization staff contacting local, state, or federal funders on a case-by-case basis to arrange for beds as needed. Staff commonly had to provide considerable education and advocacy on behalf of clients to meet their individual needs. For instance, staff often engaged funders in conversations regarding why the practice of separating beds by gender identity is not always appropriate, safe, or in the best interests of youth. Organization staff also regularly conducted training sessions with funders on "gender fluidity," particularly for transgender youth transitioning from one gender to another or undergoing gender-affirming hormone treatment. With respect to advocacy efforts, staff frequently sought permission or waivers from state funders to house transgender youth separately or with youth whose gender assigned at birth matches that of the transgender youth's identified gender in cases of bullying, discrimination, or abuse. In some cases, staff had flexibility in their organization's infrastructure to reserve single rooms for transgender youth or youth who had been victimized in shared housing. In these cases, youth often felt reassured knowing that they had various options from which to choose to ensure that their need for safe housing was met.

Staff of organizations that did not have on-site housing or whose on-site housing was over capacity referred youth to local shelters. Staff commonly noted that they would visit local emergency shelters to assess their safety, cleanliness, and livability. Staff also commonly said that they would refer youth to such shelters only if they, the staff members, would feel comfortable staying there themselves. Further, staff conducted frequent training sessions with staff from local emergency shelters about how to create safe living spaces for LGBTQ+ RHY.

Across many states, state housing regulations require organizations to house youth of the same birth-assigned gender together. In some cases, organization staff would obtain youths' sex from their driver's licenses or other identification documents. Although this practice may be affirming in some cases, it may be problematic when the sex listed on a youth's identification document does not match their gender identity. When working with youth whose gender assigned at birth did not match their gender identity, staff commonly asked the youth to identify their gender. In other cases, staff would not ask for legal documentation at all but simply ask the youth to identify their gender. In still other cases, staff would work with a youth and funders together to determine the best type of housing for the youth. In all cases, the youths' safety was at the forefront of housing placement decisions. In some states, staff would provide state funders and oversight regulatory staff with a written overview addressing all potential safety issues and concerns in housing transgender females with cisgender females or transgender males with cisgender males. Staff used these written documents to demonstrate to regulatory staff the benefit of housing transgender youth in this manner. Another strategy commonly used to ensure youths' safety was to draft a "roommate agreement" that outlined guidelines for safe, appropriate behaviors and interactions for those sharing accommodations; these were devised with and signed by the youths involved. A final strategy to ensure youths' safety was to increase staff supervision and room checks or to instate peer resident monitors to perform supervision and room checks.

At the local level, various cities have passed policies allowing youth to self-identify their gender. These more flexible policies enabled staff to house youth based on their identified gender. In these cases, staff frequently assigned transgender youth to beds according to their self-identified gender. Scattered apartments allowed transgender youth to live in their own apartments at subsidized rents. For those who wanted roommates, staff worked with youth to find appropriate roommates who were a good fit.

Despite the organizations' strategic and institutionalized efforts to ensure youths' housing safety, conflicts and tensions sometimes arose between youth, and between youth and staff, regarding youths' sexual orientation and identity and their gender identity and expression. In such cases, staff commonly addressed conflicts through individual and small-group counseling, house meetings, resident councils, conflict mediation, and cultural sensitivity trainings for both staff and youth.

In addition to their transitional living and host home programs, in 2019, the Sacramento LGBT Community Center in California introduced a short-term transitional emergency program (STEP) (Peak n.d.), which is among the first of its kind in the United States. STEP is similar to an emergency shelter in its brevity (approximately ninety days) and to a transitional living program in its trajectory toward permanent housing. The purpose is to provide immediate cover for LGBTQ+ RHY and young adults aged eighteen to twenty-four who are victims of crime and violence. The program offers "intensive case management, counseling, transportation, employment services, life skills workshops, and establishment of a support system that [youth] can maintain after exiting the program" (Peak n.d., para. 5). Such a program acknowledges the increased risk of violence and victimization to which LGBTQ+ RHY are subjected (Baams et al. 2019; Tyler and Schmitz 2018b).

Dedicated (or Separate) Services for Transgender and NBG RHY

Aria recently learned of a TLP designated for transgender and NBG young people through a street family member, who also heard of it secondhand. Aria is planning to ask about it when she visits the drop-in center later in the day. She is hesitant to appear interested, fearing that someone will try to talk her into applying for TLP housing, which she assumes would result in losing her freedom and her street family. One motivating factor that she tries to quash is her desire to become a teacher. Although not much older than those she would like to teach, Aria sees herself as a protector and nurturer, qualities she believes would make her a good teacher.

Although most organizations in our study offered integrated services for all RHY, several also addressed the unique health, mental health, employment, and legal issues related to transgender and NBG youth. Our 2012 findings are supported by a 2015 study of 124 RHY TLPs in the United States revealing that fewer than half (43.5 percent) of these programs offered LGBTQ+-specific services (Prock and Kennedy 2017). In our study, these organizations (i.e., largely mission-specific LGBTQ+ RHY organizations) commonly offered support groups specifically for LGBTQ+ RHY. In many cases, these groups were offered on-site by internal staff, staff from a collaborating organization, or peer educators from the LGBTQ+ community. Some integrated organizations employed an LGBTQ+ activity specialist who ran weekly LGBTQ+-specific groups (e.g., transgender and NBG youth groups). In other cases, youth were referred to collaborating community organizations that offered transgender and NBG youth support groups. In the latter case, the host organization was often able to provide youth with transportation (e.g., a van ride or bus tokens) to the off-site support group. Despite these groups being targeted specifically at transgender and NBG youth, all young people were welcome to attend.

Topics frequently covered in the transgender and NBG youth support groups included how to address different forms of discrimination in employment settings and in society in general; how to navigate the health care and mental health care systems before, during, and after gender transitioning; and how to make legal name changes on identification documents. Several organizations created "transgender best practices work groups" to generate solutions from both youth and staff to barriers experienced by transgender youth (e.g., changing gender markers on identification cards; obtaining public assistance, such as Medicaid; facing employment discrimination; and locating safe, appropriate, and affirming medical services) (Ferguson-Colvin and Maccio 2012). In addition to LGBTQ+ support groups and work groups, other LGBTQ+-specific services commonly offered to LGBTQ+ RHY included LGBTQ+-affirming therapy, gender-neutral facilities such as restrooms and housing or shelter units, referrals for LGBTQ+-specific medical treatments such as gender-affirming hormone therapy, and advocacy services (Prock and Kennedy 2017). Table 8.2 lists resources commonly used by staff that were designed for organizations to develop and strengthen their programming and services for transgender and NBG RHY.

Collectively, the promising integrated and dedicated (or separate) programs and services that we identified can be characterized by five key program components: a strong reliance on clinical evidence; the use of a trauma-informed approach; the provision of safe, stable, and supportive housing; the incorporation of peer providers from the LGBTQ+ community; and opportunities for reciprocal learning between LGBTQ+ and heterosexual-cisgender RHY.

THE FOUR SERVICE ENVIRONMENTS FOR RHY

We next describe the four main service environments for the general population of RHY: street outreach, drop-in centers, shelters, and TLPs. For each, we highlight best practices for LGBTQ+ RHY and the staff and organizations working with them.

Street Outreach

The Runaway and Homeless Youth Act (RHYA) (discussed in more detail in chapter 9) funds the Street Outreach Program through the Family and Youth Services Bureau, which offers grant opportunities for agencies to establish their own street outreach programs involving street-based education and outreach, access to emergency shelter, survival aid, individual assessments, trauma-informed counseling, prevention and crisis intervention services, and referrals and follow-up support to RHY who have experienced—or are at risk of experiencing—sexual abuse and exploitation. The Street Outreach Program's primary goal is to prevent the sexual abuse or exploitation of street-living and unstably housed youth and provide services for survivors (FYSB 2023b).

Street outreach programs are a typical way that organizations make services available and accessible to RHY not already connected to agency-based services. In the outreach model, service providers approach RHY in nontraditional settings (e.g., the streets, train and bus stations, parks and other public spaces) where RHY congregate and reside to provide them with basic services including food and warm clothing, harm-reduction items (e.g., safe-sex kits that include condoms and lubricant), and referrals to other agency-based services such as health care, mental health counseling, education and employment assistance, and housing. One major aim of street outreach programs—and outreach workers in particular—is to build trust with RHY (Jean 2022; Morse et al. 1996). Outreach workers acknowledge that RHY often distrust authorities and institutions and thus require emotional support and rapport to use the services and resources offered to them (Holger-Ambrose et al. 2013). Providers also recognize that their ability to work effectively with RHY depends on having established a trusting relationship with them. With a trusting relationship established, workers are able to obtain the cooperation of RHY and engage them in safe, nonjudgmental, and accessible health, mental health, and social services.

With respect to best practices in street outreach to the LGBTQ+ RHY population, it is vital that outreach workers approach youth in an affirming manner, such as by asking youth for their pronouns. Further, outreach workers should recognize that many street-involved LGBTQ+ RHY are not ready to identify with LGBTQ+ RHY-serving organizations or not ready to leave the streets. For this reason, workers should prioritize low-barrier services as a first point of entry to services for LGBTQ+ RHY, such as by asking them for only minimal information (e.g., just name or nickname and birth date). Best practices in outreach to LGBTQ+ RHY also involve the use of a nonjudgmental harm-reduction approach, such as by promoting safe-sex practices, promoting injection needle exchange in states where this practice is legal, providing preventive health education, and providing counseling and substance abuse referrals to address high-risk behaviors. In cities with public transportation systems (which can themselves be unsafe and unreliable), outreach workers should consider issuing bus passes, metro cards, or ride-sharing (e.g., Uber, Lyft) codes to facilitate access to safe, affordable, and accessible agency-based services for RHY (Ferguson-Colvin and Maccio 2012; Ferguson and Maccio 2015).

Last, since street outreach is not designed to be an ongoing daily service, outreach workers should consider handing out cards to LGBTQ+ RHY listing the agency's phone number, address, hours of operation, and available services. Such cards could also include affirming messages (e.g., "You matter to me," "Don't be afraid to ask for help," "Never forget how capable you are") or images such as symbols of diversity or caricatures created by youth working with the agency. Outreach cards could also publicize national crisis hotlines for RHY, such as the National Runaway Safeline's toll-free hotline: 1-800-RUNAWAY (1-800-786-2929) (Ferguson-Colvin and Maccio 2012). (For other hotlines for LGBTQ+ RHY, please visit https://pflag .org/resource/support-hotlines/)

Drop-In Centers

Aria relies on the two drop-in centers more than any other services available to her. She prefers the freedom that drop-in centers offer as opposed to shelters or TLPs, which exert control over youth in the form of rules for behavior and expectations for education and employment. She also wants to avoid the inevitable harassment from some of the other youth about her gender identity. Aria would like to have stable housing and a steady source of income, but she's not ready to give up what she sees as the best option for her right now: residing with her supportive, close-knit street family.

Nonresidential drop-in centers and comprehensive resource centers or youth centers serve as a bridge between street outreach and short- and long-term housing options for RHY. These centers can connect RHY to treatment, services to support their economic and self-sufficiency, and their exit from homelessness (Slesnick et al. 2008; Slesnick et al. 2016). Drop-in centers offer RHY a daily haven where they can access regular meals, clothing, laundry facilities, and showers. Case managers or dayroom counselors are also available to provide referrals to other services, such as health care, HIV and STI counseling and testing, family planning, substance abuse treatment, mental health care, educational training, and employment assistance (Kidd, Vitopoulos et al. 2019; Kipke, Unger et al. 1997). Some of these services might be offered on-site at drop-in centers, while others may be provided off-site by other organizations. Two main goals of drop-in centers—and drop-in staff in particular—are to develop an open and trusting relationship with RHY and to connect them with safe, accessible, and affordable services and resources to help their exit from homelessness.

The **program philosophy** of a drop-in center drives the development and maintenance of all programs and services offered. Drop-in centers that promote a culture of positive interpersonal relationships and trust between staff and RHY and where staff treat youth with dignity, respect, and unconditional positive regard are considered to be the centers that are most successful in engaging RHY and reintegrating them into society. Likewise, a customized and strengths-based wraparound approach that connects RHY to services across a continuum of care is considered the most effective approach to responding to the complex needs of RHY (Slesnick et al. 2008).

Regarding best practices for drop-in centers for LGBTQ+ RHY, it is vital that the physical space of the center is safe and LGBTQ+-*affirming* (validating, supporting), rather than simply LGBTQ+-*accepting* (acknowledging). Often-cited visual indications that a center is LGBTQ+-affirming include the rainbow Pride flag, safety guidelines, and antidiscrimination policies specific to sexual orientation and identity and gender identity and expression. Additionally, clients can create and maintain bulletin boards or display artwork (e.g., banners, murals) in prominent spaces with LGBTQ+-affirming messages such "All Are Welcome Here!" and various symbols of diversity (Ferguson-Colvin and Maccio 2012). Table 8.3 provides an example of an **agency assurance statement** that could be posted in a drop-in center.

It is equally important that staff who occupy the drop-in center space—both those who work directly for the host organization and those who are external, working with the organization through collaborative partnerships—display affirming values and practices. External service providers commonly present in drop-in centers through collaborative partnerships include LGBTQ+-affirming Medicaid and public assistance enrollment specialists (who assist LGBTQ+ RHY in navigating systems that can be discriminatory toward them), physicians and medical teams familiar with transgender issues (e.g., street hormones, pump parties), and veterinarians (for youth with pets). Attorneys who do pro bono work may also provide LGBTQ+ RHY with legal

TABLE 8.3 A sample agency assurance statement

[INSERT AGENCY NAME] is committed to maintaining an LGBTQ+-affirming environment. We assure this by:

- Challenging bias and hateful statements consistently.
- Using gender-affirming language or gender-neutral language. This includes calling a youth by their chosen name and pronouns.
- Understanding that sexual identity and gender expression are fluid and doing our best to respect each young person's self-identity as it changes.
- Not making assumptions. This includes not assuming someone's sexual orientation or gender identity based on appearance or behavior.
- Valuing everyone. We treat everyone, whether resident, staff, volunteer, or visitor, with unconditional professional regard.

services (e.g., changing gender markers on identification cards, addressing legal charges for sex work). Other external service providers collaborating with drop-in centers include affirming psychiatrists, mental health clinicians, and substance use counselors who support youth before, during, and after their coming-out and gender-affirming transitions, as well as with mental health challenges and substance abuse. To ensure that all staff, volunteers, and collaborating partners from external agencies are LGBTQ+-affirming in their own beliefs and practices, one best practice is to use screening questions that ask about their attitudes regarding **heterocentrism, heterosexism,** white supremacy, structural racism, sexism, classism, ableism, HIV/AIDS, and white privilege (Ferguson-Colvin and Maccio 2012).

Shelters

Agencies that are part of the Basic Center Program, also funded by the RHYA, provide temporary shelter (i.e., up to twenty-one days), trauma-informed counseling, crisis intervention, medical care, recreation programs, and after-care services to RHY after they exit shelters. The primary goal of the Basic Center Program is to develop new and strengthen existing community-based programs that serve RHY and their families. Basic Center agencies attempt to reunite RHY with their families when possible and to identify alternative longer-term placements for RHY when not possible (FYSB 2023a).

Basic Center agencies are required by the Family and Youth Services Bureau to integrate into all programs the principles of **positive youth development** (PYD): respect, dignity, building relationships, developing trust with youth, youth leadership and voice, life-goal achievement, and community service (Catalano et al. 2004; FYSB 2023a). In agencies that adopt a PYD approach, staff believe in the dignity and worth of each individual and thus create an agency climate in which all youth and staff are treated with respect. PYD agency staff also believe in the healing and empowering nature of humane, caring relationships between adults and youth in the community. Agencies can apply the PYD framework by involving RHY in developing new programs and evaluating existing programs, determining how funding is spent, serving on the agencies' boards of directors, evaluating staff in annual reviews, serving as peer counselors and peer mentors, forming advisory and resident councils, and coauthoring agency policies and program guidelines (e.g., eligibility criteria, rules, and rule-breaking consequences for TLPs). PYD agencies are solidarity based, not charity based, and staff and youth collaborate at all levels of decision-making. Youth and staff hold each other accountable, give each other permission to make mistakes, and use mistakes as learning opportunities (Catalano et al. 2004; Ferguson-Colvin and Maccio 2012).

Regarding best practices in temporary shelters for LGBTQ+ RHY, it is crucial that RHY-serving organizations advocate for additional crisis beds and emergency shelters for LGBTQ+ RHY since up to 40 percent of the more than four million youth experiencing homelessness in the United States (Morton et al. 2017) identify as LGBTQ+, and many LGBTQ+ RHY do not feel safe in existing youth and adult shelters (Ferguson-Colvin and Maccio 2012; Prock and Kennedy 2017). To ensure the availability of safe and affirming short-term shelters for LGBTQ+ youth, staff should address the unique challenges posed to transgender youth, for example, by determining whether they would feel more comfortable being housed with others of their assigned gender or of their identified gender. (See box 8.4, *What Do You Think?*)

BOX 8.4. WHAT DO YOU THINK? INTEGRATED AND DEDICATED (OR SEPARATE) SERVICES FOR LGBTQ+ RHY

- Let us take a closer look at agency principles. Write a mission statement and program philosophy for a mission-specific LGBTQ+ RHY drop-in center that are affirming and draw from PYD principles.
- Now write a mission statement and program philosophy for a drop-in center that services LGBTQ+, heterosexual, and cisgender RHY.
- Compare and contrast these two mission statements and program philosophies. How are they similar? How are they different? Which underlying values or program principles remain the same regardless of the population served and the services offered? Which values or program principles are unique to each type of center?

Transitional Living Programs

The RHYA also funds TLPs, which help RHY successfully exit homelessness and transition to independent and self-sufficient living (Landers 2019). TLPs provide RHY with a safety net of services and emotional support in four domains: extended residential shelter, service coordination, transition planning, and basic life skills. Extended residential housing (i.e., more than twenty-one days) is offered through group homes, maternity group homes, host family homes, and supervised apartments. Service coordination is offered to RHY by trained professionals through on-site services and referrals to external collaborating agencies for social services, educational services, employment training, legal services, health and mental health care, and affordable child care. RHY in TLPs develop a transition plan to facilitate their exit from supervised residential living to independent living in the community. They also learn basic life skills through individual and group counseling and psychoeducational workshops on topics such as financial literacy, interpersonal skills, educational advancement, job attainment skills, physical and mental health care, and parenting skills. Similar to the Basic Center Program, TLPs are also required to integrate components of the PYD framework, such as leadership, capacity-building, and community service, to support RHY in maximizing their potential and making a successful transition to adulthood (FYSB 2023c; Prock and Kennedy 2017).

With regard to best practices in extended residential settings for LGBTQ+ RHY, it is vital for organizations to advocate for permanent supportive housing for this population, particularly in cases in which family reunification is not possible since one of the primary reasons LGBTQ+ youth become homeless is family rejection. Further, certain subpopulations of LGBTQ+ RHY, such as older youth aged twenty-one to twenty-four, require additional long-term housing options since many of the short- and long-term housing programs funded through the RHYA are time limited and designed for youth under the ages of eighteen or twenty-one. Last, staff working with LGBTQ+ RHY should increase their focus on services for "life after housing," such as those that promote independent living skills, to ensure that once LGBTQ+ RHY secure stable housing, they can thrive in their exit from homelessness and transition to adulthood.

FUTURE DIRECTIONS FOR PROGRAMS AND SERVICES FOR LGBTQ+ RHY

The promising programs and services employed in the four service environments for LGBTQ+ RHY that we have identified in this chapter have shown success in ameliorating negative outcomes in the areas of health, mental health and substance use, case management, family issues, legal concerns, education, employment, and housing. Practitioners working with LGBTQ+ RHY will benefit from knowledge of the most commonly used interventions and service environments for this population. Intervention manuals, contact information for the developers of promising programs and services, and grant opportunities from the Family and Youth Services Bureau can support practitioners and administrators in implementing and evaluating these programs, services, and service environments.

Similarly, policymakers can use their knowledge of promising programs and services and commonly used service environments for LGBTQ+ RHY to guide their decision-making on RHY legislation. The Runaway and Homeless Youth and Trafficking Prevention Act (RHYTPA) (discussed in greater detail in chapter 9) of 2023 was introduced in the U.S. Senate (S. 3125) and House of Representatives (H.R. 6041) to reauthorize and strengthen the RHYA. Specific to protections for LGBTQ+ RHY, the RHYTPA incorporates a nondiscrimination clause to ensure that all youth are treated fairly, including LGBTQ+ RHY. The RHYTPA also contained a provision to fund a national study of the prevalence, needs, and characteristics of RHY, including LGBTQ+ RHY (RHYTPA 2023a, 2023b). However, Congressional committees failed to take up the issue, leaving the RHYA yet to be reauthorized. The information provided in this chapter could be used to inform policymakers of the importance of funding street outreach, drop-in centers, shelters, and TLPs, as well as the promising LGBTQ+-affirming programs and services provided in these service environments.

SUMMARY

Our 2012 study of twenty-four staff and administrators from nineteen organizations serving LGBTQ+ RHY yielded many promising programs and services, both integrated and dedicated, delivered in four service environments. Respondents used interventions ranging from techniques and approaches (e.g., harm reduction, group psychotherapy) to models and frameworks (e.g., transformative justice, trauma-informed care) to manualized programs and curricula (e.g., Be Proud! Be Responsible!, RISE). These programs and services focus not only on intervention, such as those that address youths' mental health and substance use needs, but also proactive with, such as those that build on youths' strengths, help transgender and NBG youth navigate the gender-affirming transition process, and educate youth on their rights. Service environments are becoming more progressive, meeting LGBTQ+ RHY where they are—creating LGBTQ+-affirming spaces, housing youth with their street families, sheltering youth according to the gender with which they identify—even if that means turning away precious government dollars. The programs and services mentioned here are merely a starting point for current and future practitioners in youth-serving organizations. The development of new programs and services and the continued refinement of existing ones will only improve outcomes for LGBTQ+ RHY.

REVISITING ARIA

- You are a dayroom counselor at a local drop-in center for RHY. Describe the engagement techniques you would use to build trust with Aria.
- Describe the assessment you would do to identify Aria's strengths, areas where growth is needed, and the goals she would like to work on in the near future.
- Describe a few promising programs that you could suggest to Aria to meet her goal of making a safe and healthy transition to her new gender.
- Would you recommend integrated or dedicated programs and services or some combination of both for Aria? Why?
- How could you describe TLPs in a way that would encourage Aria to consider applying, knowing how much she values her freedom and independence, while not omitting or mischaracterizing a TLP's expectations of resident responsibilities and behavior?

KEY CONCEPTS

- *Agency assurance statement*: a proclamation of an agency's values that clients and consumers can expect to see incorporated into their experiences with the agency
- *Dedicated (or separate) services*: services designed for specific subgroups of LGBTQ+ RHY, such as transgender and NBG youth, though all youth are welcome to participate
- *Harm-reduction approach*: an approach to care that aims to reduce or eliminate harmful behaviors through small achievable steps
- *Heterocentrism*: judging nonheterosexual orientations and identities based on heterosexual norms
- *Heterosexism*: prejudice and discrimination against nonheterosexual orientations and identities based on the belief that heterosexuality is the superior sexual orientation and identity
- *Host homes*: private homes whose owners have volunteered to house youth experiencing homelessness, often for several years, to facilitate youths' transitions to adulthood and independent living
- *Integrated services*: services designed for all RHY, including LGBTQ+ and heterosexual-cisgender youth
- *LGBTQ+-affirming*: an approach that transcends tolerance and acceptance and instead validates and supports the youth's sexual orientation and identity and gender identity and expression
- *Positive youth development*: "an intentional, prosocial approach that engages youth within their communities, schools, organizations, peer groups, and families in a manner that is productive and constructive; recognizes, utilizes, and enhances young people's strengths; and promotes positive outcomes for young people by providing opportunities, fostering positive relationships, and furnishing the support needed to build on their leadership strengths" (Youth.gov n.d.c, para. 2)
- *Program philosophy*: a guiding principle or set of principles on which a program is based
- *Social enterprises*: organizations that address a basic unmet need or solve a social or environmental problem through a market-driven approach

- *Street family*: a self-formed peer group that provides support and protection and whose members may consider themselves to be a family
- *Supported education*: "a specific type of intervention that provides supports and other assistance for persons with psychiatric disabilities for access, enrollment, retention and success in postsecondary education" (Collins and Mowbray 2005, 310)
- *Supported employment*: programs or services to assist people with disabilities and mental health challenges find and keep competitive jobs in integrated work settings (i.e., those with disabled and nondisabled employees) (Bond 2004)
- *Transformative justice model*: whereas restorative justice acknowledges the hurt and pain of victims and the culpability and accountability of offenders, transformative justice considers the role that systemic and environmental oppression play in crime and its impact on victims, offenders, and society
- *Trauma informed*: an approach "based on the knowledge and understanding of trauma and its far-reaching implications" (SAMHSA 2014, 2)

CHAPTER HIGHLIGHTS

- Much of the data discussed in this chapter comes from our 2012 study of twenty-four staff and administrators from nineteen organizations serving LGBTQ+ RHY. The study culminated in the *Toolkit for Practitioners/Researchers Working with Lesbian, Gay, Bisexual, Transgender, and Queer/Questioning (LGBTQ) Runaway and Homeless Youth (RHY)*.
- The organizations included in our study provided services that were integrated (i.e., for all RHY, including LGBTQ+ and heterosexual-cisgender youth) or dedicated (i.e., for specific subpopulations of LGBTQ+ RHY, such as transgender and NBG youth).
- Integrated programs and services address seven key areas: health, mental health and substance use, case management, family, legal and mediation concerns, education and employment, and housing.

- Organizations reported using best practices such as trauma-informed care and a harm-reduction approach to address youths' mental health and substance use challenges.
- The four most common legal services for LGBTQ+ RHY were name changes and document replacements, street encounters with the police, engagement in sex-work services, and "quality-of-life" offenses.
- Promising programs have five characteristics in common: a strong reliance on clinical evidence; the use of a trauma-informed approach; the provision of safe, stable, and supportive housing; the incorporation of peer providers from the LGBTQ+ community; and the provision of opportunities for reciprocal learning between LGBTQ+ and heterosexual-cisgender RHY.
- RHY-serving organizations delivered their services in one or more of four environments: street outreach, drop-in centers, shelters, and transitional living programs. The Sacramento LGBT Community Center has recently introduced a fifth environment: a short-term transitional emergency program.
- The Runaway and Homeless Youth Act was introduced for reauthorization in 2023 as the Runaway and Homeless Youth and Trafficking Prevention Act but failed to be voted on by its respective House and Senate committees.

9 | Policies

LEARNING OBJECTIVES

Readers of this chapter will be able to:

1. Differentiate the three branches of federal government and their functions,
2. Explain how each branch of government can affect housing and homelessness policies by way of their branch powers and functions,
3. Identify at least three key laws, executive orders, and policy interpretations that established or expanded protections for RHY, including LGBTQ+ RHY, and
4. Understand how changes in policies have contributed to advancements in policies and programs that promote mental health among LGBTQ+ RHY.

CASE VIGNETTE: DIONTE

Dionte, twenty-nine, is the director of policy for a national housing organization based in Washington, DC. He's proud of his status as the first Black person, and the youngest, to hold that position. His primary role is to supervise and help staff who write, recommend, and advocate for policy relating to housing instability and homelessness at the federal level. However, given the scope of the problem—diminishing affordable housing, the housing collapse of 2008 and the subsequent wave of mortgage foreclosures, increasing numbers of combat veterans facing housing instability, the COVID-19 pandemic, an opioid crisis that is bankrupting users and weakening the workforce, and numerous other challenges—Dionte and his staff feel overwhelmed at times. Nevertheless, the team is committed to macro-level efforts to combat homelessness with the talent and resources they have. As a foster care "survivor," Dionte is committed to the work, especially on behalf of RHY, many of whom are in foster care themselves.

INTRODUCTION

Understanding who makes policy and how policy is made can facilitate the development of advocacy strategies for intervening in the policymaking process, which will be discussed in greater depth in chapter 10. This chapter begins with a brief overview of the three branches and four levels of government. We then describe select federal and state policies designed to help the broader population of RHY and the subpopulation of LGBTQ+ RHY achieve a healthy transition to adulthood. We also identify select federal and state policies that have hindered this healthy transition to adulthood for LGBTQ+ RHY. We conclude with some future directions for political action with and on behalf of LGBTQ+ RHY.

OVERVIEW OF THE POLICYMAKING PROCESS

The U.S. political system is composed of three branches of government— executive, legislative, and judicial—and four levels of government—federal, tribal, state, and local (e.g., county, city, town, neighborhood). An understanding of how policies are made in the three governmental branches and at various levels of government allows us to identify where community members can participate in the policymaking process through political action strategies.

Policies come in many forms. For instance, at the **executive branch** (at the federal, tribal, state, and local levels), the president (federal level), chief executives of tribes (tribal level), governors (state level), and mayors (local level) can issue **executive orders** that clarify or further an existing law that was previously passed by the legislative branch or established based on the Constitution (and interpreted through the judicial branch). Executive orders commonly establish requirements or guidelines for governmental agencies and departments (Segal 2016). Likewise, the president and other executive branch officials (e.g., governors) can make policies through **executive actions**. Rather than extending existing laws, as executive orders do, executive actions are commonly statements of policy or interpretations of agency regulations (Segal 2016).

In contrast, the **legislative branch**, which includes our federal Congress, tribal councils, state legislatures, and local city councils and county boards of supervisors, can make policies by introducing and voting on policy proposals, or bills. At the federal and state levels of government, Congress and state legislatures typically introduce policy proposals in a bicameral (two-house or -chamber) process by which each house votes on the bill (or a similar version of the bill). If passed by both houses of the legislature, the bill is sent to the executive branch to be signed (or vetoed) (Blau and Abramovitz 2010).

Further, the **judicial branch**—including the Supreme Court, tribal courts, state supreme courts, and, at the local level, family courts, juvenile courts, and district circuit courts—can make policy through interpreting the Constitution (or, in the tribal court system, tribal law). In the Supreme Court, the justices' role is to scrutinize the interpretations of lower court rulings, particularly in cases in which laws might conflict with constitutional guarantees (Blau and Abramovitz 2010).

The policymaking process across the three branches of government is complex, yet one benefit of this process is that it ensures a system of checks and balances across the three branches so that no one branch has excessive power over another. However, one limitation of the process is that, because of the evenly divided and balanced power across the branches, enacting structural reforms can be challenging (Blau and Abramovitz 2010).

FEDERAL POLICY INITIATIVES SUPPORTING HETEROSEXUAL, CISGENDER, AND LGBTQ+ RHY

In this section, we describe some of the key federal policies that protect, guarantee rights, and provide for access to services and resources for LGBTQ+ RHY. We selected these policies in some of the major systems with which LGBTQ+ RHY regularly interact, namely, the homelessness, education, child welfare, and health care systems.

The Runaway and Homeless Youth Act

The Runaway and Homeless Youth Act (RHYA) is the primary federal legislation that aims to eradicate youth homelessness through funding emergency shelters, family reunification efforts, street outreach, and transitional housing. The legislation was originally passed in 1974 as the Runaway Youth Act (RYA) and as Title III of the Juvenile Justice and Delinquency Prevention Act (P.L. 93–415) to help runaway youth who were not being served by the juvenile justice and child welfare systems. Early on, the RYA authorized funding for local runaway youth shelters and for a crisis hotline in Chicago that eventually became the National Runaway Switchboard (Staller 1997) and later the National Runaway Safeline (n.d.).

The RYA has been reauthorized on six occasions. In 1977, Congress expanded the act to include youth experiencing homelessness, at which point it became known as the Runaway and Homeless Youth Act (P.L.93–415). The RHYA originally established services for homeless minors and their families through the Basic Center Program. Second, in 1988, a provision was added to the RHYA to create the Transitional Living Program (P.L. 100–690). Transitional living programs (TLPs) provide long-term residential services to youth experiencing homelessness to facilitate their transition to self-sufficiency. Third, in 1999, the administration of and funding for both the Basic Center and Transitional Living Programs were combined under the consolidated Runaway and Homeless Youth Program (P.L. 106–71) (Fernandes 2007).

The fourth reauthorization, the Runaway, Homeless, and Missing Children Protection Act, occurred in 2003 (P.L. 108–96). This act authorized federal funding for three programs—the Street Outreach Program, the Basic Center Program, and the Transitional Living Program—each of which is administered by the Department of Health and Human Services through the Family and Youth Services Bureau (Fernandes 2007; Staller 1997). The Street Outreach Program offers education, treatment, counseling, and referrals to runaway, homeless, and street youth who have experienced or are at risk of experiencing sexual abuse and exploitation. The Basic Center Program provides temporary shelter, mental health counseling, and after-care services to RHY and their families. TLPs offer youth experiencing homelessness longer-term housing and supportive services, including mental health counseling, educational and vocational training, and health care (Landers 2019).

A fifth reauthorization occurred in 2008, thus enacting the Reconnecting Homeless Youth Act of 2008 (S. 2982, Public Law 110–378). Among various updates to the 2003 legislation, this reauthorization increased funding for RHYA programs, allowed extensions in lengths of stay in both Basic Center programs and TLPs, and extended the service age for TLPs from twenty-one to twenty-two years. However, despite the disproportionate rate of LGBTQ+ youth among the broader RHY population, no mention was made in the 2008 reauthorization of the unique needs of LGBTQ+ RHY. The Center for American Progress has since called for the inclusion of the needs of LGBTQ+ RHY in subsequent reauthorizations of the RHYA to ensure that public funds are used as efficiently and effectively as possible (Dunn and Krehely 2012).

The 2008 RHYA expired in 2013 but was reauthorized for fiscal years 2019 and 2020 through the Juvenile Justice Reform Act of 2018 (Landers 2019). Many congressional bills have since been introduced, most recently one in the U.S. Senate (S. 3125) and one in the U.S. House of Representatives (H.R. 6041), both titled the Runaway and Homeless Youth and Trafficking Prevention Act (2023a, 2023b). Both bills propose important protections for LGBTQ+ RHY, including a new provision that prohibits grantees from denying services based on the sexual orientation or gender identity of youth experiencing homelessness. However, the outcome of this reauthorization is yet to be known as both bills remain in committees (i.e., the House Committee on Education & Workforce and the Senate Committee on the Judiciary). (See box 9.1, *What Do You Think?*)

BOX 9.1. WHAT DO YOU THINK? THE RUNAWAY AND HOMELESS YOUTH AND TRAFFICKING PREVENTION ACT

The **Runaway and Homeless Youth and Trafficking Prevention Act** has yet to make it through the early stages of the legislative process. What steps could you take to intervene in this political process to facilitate the successful reauthorization of the RHYA? Whom could you contact? What could you say that would be persuasive? Which interest groups and advocacy organizations are working to support the successful reauthorization of this act? Is there one such group or organization in your city or state?

The Stewart B. McKinney Homeless Assistance Act of 1987

RHY, and especially those who are homeless with their families, are supported through housing programs funded through the **Stewart B. McKinney Homeless Assistance Act of 1987**, which was the first major federal legislation to support the housing needs of people experiencing homelessness. The McKinney Act originally funded a range of housing and support programs, including the Supportive Housing Program, the Shelter Plus Care Program, the Single Room Occupancy Program, and the Emergency Shelter Grant Program. The McKinney Act also established the Interagency Council on the Homeless (later renamed the United States Interagency Council on Homelessness), which is housed within the executive branch and tasked with coordinating and catalyzing the federal response to homelessness across federal agencies (SMHAA 1987).

The McKinney Act has been reauthorized and amended numerous times since its passage. One amendment relevant to RHY was made in 2001, when the act was expanded to ensure protections for children and youth experiencing homelessness in the public education system. The **McKinney–Vento Homeless Education Assistance Improvements Act of 2001** expanded the federal government's role in addressing youth homelessness through the public education system (i.e., kindergarten through twelfth grade) through various school-based homelessness assistance programs. With this amendment, the Department of Education began requiring school districts to appoint a local education liaison to educate staff about the policy's provisions, help families experiencing homelessness (both at schools and in shelters), and ensure access to school and transportation service regardless of children's and youths' housing status (U.S. Department of Education 2017). The Homeless Children and Youth Act of 2021, an amendment to the McKinney–Vento Homeless Assistance Act, was introduced first in the U.S. Senate and then in the House (where it was referred to committees in each chamber and never voted out) to standardize the definition of *homeless* as a means of increasing access to services for those experiencing various forms of housing instability (HCYA 2021). However, some critics argue that the Department of Housing and Urban Development is not adequately funded to serve the more than 4.4 million people now covered under the McKinney-Vento definition (e.g., those living doubled up, or living with other families or youth) and that, instead, the solution to housing instability should include rental assistance and building affordable housing (National Network for Youth n.d.). The bill was reintroduced in the House in 2023 and referred to committees, where it remains (HCYA 2023).

Opening Doors

In 2010, the United States Interagency Council on Homelessness established the country's first comprehensive federal strategic plan to prevent and end homelessness: **Opening Doors**. The Opening Doors plan was presented to Congress on June 22, 2010, and updated and amended in 2012 and 2015 to reflect lessons learned. One of the five goals of Opening Doors was ending youth homelessness for those under the age of twenty-five by 2020. Within this goal, one strategy was to develop approaches in the areas of emergency assistance, housing, and social supports to serve vulnerable subpopulations of RHY, including LGBTQ+ RHY (USICH 2015).

Foster Care Legislation

Given the disproportionate percentage of LGBTQ+ youth in the foster care system in comparison to their heterosexual and cisgender peers, two pieces of foster care legislation have assisted RHY and LGBTQ+ RHY in particular. First, the **Foster Care Independence Act of 1999 (P.L. 106–169)** amended Title IV-E of the Social Security Act to provide states with more funding and greater flexibility in carrying out programs designed to help youth make the transition from foster care to self-sufficiency. Provisions of the act relevant to older youth include allowing states to use up to 30 percent of their Independent Living Program funds for room and board for youth aged eighteen to twenty-one who have left foster care and extend Medicaid to eighteen-, nineteen-, and twenty-year-olds who have been emancipated from foster care (Social Security Administration 1999).

Second, the **Fostering Connections to Success and Increasing Adoptions Act of 2008 (P.L. 110–351)** amended Title IV-E of the Social Security Act by extending the age of eligibility for foster care from eighteen to twenty-one. The act provides states with the option to continue providing Title IV-E reimbursable foster care, adoption, or guardianship assistance payments to youth up to the age of nineteen, twenty, or twenty-one if the youth is completing secondary education or a program leading to an equivalent credential, enrolled in an institution that provides postsecondary or vocational education, participating in a program or activity designed to promote or remove barriers to employment, employed for at least eighty hours per month, or is incapable of doing any of these because of a medical condition (Peters et al. 2009).

FEDERAL POLICY INITIATIVES SUPPORTING LGBTQ+ RHY

We next describe select federal policy initiatives designed to protect, promote, and guarantee the rights of LGBTQ+ individuals. These policies have benefited LGBTQ+ RHY by protecting them from discrimination in housing, employment, education, and child welfare settings; preventing and intervening in hate crimes; and guaranteeing the constitutional right of same-sex couples to marry. Although specific details regarding policy reauthorizations or continuations might change under different federal administrations in the future, it is nonetheless important to identify foundational policy initiatives upon which additional legislation protecting and promoting the rights and freedoms of LGBTQ+ RHY can build. We discuss legislation in the domains in which historical and contemporary narratives of LGBTQ+ rights and freedoms are most prevalent: civil rights, housing, workplaces, educational settings, child welfare, legal systems, and interpersonal relationships.

Justice Department Guidance

In 2012, the Justice Department issued guidance stating that the prohibition against sex discrimination in Title VII of the Civil Rights Act of 1964 includes claims of discrimination on the basis of one's gender identity, including transgender status (Milligan 2016).

Department of Housing and Urban Development Rules, Guidance, and Initiatives

In 2012 and 2015, the Department of Housing and Urban Development issued rules and guidance requiring that programs and services administered or funded by the department be made equally available to LGBT individuals. The new rules have helped LGBT people and their families across the country stay in their homes, obtain loans needed to buy homes, and access life-saving federal assistance programs to prevent homelessness (Donovan 2012).

More recently, the department spearheaded the LGBTQ+ Youth Homelessness Prevention Initiative to identify successful strategies to prevent young people from becoming homeless because of their sexual orientation and identity or their gender identity and expression. The initiative started in 2014 with two pilot communities tasked with developing and implementing local, community-wide plans to prevent homelessness among LGBTQ+ youth and intervene early when homelessness occurs (USDHUD 2017).

In June 2023, as a symbolic acknowledgment of Pride Month, the Department of Housing and Urban Development introduced the LGBTQI+ Youth Homelessness Initiative. This initiative began with nationwide listening sessions with LGBTQI+ youth and was followed by resources, training, and technical assistance for service providers and "Know Your Rights tools for direct-affected youth" (USDHUD 2023a, para. 2).

In 2021, following President Joe Biden's executive order prohibiting discrimination on the basis of sexual orientation and gender identity, the Department of Housing and Urban Development issued a memorandum titled "Implementation of Executive Order 13988 on the Enforcement of the Fair Housing Act." This memorandum bars discrimination in housing on the basis of sex as outlined in the Fair Housing Act and in the same way that Title VII of the Civil Rights Act of 1964 bars sex discrimination in employment (USDHUD 2022). It was on Title VII that the U.S. Supreme Court based their decision in *Bostock v. Clayton County, Georgia* (2019), which stated that Clayton County had discriminated against an employee, Gerald Bostock, when they fired him for joining a gay softball team.

Executive Orders

In 2014, President Barack Obama amended two previous executive orders to protect the LGBTQ+ community from discrimination in hiring and employment practices based on their sexual orientation and gender identity. **Executive Order 13672** prohibited discrimination in the civilian federal workforce based on gender identity and in hiring practices by federal contractors based on sexual orientation and gender identity (U.S. Department of Labor 2017). Soon after, President Obama issued Executive Order 13673: Fair Pay and Safe Workplaces, which added further protections for LGBTQ+ civilian federal workers. In March 2017, President Donald Trump rescinded that order with Executive Order 13782, thereby weakening protections for LGBTQ+ civilian federal workers and making them again vulnerable to discrimination. Then, in January 2021, President Joe Biden restored protections for LGBTQ+ individuals by expanding discrimination protections on the basis of sex to include both gender identity and sexual orientation through **Executive Order 13988**: Preventing and Combating

Discrimination on the Basis of Gender Identity or Sexual Orientation. That order was rescinded by President Trump in January 2025, leaving LGBTQ+ people without protection against sexual orientation and gender identity discrimination by federal agencies.

Educational Interpretations

In 2016, the Obama administration interpreted Title IX of the Education Amendments of 1972, which include protections against discrimination on the basis of sex, to mean that schools receiving federal funding must allow transgender students to use the bathroom they choose; however, this issue continues to be contested in courts across the country (Milligan 2016). In 2017, the Trump administration withdrew that interpretation, relegating transgender students to use bathrooms and locker rooms that match their "biological sex" (Battle and Wheeler 2017, para. 3). In 2021, the Biden administration issued directives allowing transgender workers and students to use bathrooms and locker rooms that match their gender identity, yet states' attorneys general and federal judges alike have used the judicial system to challenge and block these directives (Brooks 2022).

The **Administration for Children and Families** issued an information memorandum in 2011 pertaining to Titles IV-B and IV-E of the Social Security Act to encourage child welfare agencies, foster and adoptive parents, and others who work with young people in foster care to ensure that all children—regardless of their sexual orientation or gender identity—are protected and supported while they are in foster care (ACF 2011).

Hate Crimes

In 2009, President Obama signed into law the **Matthew Shepard and James Byrd Jr. Hate Crimes Prevention Act of 2009**. This legislation provides funding and technical assistance to tribal, state, and local jurisdictions to help them more effectively investigate and prosecute hate crimes, including crimes against individuals on the basis of their sexual orientation or gender identity (U.S. Department of Justice 2015).

BOX 9.2. READ ALL ABOUT IT! GOVERNMENT POLICY AND ADVOCACY RESOURCES FOR LGBTQ+ RHY

Below is a partial list of government entities and nongovernmental organizations tackling housing instability and homelessness among LGBTQ+ RHY:

Center for the Study of Social Policy: https://cssp.org/our-work /project/getreal/

Chapin Hall, University of Chicago: https://www.chapinhall.org /impact_area/youth-homelessness/

Human Rights Campaign: https://www.hrc.org/

Lambda Legal: https://lambdalegal.org/

National Network for Youth: https://nn4youth.org/lgbtq-homeless -youth/

True Colors United: https://truecolorsunited.org/

U.S. Interagency Council on Homelessness: https://www.usich .gov/

Same-Sex Marriage

In 2015, in the case of ***Obergefell v. Hodges***, the Supreme Court ruled by a vote of five to four that the Constitution guarantees the right to same-sex marriage. This ruling guaranteed same-sex couples the right to marry by both the Due Process Clause and the Equal Protection Clause of the Fourteenth Amendment to the U.S. Constitution (SCOTUSblog 2017). (See box 9.2, *Read All About It!*)

STATE POLICY INITIATIVES SUPPORTING LGBTQ+ RHY

Dionte monitors policy efforts around the country, looking for effective and promising actions that could be replicated in other states or at the national level. He is well connected and knows or is at least familiar with all of his state-level counterparts around the country. As a cisgender queer-identified man, he has also made it a point to establish professional relationships with staff at leading LGBTQ+ advocacy organizations around the country. Dionte often collaborates with a state policy agency to the benefit of both organizations, such as on legislation with both state- and national-level components. Dionte believes that helping these state organizations achieve their policy goals helps his national organization achieve its goals, and vice versa.

For public institutions serving children, youth, and families (e.g., schools, shelters, child welfare), there was at the time of this writing no comprehensive federal policy to eliminate bullying, discrimination, and harassment at a system level (with the exception of the 2011 Administration for Children and Families information memorandum). As such, states and cities across the country have enacted antidiscrimination policies in various public agencies. What follows is an example of the efforts of one state, New York State, and one city, New York City, to address bullying, discrimination, and harassment in schools, housing, family services, and child welfare. (See box 9.3, *Read All About It!*) Other states and cities have implemented similar efforts to address bullying, discrimination, and harassment; we have selected New York simply as one such example to demonstrate how states and cities use policy tools to address violence toward protected groups across multiple systems in the absence of federal law. To identify other state and local regulations, policies, and laws designed to address bullying, discrimination, and harassment, visit StopBullying.gov (https://www.stopbullying.gov/resources/laws), whose mission is to "provide information from various government agencies on what bullying is, what cyberbullying is, who is at risk, and how you can prevent and respond to bullying" (StopBullying.gov 2023, para 1).

Housing, Employment, and Public Accommodations

In 2006, the New York City Department of Homeless Services passed a policy allowing LGBTQ+ individuals to self-identify their gender for placement in New York City shelters. This policy has allowed LGBTQ+ RHY to enter shelters based on their self-identified gender rather than their birth-assigned gender (NYCDHS 2006).

In 2019, the New York State Senate and General Assembly passed the Gender Non-Discrimination Act. This law offers statewide nondiscrimination protections for transgender individuals across housing, employment, and public accommodations. The bill was originally introduced in 2003; after sixteen years of statewide debate, New York joined nineteen other states in offering comprehensive protections for LGBTQ+ people (New York State 2019).

Schools

New York State's Dignity for All Students Act of 2010 was designed to ensure that the state's public elementary and secondary schools provide students with a safe and supportive environment free from discrimination, intimidation, taunting, harassment, and bullying on school property, on school buses, and at school functions (NYSED 2017).

Family Services

In 2008, the New York State Office of Children and Family Services (OCFS) adopted the OCFS Lesbian, Gay, Bisexual, Transgender and Questioning Youth Policy, which enables LGBTQ+ youth to self-identify their gender. This policy was designed to protect youth who self-identify as LGBTQ+ and those perceived by others as LGBTQ+ from discrimination (NYSOCFS 2017).

Child Welfare

Also in 2008, New York City's Administration for Children's Services passed the Non-discrimination Policy, Youth and Families, which protects LGBTQ+ youth in care from discrimination based on actual or perceived race, color, creed, age, national origin, alienage, citizenship status, gender,

gender identity, sexual orientation, disability, marital status or partnership status, ethnicity, or religion (NYCACS n.d.).

Mental Health

In 2019, following the lead of several other states, New York State banned licensed mental health professionals from practicing conversion therapy (i.e., efforts to change or suppress a person's sexual orientation) with minors. The governor at the time, Andrew Cuomo, had issued an executive order three years earlier substantially restricting the practice and insurance coverage for it, but legislative action by the State Assembly and the State Senate resulted in a definitive ban, the Gender Expression

---

BOX 9.3. READ ALL ABOUT IT! NEW YORK STATE POLICIES AND POLICY ORGANIZATIONS

To learn more about these and other of New York's state and local policies and policy organizations, visit the following websites:

New York City Administration for Children's Services, LGBTQ Office of Policy and Practice: https://www.nyc.gov/site/acs/about/lgbtq-policies.page

New York City Human Resources Administration, LGBTQI Affairs: https://www.nyc.gov/site/hra/help/lgbtqi.page

New York State Dignity for All Students Act: https://www.nysed.gov/student-support-services/dignity-all-students-act

New York State Gender Expression Non-Discrimination Act: https://dhr.ny.gov/genda

New York State Office of Children and Family Services, Policies and Laws Regarding the LGBTQ Community: https://ocfs.ny.gov/programs/youth/lgbtq/policies.php

New York State Public High School Athletic Association Handbook, "Transgender Guidelines" (see p. 52): https://nysphsaa.org/documents/2023/8/21//NYSPHSAA_Handbook_005.pdf

Non-Discrimination Act, which the governor signed in January 2019 (New York State 2019). It is noteworthy that changes to policy to offer greater rights and protections to LGBTQ+ youth are associated with improved mental health outcomes in youth because policies and laws are the societal contexts in which mental health and well-being operate (Russell and Fish 2016). This is a particularly important point for human services practitioners as it affirms that policy advocacy and political action are necessary complements to clinical work with individuals, families, and groups and that such advocacy and action can have a positive impact on mental health outcomes among LGBTQ+ youth.

POLICIES HINDERING LGBTQ+ RHY

With his organization based in Washington, DC, Dionte is able to meet directly with U.S. representatives and senators—or more likely their staff—about policies affecting people experiencing housing instability and homelessness. When his schedule allows, he attends committee hearings and floor debates to make himself more recognizable to lawmakers and staffers and to network with others doing the same or similar work. The policy debates and discussions Dionte most frequently monitors are those focusing on pregnant and parenting teens, military veterans, people with mental health and substance use concerns, youth of color, and LGBTQ+ youth. The most challenging aspect of Dionte's job is confronting lawmakers on their policies and related actions that, at best, impose unnecessary burdens on these populations or, at worst, put them in harm's way.

Despite the policy advances that have helped protect and guarantee the rights of RHY, including LGBTQ+ RHY, states continue to pass and enforce legislation that criminalizes homelessness and restricts the rights and freedoms of LGBTQ+ people and their access to resources. For example, in the first five months of 2023 alone, state legislatures across the country introduced more than five hundred bills aimed at restricting the rights of LGBTQ+ populations and their access to resources. State policies that penalize individuals or restrict rights or access to services based on sexual orientation or gender identity are referred to as **anti-LGBTQ+ legislation**

(Peele 2023a). Similarly, some state and local policies penalize people experiencing homelessness for minor crimes associated with homelessness (e.g., panhandling, urinating in public) referred to as **quality-of-life offenses**. For instance, in our study of service providers and administrative staff from nineteen organizations serving homeless youth across the country (Ferguson and Maccio 2015; Maccio and Ferguson 2016), staff noted that policing practices have become increasingly burdensome for LGBTQ+ RHY, who are frequently targeted for their sexual orientation and identity or their gender identity and expression. Transgender youth often report being profiled as sex workers and arrested for walking in particular parts of a city at particular times of day and night. Youth also note that they are often arrested for sleeping outside and in parks in cities where there are insufficient shelter beds or where shelters are not deemed safe for LGBTQ+ RHY. Further, they note that they are frequently ticketed for turnstile jumping at subway stations (i.e., fare evasion) when trying to get to appointments with social workers or probation officers without having the needed fare. In many cities, turnstile jumping is considered a "theft of services," which is often a misdemeanor but can lead to fines, jail time, adverse impacts on immigration procedures, and other severe consequences.

FUTURE DIRECTIONS FOR POLITICAL ACTION

From this review of policies that have both helped and hindered heterosexual, cisgender, and LGBTQ+ RHY in their healthy transition to self-sufficiency, several key recommendations emerge for future policy initiatives. First, policy initiatives should prohibit discrimination on the basis of sexual orientation and identity and gender identity and expression in admissions to all housing, employment, educational, and public accommodation settings at the federal, tribal, state, and local levels. Second, policy initiatives should prevent discrimination, bullying, and harassment in the broadest sense across all levels of government. Third, policy initiatives should decriminalize youth homelessness and poverty, thus enabling RHY to pursue opportunities toward self-sufficiency without legal constraints related to their experience of being homeless. Fourth, policy initiatives should support the broader LGBTQ+ population, thereby sending the message to both housed and unhoused LGBTQ+ youth that they are valued and respected members of society. Last, physical health, mental health, and other psychosocial outcomes associated with policy and legislative changes should be tracked so that research evidence is available to inform policymaking.

SUMMARY

The legislative groundwork to support RHY was laid by the introduction of the Runaway Youth Act of 1974 and the Runaway and Homeless Youth Act of 1977. This legislation has undergone many reauthorizations over the years, having been most recently introduced for reauthorization in 2023 in both the U.S. House and Senate as the Runaway and Homeless Youth and Trafficking Prevention Act. Other RHY-supportive legislation includes the Stewart B. McKinney Homeless Assistance Act of 1987 and the McKinney–Vento Homeless Education Assistance Improvements Act of 2001, which expanded protections into the public education system.

RHY have also been supported indirectly, for example, through the Foster Care Independence Act of 1999, which in part assists youth in foster care as they transition to independence, and the Fostering Connections to Success and Increasing Adoptions Act of 2008, which increased the age of foster care eligibility from eighteen to twenty-one. Other supports, such as federal agencies (e.g., the Department of Health and Human Services, the Administration for Children and Families), policy interpretations (e.g., Title VII, Title IX), laws (e.g., the Matthew Shepard and James Byrd Jr. Hate Crimes Prevention Act of 2009), and legal decisions (e.g., *Obergefell v. Hodges*), have contributed to the protection of and equal access to services for LGBTQ+ RHY. Although isolated policies and one-off fixes make a difference, the future of LGBTQ+-affirming measures is in comprehensive, broad-based, multilevel policies and legislation that prohibit discrimination based on sexual orientation and identity and gender identity and expression.

REVISITING DIONTE

- What are some effective runaway and homeless youth laws or policy measures in your state that Dionte might want to know about and perhaps share with other states?
- If you were a member of Dionte's staff, would you want to focus on policy related to housing instability, homelessness, or both? Why? Would you want to work on prevention policy, intervention policy, or both? Why?
- If you were the director of policy at a nonprofit organization in your state, what policy actions would you pursue related to youth housing instability and homelessness?
- What are some gaps in your city's or county's RHY policies for which you might seek Dionte's assistance?

KEY CONCEPTS

- *Administration for Children and Families*: "a division of the U.S. Department of Health and Human Services . . . [that] promotes the economic and social well-being of families, children, individuals and communities with funding, strategic partnerships, guidance, training and technical assistance" (ACF 2018)
- *Anti-LGBTQ+ legislation*: a category of laws, policies, and regulations that deny rights, freedoms, and protections to individuals based on their sexual orientation or gender identity, resulting in such outcomes as unequal treatment; censorship; medical abuses; discrimination in health care, employment, and housing settings; denial of family rights; and murder
- *Executive action*: a general term for any action taken by an executive (e.g., the president), for example, executive orders and memoranda
- *Executive branch*: the branch of government that carries out and enforces laws; also known as the administrative branch
- *Executive order*: a type of executive action that carries the weight of law

- *Executive Order 13672*: an order prohibiting discrimination in the civilian federal workforce based on gender identity and in hiring practices by federal contractors based on sexual orientation and gender identity (U.S. Department of Labor 2017)
- *Executive Order 13988*: an order expanding the discrimination protections previously available on the basis of sex to include both gender identity and sexual orientation (U.S. Office of Civil Rights 2023)
- *Foster Care Independence Act of 1999*: an act that amended Title IV-E of the Social Security Act to provide states with more funding and greater flexibility in carrying out programs designed to help youth make the transition from foster care to self-sufficiency (Social Security Administration 1999)
- *Fostering Connections to Success and Increasing Adoptions Act of 2008*: an act that amended Title IV-E of the Social Security Act by extending the age of eligibility for foster care from eighteen to twenty-one. The Act provides states with the option to continue providing Title IV-E reimbursable foster care, adoption, or guardianship assistance payments to youth up to the age of nineteen, twenty, or twenty-one under certain conditions (Peters et al. 2009).
- *Judicial branch*: the branch of government that interprets laws
- *Legislative branch*: the branch of government that makes laws
- *Matthew Shepard and James Byrd Jr. Hate Crimes Prevention Act of 2009*: an act that provides funding and technical assistance to tribal, state, and local jurisdictions to help them more effectively investigate and prosecute hate crimes, including crimes against individuals on the basis of their sexual orientation or gender identity or expression (U.S. Department of Justice 2015)
- *McKinney–Vento Homeless Education Assistance Improvements Act of 2001*: an act that expanded the federal government's role in addressing youth homelessness through the public education system via various school-based homelessness assistance programs (U.S. Department of Education 2017)
- *Obergefell v. Hodges*: in 2015, the Supreme Court ruled by a vote of five to four that the Constitution guarantees the right to same-sex

marriage by both the Due Process Clause and the Equal Protection Clause of the Fourteenth Amendment to the U.S. Constitution
(SCOTUSblog 2017)

- *Opening Doors*: presented to Congress in 2010, the country's first
  comprehensive federal strategic plan to prevent and end homelessness, including youth homelessness (USICH 2015)
- *Quality-of-life offenses*: minor crimes (e.g., "public loitering, begging,
  drinking in public, using or selling drugs in public, urinating in
  public, prostitution, litter and graffiti") (Johnson et al. 2010, 19), the
  prosecution of which is perceived to negatively affect the quality of
  life of people experiencing homelessness
- *Runaway and Homeless Youth Act*: federal legislation that aims to
  eradicate youth homelessness through funding emergency shelters,
  family reunification, street outreach, and transitional housing; the act
  expired in 2013 and was reintroduced as the Runaway and Homeless
  Youth and Trafficking Prevention Act in 2022 and 2023, but it has
  not yet passed
- *Stewart B. McKinney Homeless Assistance Act of 1987*: the first major
  federal legislation to support the housing needs of people experiencing homelessness

CHAPTER HIGHLIGHTS

- The three branches of federal government—legislative, executive,
  and judicial—make, carry out, and interpret laws, respectively, and
  together serve as a system of checks and balances on each other as
  spelled out in the Constitution.
- Legislative action to support runaway youth emerged in 1974 with
  the Runaway Youth Act.
- The Runaway and Homeless Youth Act expired in 2013 and was
  reintroduced in 2022 and 2023 as the Runaway and Homeless Youth
  and Trafficking Prevention Act, but it has yet to be reauthorized.
- As an alternative to reauthorizing the Runaway and Homeless
  Youth and Trafficking Prevention Act in full, Congress extended the

Runaway and Homeless Youth Act for two years as part of the Juvenile Justice Reform Act of 2018.

- The Stewart B. McKinney Homeless Assistance Act of 1987 was the first major federal legislation to support the housing needs of people experiencing homelessness. It has been reauthorized and amended multiple times, most notably as the McKinney–Vento Homeless Education Assistance Improvements Act in 2001, when it was expanded to ensure protections for children and youth experiencing homelessness in the public education system.

- Youth aging out of foster care are vulnerable to becoming homeless. To address this, the Foster Care Independence Act of 1999 permitted more funds to be used to support independent living and expanded Medicaid up to the age of twenty-one, and the Fostering Connections to Success and Increasing Adoptions Act of 2008 extended the maximum age of foster care eligibility from eighteen to twenty-one.

- Between 2012 and 2016, the Obama administration issued guidelines and interpretations of existing policies to include protections for people based on their gender identity and expression (e.g., Title VII of the Civil Rights Act of 1964, Title IX of the Education Amendments of 1972) and for LGBTQ+ people (e.g., Department of Housing and Urban Development programs and services), thereby expanding protections and access to services and facilities for LGBTQ+ individuals. The first Trump administration reversed some of these policies and interpretations, but the Biden administration worked to restore rights and protections for members of the LGBTQ+ community, particularly in educational, housing, and workplace settings. The second Trump administration has weakened protections for LGBTQ+ people in Title VII by prioritizing meritocracy over the disparate impact experienced by protected classes (e.g., race, sex, age) (Wiessner 2025); in Title IX by reverting to the first Trump administration's policy, which had withdrawn the Obama administration's guidance that protected transgender students on the basis of sex; and in housing by no longer enforcing the 2016 Equal Access rule, which ensured access to HUD-funded housing regardless of sexual orientation or gender identity (Hollingsworth and Ho 2025).

10 | Advocacy

LEARNING OBJECTIVES

Readers of this chapter will be able to:

1. Define advocacy strategies, tactics, and targets,
2. Compare and contrast agency advocacy and legislative advocacy,
3. Explain various advocacy tactics and targets, and
4. Identify ways that one can become an ally.

CASE VIGNETTE: MIN-JI

Min-Ji, eighteen and cisgender, identifies as Korean American rather than as the more common but general "Asian American." She is a new student at a community college studying sociology with the hope of getting a job in which she can help other young people like herself. Min-Ji has been on her own for nearly a year and has struggled to stick with her plan of going to college after high school. During her junior year, Min-Ji noticed that her feelings about some girls were beginning to change from ones of friendship to ones of attraction. She'd thought about dating boys, but she never actively pursued a relationship with any. Midway through her senior year, difficulties with her parents came to a head when they assumed that their suspicions about Min-Ji "liking girls" were true and immediately restricted where she could go (mostly just to school), when and with whom she could hang out (no one, it seemed to Min-Ji), and when she was allowed to have her phone with her (only during school in case of emergency). Min-Ji often thought about leaving home, but she knew what it would do to her parents. On the other hand, she couldn't see herself not socializing and spending time with her friends until graduation— or later. She figured the longer she stayed at home, the more "stuck" she would become. Min-Ji got to a point where she needed to talk about the trouble she was having with her parents—and how it all started with her awareness that she might be lesbian. She confided in a couple of her close friends, one of whom got permission from her parents to let Min-Ji stay with them temporarily.

INTRODUCTION

Advocacy is a key component of the work of practitioners, policymakers, and researchers working with LGBTQ+ RHY. The goal of this chapter is to facilitate an increased understanding of the various strategies and tactics that LGBTQ+ RHY advocates use and of the targets at which they direct their efforts. The chapter begins with an overview of a definition of *advocacy* and a conceptual framework to guide advocacy practice in agencies and legislative settings. Next, we detail two types of strategies common among LGBTQ+ RHY advocates—agency advocacy and legislative advocacy—along with the common advocacy tactics used with each strategy. We provide examples of LGBTQ+ RHY efforts for each type of advocacy, as well as a list of advocacy organizations serving LGBTQ+ RHY. (See box 10.1, *Read All About It!*)

DEFINITION OF ADVOCACY

In Min-Ji's course on historically excluded youth, the professor mentioned that her city is home to a sizable number of "unaccompanied minors." Min-Ji felt

---

BOX 10.1. READ ALL ABOUT IT!
LGBTQ+ RHY ADVOCACY ORGANIZATIONS

- The following are advocacy organizations serving LGBTQ+ RHY:
  - Covenant House: https://www.covenanthouse.org/
  - Family Acceptance Project: http://familyproject.sfsu.edu/
  - Family Equality Council: https://www.familyequality.org/
  - GLAD Law (GLBTQ Legal Advocates and Defenders): https://www.gladlaw.org/
  - GLSEN: https://www.glsen.org
  - Human Rights Campaign: https://www.hrc.org/
  - Lambda Legal: https://www.lambdalegal.org/
  - Lyric Center for LGBTQQ+ Youth: http://lyric.org/
  - Matthew Shepard Foundation: http://www.matthewshepard.org/
  - PLFAG: https://pflag.org/
  - Safe Place: http://www.nationalsafeplace.org/
  - StandUp for Kids: http://www.standupforkids.org/
  - The Trevor Project: https://www.thetrevorproject.org/
  - True Colors United: https://truecolorsunited.org/

herself bristle at a term that sounded so clinical and impersonal. Having just turned eighteen, she knew she was no longer a minor, but she couldn't get over the fact that she fit that label as recently as a few months ago. Her instructor's description of these youths' experiences—her experiences—in what she perceived as a detached manner unsettled her. Since then, Min-Ji has thought more about serving other youth with similar experiences through advocacy, maybe even legislative advocacy, where she believes she may be able to make a greater impact than working with youth one-on-one. Min-Ji talked about her growing interest in advocacy with her academic adviser, who recommended adding social work and political science courses to her program.

Advocacy is a term with multiple definitions. In professions such as social work, advocacy is considered an ethical obligation. The *Social Work Dictionary* defines *advocacy* as "the act of directly representing or defending others" (Barker 2014, 10). Drawing from a review of more than ninety definitions of *advocacy* in the social work literature, Schneider and Lester

(2001) defined *social work advocacy* as "the exclusive and mutual representation of a client(s) or a cause in a forum, attempting to systematically influence decision-making in an unjust or unresponsive system(s)" (64–68). Similarly, Ezell (2001) defined *advocacy* as "purposive efforts to change specific existing or proposed policies or practices on behalf of or with a specific client or group of clients" (23). What these definitions have in common is that they describe advocacy as involving working with, or representing or defending, others in a systematic and purposeful way to influence or change existing or proposed policies or practices (Hoefer 2019). To accomplish this, advocates use specific **strategies** (i.e., long-range approaches and ultimate goals) and **tactics** (i.e., short-term or day-to-day maneuvers used to accomplish a strategy) to influence **targets** (i.e., an individual, group, community, or policy to be influenced or changed) (Barker 2014).

Advocacy can be performed by both members of a minoritized population and individuals outside that population who provide active support for the rights of members of the group (i.e., allies). **Allyship** is the act of demonstrating active support for the rights of members of a minoritized group and social causes of concern to the group by someone who is not a member of the group. Actions taken by allies may be on the micro level (e.g., supporting a friend's coming-out experience), the mezzo level (e.g., calling out a microaggression or act of discrimination in a school or workplace environment), or on the macro level (e.g., working for policy change that promotes equity and equality for LGBTQ+ populations, such as access to gender-affirming health care). Allyship is instrumental to advocacy efforts because it enables members of historically excluded populations to strengthen their power, status, privilege, and access to resources by building partnerships and coalitions (i.e., formal interagency relationships) across various sociodemographic groups committed to a common social cause. Allies of LGBTQ+ RHY communities show their commitment by informing themselves about definitions and issues of importance to the communities with whom they are allied; using their power and privilege to name and call out bullying, harassment, and discrimination; and supporting policies and procedures at work, at school, and in community spaces that promote equity and equality for people of diverse sexual orientations, gender identities, and housing statuses (Crawley 2021).

We outline two broad types of advocacy strategies and their accompanying tactics in this chapter and provide examples of national and local efforts around the country to change policies and practices for LGBTQ+ RHY related to discrimination in school, employment, and housing settings. It is important to note that each of these strategies can be carried out alone or in combination with each other and with other advocacy strategies outside the scope of this chapter, such as legal advocacy (e.g., litigation) and community advocacy (e.g., grassroots community organizing) (see Ezell [2001] for a review of other advocacy strategies). Further, tactics are not specific to any particular advocacy strategy; instead, advocates select the most appropriate tactic or tactics for each target they are trying to influence to accomplish their long-term goal or strategy (Ezell 2001).

TYPES OF ADVOCACY STRATEGIES

Min-Ji approached staff at a nonprofit family services agency near the college, asking if she could interview workers for an advocacy assignment. One of the program directors, Kayla, a social worker, was particularly receptive to Min-Ji's request and even suggested she play a community advocate role in helping the agency update their intake forms, a process that had been in the works for some time. Min-Ji told Kayla about her interest in helping youth who are unstably housed or experiencing homelessness, and Kayla shared that some of the families with whom her agency works are facing such challenges. Kayla encouraged Min-Ji to volunteer or consider the agency if she ever needed an internship. With that, Min-Ji was starting to see beyond her current reality and envision herself graduating from college, living independently, and making a difference in the lives of young people who are where she once was.

Agency Advocacy

One type of advocacy strategy designed to effect change in public-sector agencies or private organizations (both for-profit and nonprofit) to better serve the needs of clients and consumers is referred to as **agency advocacy**.

Using this strategy, agency advocates identify appropriate agency targets—policies, programs and services, or staff beliefs, attitudes, and practices—for change and use varied tactics to pressure agency decision-makers to make the needed changes (Ezell 2001). We discuss each of these targets next, as well as the tactics often used by advocates to influence change in agency settings.

Agency Policies

A common target for advocates is **agency policies**, which public agencies and private organizations develop to guide the development, implementation, evaluation, and monitoring of programs and services. These formal agency documents are typically put in writing and compiled in a policies-and-procedures manual or agency handbook, which is often made available for public viewing in an agency or organization. Advocates of agency change are interested in agency policies because these formal documents dictate how agencies engage, interact with, and support clients and consumers (Ezell 2001).

For organizations serving LGBTQ+ RHY, an agency advocate might adopt a tactic of meeting with private-sector agency officials to encourage (or pressure) them to adopt formal nondiscrimination or equal-employment-opportunity policies and make them available for public viewing in the agency. Posting these formal policies in public spaces can in turn contribute to the creation of a safe, respectful, and affirming agency environment. Staff from LGBTQ+-RHY-serving organizations note that these policies should not be relegated to a subsection of an agency handbook or policies-and-procedures manual but rather should permeate all agency interactions and practices (Ferguson-Colvin and Maccio 2012). These policies act as the agency's explicit commitment to LGBTQ+ RHY and guide all agency interactions with and practices for youth, staff, administration, volunteers, contractors, and members of boards of directors. Some of the commonly used policies in LGBTQ+-RHY-serving organizations are those relating to antidiscrimination, equal employment opportunities, harassment, client rights, sexuality and reproductive health, and interviewing new staff. Table 10.1 outlines a sample equal-employment-opportunity policy (Ferguson-Colvin and Maccio 2012).

TABLE 10.1 Sample equal-employment-opportunity policy

Equal Employment Opportunity Statement

[INSERT AGENCY NAME], in recognition of its responsibility, not only to its clients and employees, but also to the communities it serves, affirms its policy in regard to Executive Orders No. 11246 and 11141; Title VII of the Civil Rights Act of 1964; and the Americans with Disabilities Act of 1990, to hire qualified applicants and treat employees during their employment, without regard to race, religion, color, sex, age, national origin, sexual orientation, gender identity, and veteran status.

In carrying out the stated anti-discrimination policy, this organization will:

1. Recruit, hire and promote for all job classifications without regard to race, ethnicity, creed, color, national origin, sex, sexual orientation, gender identity or expression, disability, age, and veteran status, except when essential job functions indicate other considerations.

2. Base decisions on employment solely upon an individual's qualifications for which the individual is being considered.

3. Make promotional decisions based on the individual's qualifications for the position for which the individual is being considered.

4. Ensure that all other personnel actions, such as compensation, benefits, transfers, layoffs, return from layoff, and other related programs will be administered without regard to race, ethnicity, creed, color, national origin, sex, sexual orientation, gender identity or expression, disability, age, veteran status, and/or other characteristics prohibited by state and federal law (except where such constitutes a bona fide qualification permitted by law).

Source: New Beginnings (https://newbeginmaine.org/).

Agency advocates' work does not end once nondiscrimination or equal-employment-opportunity policies are in place. Rather, advocates then rely on additional tactics to monitor the implementation of these policies and hold agency officials and employees accountable. To ensure that LGBTQ+-RHY-serving organizations treat LGBTQ+ RHY with dignity, respect, and equality, agency advocates might also use monitoring tactics such as reviewing agency documents and annual reports, visiting the agency, and talking to agency staff and clients (Ezell 2001). Advocates recognize that respectful, inclusive, and affirming interactions between staff and youth, among staff members, and among youth depend on clear, explicit, and integrated agency policies (Ferguson-Colvin and Maccio 2012). Common areas to monitor using these tactics include proposed changes to agency rules, budget proposals, resource allocation, staff hiring, clients' outputs and outcomes, changes in agency policy or programs, and implementation practices related to agency policies and programs (Ezell 2001).

When agency advocates' efforts result in the positive outcome of LGBTQ+ RHY being treated with dignity, respect, and equality through agencies' policies and programs, advocates might use **friendly tactics** (i.e., conflict-reducing or consensus-building techniques) to share the positive findings with others (Jansson 2018). Some common friendly tactics used to disseminate positive findings include publicizing the findings with the broader public through traditional and social media outlets, sharing data and findings with policymakers, and approaching potential funders with evidence of positive client outputs and outcomes. Similarly, advocates can write to or meet with agency officials to thank them for their commitment to LGBTQ+ RHY and for creating affirming agency policies and programs. These tactics serve to reinforce the relationship between agency officials and advocates and to inform agency officials that advocates are continuing to carry out their watchdog function by monitoring the implementation of nondiscrimination policies (Ezell 2001).

Conversely, when advocates learn through their monitoring that LGBTQ+ RHY are continuing to experience discrimination, harassment, and violence in agencies, advocates have a choice of the type of tactics to employ. Advocates could again select friendly tactics by their area of concern and ask agency officials to take specific action. In this case, advocates might benefit from copying someone influential (e.g., a funder or policymaker) on a letter. They might also request a meeting with agency officials to state their case and make their request in person (Ezell 2001). If advocates do not receive their desired response, they might then consider using **adversarial tactics** (i.e., combative or conflict techniques) to pressure agency officials to make the desired change. In this case, advocates might consider exposing the agency's discriminatory practices or negative client outcomes through traditional media outlets (e.g., newspapers) or posting a negative review of the agency on social media. In these cases, advocates rely on the tactic of **shaming**, that is, publicly exposing discriminatory agency practices, to encourage policy improvements or compliance (Drinan 2002).

Agency Programs and Services

A second common target for agency advocates is programs and services. **Agency programs** are the key components of public agencies and private organizations that translate the agency's or organization's values and mission into actions that benefit clients and consumers. Programs are frequently characterized by their predefined goals and objectives, as well as the activities used to accomplish those goals and objectives (Netting et al. 2008). **Agency services** are the concrete tasks that agencies perform, which can be housed within programs (e.g., employment services), cut across programs (e.g., transportation services), or be separate from programs (e.g., intake services) (Netting et al. 2008). When agency programs and services are the target of change, advocates typically use the monitoring tactics described earlier (e.g., reviewing agency documents and annual reports, visiting the agency, talking to agency staff and clients) to ensure that program goals and objectives are being accomplished. Advocates might also use tactics such as meeting with program directors and going up the chain of command to make their case with more senior administrators if program directors are unresponsive. For particularly complex problems that arise at the programmatic or services level, advocates might develop or join a task force composed of agency staff, administrators, advocates, interested community parties, and clients to investigate problems and recommend solutions (Ezell 2001).

When advocates are involved in designing and implementing programs and services for LGBTQ+ RHY, they can be helpful to agency staff by recommending new ways to make their intake interviews (i.e., initial screening interviews with potential clients to assess their qualification for programs and services), assessment interviews (i.e., more in-depth interviews with clients in particular programs that address multiple life domains), and procedures more LGBTQ+-affirming. We next describe several recommendations for making intake and assessment interviews and procedures more LGBTQ+-affirming; these are based on our 2012 study of twenty-four staff from nineteen LGBTQ+-RHY-serving organizations across the United States (Ferguson-Colvin and Maccio 2012).

Intake Interviews Agency staff commonly recommend using short intake forms that collect just basic demographic information on young people requesting services. The purpose of the intake is to get to know the young people and make them feel welcomed and safe. The information gathered can also be used to improve agency programs and for agency funding proposals. Intake formats vary across agencies. Some agencies use an interview format in which an intake worker asks the youth questions. Others use a self-administered format in which the youth answers the questions on paper. Still others use a computer-based or online intake form in which the youth enters the information electronically. In many cases, the intake form is characteristically brief and asks demographic-related questions, and youth are allowed to use pseudonyms if desired (Ferguson-Colvin and Maccio 2012).

Intake questions regarding sexual orientation, gender identity, and gender pronouns may list common terms with check boxes that the youth can check as applicable, as well as an option of "other" with space provided for the youth to self-identify in the language they prefer. Intake forms may also include questions to identify LGBTQ+ allies, such as whether they feel they can contribute to the agency's LGBTQ+-affirming environment. Some agency staff might prefer not to directly ask about sexual orientation or gender identity at intake. In these cases, agencies can ask questions that indirectly lead to discussions of sexuality and gender identity (e.g., "Who are you attracted to?"), or they can gather the information only if the youth volunteers it. Staff at agencies that used intake forms that did not ask specifically about sexual orientation and gender identity noted that these questions are omitted early on in the interview process so that youth do not feel pressured to self-identify until they feel comfortable with staff and safe in the agency space (Ferguson-Colvin and Maccio 2012).

Assessment Interviews Agency staff commonly recommend that once youth feel more comfortable and safer at the agency and with the staff, staff should invite them to complete a lengthier, one-on-one assessment with a trusted staff member. Staff performing these assessments commonly explain to the youth that the purpose of the assessment is to determine their needs, strengths, and life goals, as well as the types of agency services or referrals they may want. Across LGBTQ+-RHY-serving agencies, assessment interviews are largely strengths based and include questions regarding the youth's holistic selves (i.e., mind, body, and spirit), such as demographics, strengths, interests, life and treatment goals, willingness to exit the streets, physical and mental health, services requested, and high-risk behaviors (Ferguson-Colvin and Maccio 2012).

Assessment interviews are typically conducted in a private room in the agency or in another private space that is comfortable and familiar to the youth. For smaller agencies with limited private space, agencies might use a sound machine or sound-masking device to reduce distractions and better protect the youth's confidentiality. An interview format is commonly used, although some agencies might use self-assessment, either paper or computer based, to enable the youth to respond privately to more personal questions (e.g., around high-risk or illegal behaviors). Assessments include questions about the youth's sexual practices and sexual partners to provide staff with more information on sexual risk and health behaviors. Table 10.2 provides sample questions about sexual orientation, gender identity, and gender pronouns that advocates might use to improve existing intake or assessment forms at LGBTQ+-RHY-serving organizations (Ferguson-Colvin and Maccio 2012).

Agency Staff Beliefs, Attitudes, and Practices

A third common target for advocates interested in agency change is the beliefs, attitudes, and practices of agency staff. Advocates recognize that staff's attitudes and beliefs influence how they interact with and administer programs and services to clients. Similarly, advocates understand that agencies frequently standardize service delivery in that service providers are trained in a particular approach and implement services according to a manual or set of practice guidelines. As such, advocates commonly rely on tactics such as monitoring agency practices and hiring decisions, conducting the training of new and existing staff, and holding meetings with agency officials to ensure that agency staff think and act in an LGBTQ+-affirming manner (Ezell 2001).

TABLE 10.2 Sample questions about sexual orientation, gender identity, and gender pronouns

What is your sexual orientation?

☐ gay, ☐ lesbian, ☐ bisexual, ☐ straight, ☐ MSM [men who have sex with men],
☐ unsure/questioning, ☐ asexual, ☐ pansexual, ☐ refused,
☐ _____ (please fill in with your own response)

What is your gender identity?

☐ male, ☐ female, ☐ trans male, ☐ trans female, ☐ genderqueer, ☐ intersex, ☐ refused,
☐ _____ (please fill in with your own response)

What gender pronouns do you use?

☐ he/him, ☐ she/her, ☐ ze/zir, ☐ none, ☐ refused,
☐ _____ (please fill in with your own response)

Other variations of these questions:

How do you identify?

☐ affirmed female, ☐ affirmed male, ☐ genderqueer, ☐ refused,
☐ _____ (please fill in with your own response)

Who are you attracted to?

☐ men/males, ☐ women/females, ☐ both, ☐ neither, ☐ refused,
☐ _____ (please fill in with your own response)

LGBTQ+-RHY-serving organizations typically screen for LGBTQ+-affirming values, beliefs, and practices among potential staff through their hiring process. Advocates have been helpful in this process by educating human resources and other hiring staff about ways in which interviewees can be screened for knowledge of LGBTQ+-related issues and their own LGBTQ+-affirming values. Table 10.3 offers some sample interview questions from LGBTQ+-RHY-serving organizations for hiring new staff (Ferguson-Colvin and Maccio 2012).

With respect to promoting LGBTQ+-affirming values among existing staff, agency advocates are helpful in offering cultural diversity and standards-of-care trainings to ensure that all staff, volunteers, and collaborating partners from external agencies are LGBTQ+-affirming in their beliefs and practices. Common themes covered in cultural diversity and

TABLE 10.3 Sample interview questions for hiring new staff

1. Administrative assistant/secretary position: We provide training on HIV/AIDS prevention and substance abuse. We provide services to gay and lesbian youth, and we have condoms and lubricant available for youth at all of our sites. What is your comfort level with these issues? What is your comfort level in answering questions about safe-sex practices and prevention methods from the youth?

2. Resident staff, shelter: A resident tells you that he/she/they is/are gay, lesbian, bisexual, transgender, queer, or questioning. How would you respond? How would you handle this youth being teased by others?

3. Dayroom counselor, drop-in center: You have the afternoon shift on the dayroom floor. A verbal argument breaks out between two youth. One youth makes a derogatory slur about the sexual orientation of the other youth. What do you do? How do you respond?

4. Administrative/bookkeeper position: A new staff member is hired and comes to you to do the necessary employment paperwork. The staff member tells you that she is married and that her wife will be on her health care plan. How would you respond? Please incorporate your existing knowledge of federal same-sex marriage laws into your response.

standards-of-care trainings include LGBTQ+ terminology (including terms related to sexual orientation, gender identity, and gender pronouns), the coming-out process, LGBTQ+-affirmative practice models, safe-sex practices, substance abuse, harm reduction, stress and resiliency, trauma-informed care, adolescent development, family conflict, anti-oppression,[1] how to interact with LGBTQ+ RHY, and how to create safe, affirming environments for LGBTQ+ RHY (Ferguson-Colvin and Maccio 2012).

In some cases, agency staff develop their training curricula from existing sources, including their own experiences working with LGBTQ+ RHY. When staff have in-house training experts (e.g., staff or youth clients), they might rely on these staff and youth clients to administer the trainings themselves. In other cases, agencies may hire external trainers (or advocates) to

---

[1] See Martin Rochlin, *Heterosexual Questionnaire* (Gender and Sexuality Center, 1972), https://www.uwgb.edu/UWGBCMS/media/pride-center/files/pdf/Heterosexual_Questionnaire.pdf; Peggy McIntosh, *White Privilege: Unpacking the Invisible Knapsack* (Wellesley Centers for Women, Wellesley College, 1988), https://www.wcwonline.org/images/pdf/Knapsack_plus_Notes-Peggy_McIntosh.pdf.

offer on-site trainings to staff. And some agencies mandate staff to attend existing trainings offered in the community at local community colleges, universities, and LGBTQ+-affirming organizations. It is common for agencies to use combinations of in-person and free online trainings and webinars for their staff. Some agencies also employ youth clients to cofacilitate portions of trainings in an effort to personalize the trainings by incorporating clients' lived experiences. Staff in-services, weekly staff forums, staff retreats, and staff meetings are all common venues at which trainings can be administered. Box 10.2, *Read All About It!*, provides information about

BOX 10.2. READ ALL ABOUT IT!
ORGANIZATIONS OFFERING CULTURAL DIVERSITY
AND STANDARDS-OF-CARE TRAINING

- **Hollywood Homeless Youth Partnership (HHYP):** "The HHYP works to shape the service environment, increase youth access to housing and supportive services, and advocate for policy changes needed to prevent and end youth homelessness" (HHYP n.d., Our Collaborative). "The HHYP sponsors regular training for member agencies. Additionally, HHYP members are available for training, consultation, information sharing and select research collaboration" (HHYP n.d.).

  ○ HHYP website: https://hhyp.org
  ○ Training website: https://nhchc.org/wp-content/uploads/2020/01/Providing-Services-for-Homeless-Youth-Supervision-Guide.pdf

- **Interagency Task Force on Trauma-Informed Care:** The Substance Abuse and Mental Health Services Administration's (SAMHSA's) Interagency Task Force "identifies, evaluates, and makes recommendations about: Best practices for supporting children, youth, and families affected by trauma [and] How Federal agencies can better respond to trauma, like substance use disorders, in families" (SAMHSA 2022b, What Are the Goals).
- **Intergroup Relations, CommonGround:** CommonGround is a student-led, student-serving program—for student organizations, residence halls, Greek life, academic courses, and other student communities—to nurture social identity development and enhance

group dynamics. Through our 1.5–3 hour interactive workshops, trained graduate and undergraduate facilitators guide your group through a series of activities and discussions, raising understanding of social identity, prejudice, stereotyping, power, privilege, and oppression—and building a community of social justice advocates on campus" (University of Michigan n.d.).

- ○ Intergroup Relations website: https://igr.umich.edu/commonground
- ○ Consultations and Training website: https://igr.umich.edu/consultations

- **National Child Traumatic Stress Initiative (NCTSI):** The NCTSI "raises awareness about the impact of trauma on children and adolescents as a behavioral health concern. NCTSI's goal is to transform mental health care for children and adolescents affected by trauma throughout the country by improving the quality of community-based trauma treatment and services and increasing access to effective trauma-focused interventions" (NCTSI n.d.).

- ○ NCTSI website: https://www.samhsa.gov/mental-health/trauma-violence/nctsi
- ○ Child Trauma resources website: https://www.samhsa.gov/mental-health/trauma-violence/child-trauma

- **National Child Traumatic Stress Network (NCTSN):** The NCTSN "was created by Congress in 2000 as part of the Children's Health Act to raise the standard of care and increase access to services for children and families who experience or witness traumatic events. Since its inception, the NCTSN has trained more than two million professionals in trauma-informed interventions" (NCTSN n.d.b).

- ○ NCTSN website: https://www.nctsn.org/
- ○ Training website: https://www.nctsn.org/resources/training

- **Runaway and Homeless Youth Training, Technical Assistance, and Capacity Building Center (RHYTTAC):** The RHYTTAC is "funded by the Department of Health and Human Services, Administration for Children and Families, Family and Youth Services Bureau (FYSB) as the training and technical assistance provider for all runaway and homeless youth (RHY) grantees. RHYTTAC will assist FYSB grantee agencies in developing effective approaches to serving runaway and homeless youth, accessing new resources, and establishing linkages with other programs with similar interests and concerns" (RHYTTAC n.d.b).

- ○ RHYTTAC website: https://www.rhyttac.net/
- ○ Training website: https://www.rhyttac.net/training

(*continued on next page*)

(continued from previous page)

- **SAMHSA Homeless and Housing Resource Center (HHRC):** "HHRC was established in August 2020 with funding from the Substance Abuse and Mental Health Services Administration (SAMHSA). Operated by Policy Research, Inc., HHRC works in partnership with national experts in homelessness, mental health, and substance use services to be a centralized hub of easily accessible, no-cost training for health and housing professionals in evidence-based practices that contributes to housing stability, recovery, and an end to homelessness" (SAMHSA 2022a).

  ○ HHRC website: https://hhrctraining.org/
  ○ Training website: https://hhrctraining.org/training-courses

- **U.S. Department of Labor:** "The Department of Labor administers programs providing employment and training services that are crucial components in the comprehensive efforts to address the cycle of homelessness. The Department offers both mainstream and targeted employment-focused programs that help lead to self-sufficiency. The DOL strategy focuses on helping homeless Americans who want to work or can become job-ready. DOL's objectives are to: 1) provide access to mainstream employment assistance and services, and 2) identify skill needs in today's workforce and address skill deficiencies of this population" (NASW n.d.).

  ○ Department of Labor website: https://www.dol.gov
  ○ Training website: https://www.dol.gov/dol/audience/aud-homeless.htm

various local and national organizations that offer free and low-cost, in-person and online (live and on-demand) trainings, webinars, and technical assistance related to cultural diversity and standards of care for LGBTQ+-RHY-serving organizations (Ferguson-Colvin and Maccio 2012).

Once affirming staff are hired and trained, advocates could continue to use tactics such as agency monitoring to ensure that staff provide a safe and affirming environment—in both the agency and partner organizations to which LGBTQ+ RHY are referred. Similarly, advocates could use initial trainings and follow-up (booster) trainings with agency staff to continue to ensure that all staff and volunteers—existing and new—undergo regular diversity trainings. Cultural humility and standards-of-care trainings, which are more specific and in-depth than diversity trainings, are recommended for all direct-services workers. Trainings for staff in LGBTQ+-RHY-serving organizations should be comprehensive, covering all aspects of LGBTQ+ youth development, biopsychosocial risks, and LGBTQ+-affirmative practice. Trainings should also rely on evidence-based curricula and reputable experts in the field of LGBTQ+ health and wellness. Trainings should incorporate topics often overlooked in LGBTQ+ trainings, such as reproductive health, legal concerns and needs, and transgender issues. Trainings should also include clear procedures for how staff should intervene and redirect youth or other staff or volunteers whenever homophobic, biphobic, transphobic, or heterophobic or cissexist comments are made in agencies (Ferguson-Colvin and Maccio 2012).

Legislative Advocacy

A second type of strategy common among LGBTQ+ RHY advocates, **legislative advocacy**, targets legislative bodies at the federal, state, or local level to change policy (i.e., federal or state laws, local ordinances, municipal codes, or budgets) to better serve clients or constituents (Ezell 2001). Legislative advocates and **lobbyists** (a lobbyist being "a provider of information on the effects of a particular piece of legislation, from the vantage point of the interest group that he or she represents") (Melton 1983, 138–39) often represent populations experiencing powerlessness, stigmatization, and oppression in an effort to influence lawmakers to defeat harmful policies, change or improve existing policies, or develop new policies to enhance clients' or constituents' overall opportunities and well-being (Jansson 2018). Advocates for legislative change identify appropriate targets (i.e., specific federal, state, or city legislators or legislative bodies) and select the most appropriate tactic or tactics for each (Ezell 2001).

Whether their targets are federal, state, or local (city or county) legislators, advocates know that to be successful in their efforts to influence policy and policymakers (i.e., targets), they must understand the policymaking process (see chapter 9 for a review of the policymaking process). The policymaking process consists of the procedures by which policy proposals (or bills) are introduced, debated, enacted, implemented, monitored, and evaluated (for a more detailed description of the making of governmental policy, see Karger and Stoesz 2014). Effective advocates know whom specifically they are targeting with their change effort at the federal, state, or local level. Common legislative targets at the federal level include U.S. representatives and U.S. senators. At the state level, common targets include state representatives (or assemblymembers) and state senators. And at the local level, common targets are members of county boards of supervisors and city council members. (See box 10.3, *Read All About It!*)

Advocates understand that one of the first steps in the policymaking process is for a bill to be assigned to a committee and that a bill's success in becoming law depends on its ability to be successfully voted out of committee. They learn which committee their bill of interest has been assigned to and who the chair overseeing that committee is. Advocates also develop

BOX 10.3. READ ALL ABOUT IT! WEBSITES TO IDENTIFY FEDERAL, STATE, AND LOCAL LEGISLATORS

- **Federal: U.S. Congress**
  - U.S. House of Representatives: http://www.house.gov/representatives/find/
  - U.S. Senate: http://www.senate.gov/states/
- **State: State legislatures**
  - Plural, "Find your Local Legislator": https://pluralpolicy.com/find-your-legislator/
  - Common Cause, "Find Your Representatives": https://www.commoncause.org/find-your-representative/
  - Visit the home page of your state's state legislature and search for your district
- **Local: County boards of supervisors or city councils**
  - Visit the home page of your city's city council or your county's county board of supervisors and search for your district

multisession plans (e.g., lasting through the current legislative session plus at least another year) to get their bills enacted and work to increase sponsorship and bipartisan support for their bills. They monitor the progress of their legislation and provide the sponsor with data and information about the bill as a resource. They may also provide testimony on the bill at hearings and maintain regular communication with bill sponsors through letter writing, position papers, phone calls, emails, and personal visits (Ezell 2001). We next discuss common targets at each of the three levels of government, as well as tactics commonly used by LGBTQ+ RHY advocates to influence changes in legislation.

Federal Policies Advocates who represent LGBTQ+ RHY and are interested in federal legislation target legislators from the U.S. House of Representatives or Senate. An example of current federal policies and policy proposals relevant to LGBTQ+ RHY is the reauthorization of the Runaway and Homeless Youth Act. (See box 10.4, *What Do You Think?*) Advocates working at the federal level might start by joining or organizing a network of advocates or coalition of organizations that work with LGBTQ+ RHY to establish a strong base of interest in and support for a policy proposal. The assumption here is that the greater the number of advocates and organizations interested in LGBTQ+ RHY issues across the country, the more policymakers these advocates will be able to reach and the greater their chances of successfully influencing policy (Ezell 2001).

Federal advocates might use the tactic of monitoring legislation to determine whether a similar existing bill has been introduced and, if so, what the bill's outcome was. Once a bill is introduced, advocates continue monitoring its progress to track how much support the bill is receiving, whether revisions have considerably changed the original bill, and what progress the bill is making through the legislative process.

Advocates might also engage in tactics such as **lobbying** (i.e., efforts to convince legislators to introduce or vote in favor or against a bill) and **testifying** before a committee at a legislative hearing (i.e., making public remarks to legislators in support of or opposition to a bill and providing specific reasons for their view). Using their network of advocates or coalition of organizations, advocates might also apply the tactic of alerting

BOX 10.4. WHAT DO YOU THINK?
LEGISLATIVE ADVOCACY

- Imagine that you are a legislative advocate whose aim is to see the Runaway and Homeless Youth Act reauthorized beyond its current funding, which expired in 2020.
    - What is a friendly tactic you could use based on past reauthorizations, most recently under the Juvenile Justice Reform Act of 2018?
    - What is an adversarial tactic you could use based on the failed reauthorization under the proposed Runaway and Homeless Youth and Trafficking Prevention Act of 2018, which would, among other provisions, "ensure trafficking is prevented and victims are served through outreach, identification, prevention, referrals and reporting" (FFCC 2018, 34)?
    - Visit Congress.gov (https://www.congress.gov/). Click on the drop-down menu in the upper left-hand corner, and change "Current Congress" to "All Congresses." In the search field, type "Runaway and Homeless Youth and Trafficking Prevention Act of 2023" (with the quotation marks). Click on each of the bills: House (H.R. 6041) and Senate (S.3125). Who were the bills' sponsors? To which committees were the bills referred? How could you use this information in your advocacy of the legislation?

constituents (i.e., registered voters) to contact the representatives in their district to voice their support for or opposition to a particular bill. Legislative advocates might also seek the signing of or an executive veto on a bill that has successfully passed Congress. In this case, advocates might rely on activities such as phoning, emailing, letter writing, and meeting in person with officials from the executive branch (i.e., the president or White House staff) to voice their support or concerns for a policy (Ezell 2001).

State Policies

Advocates who represent LGBTQ+ RHY and are interested in state legislation target legislators from their state assembly (or house) or their state senate.

In many states, people can still be terminated from employment and denied housing (when such is not funded by the U.S. Department of Housing and Urban Development) if they identify as LGBTQ+ (Becker 2014; Bradford et al. 2013; Pizer et al. 2011). These discriminatory practices are particularly problematic for LGBTQ+ RHY who depend on both employment and housing to successfully exit homelessness. The Human Rights Campaign has developed the State Equality Index (https://www.hrc.org/resources/state-equality-index), a "state-by-state summary of LGBTQ laws and policies" (HRC n.d.a, n.d.b) with which they rate all fifty states and Washington, DC, on a variety of statewide laws and policies that affect LGBTQ+ individuals and their families across many domains of law, including nondiscrimination, parenting, hate crime, youth, and health and safety. Once statewide advocates have a specific policy or policy proposal in mind and identify the most appropriate target or targets, they rely on tactics similar to those employed at the federal level, including organizing networks and coalitions, legislative monitoring, lobbying, testifying, alerting constituents, and contacting executive officials (i.e., governors or governors' staff) at the state level (Ezell 2001).

Local Policies

Advocates who represent LGBTQ+ RHY and are interested in local legislation target members of the county board of supervisors or their city council. Many cities continue to lack antidiscrimination ordinances in employment, housing, and public accommodations, as well as antibullying school policies and LGBTQ+ police liaisons or task forces (Herman et al. 2017). In addition to the State Equality Index, the Human Rights Campaign (HRC n.d.a) has developed the Municipal Equality Index (https://www.hrc.org /resources/municipal-equality-index) to evaluate the level of inclusiveness in municipal laws, policies, and services toward LGBTQ+ individuals who live and work in various cities. The Municipal Equality Index rates 506 cities from across all states on their nondiscrimination laws, the municipality as an employer, municipal services, law enforcement, and the city leadership's public position on equality.

Once local advocates identify a particular policy or policy proposal and identify the correct target or targets, they rely on tactics similar to those employed at the federal and state levels, such as organizing local networks and coalitions, monitoring city or county policies, lobbying, testifying, alerting constituents, and contacting executive officials (i.e., mayors or mayoral staff) at the local level (Ezell 2001).

In our experience over the past two decades as faculty at schools of social work, we often hear students ask, "But I am just a student. How can I get involved in legislative advocacy?" It is our experience that students can—and often do—play an important role as legislative advocates through internships and course assignments by monitoring legislation, drafting and refining bills, recruiting bill sponsors, conducting policy analyses, and applying theoretical frameworks and research evidence to the policy-making process (Sherraden et al. 2002). Table 10.4 provides a sample job description for a part-time legislative advocacy student intern (e.g., from

TABLE 10.4 Sample job description for a part-time legislative advocacy student intern

Part-time (16 hours per week) student intern to assist the communications team as follows:

Typical responsibilities and learning outcomes will include:

- Tracking legislation through the state and federal processes that could affect [*agency name*] (and the LGBTQ+ RHY population) and/or with which [*agency name*] should exert a presence
- Researching policy issues related to LGBTQ+ youth homelessness and background research on evidence-based policies and programs to prepare [*agency name*] staff for meetings with public officials
- Assisting the communications team to schedule and attend meetings with public officials
- Attending meetings and hearings with public officials for documentation and reporting purposes
- Performing follow-up work under the direction of the communications team as the result of meetings and hearings with public officials (e.g., recommending action strategies and tactics for continued advocacy)
- Under guidance/development of the communications team, creating and issuing social media alerts, advisories, infographics, and campaigns pertaining to legislative or policy issues of interest to LGBTQ+ RHY and [*agency name*]
- Under guidance/development of the communications team, developing policy position statements, papers, or articles on topical issues of interest to LGBTQ+ RHY and [*agency name*]

a Master of Social Work or related program) that could be tailored to an agency looking to incorporate a student legislative advocacy intern to track and monitor legislation that supports LGBTQ+ RHY.

SUMMARY

Advocacy with and on behalf of vulnerable populations is common practice among social workers and others in the helping professions. Given their sexual orientation and identity, their gender identity and expression, and their age (as well as other intersecting identities common among this population, such as identifying as a racial or ethnic minority, having a physical or intellectual disability, or having a mental disorder or substance use problem), LGBTQ+ youth are among society's most vulnerable. Two strategies commonly used by LGBTQ+ RHY advocates are agency advocacy and legislative advocacy, each with its own targets and tactics. Targets of agency advocacy are typically agency policies (e.g., endorsing nondiscrimination policies), programs (e.g., eliminating sexual reorientation programs), and services (e.g., promoting best practices and standards of care). Targets of legislative advocacy are typically legislative bodies (e.g., city councils), legislators (e.g., state senators or representatives or assemblymembers), or specific pieces of legislation (e.g., the Runaway and Homeless Youth and Trafficking Prevention Act).

REVISITING MIN-JI

- Min-Ji chose to shift her focus from working with youth one-on-one to working on their behalf as an advocate. She thought that by doing so, she would be able to make a greater impact. Does one approach to working with this population make more of an impact than the other? What are some similarities and differences between them?
- Min-Ji approached the agency by identifying herself as a student working on an advocacy assignment. How might the outcome have been different had Min-Ji not identified herself as a student (but

perhaps as a concerned citizen, for example) or had she not identified the purpose of her inquiry as needing to complete an advocacy assignment?

- As an unstably housed person herself, would Min-Ji be able to volunteer at an agency that saw clients and families in situations similar to hers? Should she, or would she have to, disclose her housing status and living situation?
- When Min-Ji decides to pursue legislative or other types of advocacy on this issue, what might her tactics be? What or who might her targets be? That is, what should she expect local, state, or federal legislation to contain with regard to race and ethnicity, for example?
- If you were in Min-Ji's class and had been assigned an advocacy interview, what population and topic would you choose? Which agencies might you approach for an interview? Why?
- What legislative or agency advocacy strategies and tactics have you learned about or used with or on behalf of vulnerable populations that Min-Ji could use to advocate for RHY, including LGBTQ+ youth?

KEY CONCEPTS

- *Adversarial tactics*: combative or conflict techniques to pressure agency officials to make a desired change
- *Advocacy*: working with or representing or defending others in a systematic and purposeful way to influence or change existing or proposed policies or practices (Hoefer 2019)
- *Agency advocacy*: a strategy designed to effect change in public-sector agencies or private organizations (both for-profit and nonprofit) to better serve the needs of clients and consumers
- *Agency policies*: formal agency documents that public agencies and private organizations develop to guide the development, implementation, evaluation, and monitoring of programs and services and dictate how agencies engage, interact with, and support clients and consumers

- *Agency programs*: key components of public agencies and private organizations that translate the agency's or organization's values and mission into actions that benefit clients and consumers; frequently characterized by their predefined goals and objectives and the activities used to accomplish those goals and objectives (Netting et al. 2008)
- *Agency services*: concrete tasks agencies perform, which can be housed in programs (e.g., employment services), cut across programs (e.g., transportation services), or be separate from programs (e.g., intake services) (Netting et al. 2008)
- *Allyship*: active support for members of a minoritized group (e.g., LGBTQ+ individuals) and social causes of concern to that group by someone outside the group (e.g., heterosexual individuals, cisgender individuals)
- *Friendly tactics*: conflict-reducing or consensus-building techniques
- *Legislative advocacy*: influencing legislative bodies at the federal, state, or local level to change policy (i.e., federal or state laws, local ordinances, municipal codes, or budgets) to better serve clients or constituents (Ezell 2001)
- *Lobbying*: efforts to convince legislators to introduce or vote in favor or against a bill
- *Lobbyist*: "a provider of information on the effects of a particular piece of legislation, from the vantage point of the interest group that he or she represents" (Melton 1983, 138–39)
- *Shaming*: publicly exposing agency practices that are discriminatory to encourage policy improvements or compliance
- *Strategies*: long-range approaches and ultimate goals (Barker 2014)
- *Tactics*: short-term or day-to-day maneuvers used to accomplish a strategy (Barker 2014)
- *Targets*: an individual, group, community, or policy to be influenced or changed (Barker 2014)
- *Testifying*: speaking before a committee at a legislative hearing (i.e., public remarks made to legislators in support of or opposition to a bill citing specific reasons for that support or opposition)

CHAPTER HIGHLIGHTS

- Advocacy is achieved through specific strategies (i.e., long-range approaches and ultimate goals) and tactics (i.e., short-term or day-to-day maneuvers used to accomplish a strategy) to influence targets (i.e., an individual, group, community, or policy to be influenced or changed).

- Tactics can be friendly or adversarial depending on the outcome of previous advocacy efforts. Favorable outcomes may warrant friendly tactics, whereas negative outcomes may call for adversarial tactics.

- Common advocacy strategies are agency advocacy and legislative advocacy.

- Targets of agency advocacy include policies, programs, and services, whereas legislative advocacy entails supporting or opposing legislation, legislators, or legislative bodies.

- Intake interviews and assessment interviews are two services that advocates target for improvement. Many LGBTQ+ RHY service providers adhere to LGBTQ+-affirming interview policies that dictate where, how, and by whom interviews should be conducted, as well as the nature and wording of assessment questions.

- Advocates are keen to monitor agencies' personnel decisions and professional development opportunities and may offer to educate staff about hiring practices and provide cultural humility and standards-of-care trainings.

- Legislative advocates focus their efforts at the local, state, or federal level by lobbying lawmakers or testifying during congressional committee hearings, for example.

- Students can engage in advocacy at any level, such as by interning at advocacy agencies or organizations or through service-learning or other civic engagement assignments in policy courses, for example.

- Allies of LGBTQ+RHY communities show their support by educating themselves on terms, concepts, and issues of importance to those communities; using their power and privilege to speak up and speak out against bullying, harassment, and discrimination; and supporting policies and procedures at work, at school, and in community spaces that promote equity and equality for people of diverse sexual orientations, gender identities, and housing statuses.

IV | The Future

11 | Recommendations

LEARNING OBJECTIVES

Readers of this chapter will be able to:

1. Identify gaps in LGBTQ+ RHY programs, research, and policies,
2. Summarize the impact that those gaps have on the LGBTQ+ RHY population, and
3. Describe recommendations to fill these gaps.

CASE VIGNETTE: AARON

Aaron, nineteen, proudly identifies as a young, Black transgender man, but that wasn't the case not too long ago. During the ninth and tenth grades, before he came out, he considered himself an ally to the LGBTQ+ community and was a member of his high school's gay–straight alliance. Toward the end of tenth grade, Aaron came out as lesbian, an identity that seemed to fit with what he was feeling. However, after about a year, Aaron noticed that "something still didn't seem right." The more he heard transgender youth in the gay–straight alliance talk about their experience of realizing their true gender, the more he thought their narrative sounded a lot like what he was experiencing. After several months, Aaron felt safe enough in the group to disclose his gender identity as a transgender man—his true, authentic self.

INTRODUCTION

After reading this book, it might seem that, although there are areas in the field of LGBTQ+ RHY that are rich in knowledge and activity, there are many others where apparently little is known or being done. Keep in mind, though, that, with the exception of chapter 8, much of what we have presented here reflects the current state of **research knowledge**. Equally valid (or, as some might argue, more valid), is **practice knowledge**: knowledge gained by doing. The seasoned practitioner reading the preceding chapters could likely inform responses to many of the unanswered questions posed by the extant literature based on their own encounters with LGBTQ+ RHY. Practitioner knowledge is disseminated through trainee supervision, professional development workshops, classroom lectures, conference presentations, and other interfaces where knowledge is shared. Even though it may not be reflected here, much of the knowledge to fill the gaps is out there. It exists in the practice and education communities, as well as in the LGBTQ+ RHY who teach us.

Valid, too, is **practice wisdom**, which is harder to define and capture but is no less critical to the services provided to LGBTQ+ RHY. Practice wisdom, as Higgs (2019) explains, is a combination of **theoretical knowledge** and **experiential learning**, a blend of epistemology and ontology that creates a new form of knowing:

> Practice knowledge incorporates learned propositional knowledge about practice, and is enriched through experience-based knowledge gained through professional practice. The sum of a practitioner's professional knowledge and capacity to use this knowledge in practice is progressively transformed and enhanced, becoming qualitatively different. This

increasingly complex phenomenon becomes practice wisdom when it is practised and actuated wisely. This is illustrated in the use of professional judgement, particularly in situations of great complexity and uncertainty where rules and prescribed findings from research are inadequate to deal with wicked problems and lack the essential wisdom of particularity and situatedness. Practice wisdom occurs in spaces beyond the notion of expertise and learned reasoning. Such practice wisdom holds no less responsibility for the quality of practice for the client, but rests on an inherently richer, deeper and more humanly complex realisation of lived reality, creative understanding and human interests. (4)

By blending their praxis and theoretical knowledge, practitioners can meet the client, as Higgs (2019) suggested, "in spaces beyond the notion of expertise and learned reasoning" (4) to answer questions, solve problems, and resolve ethical dilemmas not always addressed by theoretical knowledge. As the clinical psychologist Cynthia Baum-Baicker (2018) wrote, "*Clinical Wisdom* is the linchpin between theory and practice" (emphasis in the original). We encourage you to draw on various sources of knowledge, including what we have amassed here. This chapter summarizes our recommendations for practice, research, and policy based on what we have found (or not found) in the literature, as well as on our own research with LGBTQ+ RHY and the providers who serve them.

PRACTICE

RHY-serving agencies and organizations operate largely in the nonprofit sector, forcing them to compete for precious dollars that seem to be increasingly scarce. Program directors and other administrators and staff are having to do more with less while maintaining a standard of care that meets the needs of a very vulnerable population and keeps them safe in the process. Some of the recommendations we pose here, although ideal, may not be feasible, given the funding challenges RHY organizations often face. Others require little to no funding, just a desire to meet LGBTQ+ RHY where they are.

Sexual Orientation and Gender Identity Data

Agencies collect demographic and other background information on their clients and consumers for several reasons: to identify a profile of the clients they serve, to apply for demographic-determinant funding, and to report outcomes to interested parties. However, demographic questions are not always standardized, and questions about sexual orientation and gender identity are sometimes exclusionary (e.g., "Do you identify as lesbian, gay, or straight?"), archaic (e.g., "Do you identify as heterosexual or homosexual?"), or mutually exclusive (i.e., "Do you identify as straight, lesbian, gay, bisexual, or transgender?"), if they are asked at all. Asking LGBTQ+ RHY about their sexual orientation and gender identity, and doing so in clear, affirming ways, gives them the opportunity to identify themselves at intake if they choose to do so, making visible an often invisible population. Having this information helps agencies meet the needs of their LGBTQ+ RHY clients in a culturally competent and LGBTQ+-affirming manner. Conversely, some staff may not collect this information because they do not want to know the youths' sexual orientation or gender identity, either based on an unwritten "don't ask, don't tell" policy or because they do not wish to serve LGBTQ+ youth. Some agencies require LGBTQ+ youth to keep quiet about their sexual and gender identities ("don't say gay"), while others bar these youth from accessing their programs and services altogether (Nolan 2018; Woronoff et al. 2006). LGBTQ+ RHY should be validated, not silenced or turned away.

Professional Mental Health Staff

Given the high rates of depression, anxiety, post-traumatic stress disorder (PTSD), and suicide among this population (Bidell 2014; Rhoades et al. 2018), mental health professionals should be fixtures of all RHY agencies. Licensed social workers, counselors, and psychologists, among others, can provide weekly psychotherapy and counseling sessions, respond to acute mental health crises, and make referrals for inpatient or intensive outpatient treatment, substance abuse treatment, or other supportive services. A repertoire of assessment and screening instruments can help clinicians spot mental and behavioral health problems that might not be evident on the surface. When administered during or soon after a youth's intake session, needs and challenges can be addressed sooner rather than later, stemming problematic and distressing symptoms. Prevention and early intervention can mitigate negative outcomes by getting youth the help they need when they need it.

Transgender and Nonbinary Youth Housing

When it comes to housing transgender and nonbinary RHY in shared living spaces, agencies must consider inclusivity, safety, and funding constraints. Inclusive housing allows all youth equal access to available rooms, floors, or apartments. Ideally, transgender and nonbinary RHY are given the choice to be housed where they feel most comfortable, whether with peers based on their gender identity or in a space by themselves. However, some funding sources require youth to be housed according to the gender they were assigned at birth, which poses risks to privacy and safety. Some agencies circumvent this mandate by forgoing funding from those sources. The goal is to house transgender and nonbinary RHY in a way that keeps them safe yet not isolated. One alternative is to provide living spaces dedicated to transgender and nonbinary youth and their allies. While this option segregates these youth from their cisgender peers, many may prefer it.

Trauma-Informed Care

RHY agencies routinely encounter youth with extensive histories of abuse and violence. Thus, all staff who interact with these youth should be trained in a trauma-informed approach. According to the Substance Abuse and Mental Health Services Administration (SAMHSA 2014), the six key principles to such an approach are safety; trustworthiness and transparency; peer support; collaboration and mutuality; empowerment, voice, and choice; and (responsiveness to) cultural, historical, and gender issues. For programs that provide clinical services and have the resources to fund professional development, trauma-focused cognitive-behavioral therapy (TF-CBT) is an evidence-based model suitable for LGBTQ+ RHY. TF-CBT was developed specifically for use with children and adolescents who have experienced trauma and who consequently exhibit mental health problems, such as PTSD (Cohen et al. 2006). Judith Cohen and her colleagues (2018) developed a manual for implementing TF-CBT with LGBTQ+ youth, incorporating the family support component of the Family Acceptance Project into the model. The approach with LGBTQ+ youth can be used in conjunction with Cohen et al.'s (2017) work on TF-CBT with sexually exploited youth, such as survivors of sex trafficking. At a minimum, agency staff would benefit from training that involves learning how to identify trauma-affected youth and develop a plan to refer these youth to the resources that can best help them.

Sexual Health and Wellness

Approximately 10 percent of adolescents have had sexual intercourse by age twelve (Cavazos-Rehg et al. 2009), 20 percent by age fifteen, and 60 percent by age eighteen (Philbin, as cited in Boyer 2018). Cavazos-Rehg et al. (2009) and Boyer (2018) point to these statistics as evidence that sex education is failing students in the United States. Moreover, LGBTQ+ youth typically do not see themselves represented in sex education curricula, which is problematic for several reasons, not the least of which is because LGBTQ+ RHY are more likely than heterosexual-cisgender RHY to engage in high-risk sexual behaviors such as survival sex, unprotected sex, and having multiple sex partners (Kattari et al. 2017; Marshall et al. 2010; Tyler 2013; Tyler and Schmitz 2018b; Walls and Bell 2011). It falls to youth-serving agencies, then, to provide LGBTQ+ RHY with the information they need to keep themselves safe to the extent they are able to do so while unstably housed or homeless. Northwestern University provides sex education information online through their Institute for Sexual and Gender Minority Health and Wellbeing (https://isgmh.northwestern.edu/). Agencies can incorporate the institute's many resources into a curriculum of their own or point youth to the website as part of a self-directed learning activity.

Comprehensive sex education also covers the transmission, symptoms, and treatment of sexually transmitted infections (STIs) (including HIV and the hepatitis viruses) and how to prevent them, such as by practicing safer sex. Youth should also be encouraged to get tested for STIs as part of their overall health care regimen and to consider vaccination, if available, and treatment, as recommended by a physician. LGBTQ+ RHY would also benefit from personal safety training and information on rape crisis services. Short- and long-term safety planning benefits youth while they are receiving services and potentially long after service termination.

Parents and Families

Prevention and intervention efforts that involve the families, especially parents, of RHY have shown promise in keeping youth in the home and reuniting them after they leave. However, only a few family-centered approaches have been studied with LGBTQ+ youth. The Family Acceptance Project (Ryan 2014), with its focus on supporting parents and caregivers while they learn to support their LGBTQ+ children, is perhaps the most well known of these approaches. Training is available through the Family Acceptance Project, but practitioners can also avail themselves of the many resources provided for free on the organization's websites (https://familyproject.sfsu.edu/ and https://lgbtqfamilyacceptance.org/). The Child Welfare Information Gateway, under the U.S. Department of Health and Human Services, also provides resources on its "Equity for LGBTQIA2S+ Individuals" web page (https://web.archive.org/web/20250117211335/https://www.childwelfare .gov/topics/equitable-practice/equity-lgbtqia2s-individuals/?top=1392). Reunification is a priority when it is safe and appropriate to do so, and services such as the Family Acceptance Project may help LGBTQ+ RHY and their families reach that goal.

RESEARCH

Aaron had been living with the same foster family since he was seven, and although they had always been supportive and felt like more of a family than he had ever had, his foster parents had become increasingly distant, uncomfortable with the changes they were noticing in Aaron's gender expression. The support he thought he would have after he turned eighteen was now uncertain as they made it ever clearer that when he graduated from high school, they expected him to move out, which he did. Aaron was able to find places to stay during the summer between graduation and the start of the semester at a nearby university, where he now resides in a dorm. When the university shuts down during long breaks and closes their student housing, Aaron is able to find friends and classmates who will let him stay at their place until housing opens up again. He has a basic residential meal plan, which he supplements with staples from the student food pantry. He has disclosed his foster care history, family discord, and housing status to his academic adviser, who referred him to the university's student support center, who in turn connected him with a program in the community to help him develop his independent living skills.

The field of LGBTQ+ RHY is a relatively new one and perhaps as a result is still fairly narrow. Mental disorders, suicide, substance abuse, and high-risk sexual behaviors dominate LGBTQ+ RHY research while other areas of interest, such as education, employment, family intervention, and others are understudied. The LGBTQ+ RHY literature also varies in its definitions, categorizations, and language regarding sexual orientation and identity and gender identity and expression. What we pose here are recommendations for a more thorough and standardized approach to data collection with this population.

Demographic Scope

A core element of published research is a description of the study sample. Research involving human participants typically includes an overview of participant demographics, such as race, age, and gender at the very least. Since LGBTQ+ RHY span the spectrum of human diversity, the literature would also benefit from knowing participants' ethnicity, disability identity, and immigration status. In much of the literature, Hispanic/Latinx youth are counted according to their race, making their ethnicity invisible. This oversight serves to reinforce a white European standard, which has historically been the problematic paradigm for research (Dresser 1992). An inclusive approach extends to other minority identities, too, such as disability and citizenship or immigration status. The better defined the sample, the more explicable and useful the findings.

Sexual Orientation and Gender Identity Categories

At a minimum, researchers studying LGBTQ+ RHY must report participants' gender, gender identity, and sexual orientation or identity—the very heart of LGBTQ+ research—and do so with precision. Researchers should take care not to conflate sexual orientation and identity with gender identity; truncate sexual orientation and identity to lesbian, gay, and bisexual; or omit gender identity altogether. The sexual and gender minorities, while covered under the same LGBTQ+ initialism, occupy distinct categories and should not be referred to collectively as a single sexual orientation or identity. Gender identity must be captured separately from sexual orientation and identity, and transgender participants should be able to specify the gender or genders with which they identify (or whether no gender applies), rather than being assigned the singular, nonspecific term *transgender*. Similarly, when response options are limited to "heterosexual or LGB" and "cisgender or transgender," individuals outside those binaries are denied representation (i.e., they are made invisible) and must instead choose the label that best (even if poorly) defines them. To that point, an increasing number of youth are identifying as queer, which can refer to either sexuality or gender identity. Thus, "queer" should be added as a response option, and it should appear in both categories.

As researchers ourselves, we are aware that not every sexual orientation and identity and every gender identity can be presented as options to research participants. However, it only serves to improve the quality of research by allowing participants to self-identify: it is better to have a variety of responses and be forced to collapse categories than to have too few and subsequently overlook or misrepresent participants' identities. Findings are only as accurate as the data collected. As disinclined as some researchers might be to allowing open-ended responses to demographic questions, there may be occasions when doing so provides the best data. The impersonal "other" response is also an option, as off-putting as it is for some, given its literal "otherizing" of anyone not represented in the traditional list of sexual and gender identities. However, when accompanied by space for participants to provide qualitative responses, "other" allows participants to self-identify in a way that is less burdensome than choosing from a list of a dozen or more identity categories. Capturing the nuances of sexual orientation and identity and gender identity adds to the richness of research data and enhances our understanding of sexual and gender diversity and of the LGBTQ+ RHY who embody those identities.

Education and Employment

We also recommend reporting participants' education and employment status and history. The research on LGBTQ+ RHY experiences in education and employment is limited, but we know that LGBTQ+ people, including youth, in the general population are subjected to prejudice and discrimination in these settings. We also know little about the educational experiences of LGBTQ+ RHY, particularly beyond high school. They aspire to attend college, but what do we know about their attempts to get there and their experiences once they do, if they do? LGBTQ+ RHY recruitment and retention efforts at postsecondary institutions are largely an untapped field of research.

Disease and Mortality

LGBTQ+ RHY are exposed to a number of risk factors that jeopardize their physical health. The most commonly reported consequences are infectious diseases, especially those that are blood-borne, and injuries, given the high rate of violence and victimization they experience. The prevalence of infectious diseases, especially STIs including HIV, in this population is not well understood, although HIV prevention studies abound. A more comprehensive picture of the presence and impact of STIs and other infectious diseases, such as those transmitted via needle sharing (as with injection drug use, street hormones, and silicone injections), is needed. Perhaps even more alarming is the dearth of reported mortality rates for any RHY population, but especially LGBTQ+ RHY. If the ultimate peril facing LGBTQ+ RHY is death, we must take note and account for it.

Resilience

LGBTQ+ RHY possess a wealth of protective factors that sustain them during challenging times and sometimes treacherous circumstances. Social support and social networks, resilience, coping and adaptability, and inner strength are just some of the reserves on which LGBTQ+ RHY can draw as they work toward their nearly universal goal of stable housing. Tyler (2013) asserted that we have yet to come to a consensus on how resilience among RHY should be defined. The term is often used as a catch-all for other ideas related to withstanding adversity. Is resilience a singular, discrete concept, or is it an umbrella term for other survival mechanisms? To Tyler's (2013) point, we would add that there exists great overlap in many of these terms, with scholars using *resilience, support, coping, adaptability,* and *strength* interchangeably. Perhaps, then, the first task of research into protective factors is to differentiate these concepts to clarify what RHY are really exhibiting and what kinds of interventions tap into each. Standardizing the definitions of resilience-related terms is necessary for practitioners, researchers, and policymakers to target factors that contribute to positive outcomes, measure them across standardized parameters, and interpret findings using the same language. How these terms are defined may also uncover other protective factors heretofore unseen. To capitalize on these resources, they need to be explored in greater detail. A deeper dive might include examining the sources and types of protective factors, the level or degree of protection offered by each factor, how LGBTQ+ RHY acquire them, and how they contribute to positive outcomes among this population.

Family Intervention

Youth homelessness often starts with family conflict. Intervening early is the best hope for interrupting a youth's path to winding up on the streets either because they have been kicked out or because the situation at home has become so untenable that they feel they have no choice but to leave. The Family Acceptance Project was developed for use specifically with LGBTQ+ youth and their families, and it is well studied and has demonstrated positive outcomes. Nevertheless, opportunities exist for additional research on this and other models used with LGBTQ+ RHY already living outside the home, and we need to develop entirely novel approaches, especially those tailored to transgender and nonbinary youth and their families. Reunification strategies exist, but their use with and effect on LGBTQ+ RHY and their families is not well understood. It is possible that current reunification approaches could be used as is or with just minor adaptations for this population.

Permanency and Emancipation

When prevention and reunification measures fail, the task becomes providing temporary housing for LGBTQ+ RHY until permanency goals are achieved. Most LGBTQ+ youth in foster care age out of the system, unlike their heterosexual-cisgender counterparts, who are more likely to be reunited with their families of origin or adopted before their eighteenth birthday. Given their lengthy involvement in the child welfare system, LGBTQ+ youth have received considerable attention in the child welfare literature. Less studied is their experience with adoption, and questions remain about barriers to the adoption of LGBTQ+ youth, factors associated with their successful adoption, and ways to promote adoption for this population. At the other end of the outcome spectrum, little is known about LGBTQ+ RHY who choose to judicially emancipate: how many there are, why they choose to do so, and how they fare in the months and years that follow.

Transformative Justice

A thorough search of the extant literature turned up no research on the use of the transformative justice model with LGBTQ+ RHY. However, service providers working with this population are currently employing this strategy. Research would be able to evaluate the effectiveness of transformative justice with LGBTQ+ RHY and demonstrate its potential applicability across subpopulations, settings, and problem areas.

Policy Research and Advocacy

Researchers typically disseminate their findings through sober academic journals and cloistered professional conferences. However, as experts in their field, researchers are in a position to be effective influencers of policy. Despite being skilled communicators, researchers face challenges when it comes to engaging in policy advocacy (Scott et al. 2019; Ward et al. 2009). Influencing policy involves, first and foremost, having the occasion to interact with policymakers. Researchers and policymakers occupy different professional realms, each with its own culture, pace, communication style, sources of information, and sense of distrust of the other. Moreover, researchers are not always supported by their institutions to engage in policy advocacy (Scott et al. 2019). Policy advocacy takes time and requires training for the uninitiated, resources that are often in short supply among researchers (Scott et al. 2019; Ward et al. 2009). Bringing research to bear on policy may warrant a culture shift from perceiving policy advocacy as a separate activity to embracing it as one part of the dissemination process. This means educating researchers through direct instruction and experiential learning (Scott et al. 2019) on the policymaking process and developing their competency to translate and convey their findings to those who have the power to effect policy change. Scholars studying LGBTQ+ RHY are encouraged to develop their policy advocacy skills and transform their research into action, whether through written policy briefs, by meeting directly with policymakers, or, ideally, both (Arnautu and Dagenais 2021). (See box 11.1, *Read All About It!*) As the professor and public policy advocate Chuck Rice cautioned, " 'If [policymakers] don't hear from the science community, then they're going to get their information on perceived science needs from other sources' " (Robbins 2021).

BOX 11.1. READ ALL ABOUT IT!
TRANSLATING RESEARCH INTO POLICY

- The national policy advisers and scholars MaryEllen McGuire and Laura W. Perna (2023), offer "six recommendations for faculty and academic researchers":

  ○ *Write with policymakers in mind.* Keep written communication short, concise, and jargon free.
  ○ *Share findings in outlets that are accessible to policymakers and their staff.* Use social media to point policymakers and their staff to your findings, providing a clear link to current relevance.
  ○ *Build relationships.* Engage directly with policymakers and their staff to discuss research findings and how they relate to their priorities. Follow up to maintain the relationship over time.
  ○ *Know your audience.* Identify the policymakers who share your field of interest, and convey the implications of your findings and recommendations for action.
  ○ *Work with trusted intermediaries.* Intermediaries are third parties, such as "think tanks, . . . advocacy organizations, and grant-making organizations," who can assist researchers with getting their findings in the hands of policymakers.
  ○ *Talk to journalists.* Journalists, too, are conduits for disseminating findings to policymakers, among others. Researchers can provide a scientific perspective on problems and solutions that involve policies. (17–18)

Involvement in policymaking has never been more important given the recent onslaught of anti-LGBTQ+ legislation being promulgated throughout the United States. Between January 1 and May 31, 2023, a record 520 bills made their way through state legislatures (Peele 2023b), nearly double that of the previous twelve months (ACLU 2022). That record was broken the following year, with more than 530 anti-LGBTQ+ bills introduced in state legislatures across the country (ACLU 2024). Among the plethora of bills are those targeting transgender student athletes (i.e., prohibiting primarily transgender girls from participating in girls' sports), library books (i.e., banning books with LGBTQ+ content), bathrooms and locker rooms (i.e., requiring transgender and nonbinary individuals to use facilities according to the gender they were assigned at birth), gender-affirming care (i.e., prohibiting health care professionals from providing gender-affirming hormone therapy, puberty-blocking medications, surgeries, and other treatments to minors), school curricula (i.e., banning lectures and materials depicting LGBTQ+ history or historical figures or other content that could be deemed LGBTQ+-affirming), classroom speech (i.e., prohibiting teachers from discussing sexual orientation and gender identity with students, for example, via the "don't say gay" bills), and drag performances (i.e., prohibiting minors from attending them or banning them altogether). Researchers can play a critical role in the life of these bills and future ones by collecting data on the impact they have on LGBTQ+ people, including RHY, both individually and collectively.

POLICY

Now a sophomore, Aaron attends an LGBTQ+/ally youth group at his church. He also belongs to an African American fraternity that supports its queer members, and he often participates in the activities sponsored by the university's diversity office and LGBTQ+ student organizations. Aaron has his sights set on a career in government, politics, or law, so for now he is content being a political science major. He knows he wants to make an impact supporting the LGBTQ+ RHY population, but he's not sure how or at what level, whether as an advocate at an agency or organization, as a researcher at a policy center or institute, or as a politician in government. After attending a recent panel discussion about youth experiencing homelessness by professionals from the local community, he realizes there's a lot that needs to be done—and how close he is to being counted among that population. He dreams about influencing policy that would benefit LGBTQ+ RHY, such as improving standards of care in basic shelters and transitional living programs. Aaron figures a career as a lobbyist or politician might make him a more visible role model for youth of color, for which there would be no greater satisfaction.

LGBTQ+-affirming policy is sometimes the last entity to align with prevailing public sentiment, but it is nonetheless necessary for promoting and enforcing best practices. What we outline next are six unprotected or minimally protected areas affecting the lives and well-being of LGBTQ+ RHY that must be addressed. These recommendations pertain to governmental policies, particularly at the federal level, where they would have the broadest scope and carry the most weight. They are intended for policymakers, as well as for the practitioners and researchers who can assist them.

Human Rights

No discussion of LGBTQ+ RHY policy change can begin without first advocating for the most fundamental of reforms: discrimination, bullying, and harassment on the basis of sexual orientation and identity and gender identity and expression must be prohibited by all levels of government. Protection must be broad based and cover basic human rights (see UN 1948). LGBTQ+ youth and young adults are discriminated against, bullied, and harassed in education (Kosciw et al. 2022), employment (Sabia 2014; Singh et al. 2014), and housing settings (Casey et al. 2019) and in public accommodations (Rossman et al. 2017) in ways that lead to housing instability and homelessness. Without such legislation, LGBTQ+ youth already experiencing housing instability and homelessness will continue to endure discrimination, harassment, and violence in shelters and other spaces meant to protect them (Wagner 2010; Yu 2010) and find it difficult, if not impossible, to escape poverty and homelessness.

Nondiscrimination

Despite recent advances in LGBTQ+ equality—or perhaps because of them—discrimination and prejudice on the basis of sexual orientation and identity and gender identity and expression have taken on new life in ways not seen before. The recent proliferation of religious freedom laws appears to be a reaction to the U.S. Supreme Court's 2015 decision in *Obergefell v. Hodges* that same-sex couples have a constitutional right to marriage, thus rendering state same-sex marriage bans null and void. Aside from the bakers and florists who no longer cater to LGBTQ+ celebrants, these laws have the potential to do real harm to youth, some of whom are not even old enough to marry. What happens to a gay boy in a small city where the only runaway youth program is operated by a local church with a reputation for being unwelcoming to LGBTQ+ people, or to the young trans woman forced to room with a young cisgender man and wear men's clothes in an emergency shelter run by a faith-based organization? Such scenarios pose a substantial moral dilemma that pits human safety and well-being against religious freedom. (See box 11.2, *What Do You Think?*) Policymakers must find ways to protect LGBTQ+ RHY from prejudice and discrimination that puts their safety at risk.

BOX 11.2. WHAT DO YOU THINK? RELIGIOUS FREEDOM

- **Religious freedom legislation** is designed to protect individuals, organizations, and businesses from being forced to serve LGBTQ+ people; it is based on the claim of some such individuals, organizations, and businesses that doing so violates their religious beliefs. Those in support of such legislation cite their First Amendment right to express their religion, interpreting this right to include the freedom to deny services that they believe contradict their religious beliefs. Those opposed decry such policies as legalizing discrimination under the guise of religious freedom, comparing it to bygone legislation that discriminated against other marginalized groups on the basis of religious justification.

  o What are the pros and cons of establishing religious freedom legislation? What are the pros and cons of barring such legislation?

  o Under what circumstances, if any, could religious freedom be incited against LGBTQ+ people? Under what circumstances could religious freedom not be incited against LGBTQ+ people?

Gender-Affirming Care

Nearly half (220) of the 520 anti-LGBTQ+ bills proposed in early 2023 were aimed specifically at transgender and nonbinary people, including youth (Peele 2023b). Many of these bills targeted books and school curricula, but many more targeted gender-affirming care, which transgender individuals and health care providers have deemed medically necessary and lifesaving. For transgender youth especially, having access to puberty blockers early in their sexual development is critical because the development of many secondary sex characteristics is irreversible (e.g., the deepening of the voice in natal males, the widening of hips in natal females) or reversible but painful and financially costly (e.g., gender-affirming surgeries and aesthetic treatments). More importantly, youth who receive such care have lower rates of depression, suicidal ideation, and suicide attempts (Green et al. 2022; Tordoff et al. 2022), suggesting that those who are denied access to gender-affirming care suffer the consequences. Gender-affirming care should be accessible to those who need it. For some, it is a matter of life or death.

Sexuality Education

Perhaps nothing denies a minority culture's existence more than the majority's silence, and nowhere is this seen more than in schools. Eighteen states (GLSEN 2024), representing 18.5 million public school children (NCES 2022), have prohibited the mention of LGBTQ+ topics in the classroom. So-called no-promo-homo laws emerged in the 1980s and 1990s as a result of the HIV/AIDS pandemic, with some states directing their public school systems to refrain from discussing homosexuality in a positive light, and some even promoting negative portrayals (GLSEN 2018). "Don't say gay" laws, more generally, have replaced "no promo homo" laws, although the two phrases are now sometimes used synonymously. In addition, five states have enacted "opt-in" or "opt-out" laws that allow parents to choose whether their children receive sex education in school (MAP 2024; SIECUS 2018). Together, these policies, largely aimed at health and sex education curricula, prevent LGBTQ+ youth, some of whom are or may become homeless, from receiving the information they need to keep themselves and their partners safe, information that otherwise poses no harm to the student body at large (table 11.1). "On the contrary," say Gegenfurtner and Gebhardt (2017), "on the basis of the reviewed evidence, there are good reasons to expect that the educational benefits will be overwhelmingly positive, particularly for at-risk students belonging to a sexual minority" (219). Such legislation does nothing to protect heterosexual-cisgender students and much to harm LGBTQ+ ones.

RHY Legislation

Lawmakers must finish the job that their predecessors started and reintroduce stalled bills or introduce new ones that benefit LGBTQ+ RHY, their families, and those who serve them. First among them is the Runaway and Homeless Youth and Trafficking Prevention Act (RHYTPA), which has yet to be put to a vote. This bill would replace the Runaway and Homeless Youth Act of 2008, which expired in 2013 and was reauthorized only as part of the Juvenile Justice Reform Act of 2018 (Landers 2019). The RHYTPA would prohibit discrimination on the basis of sexual orientation and gender identity, among other characteristics, meaning that LGBTQ+ RHY would have access to the services they need and deserve without fear of discrimination, harassment, or mistreatment. Reauthorizing the RHYTPA would return it to its previous five-year funding cycle as a stand-alone bill, a status conveying its importance.

Another abandoned policy is then-Senator John Kerry's Reconnecting Youth to Prevent Homelessness Act, which would direct the secretary of health and human services to "establish a demonstration project to develop programs that are focused on improving family relationships and reducing homelessness for lesbian, gay, bisexual, and transgender youth" through family interventions, risk assessment, and educational resources (RYPHA 2011, section 106). With family conflict among the leading factors behind youth being forced or compelled to leave home and potentially becoming homeless, passing legislation to remedy this outcome should be a priority.

TABLE 11.1 U.S. state laws regulating the mention of sexual orientation and identity and gender identity in public school curricula

State	State law sets a standard for LGBTQI+ inclusion in one or more academic subject	State education agency sets a standard for LGBTQI+ inclusion in one or more academic subject	State policy sets a standard for LGBTQI+ inclusion in sex education	State policy encourages LGBTQI+ inclusion in locally adopted curriculum	State has no policies supporting or restricting LGBTQI+ inclusive instruction	State law permits opting out of LGBTQI+ inclusive instruction	State law prohibits LGBTQI+ inclusive instruction without parental approval	State law censors LGBTQI+ inclusive instruction	State law censors teaching about structural inequality and its impacts on people of color, women, and LGBTQI+ people
AL								X	X
AK					X				
AZ							X		
AR								X	X
CA	X		X						
CO	X		X						
CT				X					
DE				X					
FL								X	X
GA									X
HI					X				
ID									X
IL	X		X						
IN								X	
IA								X	X
KS					X				
KY								X	X
LA								X	
ME					X				

State	State law sets a standard for LGBTQI+ inclusion in one or more academic subject	State education agency sets a standard for LGBTQI+ inclusion in one or more academic subject	State policy sets a standard for LGBTQI+ inclusion in sex education	State policy encourages LGBTQI+ inclusion in locally adopted curriculum	State has no policies supporting or restricting LGBTQI+ inclusive instruction	State law permits opting out of LGBTQI+ inclusive instruction	State law prohibits LGBTQI+ inclusive instruction without parental approval	State law censors LGBTQI+ inclusive instruction	State law censors teaching about structural inequality and its impacts on people of color, women, and LGBTQI+ people
MD			X						
MA		X	X	X					
MI					X				
MN					X				
MS								X	X
MO					X				
MT						X			
NE					X				
NV	X								
NH	X	X				X			X
NJ	X		X						
NM					X				
NY					X				
NC								X	
ND									X
OH					X				
OK								X	X
OR	X		X						

(continued)

TABLE 11.1 (*continued*)

State	State law sets a standard for LGBTQI+ inclusion in one or more academic subject	State education agency sets a standard for LGBTQI+ inclusion in one or more academic subject	State policy sets a standard for LGBTQI+ inclusion in sex education	State policy encourages LGBTQI+ inclusion in locally adopted curriculum	State has no policies supporting or restricting LGBTQI+ inclusive instruction	State law permits opting out of LGBTQI+ inclusive instruction	State law prohibits LGBTQI+ inclusive instruction without parental approval	State law censors LGBTQI+ inclusive instruction	State law censors teaching about structural inequality and its impacts on people of color, women, and LGBTQI+ people
PA					X				
RI			X						
SC									X
SD					X				
TN							X		X
TX								X	X
UT									X
VT									
VA					X				
WA	X		X						
WV					X				
WI					X				
WY							X		

Abbreviation: LGBTQI+, lesbian, gay, bisexual, transgender, queer and/or questioning, intersex, and other sexual and gender identities.
Source: GLSEN 2024. Copyright 2024 by GLSEN. Reprinted with permission.

Legislation targeting LGBTQ+ RHY must, when possible, make provisions (e.g., allot funding and resources) for physical and mental health care and substance abuse treatment. Exposure to the elements, living in close quarters and squalid conditions, trading sex, and not receiving medical attention when needed puts these youths' health at risk. Exploitation, violence and victimization (both past and present), and the resulting trauma have the potential to leave any individual, particularly children and adolescents, vulnerable to depression, anxiety, PTSD, and other mental health problems, as well as substance abuse in an attempt to self-medicate and suicide to end emotional suffering or escape current traumatic experiences. Unaccompanied minors may not seek or even know where they can receive physical and mental health care or substance abuse treatment. And when they do, they may be turned away for lack of parental consent or proof of financial responsibility, or they may be handed a hefty bill they cannot afford.

Decriminalization

Anti-homeless legislation (i.e., that relating to quality-of-life offenses) criminalizes individuals on the basis of factors over which they have little control. Couched in terms of public health and the best interest of individuals experiencing homelessness (Wiltz 2015), these policies limit the movement, behaviors, and freedom of people living on the streets, including LGBTQ+ RHY. Panhandling, loitering, sleeping in public, and living in vehicles, among other common survival needs and behaviors, are criminalized to some degree in many municipalities (NLCHP 2014). Not only do these laws not serve their purported purpose (ostensibly to help those who are homeless), but they actually end up hurting many people, unhoused and housed alike. Using the economic cost of homelessness as an example, taxpayers in Seattle and Spokane, Washington, spent more than $3.7 million on enforcing ordinances that criminalize people experiencing homelessness; an affordable housing program would have saved them nearly three times that much (Howard et al. 2015). Resources should instead be focused on helping people experiencing homelessness to find and maintain stable housing, get the health care they need, and develop the skills they need to be self-sufficient if they so choose.

GENERAL RECOMMENDATIONS

In addition to the specific roads to improvement just discussed, we also have some general recommendations for practitioners, researchers, and policymakers to consider.

Language and Terminology

Young people are often immersed in contemporary culture in ways that generations ahead of them are not. Technology allows its users to stay abreast of cultural events and trends in intimate and immediate ways, and young people are frequent—and savvy—tech consumers. It makes sense, then, that young people, heterosexual-cisgender and LGBTQ+ alike, are typically the first to know—and to let everyone else know—when socially acceptable terminology around sexuality and gender identity changes. Practitioners, researchers, and policymakers would be wise to listen for and incorporate these language changes as they arise. Accurately and effectively serving, studying, and protecting LGBTQ+ RHY begins with correct and respectful identification and naming.

Inclusion

LGBTQ+ youth compose 20 to 40 percent of the RHY population. Anyone—practitioners and program developers, researchers, and policymakers—whose efforts touch on minoritized youth populations in general or RHY in particular must consider how their work includes or potentially excludes this RHY subpopulation. More than just being accommodating, professionals should be intentional in their efforts to include LGBTQ+ youth in their services, programs, research, and policies. Keep in mind, too, the intersectionality that runs through this population, that is, the presence of individuals with multiple identities, particularly multiple minority identities, such as youth from historically excluded racial and ethnic groups, youth with physical disabilities and mental health problems, and immigrant and undocumented youth.

Family Support

The U.S. Interagency Council on Homelessness (USICH 2015) has acknowledged family conflict as the number one reason for youth homelessness. This is especially true for LGBTQ+ youth. With the promise that the Family Acceptance Project has shown by engaging families in treatment, the case has been made for incorporating this approach in agencies, studying it in greater depth and breadth, and supporting it in policies that address homeless youth prevention and intervention. Practitioners can help young people who are thinking of coming out to their parents and caregivers, as well as those who have had their disclosure received poorly and are thus at risk of being kicked out or compelled to leave home. Practitioners and researchers can work in collaboration to develop protocols for LGBTQ+ youth and their families, and policymakers can mandate the use of evidence-based programs targeting youth and their families.

SUMMARY

On the face of it, eliminating LGBTQ+ youth homelessness seems a daunting task, overwhelming even. Doing so requires qualified personnel, adequate funding, and political influence that, in the nonprofit sector, are in short supply. LGBTQ+-affirming practice meets these youth where they are and ensures their immediate well-being; research identifies best practices and informs practice and legislation; and policy sets the boundaries that protect the rights of this vulnerable population. All of these promote the message that LGBTQ+ RHY are valuable members of society worth investing in.

Considerable work lies ahead, but having a road map (of where to go), a plan (of how to get there), and a team (to help along the way) is a good place to start. It begins with each of us exploring the various avenues—practice and programs, research, and policy—that lead to the destination of better outcomes.

REVISITING AARON

- Assume that Aaron lives in your state. Can his foster parents be forced to continue supporting him financially or otherwise? If not, does your state allow foster youth who left care after the age of eighteen to return to care until they are twenty-one?
- Aaron is currently a political science major. What other majors and disciplines might lead to careers that make a positive difference in the lives of LGBTQ+ RHY? In what ways would they make a difference?
- Aaron's career interests range from working for an RHY agency or organization as an advocate to conducting research at a think tank to becoming a policymaker himself. How might each of these careers make a positive difference in the lives of LGBTQ+ RHY?
- What limits or drawbacks do advocacy, lobbying, research, and policymaking pose in the type or scope of impact each can make? On what audience might each have its biggest influence?
- If you were in Aaron's position, would you tackle recommendations in practice, research, or policy? Why?
- Which policy, research, and practice recommendations from this chapter might you suggest to Aaron as having the potential to make a substantial impact? Why did you choose those recommendations? How would they make an impact? How far-reaching would you estimate that impact to be?

KEY CONCEPTS

- *Experiential learning*: learning that occurs in a simulated or real-world setting; "hands-on" learning

- *Practice knowledge*: knowledge gained by enacting theoretical knowledge in practice settings
- *Practice wisdom*: wisdom created by the intersection of theoretical and practice knowledge that is "transformed and enhanced" over time (Higgs 2019, 4)
- *Religious freedom legislation*: laws meant to protect individuals from the infringement of their religious beliefs and practices; in some cases, the mere enactment of these laws results in legalized discrimination against others; these laws are thus sometimes referred to as a "license to discriminate"
- *Research knowledge*: knowledge gained through quantitative or qualitative observations that can be used to inform practice and policy
- *Theoretical knowledge*: knowledge based on ideas that have been investigated through quantitative or qualitative research

CHAPTER HIGHLIGHTS

- Agencies and researchers collect demographic data, such as age, gender, race, sexual orientation and identity, and gender identity. These data provide the size and characteristics of the LGBTQ+ RHY population, information that can be used to make the case for funding and legislation; thus, thorough and accurate collection and reporting of demographic data is important.
- Trauma-focused cognitive-behavioral therapy in combination with the family support model of the Family Acceptance Project helps LGBTQ+ RHY and their families address and overcome conflict and associated abuse and violence; these interventions are used to prevent or minimize youth homelessness.
- HIV prevalence, mortality rates, employment seeking, and adoption experiences are just some of the research gaps that persist in the field of LGBTQ+ RHY. Insight into these areas would help inform practice and policy that could shore up risks and negative outcomes.
- Researchers in the field of LGBTQ+ RHY are not trained to transform their expertise into policy advocacy, yet their voices can be

effective in influencing legislation that benefits this vulnerable population.

- Unlike the categories of age, disability, gender, and race, sexual orientation and identity and gender identity remain unprotected statuses at the federal and, to a lesser extent, state levels. Until legislation is passed, LGBTQ+ RHY will continue to experience discrimination in shelters, drop-in centers, and other services meant to protect them.
- RHY legislation that saw fairly consistent reauthorization through the first decade of the millennium was interrupted in 2013 until returning in 2019 under the Juvenile Justice Reform Act of 2018.
- Language and terminology regarding sexuality and gender identity changes often, potentially making it difficult for practitioners, researchers, and policymakers to keep up. Including LGBTQ+ youth voices in these arenas is a meaningful way to stay abreast of appropriate language and terminology.

References

A4TE (Advocates for Trans Equality). n.d.a. "Supporting Transgender People." Accessed August 5, 2025 October 16, 2024. https://transequality.org/trans-101/supporting-transgender-people

——. n.d.b. "Understanding Nonbinary People: How to Be Respectful and Supportive." Accessed October 16, 2024. https://transequality.org/issues/resources/understanding-nonbinary-people-how-to-be-respectful-and-supportive.

Abramovich, A. 2017. "Understanding How Policy and Culture Create Oppressive Conditions for LGBTQ2S Youth in the Shelter System." *Journal of Homosexuality* 64 (11): 1484–1501. https://doi.org/10.1080/00918369.2016.1244449.

ACF (Administration for Children and Families). 2011. *Information Memorandum ACYF-CB-IM-11-03*. https://www.acf.hhs.gov/sites/default/files/documents/cb/im1103.pdf.

——. 2018. "About: What We Do." https://www.acf.hhs.gov/about.

Achenbach, T. M. 1978. "The Child Behavior Profile: An Empirically Based System for Assessing Children's Behavioral Problems and Competencies." *International Journal of Mental Health* 7 (3–4): 24–42.

ACLU (American Civil Liberties Union). 2022. "Past Legislation Affecting LGBTQ Rights Across the Country 2022." https://www.aclu.org/documents/legislation-affecting-lgbtq-rights-across-country-2022.

——. 2024. "Mapping Attacks on LGBTQ Rights in U.S. State Legislatures in 2024." https://www.aclu.org/legislative-attacks-on-lgbtq-rights-2024.

Alessi, E. J., B. Greenfield, D. Manning, and M. Dank. 2021. "Victimization and Resilience Among Sexual and Gender Minority Homeless Youth Engaging in Survival Sex." *Journal of Interpersonal Violence* 36 (23–24): 11236–59. https://doi.org/10.1177/0886260519898434.

Alexander, J. F., and M. S. Robbins. 2010. "Functional Family Therapy: A Phase-Based and Multi-Component Approach to Change." In *Clinical Handbook of Assessing and Treating Conduct Problems in Youth*, ed. R. C. Murrihy, A. D. Kidman, and T. H. Ollendick. Springer. https://doi.org/10.1007/978-1-4419-6297-3_10.

Ali Forney Center. n.d. "About Us." Accessed November 1, 2024. https://www.aliforneycenter .org/about-us/lgbtq-youth-crisis/.

Altena, A. M., S. N. Brilleslijper-Kater, and J. R. Wolf. 2010. "Effective Interventions for Homeless Youth: A Systematic Review." *American Journal of Preventive Medicine* 38 (6): 637–45. https://doi.org/10.1016/j.amepre.2010.02.017.

American Psychological Association. 2022a. "Gender." APA Style. Accessed October 16, 2024. https://apastyle.apa.org/style-grammar-guidelines/bias-free-language/gender.

——. 2022b. "Sexual Orientation." APA Style. Accessed October 16, 2024. https://apastyle .apa.org/style-grammar-guidelines/bias-free-language/sexual-orientation.

Anspach, R. 2017. "Why Trans Youth Are More at Risk for Deportation." *Teen Vogue*. https:// www.teenvogue.com/story/why-transgender-youth-more-likely-to-be-deported.

Anzaldúa, G. 2009. "To(o) Queer the Writer: *Loca, Escritora y Chicana*." In *The Gloria Anzaldúa Reader*, ed. A. Keating. Duke University Press. https://doi.org/10.1215 /9780822391272-024.

APA (American Psychiatric Association). n.d. "DSM History." Accessed June 30, 2023. https://www.psychiatry.org/psychiatrists/practice/dsm/about-dsm/history-of-the-dsm.

——. 1973. Homosexuality and Sexual Orientation Disturbance: Proposed Change in DSM-II, 6th Printing, Page 44—Position Statement (Retired). APA document reference no.730008.https://pages.uoregon.edu/eherman/teaching/texts/DSM-II_Homosexuality _Revision.pdf.

——, ed. 2022. *Diagnostic and Statistical Manual of Mental Disorders*, 5th ed. Text rev. American Psychiatric Association. https://doi.org/10.1176/appi.books.9780890425787.

Arnautu, D., and C. Dagenais. 2021. "Use and Effectiveness of Policy Briefs as a Knowledge Transfer Tool: A Scoping Review." *Humanities and Social Sciences Communications* 8: 211. https://doi.org/10.1057/s41599-021-00885-9.

Arnold, E. M., A. K. Walsh, M. S. Oldham, and C. A. Rapp. 2007. "Strengths-Based Case Management: Implementation with High-Risk Youth." *Families in Society* 88 (1): 86–94. https://doi.org/10.1606%2F1044-3894.3595.

Ashcraft, L., and W. A. Anthony. 2006. "Crisis Services in the 'Living Room': An Environment with Peer Supports Helps People in Crisis." *Behavioral Healthcare* 26 (7): 12, 14. https://link.gale.com/apps/doc/A150553366/AONE?u=anon~3979f145&sid=google Scholar&xid=80f69ad6.

Ashley, F. 2019. "Puberty Blockers Are Necessary, but They Don't Prevent Homelessness: Caring for Transgender Youth by Supporting Unsupportive Parents." *American Journal of Bioethics* 19 (2): 87–89. https://doi.org/10.1080/15265161.2018.1557277.

Associated Press. 2016. "Illinois Agency Urges Foster Parents to Take in LGBT Youth." WQAD-TV, July 9. https://www.wqad.com/article/news/local/drone/8-in-the-air/illinois -agency-urges-foster-parents-to-take-in-lgbt-youth/526-a2768c51-4c4a-4c9e-95a6 -1bb7633d38b8.

Auerswald, C. L., J. S. Lin, and A. Parriott. 2016. "Six-Year Mortality in a Street-Recruited Cohort of Homeless Youth in San Francisco, California." *PeerJ* 4. https://doi.org/10.7717/peerj.1909.

Austin, A., and R. Papciak. 2022. "Practice with Transgender and Gender Diverse Clients." In *Social Work Practice with the LGBTQ+ Community: The Intersection of History, Health, Mental Health, and Policy Factors*, 2nd ed., ed. M. P. Dentato. Oxford University Press.

Avenues for Youth. n.d. "ConneQT." Accessed January 30, 2022. https://avenuesforyouth.org/host-home-landing-page/.

Aykanian, A. 2018. "Service and Policy Considerations When Working with Highly Mobile Homeless Youth: Perspectives from the Frontlines." *Children and Youth Services Review* 84: 9–16. https://doi-org.libezp.lib.lsu.edu/10.1016/j.childyouth.2017.11.014.

Baams, L., B. D. M. Wilson, and S. T. Russell. 2019. "LGBTQ Youth in Unstable Housing and Foster Care." *Pediatrics* 143 (3): e20174211. https://doi.org/10.1542/peds.2017-4211.

Babits, C. 2019. "Kent Philpott and the Charismatic Roots of Contemporary Conversion Therapy." *Journal of Faith, Education, and Society* 3 (1): 6. https://scholarworks.sfasu.edu/cgi/viewcontent.cgi?article=1021&context=jfec.

Bailey, J. M., and R. C. Pillard. 1991. "A Genetic Study of Male Sexual Orientation." *Archives of General Psychiatry* 48 (12): 1089–96. https://doi.org/10.1001/archpsyc.1991.01810360053008.

Bailey, J. M., P. L. Vasey, L. M. Diamond, S. M. Breedlove, E. Vilain, and M. Epprecht. 2016. "Sexual Orientation, Controversy, and Science." *Psychological Science in the Public Interest* 17 (2): 45–101. https://doi.org/10.1177/1529100616637616.

Banks, A. M. 2009. "New Groups Help Make Exodus with Merger." *Religion News Service*, July 17. https://religionnews.com/2009/07/17/new-groups-help-make-exodus-with-merger/.

Barker, R. L. 2014. *The Social Work Dictionary*, 6th ed. NASW.

Barman-Adhikari, A., E. Bowen, K. Bender, S. Brown, and E. Rice. 2016. "A Social Capital Approach to Identifying Correlates of Perceived Social Support Among Homeless Youth." *Child & Youth Care Forum* 45 (5): 691–708. https://doi.org/10.1007/s10566-016-9352-3.

Baron, R. M., and D. A. Kenny. 1986. "The Moderator-Mediator Variable Distinction in Social Psychological Research: Conceptual, Strategic, and Statistical Considerations." *Journal of Personality and Social Psychology* 51 (6): 1173–82. https://doi.org/10.1037/0022-3514.51.6.1173.

Baruch, G., I. Vrouva, and P. Fearon. 2009. "A Follow-Up Study of Characteristics of Young People That Dropout and Continue Psychotherapy: Service Implications for a Clinic in the Community." *Child and Adolescent Mental Health* 14 (2): 69–75. https://doi.org/10.1111/j.1475-3588.2008.00492.x.

Basile, K. C., S. G. Smith, M. J. Breiding, M. C. Black, and R. Mahendra. 2014. *Sexual Violence Surveillance: Uniform Definitions and Recommended Data Elements*. Centers for Disease Control and Prevention. https://stacks.cdc.gov/view/cdc/26326/cdc_26326_DS1.pdf.

Basile, K. C., S. G. Smith, M. Kresnow, S. Khatiwada, and R. W. Leemis. 2022. *The National Intimate Partner and Sexual Violence Survey: 2016/2017 Report on Sexual Violence.*

Centers for Disease Control and Prevention. https://www.cdc.gov/nisvs/documentation/nisvsReportonSexualViolence.pdf.

Battle, S., and T. E. Wheeler II. 2017. *Dear Colleague Letter: Notice of Language Assistance.* U.S. Department of Justice, U.S. Department of Education, February 22. https://www2.ed.gov/about/offices/list/ocr/letters/colleague-201702-title-ix.pdf.

Bauer, G. R., J. Braimoh, A. I. Scheim, and C. Dharma. 2017. "Transgender-Inclusive Measures of Sex/Gender for Population Surveys: Mixed-Methods Evaluation and Recommendations." *PLoS One* 12 (5). https://doi.org/10.1371/journal.pone.0178043.

Baum-Baicker, C. 2018. "Clinical Wisdom in Professional Practice." University of Chicago, September 24. https://wisdomcenter.uchicago.edu/news/discussions/clinical-wisdom-professional-practice.

Bayer, R. 1987. *Homosexuality and American Psychiatry: The Politics of Diagnosis.* Princeton University Press.

Becker, A. B. 2014. "Employment Discrimination, Local School Boards, and LGBT Civil Rights: Reviewing 25 Years of Public Opinion Data." *International Journal of Public Opinion Research* 26 (3): 342–54.

Begun, S., C. Frey, K. M. Combs, and M. Torrie. 2019. "'I Guess It Would Be a Good Shock': A Qualitative Examination of Homeless Youths' Diverse Pregnancy Attitudes." *Children and Youth Services Review* 99: 87–96. https://doi.org/10.1016/j.childyouth.2019.01.029.

Bender, K., N. Schau, S. Begun, B. Haffejee, A. Barman-Adhikari, and J. Hathaway. 2015. "Electronic Case Management with Homeless Youth." *Evaluation and Program Planning* 50: 36–42. https://doi.org/10.1016/j.evalprogplan.2015.02.002.

Benoit-Bryan, J. 2011. *The Runaway Youth Longitudinal Study.* National Runaway Safeline. https://www.nationalrunawaysafeline.org/wp-content/uploads/2015/05/NRS-Longitudinal-study-full-report.pdf.

Berberet, H. M. 2006. "Putting the Pieces Together for Queer Youth: A Model of Integrated Assessment of Need and Program Planning." *Child Welfare* 85 (2): 361–84.

Berking, M., and B. Whitley. 2014. *Affect Regulation Training: A Practitioner's Manual.* Springer. https://doi.org/10.1007/978-1-4939-1022-9.

Besen, W. R. 2003. *Anything but Straight: Unlocking the Scandals and Lies Behind the Ex-Gay Myth.* Harrington Park.

Besen, W. 2014. "Discredited 'Ex-Gay' Therapy Group, NARTH, Undergoes Major Rebranding Effort." TWO Care Center Against Religious Extremism, August 6. https://twocare.org/discredited-ex-gay-therapy-group-narth-undergoes-major-rebranding-effort/?utm_source=Discredited+%27Ex-Gay%27+Therapy+Group%2C+NARTH%2C+Undergoes+Major+Rebranding+Effort&utm_campaign=worldvision&utm_medium=email.

Bidell, M. P. 2014. "Is There an Emotional Cost of Completing High School? Ecological Factors and Psychological Distress Among LGBT Homeless Youth." *Journal of Homosexuality* 61 (3): 366–81. https://doi.org/10.1080/00918369.2013.842426.

——. 2017. "The Lesbian, Gay, Bisexual, and Transgender Development of Clinical Skills Scale (LGBT-DOCSS): Establishing a New Interdisciplinary Self-Assessment for Health Providers." *Journal of Homosexuality* 64 (10): 1432–60. https://doi.org/10.1080/00918369.2017.1321389.

Blackless, M., A. Charuvastra, A. Derryck, A. Fausto-Serling, K. Lauzanne, and E. Lee. 2000. "How Sexually Dimorphic Are We? Review and Synthesis." *American Journal of Human Biology* 12 (2): 151–66. https://doi.org/10.1002/(sici)1520-6300(200003/04)12:2%3C151::aid-ajhb1%3E3.0.co;2-f.

Blau, J., and M. Abramovitz. 2010. *The Dynamics of Social Welfare Policy.* Oxford University Press.

Bloom, S. 1997. *Creating Sanctuary: Toward the Evolution of Sane Societies.* Routledge.

Bond, G. R. 2004. "Supported Employment: Evidence for an Evidence-Based Practice." *Psychiatric Rehabilitation Journal* 27 (4): 345–59. https://doi.org/10.2975/27.2004.345.359.

Bostock v. Clayton County, Georgia, 590 U.S. 644. 2019. https://www.supremecourt.gov/opinions/19pdf/17-1618_hfci.pdf.

Boyer, J. 2018. "New Name, Same Harm: Rebranding of Federal Abstinence-Only Programs." *Guttmacher Policy Review* 21: 11–16. https://www.guttmacher.org/sites/default/files/article_files/gpr2101118.pdf.

Bradford, J., S. L. Reisner, J. A. Honnold, and J. Xavier. 2013. "Experiences of Transgender-Related Discrimination and Implications for Health: Results from the Virginia Transgender Health Initiative Study." *American Journal of Public Health* 103 (10): 1820–29.

Brakenhoff, B., and N. Slesnick. 2018. "Substance Use & Mental Health Interventions for Youth Who Are Homeless: The Community Reinforcement Approach & Motivational Enhancement Therapy." In *Mental Health & Addiction Interventions for Youth Experiencing Homelessness: Practical Strategies for Front-Line Providers,* ed. S. Kidd, N. Slesnick, T. Frederick, J. Karabanow, and S. Gaetz. Canadian Observatory on Homelessness. https://www.homelesshub.ca/sites/default/files/attachments/Ch1-1-MentalHealthBook.pdf.

Brands, B., K. Leslie, L. Catz-Biro, and S. Li. 2005. "Heroin Use and Barriers to Treatment in Street-Involved Youth." *Addiction Research & Theory* 13 (5): 477–87. https://doi.org/10.1080/16066350500150624.

Bregman, H. R., N. M. Malik, M. J. L. Page, E. Makynen, and K. M. Lindahl. 2013. "Identity Profiles in Lesbian, Gay, and Bisexual Youth: The Role of Family Influences." *Journal of Youth and Adolescence* 42 (3): 417–30. https://doi.org/10.1007/s10964-012-9798-z.

Brooks, B. 2022. "Judge Blocks Biden Administration's Directives on Transgender Athletes, Bathrooms." *Reuters,* July 18. https://www.reuters.com/world/us/judge-blocks-biden-admin-directives-transgender-athletes-bathrooms-2022-07-16/#:~:text=July%2016%20(Reuters)%20%2D%20A,correspond%20with%20their%20gender%20identity.

Brown, C., C. M. Porta, M. E. Eisenberg, B. J. McMorris, and R. E. Sieving. 2020. "Family Relationships and the Health and Well-Being of Transgender and Gender-Diverse Youth: A Critical Review." *LGBT Health* 7 (8): 407–19. https://doi.org/10.1089/lgbt.2019.0200.

Brown, L. B. 2016. "What's in a Name? Examining the Creation and Use of Sexual Orientation and Gender Identity Labels." *Issues in Religion and Psychotherapy* 37 (1): 23–32. https://scholarsarchive.byu.edu/cgi/viewcontent.cgi?article=1554&context=irp.

Brown, T. 2002. "A Proposed Model of Bisexual Identity Development That Elaborates on Experiential Differences of Women and Men." *Journal of Bisexuality* 2 (4): 67–91. https://doi.org/10.1300/j159v02n04_05.

Brown, T. M., and E. Fee. 2003. "Alfred C. Kinsey: A Pioneer of Sex Research." *American Journal of Public Health* 93 (6): 896–97. https://doi.org/10.2105/ajph.93.6.896.

Bruce, D., R. Stall, A. Fata, and R. T. Campbell. 2014. "Modeling Minority Stress Effects on Homelessness and Health Disparities Among Young Men Who Have Sex with Men." *Journal of Urban Health* 91 (3): 568–80. https://doi.org/10.1007/s11524-014-9876-5.

Budescu, M., A. Sisselman-Borgia, and G. C. Torino. 2022. "Discrimination, Self-Harming Behaviors and Emotional Quality of Life Among Youth Experiencing Homelessness." *Journal of Social Distress and Homelessness* 31 (1): 55–64. https://doi.org/10.1080/1053 0789.2021.1879616.

Burkard, A. W., N. T. Pruitt, B. R. Medler, and A. M. Stark-Booth. 2009. "Validity and Reliability of the Lesbian, Gay, Bisexual Working Alliance Self-Efficacy Scales." *Training and Education in Professional Psychology* 3 (1): 37–46. https://psycnet.apa.org/doi /10.1037/1931-3918.3.1.37.

Bussee, M. n.d. "Statement of Apology by Former Exodus Leaders." Beyond Ex-Gay. Accessed July 13, 2023. https://www.beyondexgay.com/article/busseeapology.html.

Caccamo, A., R. Kachur, and S. P. Williams. 2017. "Narrative Review: Sexually Transmitted Diseases and Homeless Youth—What Do We Know About Sexually Transmitted Disease Prevalence and Risk?" *Sexually Transmitted Diseases* 44 (8): 466–76. https://doi .org/10.1097/OLQ.0000000000000633.

CAPTA (Child Abuse Prevention and Treatment Act) of 1974, Pub. L. No. 93–247, 88 Stat. 5. 1974. Codified as Amended at 42 U.S.C. § 5101, Note. https://www.govinfo.gov /content/pkg/COMPS-805/uslm/COMPS-805.xml.

Casey, L. S., S. L. Reisner, M. G. Findling et al. 2019. "Discrimination in the United States: Experiences of Lesbian, Gay, Bisexual, Transgender, and Queer Americans." *Health Services Research* 54 (S2): 1454–66. https://doi.org/10.1111/1475-6773.13229.

Cass, V. C. 1979. "Homosexual Identity Formation: A Theoretical Model." *Journal of Homosexuality* 4 (3): 219–35. https://doi.org/10.1300/j082v04n03_01.

Castellanos, H. D. 2016. "The Role of Institutional Placement, Family Conflict, and Homosexuality in Homelessness Pathways Among Latino LGBT Youth in New York City." *Journal of Homosexuality* 63 (5): 601–32. https://doi.org/10.1080/00918369.2015.1111108.

Castro, A. L., E. L. Gustafson, A. E. Ford et al. 2014. "Psychiatric Disorders, High-Risk Behaviors, and Chronicity of Episodes Among Predominantly African American Homeless Chicago Youth." *Journal of Health Care for the Poor and Underserved* 25 (3): 1201–16. https://doi.org/10.1353/hpu.2014.0124.

Catalano, R. F., M. L. Berglund, J. A. Ryan, H. S. Lonczak, and J. D. Hawkins. 2004. "Positive Youth Development in the United States: Research Findings on Evaluations of Positive Youth Development Programs." *Annals of the American Academy of Political and Social Science* 591 (1): 98–124. https://doi.org/10.1037/1522-3736.5.1.515a.

Cataldo, M. A. 2014. "Safe Haven: Granting Support to Victims of Child Abuse Who Have Been Judicially Emancipated." *Family Court Review* 52 (3): 592–609. https://doi .org/10.1111/fcre.12109.

Cauce, A. M., M. Paradise, J. A. Ginzler et al. 2000. "The Characteristics and Mental Health of Homeless Adolescents: Age and Gender Differences." *Journal of Emotional and Behavioral Disorders* 8 (4): 230–39. https://doi.org/10.1177/106342660000800403.

Cavazos-Rehg, P. A., M. J. Krauss, E. L. Spitznagel et al. 2009. "Age of Sexual Debut Among US Adolescents." *Contraception* 80 (2): 158–62. https://doi.org/10.1016/j.contraception .2009.02.014.

CDC (Centers for Disease Control and Prevention). n.d. "STI Prevalence and Incidence in the US." Accessed November 2, 2024. https://www.cdc.gov/sti/media/images/SPICE -prevalence-vs-incidence.png.

——. 2020. "Street Smart: Reducing HIV Risk Among Runaway and Homeless Youth." Internet Archive. https://web.archive.org/web/20200920152733/https://www.cdc.gov/hiv /research/interventionresearch/rep/packages/streetsmart.html.

——. 2021. "Chlamydial Infections." https://www.cdc.gov/std/treatment-guidelines/chlamydia .htm.

——. 2022a. "HIV and Transgender People: What CDC Is Doing." Internet Archive. https://web.archive.org/web/20240412204759/https://www.cdc.gov/hiv/group/gender /transgender/what-cdc-is-doing.html.

——. 2022b. "Number of Reported Cases of Acute Hepatitis C Virus Infection and Estimated Infections—United States, 2013–2020." https://www.cdc.gov/hepatitis/statistics /2020surveillance/hepatitis-c/figure-3.1.htm.

——. 2023a. "About Syphilis." https://www.cdc.gov/syphilis/about/index.html.

——. 2023b. "About Trichomoniasis." https://www.cdc.gov/trichomoniasis/about/index .html.

——. 2023c. "Gonorrhea (*Neisseria gonorrhoeae* Infection): 2023 Case Definition." https:// ndc.services.cdc.gov/case-definitions/gonorrhea-neisseria-gonorrhoeae-2023/.

——. 2024a. "About Genital Herpes." https://www.cdc.gov/herpes/about/index.html.

——. 2024b. "About HIV." https://www.cdc.gov/hiv/about/index.html.

——. 2024c. "About HPV." https://www.cdc.gov/hpv/about/index.html.

——. 2024d. "Estimated HIV Incidence and Prevalence in the United States, 2018–2022." *HIV Surveillance Supplemental Report* 29 (1). https://stacks.cdc.gov/view/cdc/156513 /cdc_156513_DS1.pdf.

——. 2024e. "Hepatitis B Surveillance." https://www.cdc.gov/hepatitis-surveillance-2022 /hepatitis-b/index.html.

——. 2024f. "Hepatitis C Surveillance." https://www.cdc.gov/hepatitis-surveillance-2022 /hepatitis-c/index.html.

——. 2024g. "How HIV Spreads." https://www.cdc.gov/hiv/causes/index.html.

——. 2024h. "Sexually Transmitted Infections Prevalence, Incidence, and Cost Estimates in the United States." https://www.cdc.gov/sti/php/communication-resources/prevalence -incidence-and-cost-estimates.html.

——. 2024i. "Syphilis." https://www.cdc.gov/std/treatment-guidelines/syphilis.htm.

Center for Substance Abuse Treatment. 2015. *Comprehensive Case Management for Substance Abuse Treatment.* Treatment Improvement Protocol (TIP) Series No. 27. Substance Abuse and Mental Health Services Administration. https://library.samhsa.gov /sites/default/files/sma15-4215.pdf.

Centrepoint. 2016. *Families Under Pressure: Preventing Family Breakdown and Youth Homelessness.* https://centrepoint.org.uk/sites/default/files/2023-06/families-under-pressure .pdf.

———. 2023. *Human Costs and Lost Potential: The Real Cost of Youth Homelessness.* https:// centrepoint.org.uk/sites/default/files/2023-09/Cost%20of%20Youth%20Home lessness%20Research%20Report%20-%20Full%20report%202023.pdf.

Chang, S. C., A. A. Singh, and K. Rossman. 2017. "Gender and Sexual Orientation Diversity Within the TGNC Community." In *Affirmative Counseling and Psychological Practice with Transgender and Gender Nonconforming Clients,* ed. A. A. Singh and L. M. Dickey. American Psychological Association. https://doi.org/10.1037/14957-002.

Chaturvedi, S. 2016. "Accessing Psychological Therapies: Homeless Young People's Views on Barriers and Facilitators." *Counselling and Psychotherapy Research* 16 (1): 54–63.

Chen, X., L. Thrane, L. B. Whitbeck, and K. Johnson. 2006. "Mental Disorders, Comorbidity, and Postrunaway Arrests Among Homeless and Runaway Adolescents." *Journal of Research on Adolescence* 16 (3): 379–402. https://doi.org/10.1111/j.1532-7795.2006.00499.x.

Children's Bureau. 2023. *The AFCARS Report.* Administration for Children and Families. https://www.acf.hhs.gov/sites/default/files/documents/cb/afcars-report-30.pdf.

———. 2024. *Child Maltreatment 2022.* Administration for Children and Families. https:// www.acf.hhs.gov/sites/default/files/documents/cb/cm2022.pdf.

Choi, S. K., B. D. M. Wilson, J. Shelton, and G. Gates. 2015. *Serving Our Youth 2015: The Needs and Experiences of Lesbian, Gay, Bisexual, Transgender, and Questioning Youth Experiencing Homelessness.* Williams Institute. https://williamsinstitute.law.ucla.edu/wp -content/uploads/Serving-Our-Youth-Update-Jun-2015.pdf.

Clark, C. M., and J. G. Kosciw. 2022. *Considerations for Measuring Sexual Orientation and Gender Identity in Surveys of Secondary School Students: Research Brief.* GLSEN. https://www.glsen.org/sites/default/files/2022-05/GLSEN_LGBTQ_Data_Inclusion _Research_Brief.pdf.

Clatts, M. C., W. R. Davis, J. L. Sotheran, and A. Atillasoy. 1998. "Correlates and Distribu-tion of HIV Risk Behaviors Among Homeless Youths in New York City: Implications for Prevention and Policy." *Child Welfare* 77 (2): 195–207.

Clatts, M. C., L. Goldsamt, H. Yi, and M. V. Gwadz. 2005. "Homelessness and Drug Abuse Among Young Men Who Have Sex with Men in New York City: A Preliminary Epide-miological Trajectory." *Journal of Adolescence* 28 (2): 201–14. https://doi.org/10.1016/j .adolescence.2005.02.003.

Cochran, B. N., A. J. Stewart, J. A. Ginzler, and A. M. Cauce. 2002. "Challenges Faced by Homeless Sexual Minorities: Comparison of Gay, Lesbian, Bisexual, and Transgender Homeless Adolescents with Their Heterosexual Counterparts." *American Journal of Public Health* 92 (5): 773–77. https://doi.org/10.2105/ajph.92.5.773.

Cohen, J. A., A. P. Mannarino, and E. Deblinger. 2006. *Treating Trauma and Traumatic Grief in Children and Adolescents.* Guilford.

Cohen, J. A., A. P. Mannarino, and K. Kinnish. 2017. "Trauma-Focused Cognitive Behav-ioral Therapy for Commercially Sexually Exploited Youth." *Journal of Child and Adoles-cent Trauma* 10: 175–85. https://link.springer.com/article/10.1007/s40653-015-0073-9.

Cohen, J. A., A. P. Mannarino, K. Wilson, and A. Zinny. 2018. *Implementing Trauma-Focused Cognitive Behavioral Therapy for LGBTQ Youth and Their Caregivers.* Allegh-eny Health Network. https://tfcbt.org/wp-content/uploads/2019/10/TF-CBT-LGBTQ -Implementation-Manual-FINAL.pdf.

Collins, M. E., and C. T. Mowbray. 2005. "Higher Education and Psychiatric Disabilities: National Survey of Campus Disability Services." *American Journal of Orthopsychiatry* 75 (2): 304–15. https://doi.org/10.1037/0002-9432.75.2.304.

Conner, B. M. 2016. "Salvaging 'Safe Spaces': Toward Model Standards for LGBTQ Youth-Serving Professionals Encountering Law Enforcement." *Journal of Gender, Social Policy & the Law* 24 (2): 199–241. https://digitalcommons.wcl.american.edu/cgi/viewcontent.cgi?article=1680&context=jgspl.

Conron, K. J. 2020. *LGBT Youth Population in the United States.* Williams Institute. https://williamsinstitute.law.ucla.edu/wp-content/uploads/LGBT-Youth-US-Pop-Sep-2020.pdf.

Cooley, S. J., M. L. Quinton, M. J. G. Holland, B. J. Parry, and J. Cumming. 2019. "The Experiences of Homeless Youth When Using Strengths Profiling to Identify Their Character Strengths." *Frontiers in Psychology* 10: 2036. https://doi.org/10.3389/fpsyg.2019.02036.

Coolhart, D., and M. T. Brown. 2017. "The Need for Safe Spaces: Exploring the Experiences of Homeless LGBTQ Youth in Shelters." *Children and Youth Services Review* 82: 230–38. https://doi.org/10.1016/j.childyouth.2017.09.021.

Copen, C. E., A. Chandra, and I. Febo-Vazquez. 2016. *Sexual Behavior, Sexual Attraction, and Sexual Orientation Among Adults Aged 18–44 in the United States: Data from the 2011–2013 National Survey of Family Growth.* National Health Statistics Reports No. 88. National Center for Health Statistics. https://www.cdc.gov/nchs//data/nhsr/nhsr088.pdf.

Corliss, H. L., C. S. Goodenow, L. Nichols, and S. B. Austin. 2011. "High Burden of Homelessness Among Sexual-Minority Adolescents: Findings from a Representative Massachusetts High School Sample." *American Journal of Public Health* 101 (9): 1683–89. https://doi.org/10.2105/ajph.test.2011.300155.

Côté, P.-B., and M. Blais. 2019. "Between Resignation, Resistance and Recognition: A Qualitative Analysis of LGBTQ+ Youth Profiles of Homelessness Agencies Utilization." *Children and Youth Services Review* 100: 437–43. https://doi.org/10.1016/j.childyouth.2019.03.024.

Craig, S. L. 2012. "Strengths First: An Empowering Case Management Model for Multi-ethnic Sexual Minority Youth." *Journal of Gay & Lesbian Social Services* 24 (3): 274–88. https://doi.org/10.1080/10538720.2012.697833.

Craig, S. L., A. D. Eaton, A. Kirkland et al. 2021. "Towards an Integrative Self: A Digital Photo Elicitation Study of Resilience Among Key Marginalized Populations of Sexual and Gender Minority Youth." *International Journal of Qualitative Studies on Health and Well-Being* 16. https://doi.org/10.1080/17482631.2021.1961572.

Crawford, D. M., L. B. Whitbeck, and D. R. Hoyt. 2011. "Propensity for Violence Among Homeless and Runaway Adolescents: An Event History Analysis." *Crime and Delinquency* 57 (6): 950–68. https://doi.org/10.1177/0011128709335100.

Crawley, S. A. 2021. "Allies and Allyship." In *Critical Understanding in Education: Encyclopedia of Queer Studies in Education*, ed. K. K. Strunk and S. A. Shelton. Brill. https://doi.org/10.1163/9789004506725_005.

Crosland, K., R. D. Haynes Jr., and S. Clarke. 2020. "The Functional Assessment Interview for Runaways (FAIR): An Assessment Tool to Assist with Behavior Support Plan

Development to Reduce Runaway Behavior." *Child and Adolescent Social Work Journal* 37 (1): 73–82. https://doi.org/10.1007/s10560-019-00626-7.

Cutuli, J. J., D. Treglia, and J. E. Herbers. 2020. "Adolescent Homelessness and Associated Features: Prevalence and Risk Across Eight States." *Child Psychiatry & Human Development* 51 (1): 48–58. https://doi.org/10.1007/s10578-019-00909-1.

CWIG (Child Welfare Information Gateway). 2021. *Foster Care Statistics 2019.* Child Welfare Information Gateway; Children's Bureau, Office of the Administration for Children & Families. https://cwlibrary.childwelfare.gov/discovery/delivery/01CWIG_INST:01CWIG /1218691630007651.

Damian, A. J., D. Ponce, A. Ortiz-Siberon et al. 2022. "Understanding the Health and Health-Related Social Needs of Youth Experiencing Homelessness: A Photovoice Study." *International Journal of Environmental Research and Public Health* 19 (16). https://doi .org/10.3390/ijerph19169799.

Darbyshire, P., E. Muir-Cochrane, J. Fereday, J. Jureidini, and A. Drummond. 2006. "Engagement with Health and Social Care Services: Perceptions of Homeless Young People with Mental Health Problems." *Health and Social Care in the Community* 14 (6): 553–62. https://doi.org/10.1111/j.1365-2524.2006.00643.x.

D'Augelli, A. R., A. H. Grossman, and M. T. Starks. 2005. "Parents' Awareness of Lesbian, Gay, and Bisexual Youth's Sexual Orientation." *Journal of Marriage and Family* 67 (2): 474–82. https://doi.org/10.1111/j.0022-2445.2005.00129.x.

Davidson, M. 2007. "Seeking Refuge Under the Umbrella: Inclusion, Exclusion, and Organizing Within the Category *Transgender.*" *Sexuality Research & Social Policy* 4 (4): 60–80. https://doi.org/10.1525/srsp.2007.4.4.60.

Davies, D. 1996. "Towards a Model of Gay Affirmative Therapy." In *Pink Therapy: A Guide for Counsellors and Therapists Working with Lesbian, Gay and Bisexual Clients*, ed. D. Davies and C. Neal. Open University Press.

——. 1998. "The Six Necessary and Sufficient Conditions Applied to Working with Lesbian, Gay, and Bisexual Clients." *Person-Centered Journal* 5 (2): 111–20.

Davila, J., J. Jabbour, C. Dyar, and B. A. Feinstein. 2019. "Bi+ Visibility: Characteristics of Those Who Attempt to Make Their Bisexual+ Identity Visible and the Strategies They Use." *Archives of Sexual Behavior* 48 (1): 199–211. https://doi.org/10.1007/s10508-018-1284-6.

Davy, Z. 2015. "The DSM-5 and the Politics of Diagnosing Transpeople." *Archives of Sexual Behavior* 44 (5): 1165–76. https://doi.org/10.1007/s10508-015-0573-6.

de Kervor, D. N. 2004. *City Enters Partnership to Assist Lesbian and Gay Homeless Youth.* FreeLibrary.http://www.thefreelibrary.com/City+enters+partnership+to+assist+lesbian +and+gay+homeless+youth.-a0114238855.

de Sousa, T., and M. Henry. 2024. *The 2024 Annual Homelessness Assessment Report (AHAR) to Congress: Part 1: Point-in-Time Estimates of Homelessness.* U.S. Department of Housing and Urban Development. https://www.huduser.gov/portal/sites/default/ files/pdf/2024-AHAR-Part-1.pdf.

DeChants, J. P., A. E. Green, M. N. Price, and C. K. Davis. 2021. *Homelessness and Housing Instability Among LGBTQ Youth.* Trevor Project. https://www.thetrevorproject.org /wp-content/uploads/2022/02/Trevor-Project-Homelessness-Report.pdf.

DeChants, J. P., J. Shelton, Y. Anyon, and K. Bender. 2022. "'I Just Want to Move Forward': Themes of Resilience Among LGBTQ Young Adults Experiencing Family Rejection and Housing Insecurity." *Children and Youth Services Review* 139. https://doi.org/10.1016/j .childyouth.2022.106552.

DeHart, D., B. Anderson, and J. Martin. 2021. "Transition-Aged Youth Who Are Homeless and Misuse Substances: A Qualitative Study of Service Needs." *Journal of Social Service Research* 47 (6): 872–85. https://doi.org/10.1080/01488376.2021.1941503.

Denning, P. 2001. "Strategies for Implementation of Harm Reduction in Treatment Settings." *Journal of Psychoactive Drugs* 33 (1): 23–26. https://doi.org/10.1080/02791072.2001.10400464.

DESC (Downtown Emergency Service Center). n.d. *Vulnerability Assessment Tool.* Accessed July 13, 2023. https://www.desc.org/what-we-do/vulnerability-assessment-tool/.

Desgarennes, P. R. 2017. "This Young Advocate Is Helping Providers Serve Undocumented LGBTQ Youth." True Colors United. https://truecolorsunited.org/young-advocate-developing -tool-help-providers-serve-undocumented-lgbtq-youth/.

Dettlaff, A. J., M. Washburn, L. C. Carr, and A. N. Vogel. 2018. "Lesbian, Gay, and Bisexual (LGB) Youth Within in Welfare: Prevalence, Risk and Outcomes." *Child Abuse & Neglect* 80: 183–93. https://doi.org/10.1016/j.chiabu.2018.03.009.

dickey, l. m., and J. A. Puckett. 2023. *Affirmative Counseling for Transgender and Gender Diverse Clients.* Hogrefe.

Dillon, F. R., E. J. Alessi, S. Craig, R. C. Eber-Sole, S. M. Kumar, and C. Spadola. 2015. "Development of the Lesbian, Gay, and Bisexual Affirmative Counseling Self-Efficacy Inventory–Short Form (LGB-CSI-SF)." *Psychology of Sexual Orientation and Gender Diversity* 2 (1): 86–95. https://doi.org/10.1037/sgd0000087.

Donovan, S. 2012. "Remarks of Secretary Shaun Donovan, National Gay and Lesbian Task Force, Creating Change Conference, Hilton Baltimore, Saturday, January 28, 2012." U.S. Department of Housing and Urban Development Archives. https://archives.hud.gov /remarks/donovan/speeches/2012-01-28.cfm.

Drescher, J. 2015. "Out of DSM: Depathologizing Homosexuality." *Behavioral Sciences* 5: 565–75. https://doi.org/10.3390/bs5040565.

Dresser, R. 1992. "Wanted. Single, White Male for Medical Research." *Hastings Center Report* 22 (1): 24–29.

Drinan, R. F. 2002. *The Mobilization of Shame: A World View of Human Rights.* Yale University Press.

Duggan, L. 2003. *The Twilight of Equality? Neoliberalism, Cultural Politics, and the Attack on Democracy.* Beacon.

Dunn, M., and J. Krehely. 2012. *Runaway and Homeless Youth Act Should Include Gay and Transgender Youth.* Center for American Progress. https://www.americanprogress.org /issues/lgbt/news/2012/05/10/11572/runaway-and-homeless-youth-act-should-include -gay-and-transgender-youth/.

Durso, L. E., and G. J. Gates. 2012. *Serving Our Youth: Findings from a National Survey of Services Providers Working with Lesbian, Gay, Bisexual and Transgender Youth Who Are Homeless or at Risk of Becoming Homeless.* Williams Institute. https://williamsinstitute .law.ucla.edu/wp-content/uploads/Serving-Our-Youth-July-2012.pdf.

Edidin, J. P., Z. Ganim, S. J. Hunter, and N. S. Karnik. 2012. "The Mental and Physical Health of Homeless Youth: A Literature Review." *Child Psychiatry & Human Development* 43 (3): 354–75. https://doi.org/10.1007/s10578-011-0270-1.

Eisenberg, M. E., E. D. Kelly, A.-L. McRee, S. S. Brady, and A. J. Barnes. 2017. "Homelessness Experiences and Gender Identity in a Population-Based Sample of Adolescents." *Preventive Medicine Reports* 16: 1–3. https://doi.org/10.1016/j.pmedr.2019.100986.

Erney, R., and K. Weber. 2018. "Not All Children Are Straight and White: Strategies for Serving Youth of Color in Out-of-Home Care Who Identify as LGBTQ." *Child Welfare* 96 (2): 151–77. https://www.jstor.org/stable/48624548.

Erzen, T. 2006. *Straight to Jesus: Sexual and Christian Conversions in the Ex-Gay Movement.* University of California Press.

Estrada, G. S. 2011. "*Two Spirits, Nádleeh*, and LGBTQ2 Navajo Gaze." *American Indian Culture and Research Journal* 35 (4): 167–90. https://masculinisation.files.wordpress.com/2015/05/two-spirits-nadleeh-and-lgbtq2-navajo-gaze-by-gabriel-s-estrada.pdf.

ETR (Education Training Research). n.d. *Be Proud! Be Responsible!* https://www.etr.org/ebi/programs/be-proud-be-responsible/.

Ewing, J. A. 1984. "Detecting Alcoholism: The CAGE Questionnaire." *Journal of the American Medical Association* 252 (14): 1905–7. https://doi.org/10.1001/jama.252.14.1905.

Executive Order 13782, 3 C.F.R. 15607. 2017.

Eysenck, H. J. 1996. "Personality and Crime: Where Do We Stand." *Psychology, Crime & Law* 2 (3): 143–52.

Ezell, M. 2001. *Advocacy in the Human Services.* Brooks/Cole.

Factor, R., and E. Rothblum. 2008. "Exploring Gender Identity and Community Among Three Groups of Transgender Individuals in the United States: MTFs, FTMs, and Genderqueers." *Health Sociology Review* 17 (3): 235–53. https://doi.org/10.5172/hesr.451.17.3.235.

Family Acceptance Project. n.d. "Welcome to the Family Acceptance Project." Accessed December 28, 2017. https://familyproject.sfsu.edu/.

Family Support Services of the Bay Area. n.d. "Family Preservation Program." Accessed December 28, 2017. http://fssba.org/family-preservation-program/.

FBI (Federal Bureau of Investigation). 2020. "2019 Hate Crime Statistics: Table 1—Incidents, Offenses, Victims, and Known Offenders, by Bias Motivation, 2019." FBI: UCR. https://ucr.fbi.gov/hate-crime/2019/topic-pages/tables/table-1.xls.

Ferguson, K. M., B. Xie, and S. Glynn. 2012. "Adapting the Individual Placement and Support Model with Homeless Young Adults." *Child & Youth Care Forum* 41 (3): 277–94. https://doi.org/10.1007/s10566-011-9163-5.

Ferguson, K. M., and E. M. Maccio. 2015. "Promising Programs for Lesbian, Gay, Bisexual, Transgender, and Queer/Questioning Runaway and Homeless Youth." *Journal of Social Service Research* 41 (5): 659–83. https://doi.org/10.1080/01488376.2015.1058879.

Ferguson-Colvin, K. M., and E. M. Maccio. 2012. *Toolkit for Practitioners/Researchers Working with Lesbian, Gay, Bisexual, Transgender, and Queer/Questioning (LGBTQ) Runaway and Homeless Youth (RHY).* National Resource Center for Permanency and Family Connections, Silberman School of Social Work at Hunter College. https://cwlibrary.childwelfare.gov/discovery/delivery/01CWIG_INST:01CWIG/1218286110007651.

Fernandes, A. L. 2007. *Runaway and Homeless Youth: Demographics, Programs, and Emerging Issues*. CRS Report for Congress. Order Code RL33785. https://www.everycrsreport.com/files/20070615_RL33785_998803589e285a5a6081f39535571bd1f632d1b4.pdf.

FFCC (First Focus Campaign for Children). 2018. *Proactive Kids Agenda: How to Create Lasting, Positive Change in the Lives of Children and Families During the 116th Congress*. https://campaignforchildren.org/wp-content/uploads/sites/2/2018/12/Proactive-Kids-Agenda-FFCC-1.22.19.pdf.

Fish, J. N., L. Baams, A. S. Wojciak, and S. T. Russell. 2019. "Are Sexual Minority Youth Overrepresented in Foster Care, Child Welfare, and Out-of-Home Placement? Findings from Nationally Representative Data." *Child Abuse & Neglect* 89: 203–11. https://doi.org/10.1016/j.chiabu.2019.01.005.

Fisher, T. 2006. "Transformative Mediation: Differentiating Principles from Illusions—Part 1." *ADR Bulletin* 9 (3): 2. https://librarysearch.bond.edu.au/discovery/delivery/61BOND_INST:BOND/1281272900002381.

——. 2007. "Transformative Mediation: Differentiating Principles from Illusions—Part 2." *ADR Bulletin* 9 (5): 4. https://librarysearch.bond.edu.au/discovery/delivery/61BOND_INST:BOND/1281273590002381.

Flentje, A., N. C. Heck, and B. N. Cochran. 2014. "Experiences of Ex-Ex-Gay Individuals in Sexual Reorientation Therapy: Reasons for Seeking Treatment, Perceived Helpfulness and Harmfulness of Treatment, and Post-Treatment Identification." *Journal of Homosexuality* 61 (9): 1242–68. https://doi.org/10.1080/00918369.2014.926763.

Ford, C. L., T. Slavin, K. L. Hilton, and S. L. Holt. 2013. "Intimate Partner Violence Prevention Services and Resources in Los Angeles: Issues, Needs, and Challenges for Assisting Lesbian, Gay, Bisexual, and Transgender Clients." *Health Promotion Practice* 14 (6): 841–49. https://doi.org/10.1177/1524839912467645.

Forge, N., R. Hartinger-Saunders, E. Wright, and E. Ruel. 2018. "Out of the System and Onto the Streets: LGBTQ-Identified Youth Experiencing Homelessness with Past Child Welfare System Involvement." *Child Welfare* 96 (2): 47–74.

Forge, N., T. Lewinson, B. M. Garner, C. Braxton, L. Greenwald, and O. Maley. 2018. "'Humbling Experiences': A Photovoice Project with Sexual and Gender-Expansive Youth Experiencing Homelessness." *Journal of Community Psychology* 46: 806–22. https://doi.org/10.1002/jcop.21974.

Foucault, M. 1990. *The History of Sexuality*, vol. 1, *An Introduction*. Vantage. Originally published in 1976 by Éditions Gallimard.

Freeman, L., and D. Hamilton. 2008. *A Count of Homeless Youth in New York City*. Report prepared for the Empire State Coalition of Youth and Family Services.

——. 2013. *A Count of Unaccompanied Homeless Youths in New York City*. Supportive Housing Network of New York. https://shnny.org/images/uploads/2013-NYC-Homeless-Youth-Report.pdf.

French, R., M. Reardon, and P. Smith. 2003. "Engaging with a Mental Health Service: Perspectives of At-Risk Youth." *Child and Adolescent Social Work Journal* 20 (6): 529–48.

Frydenberg, E., and R. Lewis. 1996. "A Replication Study of the Structure of the Adolescent Coping Scale: Multiple Forms and Applications of a Self-Report Inventory in a

Counseling and Research Context." *European Journal of Psychological Assessment* 12 (3): 224–35. https://doi.org/10.1027/1015-5759.12.3.224.

Fuechtner, V., D. E. Haynes, and R. M. Jones. 2018. "Toward a Global History of Sexual Science: Movements, Networks, and Deployments." In *A Global History of Sexual Science, 1880–1960*, ed. V. Fuechtner, D. E. Haynes, and R. M. Jones. University of California Press. https://doi.org/10.1525/california/9780520293373.003.0001.

Fulginiti, A., E. Rice, H.-T. Hsu, H. Rhoades, and H. Winetrobe. 2016. "Risky Integration: A Social Network Analysis of Network Position, Exposure, and Suicidal Ideation Among Homeless Youth." *Crisis* 37 (3): 184–93. https://doi.org/10.1027/0227-5910/a000374.

FYSB (Family and Youth Services Bureau). 2023a. *Fact Sheet: Basic Center Program*. https://www.acf.hhs.gov/sites/default/files/documents/fysb/BCP_Fact_Sheet_2023.pdf.

——. 2023b. *Fact Sheet: Street Outreach Program*. https://www.acf.hhs.gov/sites/default/files/documents/fysb/SOP_Fact_Sheet_2023.pdf.

——. 2023c. *Fact Sheet: Transitional Living Program*. https://acf.gov/system/files/documents/fysb/rhy-sop-fact-sheet-508.pdf

Gallardo, K. R., S. C. Narendorf, C. M. Markham, M. D. Swartz, and D. Santa Maria. 2023. "Hidden Champions: Exploring Supportive Family Relationships of Youth Experiencing Homelessness." *Child & Family Social Work* 28 (1): 248–57. https://doi.org/10.1111/cfs.12957.

Gangamma, R., N. Slesnick, P. Toviessi, and J. Serovich. 2008. "Comparison of HIV Risks Among Gay, Lesbian, Bisexual and Heterosexual Homeless Youth." *Journal of Youth and Adolescence* 37 (4): 456–64. https://doi.org/10.1007/s10964-007-9171-9.

Garrett, S. B., D. H. Higa, M. M. Phares, P. L. Peterson, E. A. Wells, and J. S. Baer. 2008. "Homeless Youths' Perceptions of Services and Transitions to Stable Housing." *Evaluation and Program Planning* 31 (4): 436–44. https://doi.org/10.1016/j.evalprogplan.2008.04.012.

Garvey, R., E. R. Pedersen, E. J. D'Amico, B. A. Ewing, and J. S. Tucker. 2018. "Recruitment and Retention of Homeless Youth in a Substance Use and HIV-Risk Reduction Program." *Field Methods* 30 (1): 22–36. https://doi.org/10.1177/1525822X17728346.

Gattis, M. N. 2013. "An Ecological Systems Comparison Between Homeless Sexual Minority Youths and Homeless Heterosexual Youths." *Journal of Social Service Research* 39 (1): 38–49. https://doi.org/10.1080/01488376.2011.633814.

Gattis, M. N., and A. Larson. 2016. "Perceived Racial, Sexual Identity, and Homeless Status-Related Discrimination Among Black Adolescents and Young Adults Experiencing Homelessness: Relations with Depressive Symptoms and Suicidality." *American Journal of Orthopsychiatry* 86 (1): 79–90. https://doi.org/10.1037/ort0000096.

——. 2017. "Perceived Microaggressions and Mental Health in a Sample of Black Youths Experiencing Homelessness." *Social Work Research* 41 (1): 7–17. https://doi.org/10.1093/swr/svw030.

Gearing, R. E., C. S. J. Schwalbe, R. H. Lee, and K. E. Hoagwood. 2013. "The Effectiveness of Booster Sessions in CBT Treatment for Child and Adolescent Mood and Anxiety Disorders." *Depression and Anxiety* 30 (9): 800–808. https://doi.org/10.1002/da.22118.

Gegenfurtner, A., and M. Gebhardt. 2017. "Sexuality Education Including Lesbian, Gay, Bisexual, and Transgender (LGBT) Issues in Schools." *Educational Research Review* 22: 215–22. https://doi.org/10.1016/j.edurev.2017.10.002.

Georgevich, M. 2013. "Rethink Immigration: A Homeless, Undocumented & Detained LGBT Teen's Struggle for Due Process." National Immigrant Justice Center. https://www.immigrantjustice.org/staff/blog/rethink-immigration-homeless-undocumented-detained-lgbt-teens-struggle-due-process.

GLAAD. 2021. "Tips for Allies of Transgender People." https://www.glaad.org/transgender/allies.

——. 2022a. *Glossary of Terms: LGBTQ.* In *GLAAD Media Reference Guide*, 11th ed. https://www.glaad.org/reference/terms.

——. 2022b. *Glossary of Terms: Transgender.* In *GLAAD Media Reference Guide*, 11th ed. https://www.glaad.org/reference/trans-terms.

Glasser, A. M., A. Hinton, A. Wermert, J. Macisco, and J. M. Nemeth. 2022. "Characterizing Tobacco and Marijuana Use Among Youth Combustible Tobacco Users Experiencing Homelessness: Considering Product Type, Brand, Flavor, Frequency, and Higher-Risk Use Patterns and Predictors." *BMC Public Health* 22 (1). https://doi.org/10.1186/s12889-022-13244-3.

GLSEN. n.d. "Solidarity Week." Accessed August 4, 2022. https://www.glsen.org/programs/solidarity-week.

——. 2018. *Laws Prohibiting "Promotion of Homosexuality" in Schools: Impacts and Implications.* https://www.glsen.org/sites/default/files/2019-10/GLSEN-Research-Laws-that-Prohibit-Promotion-of-Homosexuality-Implications.pdf.

——. 2024. "Inclusive Curricular Standards Policies." https://maps.glsen.org/inclusive-curricular-standards-policies/.

Gonsiorek, J. C., R. L. Sell, and J. D. Weinrich. 1995. "Definition and Measurement of Sexual Orientation." *Suicide and Life-Threatening Behavior* 25 (S1): 40–51. https://doi.org/10.1111/j.1943-278x.1995.tb00489.x.

Gordon, L. E., and T. J. Silva. 2015. "Inhabiting the Sexual Landscape: Toward an Interpretive Theory of the Development of Sexual Orientation and Identity." *Journal of Homosexuality* 62 (4): 495–530. https://doi.org/10.1080/00918369.2014.986417.

Gordon, N., and J. Krehely. 2011. *Combating LGBT Youth Homelessness.* Center for American Progress. https://www.americanprogress.org/article/combating-lgbt-youth-homelessness/.

Grabbe, L., S. T. Nguy, and M. K. Higgins. 2012. "Spirituality Development for Homeless Youth: A Mindfulness Meditation Feasibility Pilot." *Journal of Child and Family Studies* 21 (6): 925–37. https://doi.org/10.1007/s10826-011-9552-2.

Grafsky, E. L., A. Letcher, N. Slesnick, and J. M. Serovich. 2011. "Comparison of Treatment Response Among GLB and Non-GLB Street-Living Youth." *Children and Youth Services Review* 33 (5): 569–74. https://doi.org/10.1016/j.childyouth.2010.10.007.

Gready, P., and S. Robins. 2014. "From Transitional to Transformative Justice: A New Agenda for Practice." *International Journal of Transitional Justice* 8 (3): 339–61. https://doi.org/10.1017/9781316676028.002.

Green, A. E., J. P. DeChants, M. N. Price, and C. K. Davis. 2022. "Association of Gender-Affirming Hormone Therapy with Depression, Thoughts of Suicide, and Attempted Suicide Among Transgender and Nonbinary Youth." *Journal of Adolescent Health* 70 (4): 643–49. https://doi.org/10.1016/j.jadohealth.2021.10.036.

Greenfield, B., E. J. Alessi, D. Manning, C. Dato, and M. Dank. 2020. "Learning to Endure: A Qualitative Examination of the Protective Factors of Homeless Transgender and Gender Expansive Youth Engaged in Survival Sex." *International Journal of Transgender Health* 22 (3): 316–29. https://doi.org/10.1080/26895269.2020.1838387.

Greeson, J. K. P., D. Treglia, S. Morones, M. Hopkins, and D. Mikell. 2020. "Youth Matters: Philly (YMP): Development, Usability, Usefulness, & Accessibility of a Mobile Web-Based App for Homeless and Unstably Housed Youth." *Children and Youth Services Review* 108: 1–8. https://doi.org/10.1016/j.childyouth.2019.104586.

Greeson, J. K. P., D. Treglia, D. S. Wolfe, and S. Wasch. 2019. "Prevalence and Correlates of Sex Trafficking Among Homeless and Runaway Youths Presenting for Shelter Services." *Social Work Research* 43 (2): 91–100. https://doi.org/10.1093/swr/svz001.

Grossman, A. H., A. R. D'Augelli, and N. P. Salter. 2006. "Male-to-Female Transgender Youth: Gender Expression Milestones, Gender Atypicality, Victimization, and Parents' Responses." *Journal of GLBT Family Studies* 2 (1): 71–92. https://doi.org/10.1300/J461v02n01_04.

Grossman, A. H., A. R. D'Augelli, N. P. Salter, and S. M. Hubbard. 2005. "Comparing Gender Expression, Gender Nonconformity, and Parents' Responses to Female-to-Male and Male-to Female Transgender Youth: Implications for Counseling." *Journal of LGBT Issues in Counseling* 1 (1): 41–59. https://doi.org/10.1300/j462v01n01_04.

Grov, C., D. S. Bimbi, J. E. Nanin, and J. T. Parsons. 2006. "Race, Ethnicity, Gender, and Generational Factors Associated with the Coming-Out Process Among Gay, Lesbian, and Bisexual Individuals." *Journal of Sex Research* 43 (2): 115–21. https://doi.org/10.1080/00224490609552306.

Hadland, S. E., T. Kerr, K. Li, J. S. Montaner, and W. Wood. 2009. "Access to Drug and Alcohol Treatment Among a Cohort of Street-Involved Youth." *Drug and Alcohol Dependence* 101 (1–2): 1–7. https://doi.org/10.1016/j.drugalcdep.2008.10.012.

Haldeman, D. C. 1994. "The Practice and Ethics of Sexual Orientation Conversion Therapy." *Journal of Consulting and Clinical Psychology* 62 (2): 221–27.

Halkitis, P. N., F. Kapadia, D. E. Siconolfi et al. 2013. "Individual, Psychosocial, and Social Correlates of Unprotected Anal Intercourse in a New Generation of Young Men Who Have Sex with Men in New York City." *American Journal of Public Health* 103 (5): 889–95. https://doi.org/10.2105/AJPH.2012.300963.

Hammer, H., D. Finkelhor, and A. J. Sedlak. 2002. *Runaway/Thrownaway Children: National Estimates and Characteristics*. National Criminal Justice Reference Service. https://www.ncjrs.gov/pdffiles1/ojjdp/196469.pdf.

Harrington-Motley, K., E. Lulow, N. Kozloff et al. 2017. *Frequently Asked Questions for Child, Adolescent, and Adult Psychiatrists and Other Professionals Working with Transitional Age Youth with Substance Use Disorders*. American Academy of Child and Adolescent Psychiatry. https://www.aacap.org/App_Themes/AACAP/Docs/clinical_practice_center/systems_of_care/sud-tay.pdf.

Harvey, R. G., and L. Stone Fish. 2015. "Queer Youth in Family Therapy." *Family Process* 54 (3): 396–417. https://doi.org/10.1111/famp.12170.

Hatchel, T., D. L. Espelage, and Y. Huang. 2018. "Sexual Harassment Victimization, School Belonging, and Depressive Symptoms Among LGBTQ Adolescents: Temporal Insights." *American Journal of Orthopsychiatry* 88 (4): 422–30. https://doi.org/10.1037/ort0000279.

Havighurst, R. J. 1953. *Human Development and Education.* D. McKay.

HCYA (Homeless Children and Youth Act), H.R. 5221, 118th Congress. 2023. https://www.congress.gov/bill/118th-congress/house-bill/5221/all-actions.

——, S. 1469, 117th Congress. 2021. https://www.congress.gov/bill/117th-congress/senate-bill/1469.

Hein, L. C. 2010. "Where Did You Sleep Last Night? Homeless Male Adolescents: Gay, Bisexual, Transgender and Heterosexual Compared." *Southern Online Journal of Nursing Research* 10 (1).

Herek, G. M. 2003. "Evaluating Interventions to Alter Sexual Orientation: Methodological and Ethical Considerations." *Archives of Sexual Behavior* 32 (5): 438–39.

Herman, J. L., A. R. Flores, T. N. T. Brown, B. D. M. Wilson, and K. J. Conron. 2017. *Age of Individuals Who Identify as Transgender in the United States.* Williams Institute. https://williamsinstitute.law.ucla.edu/wp-content/uploads/Age-Trans-Individuals-Jan-2017.pdf.

Herting, M. M., and E. R. Sowell. 2017. "Puberty and Structural Brain Development in Humans." *Frontiers in Neuroendocrinology* 44: 122–37. https://doi.org/10.1016/j.yfrne.2016.12.003.

HHYP (Hollywood Homeless Youth Partnership). n.d. "What We Do." Accessed August 6, 2022. https://5mt.2b2.myftpupload.com/what-we-do/.

Higbee, M., E. R. Wright, and R. M. Roemerman. 2022. "Conversion Therapy in the Southern United States: Prevalence and Experiences of the Survivors." *Journal of Homosexuality* 69 (4): 612–31. https://doi.org/10.1080/00918369.2020.1840213.

Higgs, J. 2019. "Appreciating Practice Wisdom." In *Practice Wisdom: Values and Interpretations,* ed. J. Higgs. Brill.

Hishida, J. 2016. *Engaging Youth Experiencing Homelessness: Core Practices & Services.* National Health Care for the Homeless Council. https://nhchc.org/wp-content/uploads/2019/08/engaging-youth-experiencing-homelessness.pdf.

Hoefer, R. 2019. *Advocacy Practice for Social Justice,* 4th ed. Oxford University Press.

Hoffman, R. M. 2001. "The Measurement of Masculinity and Femininity: Historical Perspective and Implications for Counseling." *Journal of Counseling & Development* 79 (4): 472–85. https://doi.org/10.1002/j.1556-6676.2001.tb01995.x.

Holger-Ambrose, B., C. Langmade, L. D. Edinburgh, and E. Saewyc. 2013. "The Illusions and Juxtapositions of Commercial Sexual Exploitation Among Youth: Identifying Effective Street-Outreach Strategies." *Journal of Child Sexual Abuse* 22 (3): 326–40. https://doi.org/10.1080/10538712.2013.737443.

Hollingsworth, H., and S. Ho. 2025. "In Battle Against Transgender Rights, Trump Targets HUD's Housing Policies." Associated Press. https://www.ap.org/news-highlights/spotlights/2025/in-battle-against-transgender-rights-trump-targets-huds-housing-policies/.

Holm, J. M., and C. A. B. Minton. 2016. "A Predictive Model of Adolescent Persistence in Counseling." *Children and Youth Services Review* 67: 161–67. https://doi.org/10.1016/j.childyouth.2016.06.005.

Horvath, A. O., and L. S. Greenberg. 1986. "The Development of the Working Alliance Inventory." In *The Psychotherapeutic Process: A Research Handbook,* ed. L. S. Greenberg and W. M. Pinsof. Guilford.

Hotton, A. L., R. Garofalo, L. M. Kuhns, and A. K. Johnson. 2013. "Substance Use as a Mediator of the Relationship Between Life Stress and Sexual Risk Among Young Transgender Women." *AIDS Education and Prevention* 25 (1): 62–71. https://doi.org/10.1521/aeap.2013.25.1.62.

Howard, J. 2020. "Substance Use Among Young People Experiencing Homelessness: A Brief Motivational Enhancement Approach." In *Clinical Care for Homeless, Runaway and Refugee Youth: Intervention Approaches, Education and Research Directions*, ed. C. Warf and G. Charles. Springer.

Howard, J., D. Tran, and S. Rankin. 2015. *At What Cost: The Minimum Cost of Criminalizing Homelessness in Seattle and Spokane*. Seattle University School of Law. https://digital commons.law.seattleu.edu/cgi/viewcontent.cgi?article=1000&context=hrap.

HRC (Human Rights Campaign). n.d.a. "Municipal Equality Index 2024." Accessed August 8. 2025. https://www.hrc.org/resources/municipal-equality-index.

——. n.d.b. "State Equality Index 2024." Accessed August 8, 2025. https://www.hrc.org/resources/state-equality-index.

——. n.d.c. Why We Ask Each Other Our Pronouns https://www.hrc.org/resources/why-we-ask-each-other-our-pronouns.

HRCF (Human Rights Campaign Foundation). 2022. *Being an LGBTQ+ Ally*. https://reports.hrc.org/being-an-lgbtq-ally.

Hudson, A. L., A. Nyamathi, B. Greengold et al. 2010. "Health-Seeking Challenges Among Homeless Youth." *Nursing Research* 59 (3): 212–18. https://doi.org/10.1097/NNR.0b013e3181d1a8a9.

Institute of Medicine. 2011. *What You Need to Know About Infectious Disease*. National Academies Press. https://doi.org/10.17226/13006.

IPS Employment Center at Research Foundation for Mental Hygiene. 2024. "IPS Supported Employment Practice & Principles." https://ipsworks.org/wp-content/uploads/2017/08/IPS-Practice-Principles-rev-6.2024.pdf.

Jacobs, J., and M. Freundlich. 2006. "Achieving Permanency for LGBTQ Youth." *Child Welfare* 85 (2): 299–316.

Jadidzadeh, A., and R. Kneebone. 2022. "How Do Youth Use Homeless Shelters?" *Journal of Poverty* 26 (4): 322–36. https://doi.org/10.1080/10875549.2021.1910106.

Jansson, B. S. 2018. *Becoming an Effective Policy Advocate: From Policy Practice to Social Justice*, 8th ed. Cengage Learning.

Jean, M. 2022. *Healing Hands: Street Medicine and Outreach—Bringing Care to People Where They Are*. National Health Care for the Homeless Council. https://nhchc.org/wp-content/uploads/2022/06/healing-hands-june-2022.pdf.

Jessor, R., M. S. Turbin, and F. M. Costa. 1998. "Risk and Protection in Successful Outcomes Among Disadvantaged Adolescents." *Applied Developmental Science* 2 (4): 194–208. https://doi.org/10.1207/s1532480xads0204_3.

Job Corps. n.d. "Job Corps Basics." Accessed May 26, 2025. https://www.jobcorps.gov/faqs.

Johnson, B. D., A. Golub, and J. McCabe. 2010. "The International Implications of Quality-of-Life Policing as Practiced in New York City." *Police Practice and Research* 11 (1): 17–29. http://doi.org/10.1080/15614260802586368.

Johnson, R. J., L. Rew, and K. Kouzekanani. 2006. "Gender Differences in Victimized Homeless Adolescents." *Adolescence* 41 (161): 39–53.

Justia. n.d. *Diamond v. Diamond*. Accessed February 21, 2020. https://law.justia.com/cases /new-mexico/supreme-court/2012/32-695.html.

Kalton, G. 1983. "Introduction to Survey Sampling." In *Quantitative Applications in the Social Sciences*, vol. 35, ed. M. S. Lewis-Beck. Sage.

Karger, H. J., and D. Stoesz. 2014. *American Social Welfare Policy: A Pluralist Approach*, 8th ed. Pearson.

Kattari, S. K., A. Barman-Adhikari, J. DeChants, and E. Rice. 2017. "Social Networks and Sexual Risk Factor Differences Between Cisgender Heterosexual and Cisgender LGBQ Homeless Youths." *Journal of Gay & Lesbian Social Services* 29 (2): 182–200. https://doi .org/10.1080/10538720.2017.1296800.

Katz-Wise, S. L., M. Rosario, and M. Tsappis. 2016. "LGBT Youth and Family Acceptance." *Pediatric Clinics of North America* 63 (6): 1011–25. https://doi.org/10.1016/j.pcl .2016.07.005.

Kelleher, C. 2009. "Minority Stress and Health: Implications for Lesbian, Gay, Bisexual, Transgender, and Questioning (LGBTQ) Young People." *Counselling Psychology Quarterly* 22 (4): 373–79. https://doi.org/10.1080/09515070903334995.

Kennedy, H. 1997. "Karl Heinrich Ulrichs: First Theorist of Homosexuality." In *Science and Homosexualities*, ed. V. A. Rosario. Routledge.

Kennedy, M. R. 1991. "Homeless and Runaway Youth Mental Health Issues: No Access to the System." *Journal of Adolescent Health* 12 (7): 575–79. https://doi.org/10.1016 /0197-0070(91)90091-y.

Keuroghlian, A. S., D. Shtasel, and E. L. Bassuk. 2014. "Out on the Street: A Public Health and Policy Agenda for Lesbian, Gay, Bisexual, and Transgender Youth Who Are Homeless." *American Journal of Orthopsychiatry* 84 (1): 66–72. https://doi.org/10.1037/h0098852.

Kidd, S. A. 2003. "Street Youth: Coping and Interventions." *Child and Adolescent Social Work Journal* 20 (4): 235–61.

Kidd, S. A., J. Thistle, T. Beaulieu, B. O'Grady, and S. Gaetz. 2019. "A National Study of Indigenous Youth Homelessness in Canada." *Public Health* 176: 163–71. https://doi.org /10.1016/j.puhe.2018.06.012.

Kidd, S. A., N. Vitopoulos, T. Frederick, S. Leon, J. Karabanow, and K. McKenzie. 2019. "More Than Four Walls and a Roof Needed: A Complex Tertiary Prevention Approach for Recently Homeless Youth." *American Journal of Orthopsychiatry* 89 (2): 248–57. https://doi.org/10.1037/ort0000335.

Kinsey, A. C., W. R. Pomeroy, and C. E. Martin. 1948. *Sexual Behavior in the Human Male*. W. B. Saunders.

Kipke, M. D., S. B. Montgomery, T. R. Simon, J. B. Unger, and C. J. Johnson. 1997. "Homeless Youth: Drug Use Patterns and HIV Risk Profiles According to Peer Group Affiliation." *AIDS and Behavior* 1 (4): 247–59. https://doi.org/10.1023/a:1026279402791.

Kipke, M. D., J. B. Unger, S. O'Connor, R. F. Palmer, and S. R. LaFrance. 1997. "Street Youth, Their Peer Group Affiliation and Differences According to Residential Status, Subsistence Patterns, and Use of Services." *Adolescence* 32: 655–69.

Kirk, K. M., J. M. Bailey, and N. G. Martin. 2000. "Etiology of Male Sexual Orientation in an Australian Twin Sample." *Psychology, Evolution & Gender* 2 (3): 301–11. https://doi.org/10.1080/14616660010024418.

Klonsky, D. E., and J. J. Muehlenkamp. 2007. "Self-Injury: A Research Review for the Practitioner." *Journal of Clinical Psychology* 63 (11): 1045–56. https://doi.org/10.1002/jclp.20412.

Koch, K., and R. Bales. 2008. "Transgender Employment Discrimination." *UCLA Women's Law Journal* 17 (2): 243–67. https://doi.org/10.5070/l3172017813.

Kosciw, J. G., C. M. Clark, and L. Menard. 2022. *The 2021 National School Climate Survey: The Experiences of LGBTQ+ Youth in Our Nation's Schools.* GLSEN. https://www.glsen.org/sites/default/files/2022-10/NSCS-2021-Full-Report.pdf.

Kozloff, N., A. H. Cheung, L. E. Ross et al. 2013. "Factors Influencing Service Use Among Homeless Youths with Co-occurring Disorders." *Psychiatric Services* 64 (9): 925–28.

Krause, K. D., F. Kapadia, D. C. Ompad, P. A. D'Avanzo, D. T. Duncan, and P. N. Halkitis. 2016. "Early Life Psychosocial Stressors and Housing Instability Among Young Sexual Minority Men: The P18 Cohort Study." *Journal of Urban Health* 93 (3): 511–25. https://doi.org/10.1007/s11524-016-0049-6.

Kroenke, K., R. L. Spitzer, and J. B. W. Williams. 2001. "The PHQ-9: Validity of a Brief Depression Severity Measure." *Journal of General Internal Medicine* 16 (9): 606–13. https://doi.org/10.1046/j.1525-1497.2001.016009606.x.

Kulik, D. M., S. Gaetz, C. Crowe, and E. L. Ford-Jones. 2011. "Homeless Youth's Overwhelming Health Burden: A Review of the Literature." *Paediatrics & Child Health* 16 (6): e43–47. https://doi.org/10.1093/pch/16.6.e43.

Kuperberg, A., and A. M. Walker. 2018. "Heterosexual College Students Who Hookup with Same-Sex Partners." *Archives of Sexual Behavior* 47 (5): 1387–1403. https://doi.org/10.1007/s10508-018-1194-7.

LaLota, M., B. W. Kwan, M. Waters, L. E. Hernandez, and T. M. Liberti. 2005. "The Miami, Florida, Young Men's Survey: HIV Prevalence and Risk Behaviors Among Urban Young Men Who Have Sex with Men Who Have Ever Run Away." *Journal of Urban Health* 82 (2): 327–38. https://doi.org/10.1093/jurban/jti056.

Lambda Legal. n.d. "Know Your Rights." Accessed May 18, 2019. https://www.lambdalegal.org/know-your-rights.

Landers, P. A. 2019. *Runaway and Homeless Youth: Demographics and Programs* (RL33785). Congressional Research Service. https://crsreports.congress.gov/product/pdf/RL/RL33785.

Langenderfer-Magruder, L., N. E. Walls, D. L. Whitfield, S. M. Brown, and C. M. Barrett. 2016. "Partner Violence Victimization Among Lesbian, Gay, Bisexual, Transgender, and Queer Youth: Associations Among Risk Factors." *Child & Adolescent Social Work Journal* 33 (1): 55–68. https://doi.org/10.1007/s10560-015-0402-8.

Larson, K. 2008. "New Campaign Seeks to Place Gay Foster Youth." *Bay Area Reporter*, January 16.

Lazarus, S. A., and J. S. Cheavens. 2017. "An Examination of Social Network Quality and Composition in Women with and Without Borderline Personality Disorder." *Personality Disorders* 8 (4): 340–48. https://doi.org/10.1037/per0000201.

Legal Information Institute. 2022. "Emancipation of Minors." Cornell Law School. https://www.law.cornell.edu/wex/emancipation_of_minors.

Leitch, J., M. Gandy-Guedes, and L. Messinger. 2021. "The Psychometric Properties of the Competency Assessment Tool for Lesbian, Gay, Bisexual, and Transgender Clients." *Journal of Homosexuality* 68 (11): 1785–1812. https://doi.org/10.1080/00918369.2020.1712138.

Lev, A. I. 2004. *Transgender Emergence: Therapeutic Guidelines for Working with Gender-Variant People and Their Families*. Routledge. https://doi.org/10.4324/9780203047781.

Lim, C., E. Rice, and H. Rhoades. 2016. "Depressive Symptoms and Their Association with Adverse Environmental Factors and Substance Use in Runaway and Homeless Youths." *Journal of Research on Adolescence* 26 (3): 403–17. https://doi.org/10.1111/jora.12200.

Linehan, M. 1987. "Dialectical Behavior Therapy for Borderline Personality Disorder: Theory and Methods." *Bulletin of the Menninger Clinic* 51 (3): 261–76.

Lo, B. C. Y., W. Y. So, J. H. T. Yang, and T. K. C. Ng. 2019. "Assessment of Adolescent Mental Disorders: Cross-Cultural Issues." In *The Encyclopedia of Child and Adolescent Development: History, Theory, and Culture in Adolescence*, ed. S. Hup and J. D. Jewell. Wiley. https://doi.org/10.1002/9781119171492.wecad338.

Logan, J. L., A. Frye, H. O. Pursell, M. Anderson-Nathe, J. E. Scholl, and P. T. Korthuis. 2013. "Correlates of HIV Risk Behaviors Among Homeless and Unstably Housed Young Adults." *Public Health Reports* 128 (3): 153–60. https://doi.org/10.1177/003335491312800305.

Los Angeles LGBT Center. n.d. "Legal Services." Accessed May 18, 2019. https://lalgbtcenter.org/services/legal-services/.

Lund, S., and C. Renna. 2003. "An Analysis of the Media Response to the Spitzer Study." *Journal of Gay & Lesbian Psychotherapy* 7 (3): 55–67. https://doi.org/10.1300/J236v07n03_04.

Lynk, M., E. McCay, C. Carter, A. Aiello, and F. Donald. 2015. "Engaging Street-Involved Youth in Dialectical Behavior Therapy: A Secondary Analysis." *Journal of the Canadian Academy of Child and Adolescent Psychiatry* 24 (2): 116–22.

Maccio, E. M., and K. M. Ferguson. 2016. "Services to LGBTQ Runaway and Homeless Youth: Gaps and Recommendations." *Children and Youth Services Review* 63: 47–57. https://doi.org/10.1016/j.childyouth.2016.02.008.

Madrigal-Borloz, V., and L. Farha. 2019. *The Right to Housing of LGBT Youth: An Urgent Task in the SDG Agenda Setting*. United Nations Human Rights Council. https://www.ohchr.org/en/statements/2019/08/right-housing-lgbt-youth-urgent-task-sdg-agenda-setting.

Mallory, A. B., J. K. Martin, M. M. Fitzpatrick, T. Yilmazer, L. Chavez, and N. Slesnick. 2025. "Differences in Mental Health Between Female Sexual Minority and Heterosexual Youth with a Substance Use Disorder Who Are Experiencing Homelessness." *LGBT Health* 12 (3): 183–92. https://doi.org/10.1089/lgbt.2023.0230.

Mallory, C., T. N. T. Brown, and K. J. Conron. 2019. *Conversion Therapy and LGBT Youth: Update*. Williams Institute. https://williamsinstitute.law.ucla.edu/wp-content/uploads/Conversion-Therapy-Update-Jun-2019.pdf.

Malpas, J. 2011. "Between Pink and Blue: A Multi-Dimensional Family Approach to Gender Nonconforming Children and Their Families." *Family Process* 50 (4): 453–70. https://doi.org/10.1111/j.1545-5300.2011.01371.x.

Malyon, A. K. 1982. "Psychotherapeutic Implications of Internalized Homophobia in Gay Men." *Journal of Homosexuality* 7 (2–3): 59–69. https://doi.org/10.1300/J082v07n02_08.

Manthey, T., M. Coffman, R. Goscha, G. Bond, A. Mabry, L. Carlson, J. Davis, and C. Rapp. 2012. "The University of Kansas Supported Education Toolkit 3.0." The Office of Mental Health Research and Training, The University of Kansas School of Social Welfare.

MAP (Movement Advancement Project). 2024. "LGBTQ Curricular Laws." https://www .lgbtmap.org/equality-maps/curricular_laws.

Marchionda, D. M., and N. Slesnick. 2013. "Family Therapy Retention: An Observation of First-Session Communication." *Journal of Marital and Family Therapy* 39 (1): 87–97. https://doi.org/10.1111/j.1752-0606.2011.00279.x.

Marshall, B. D., K. Shannon, T. Kerr, R. Zhang, and E. Wood. 2010. "Survival Sex and Increased HIV Risk Among Sexual Minority Street-Involved Youth." *Journal of Acquired Immune Deficiency Syndrome* 53 (5): 661–64. https://doi.org/10.1097/qai .0b013e3181c300d7.

Marsiglia, F. F., T. Nieri, E. Valdez, M. Gurrola, and C. Marrs. 2009. "History of Violence as a Predictor of HIV Risk Among Multi-Ethnic, Urban Youth in the Southwest." *Journal of HIV/AIDS and Social Services* 8 (2): 144–65. https://doi.org/10.1080/15381500903025589.

Martin, J. I. 2008. "Nosology, Etiology, and Course of Gender Identity Disorder in Children." *Journal of Gay & Lesbian Mental Health* 12 (1/2): 81–94. https://doi.org/10.1300 /J529v12n01_06.

Martin, J. K., and T. R. Howe. 2016. "Attitudes Toward Mental Health Services Among Homeless and Matched Housed Youth." *Child & Youth Services* 37 (1): 49–64. https:// doi.org/10.1080/0145935x.2015.1052135.

Martin, M., L. Down, and R. Erney. 2016. *Out of the Shadows: Supporting LGBTQ Youth in Child Welfare Through Cross-System Collaboration.* Center for the Study of Social Policy. https://www.floridaschildrenfirst.org/wp-content/uploads/2016/06/Out-of-the -Shadows-Supporting-LGBTQ-youth-in-child-welfare-through-cross-system-collaboration -web.pdf.

Martos, A. J., S. Nezhad, and I. H. Meyer. 2015. "Variations in Sexual Identity Milestones Among Lesbians, Gay Men, and Bisexuals." *Sexuality Research and Social Policy* 12 (1): 24–33. https://doi.org/10.1007/s13178-014-0167-4.

Marzullo, M. A., and A. J. Libman. 2009. *Research Overview: Hate Crimes and Violence Against Lesbian, Gay, Bisexual and Transgender People.* Human Rights Campaign Foundation. http://hrc-assets.s3-website-us-east-1.amazonaws.com//files/assets/resources /Hatecrimesandviolenceagainstlgbtpeople_2009.pdf.

McCay, E., C. Carter, A. Aiello et al. 2015. "Dialectical Behavior Therapy as a Catalyst for Change in Street-Involved Youth: A Mixed Methods Study." *Children and Youth Services Review* 58: 187–99. http://dx.doi.org/10.1016/j.childyouth.2015.09.021.

McCay, E., S. Quesnel, J. Langley et al. 2011. "A Relationship-Based Intervention to Improve Social Connectedness in Street-Involved Youth: A Pilot Study." *Journal of Child and Adolescent Psychiatric Nursing* 24: 208–15. https://doi.org/10.1111/j.1744-6171.2011.00301.x.

McCormick, A., K. Schmidt, and S. R. Terrazas. 2016. "Foster Family Acceptance: Understanding the Role of Foster Family Acceptance in the Lives of LGBTQ Youth." *Children and Youth Services Review* 61: 69–74. https://doi.org/10.1016/j.childyouth.2015.12.005.

McGuire, M., and L. W. Perna. 2023. "Connecting Policymakers with Academic Research to Inform Public Policy." *Change: The Magazine of Higher Learning* 55 (6): 15–20. https://doi.org/10.1080/00091383.2023.2263188.

McGuirk, S., M. Niedzwiecki, T. Oke, and A. Volkova. 2015. *Stronger Together: Supporting LGBT Asylum Seekers in the United States.* LGBT Freedom and Asylum Network. http://assets2.hrc.org/files/assets/resources/LGBT_Asylum_Seekers_FINAL.pdf.

McKinney–Vento Homeless Assistance Act of 1987, 42 USC § 11434a(6). 1987. https://uscode.house.gov/view.xhtml?req=(title:42%20section:11434a%20edition:prelim) #sourcecredit.

McLaughlin, K. A., M. L. Hatzenbuehler, Z. Xuan, and K. J. Conron. 2012. "Disproportionate Exposure to Early-Life Adversity and Sexual Orientation Disparities in Psychiatric Morbidity." *Child Abuse & Neglect* 36 (9): 645–55. https://doi.org/10.1016/j.chiabu.2012.07.004.

Meites, E., P. G. Szilagyi, H. W. Chesson, E. R. Unger, J. R. Romero, and L. E. Markowitz. 2019. "Human Papillomavirus Vaccination for Adults: Updated Recommendations of the Advisory Committee on Immunization Practices." *Morbidity and Mortality Weekly Report* 68 (32): 698–702. https://www.cdc.gov/mmwr/volumes/68/wr/pdfs/mm6832a3 -H.pdf.

Melton, G. B. 1983. *Child Advocacy: Psychological Issues and Interventions.* Plenum.

Mereish, E. H., and V. P. Poteat. 2015. "A Relational Model of Sexual Minority Mental and Physical Health: The Negative Effects of Shame on Relationships, Loneliness, and Health." *Journal of Counseling Psychology* 62 (3): 425–37. https://doi.org/10.1037/cou0000088.

Meyer, I. H. 2018. *Young People in the U.S. Identify as LGB and Come Out Earlier Than Previous Generations.* Williams Institute. http://williamsinstitute.law.ucla.edu/wp-content /uploads/Coming-Out-Milestones-Oct-2018.pdf.

Meyers, R. J., H. G. Roozen, and J. E. Smith. 2011. "The Community Reinforcement Approach: An Update of the Evidence." *Alcohol Research & Health* 33 (4): 380–88.

Michael Ferguson, Benjamin Unger, Chaim Levin, Jo Bruck, Bella Levin v. JONAH (Jews Offering New Alternatives for Healing f/k/a Jews Offering New Alternatives to Homosexuality), Arthur Goldberg, Alan Downing, Alan Downing Life Coach LLC. No. L-5473 -12. N.J. Super. Ct. Law Div. 2015. https://www.njcourts.gov/system/files/court-opinions /2019/fergusonvjonah.pdf.

Milburn, N. G., G. Ayala, E. Rice, P. Batterham, and M. J. Rotheram-Borus. 2006. "Discrimination and Exiting Homelessness Among Homeless Adolescents." *Cultural Diversity and Ethnic Minority Psychology* 12 (4): 658–72. https://doi.org/10.1037/1099-9809 .12.4.658.

Milburn, N. G., F. J. Iribarren, E. Rice et al. 2012. "A Family Intervention to Reduce Sexual Risk Behavior, Substance Use, and Delinquency Among Newly Homeless Youth." *Journal of Adolescent Health* 50: 358–64. https://doi.org/10.1016/j.jadohealth.2011.08.009.

Milburn, N. G., D. Rosenthal, M. J. Rotheram-Borus et al. 2007. "Newly Homeless Youth Typically Return Home." *Journal of Adolescent Health* 40 (6): 574–76. https://doi.org /10.1016/j.jadohealth.2006.12.017.

Miller, W. R., and S. Rollnick. 1991. *Motivational Interviewing: Preparing People to Change Addictive Behavior.* Guilford.

——. 2023. *Motivational Interviewing: Helping People Change and Grow*, 4th ed. Guilford.

Miller, W. R., A. Zweben, C. C. DiClemente, and R. G. Rychtarik. 1999. *Motivational Enhancement Therapy Manual: A Clinical Research Guide for Therapists Treating Individuals with Alcohol Abuse and Dependence*. Vol. 2 of *Project MATCH Monograph Series*, ed. M. E. Mattson. U.S. Department of Health and Human Services. https://www.niaaa .nih.gov/sites/default/files/match02.pdf.

Milligan, S. 2016. "The Devil Is in the Details. Donald Trump Could Undo a Lot of President Obama's Work Through Rules, Regulations and Executive Orders." *USA Today*, December 16. http://www.usnews.com/news/the-report/articles/2016-12-16/donald -trump-could-use-executive-orders-to-undo-barack-obamas-work.

Minkin, R., J. Horowitz., L. Lin, and D. Braga. 2025. The Experiences of LGBTQ Americans Today. Pew Research Center. https://www.pewresearch.org/wp-content/uploads /sites/20/2025/05/ST_2025.5.29_LGBTQ-experiences_report.pdf

Monro, S., S. Hines, and A. Osborne. 2017. "Is Bisexuality Invisible? A Review of Sexualities Scholarship 1970–2015." *Sociological Review* 65 (4): 663–81. https://doi.org/10.1177 %2F0038026117695488.

Moon, M. W., W. McFarland, T. Kellogg et al. 2000. "HIV Risk Behavior of Runaway Youth in San Francisco: Age of Onset and Relation to Sexual Orientation." *Youth & Society* 32 (2): 184–201. https://doi.org/10.1177/0044118x00032002003.

Morse, G. A., R. J. Calsyn, J. Miller, P. Rosenberg, L. West, and J. Gilliland. 1996. "Outreach to Homeless Mentally Ill People: Conceptual and Clinical Considerations." *Community Mental Health Journal* 32 (3): 261–74. https://doi.org/10.1007/bf02249427.

Morton, M. H., R. Chávez, and K. Moore. 2019. "Prevalence and Correlates of Homelessness Among American Indian and Alaska Native Youth." *Journal of Primary Prevention* 40: 643–60. https://doi.org/10.1007/s10935-019-00571-2.

Morton, M. H., A. Dworsky, J. L. Matjasko et al. 2018. "Prevalence and Correlates of Youth Homelessness in the United States." *Journal of Adolescent Health* 62: 14–21. https://doi .org/10.1016/j.jadohealth.2017.10.006.

Morton, M. H., A. Dworsky, and G. M. Samuels. 2017. *Missed Opportunities: Youth Homelessness in America. National Estimates*. Chapin Hall, University of Chicago. https://www .chapinhall.org/wp-content/uploads/ChapinHall_VoYC_NationalReport_Final.pdf.

Morton, M. H., S. Kugley, R. A. Epstein, and A. F. Farrell. 2019. *Missed Opportunities: Evidence on Interventions for Addressing Youth Homelessness*. Chapin Hall, University of Chicago. https://www.chapinhall.org/wp-content/uploads/Evidence-Review-Brief.pdf.

Morton, M. H., G. M. Samuels, A. Dworsky, and S. Patel. 2018. *Missed Opportunities: LGBTQ Youth Homelessness in America*. Chapin Hall, University of Chicago. https:// www.chapinhall.org/wp-content/uploads/VoYC-LGBTQ-Brief-FINAL.pdf.

Moser, C. 2016. "Defining Sexual Orientation." *Archives of Sexual Behavior* 45 (3): 505–8. https://doi.org/10.1007/s10508-015-0625-y.

Moskowitz, A., J. A. Stein, and M. Lightfoot. 2013. "The Mediating Roles of Stress and Maladaptive Behaviors on Self-Harm and Suicide Attempts Among Runaway and Homeless Youth." *Journal of Youth and Adolescence* 42 (7): 1015–27. https://doi.org/10.1007 /s10964-012-9793-4.

Moss, N. E., and L. Moss-Racusin. 2021. *Practical Guide to Child and Adolescent Psychological Testing*. Springer.

Motivational Interviewing Network of Trainers. n.d. "Understanding Motivational Interviewing." Accessed May 26, 2025. https://motivationalinterviewing.org/understanding-motivational-interviewing.

Mountz, S., and M. Capous-Desyllas. 2020. "Exploring the Families of Origin of LBTQ Former Foster Youth and Their Trajectories Throughout Care." *Children and Youth Services Review* 109. https://doi.org/10.1016/j.childyouth.2019.104622.

Murphy, T. F. 1992. "Redirecting Sexual Orientation: Techniques and Justifications." *Journal of Sex Research* 29 (4): 501–23. https://doi.org/10.1080/00224499209551664.

Mustanski, B., G. J. Greene, D. Ryan, and S. W. Whitton. 2015. "Feasibility, Acceptability, and Initial Efficacy of an Online Sexual Health Promotion Program for LGBT Youth: The Queer Sex Ed Intervention." *Journal of Sex Research* 52 (2): 220–30. https://doi.org/10.1080/00224499.2013.867924.

Najavits, L. M. 2002. *Seeking Safety: A Treatment Manual for PTSD and Substance Abuse*. Guilford.

Narendorf, S. C., M. B. Cross, D. Santa Maria, P. R. Swank, and P. S. Bordnick. 2017. "Relations Between Mental Health Diagnoses, Mental Health Treatment, and Substance Use in Homeless Youth." *Drug and Alcohol Dependence* 175 (1): 1–8. https://doi.org/10.1016/j.drugalcdep.2017.01.028.

NASEM (National Academies of Sciences, Engineering, and Medicine). 2019. *The Promise of Adolescence: Realizing Opportunity for All Youth*. National Academies Press. https://doi.org/10.17226/25388.

NASW (National Association of Social Workers). n.d. "Homelessness: Resources for Social Workers." Accessed October 30, 2024. https://www.socialworkers.org/News/Research-Data/Social-Work-Policy-Research/Homelessness-Resources-for-Social-Workers.

National Institute of Justice. 2022. *Overview of Human Trafficking and NIJ's Role*. https://nij.ojp.gov/topics/articles/overview-human-trafficking-and-nijs-role.

National Network for Youth. n.d. "Federal Definitions of Homelessness Should Not Be Different." Accessed October 29, 2024. https://nn4youth.org/policy/federal-policy-on-youth-homelessness/hcya/.

National Runaway Safeline. n.d. "About Us: History." Accessed August 4, 2022. https://www.nationalrunawaysafeline.org/about-us.

NCES (National Center for Education Statistics). 2022. "Table 203.20: Enrollment in Public Elementary and Secondary Schools, by Region, State, and Jurisdiction: Selected Years, Fall 1990 Through Fall 2031." https://nces.ed.gov/programs/digest/d22/tables/dt22_203.20.asp.

NCTSI (National Child Traumatic Stress Initiative). n.d. "About NCTSI." Accessed August 8, 2025. https://www.samhsa.gov/mental-health/trauma-violence/nctsi.

NCTSN (National Child Traumatic Stress Network). n.d.a. "All NCTSN Resources." Accessed May 26, 2025. https://www.nctsn.org/resources/all-nctsn-resources.

——. n.d.b. "Who We Are." Accessed October 30, 2024. https://www.nctsn.org/about-us/who-we-are.

——. 2012. *SPARCS: Structured Psychotherapy for Adolescents Responding to Chronic Stress.* https://www.nctsn.org/sites/default/files/interventions/sparcs_fact_sheet.pdf.

Netting, F. E., M. K. O'Connor, and D. P. Fauri. 2008. *Comparative Approaches to Program Planning.* Wiley.

New York Civil Liberties Union. 2008. "Know Your Rights: LGBTQ Youth in Schools." https://www.nyclu.org/migrated-page/trainings-and-workshops-0#lgbtq.

New York State. 2019. "Governor Cuomo Signs Landmark Legislation Protecting LGBTQ Rights." https://dhr.ny.gov/news/governor-cuomo-signs-landmark-legislation-protecting-lgbtq-rights.

NIAMSD (National Institute of Arthritis and Musculoskeletal and Skin Diseases). 2024. "Reactive Arthritis." https://www.niams.nih.gov/health-topics/reactive-arthritis.

NLCHP (National Law Center on Homelessness & Poverty). 2014. *No Safe Place: The Criminalization of Homelessness in U.S. Cities.* https://homelesslaw.org/wp-content/uploads/2019/02/No_Safe_Place.pdf.

Noell, J. W., and L. M. Ochs. 2001. "Relationship of Sexual Orientation to Substance Use, Suicidal Ideation, Suicide Attempts, and Other Factors in a Population of Homeless Adolescents." *Journal of Adolescent Health* 29 (1): 31–36. https://doi.org/10.1016/S1054-139X(01)00205-1.

Nolan, K. 2018. "Foster Care: Can the System Handle Soaring Demand?" *CQ Researcher* 28 (26): 609–32. CQ. https://9pp.8cf.myftpupload.com/wp-content/uploads/2020/03/foster-are-report.pdf.

NYC Mayor's Office of Immigrant Affairs. 2023. *2023 Annual Report on New York City's Immigrant Population and Initiatives of the Office.* https://www.nyc.gov/assets/immigrants/downloads/pdf/MOIA-Annual-Report-2023_Final.pdf.

NYCACS (New York City Administration for Children's Services). n.d. "LGBTQAI+ Policies." https://www.nyc.gov/site/acs/about/lgbtq-policies.page.

NYCDHS (New York City Department of Homeless Services). 2006. *Procedure No. 06-1-31.* http://srlp.org/files/DHS_trans_policy.pdf.

NYSED (New York State Education Department). 2017. "The Dignity for All Students Act (DASA)." http://www.p12.nysed.gov/dignityact/.

NYSOCFS (New York State Office of Children and Family Services). 2017. "LGBTQ Homepage." http://ocfs.ny.gov/main/LGBTQ/.

O'Connor, M. E., T. Boat, and K. E. Warner, eds. 2009. *Preventing Mental, Emotional, and Behavioral Disorders Among Young People: Progress and Possibilities.* National Academies Press. https://www.nap.edu/catalog/12480/preventing-mental-emotional-and-behavioral-disorders-among-young-people-progress.

OrgCode Consulting, Inc. 2015a. *Transition Age Youth–Vulnerability Index–Service Prioritization Decision Assistance Tool (TAY-VI-SPDAT): Next Step Tool for Homeless Youth.* Community Technology Alliance. http://ctagroup.org/wp-content/uploads/2015/10/TAY-VI-SPDAT-v1.0-US-Print.pdf.

——. 2015b. *Youth Service Prioritization Decision Assistance Tool (Y-SPDAT).* Community Technology Alliance. https://ctagroup.org/wp-content/uploads/2015/10/Y-SPDAT-v1.0-Youth-Print.pdf.

Palmiter, D. J., Jr. 2016. *Practicing Cognitive Behavioral Therapy with Children and Adolescents: A Guide for Students and Early Career Professionals.* Springer.

Parks, C. A., T. L. Hughes, and L. Werkmeister-Rozas. 2009. "Defining Sexual Identity and Sexual Orientation in Research with Lesbians, Gay Men, and Bisexuals." In *Handbook of Research with Gay, Lesbian, Bisexual & Transgender Populations*, ed. W. Meezan and J. I. Martin. Routledge.

Parry, B. J., M. L. Quinton, M. J. G. Holland, J. L. Thompson, and J. Cumming. 2021. "Improving Outcomes in Young People Experiencing Homelessness with My Strengths Training for Life (MST4Life): A Qualitative Realist Evaluation." *Children and Youth Services Review* 121: 105793. https://doi.org/10.1016/j.childyouth.2020.105793.

Peak, K. n.d. "Exciting New Housing Program for LGBTQ+ Youth Proposed in Sacramento." Sacramento LGBT Community Center. Accessed May 18, 2019. https://saccenter.org/exciting-new-housing-program-for-lgbtq-youth-proposed-in-sacramento/.

Pearson, J., L. Thrane, and L. Wilkinson. 2017. "Consequences of Runaway and Thrownaway Experiences for Sexual Minority Health During the Transition to Adulthood." *Journal of LGBT Youth* 14 (2): 15–171. https://doi.org/10.1080/19361653.2016.1264909.

Pedersen, E. R., J. S. Tucker, and S. A. Kovalchik. 2016. "Facilitators and Barriers of Drop-In Center Use Among Homeless Youth." *Journal of Adolescent Health* 59 (2): 144–53. https://doi.org/10.1016/j.jadohealth.2016.03.035.

Peele, C. 2023a. "Weekly Roundup of Anti-LGBTQ+ Legislation Advancing in States Across the Country." Press release. Human Rights Campaign, May 2. https://www.hrc.org/press-releases/weekly-roundup-of-anti-lgbtq-legislation-advancing-in-states-across-the-country-3.

——. 2023b. "Weekly Roundup of Anti-LGBTQ+ Legislation Advancing in States Across the Country." Press release. Human Rights Campaign, May 31. https://www.hrc.org/press-releases/weekly-roundup-of-anti-lgbtq-legislation-advancing-in-states-across-the-country-6.

Perez, R. M. 2007. "The 'Boring' State of Research and Psychotherapy with Lesbian, Gay, Bisexual, and Transgender Clients: Revisiting Barón (1991)." In *Handbook of Counseling and Psychotherapy with Lesbian, Gay, Bisexual, and Transgender Clients*, 2nd ed., ed. K. J. Bieschke, R. M. Perez, and K. A. DeBord. American Psychological Association.

Pérez, Z. J. 2014. *Left Behind: How LGBT Young People Are Excluded from Economic Prosperity.* Center for American Progress. https://www.americanprogress.org/article/left-behind/.

Pergamit, M. R. 2010. *On the Lifetime Prevalence of Running Away from Home.* Urban Institute. https://www.urban.org/sites/default/files/publication/28616/412087-On-the-Prevalence-of-Running-Away-from-Home.PDF.

Pergamit, M., M. Ernst, J. Benoit-Bryan, and J. Kessel. 2010. *Why They Run: An In-Depth Look at America's Runaway Youth.* National Runaway Safeline. https://montrosecenter.org/wp-content/uploads/2010/12/Why_They_Run_NRS.pdf.

Pergamit, M., J. Gelatt, B. Stratford, S. Beckwith, and M. C. Martin. 2016. *Family Interventions for Youth Experiencing or at Risk of Homelessness.* Urban Institute. https://www.urban.org/sites/default/files/publication/82876/2000873-Family-Interventions-for-Youth-Experiencing-or-at-Risk-of-Homelessness.pdf.

Petering, R., N. Barr, A. Srivastava, L. Onasch-Vera, N. Thompson, and E. Rice. 2021. "Examining Impacts of a Peer-Based Mindfulness and Yoga Intervention to Reduce Interpersonal Violence Among Young Adults Experiencing Homelessness." *Journal of the Society for Social Work and Research* 12 (1): 41–57. http://doi.org/10.1086/712957.

Peters, C. M., A. Dworsky, M. E. Courtney, and H. Pollack. 2009. *Extending Foster Care to Age 21: Weighing the Costs to Government Against the Benefits to Youth.* Chapin Hall, University of Chicago. https://www.chapinhall.org/wp-content/uploads/Peters-Extending-foster-care-to-age-21.pdf.

Peterson, P. L., J. S. Baer, E. A. Wells, J. A. Ginzler, and S. B. Garrett. 2006. "Short-Term Effects of a Brief Motivational Intervention to Reduce Alcohol and Drug Risk Among Homeless Adolescents." *Psychology of Addictive Behaviors* 20 (3): 254–64. https://doi.org/10.1037/0893-164X.20.3.254.

PFLAG. n.d. "Our Story." Accessed February 21, 2020. https://pflag.org/our-story.

——. 2019. *Guide to Being an Ally to LGBTQ+ People.* https://pflag.org/wp-content/uploads/2025/06/S4E-LGBTQ-Ally-Guide-FY25.pdf.

——. 2024. *Guide to Being an Ally to Trans and Nonbinary People.* https://pflag.org/wp-content/uploads/2016/04/S4E-Trans-Ally-Guide-FINAL.pdf.

Phillips, D., S. C. Fischer, G. A. Groves, and R. Singh. 1976. "Alternative Behavioral Approaches to the Treatment of Homosexuality." *Archives of Sexual Behavior* 5: 223–28.

Pierce, C. 1970. "Offensive Mechanisms." In *The Black Seventies*, ed. F. B. Barbour. Porter Sargent.

Pierce, C. M., J. V. Carew, D. Pierce-Gonzalez, and D. Wills. 1977. "An Experiment in Racism: TV Commercials." *Education and Urban Society* 10 (1): 61–87.

Los Angeles LGBT Center. n.d. *Recognize. Intervene. Support. Empower.* Accessed August 8, 2025. https://rise.lalgbtcenter.org/

PIIET (Permanency Innovations Initiative Evaluation Team). 2016. *Findings from the RISE Youth Qualitative Interviews.* OPRE Report 2016–05. Department of Health and Human Services, Administration for Children and Families, Children's Bureau, and Office of Planning, Research and Evaluation. https://www.acf.hhs.gov/sites/default/files/documents/opre/rise_youth_interview_brief_2016_final_2_b508.pdf.

Pine, B. A., R. Spath, and S. Gosteli. 2014. "Reunification." In *Child Welfare for the 21st Century: A Handbook of Practices, Policies, and Programs*, 2nd ed., ed. G. P. Mallon and P. M. Hess. Columbia University Press.

Pizer, J. C., B. Sears, C. Mallory, and N. D. Hunter. 2011. "Evidence of Persistent and Pervasive Workplace Discrimination Against LGBT People: The Need for Federal Legislation Prohibiting Discrimination and Providing for Equal Employment Benefits." *Loyola of Los Angeles Law Review* 45: 715–79. https://escholarship.org/uc/item/3wf4t3q9.

Pleace, N. 2015. *At What Cost? As Estimation of the Financial Costs of Single Homelessness in the UK.* Crisis. https://www.crisis.org.uk/media/20677/crisis_at_what_cost_2015.pdf.

Poirier, J. M., S. Wilkie, K. Sepulveda, and T. Uruchima. 2018. "Jim Casey Youth Opportunities Initiative: Experiences and Outcomes of Youth Who Are LGBTQ." *Child Welfare* 96 (1): 1–26. https://www.jstor.org/stable/48628033.

Powell, C., I. Ellasante, J. D. Korchmaros, K. Haverly, and S. Stevens. 2016. "iTEAM: Outcomes of an Affirming System of Care Serving LGBTQ Youth Experiencing Homelessness." *Families in Society* 97 (3): 181–90. https://doi.org/10.1606/1044-3894.2016.97.24.

Prochaska, J., and C. DiClemente. 1983. "Stages and Processes of Self-Change of Smoking: Toward an Integrative Model of Change." *Journal of Consulting and Clinical Psychology* 51 (3): 390–95.

Prock, K. A., and A. C. Kennedy. 2020. "Characteristics, Experiences, and Service Utilization Patterns of Homeless Youth in a Transitional Living Program: Differences by LGBQ Identity." *Children and Youth Services Review* 116: 105176. https://doi.org/10.1016/j .childyouth.2020.105176.

——. 2017. "Federally-Funded Transitional Living Programs and Services for LGBTQ-Identified Homeless Youth: A Profile in Unmet Need." *Children and Youth Services Review* 83: 17–24. https://doi.org/10.1016/j.childyouth.2017.10.023.

Prosser, J. 1998. *Second Skins: The Body Narratives of Transsexuality.* Columbia University Press.

Przeworski, A., E. Peterson, and A. Piedra. 2021. "A Systematic Review of the Efficacy, Harmful Effects, and Ethical Issues Related to Sexual Orientation Change Efforts." *Clinical Psychology* 28 (1): 81–100. http://doi.org/10.1111/cpsp.12377.

Quintana, N. S., J. Rosenthal, and J. Krehely. 2010. *On the Streets: The Federal Response to Gay and Transgender Homeless Youth.* Center for American Progress. https://cdn.american progress.org/wp-content/uploads/issues/2010/06/pdf/lgbtyouthhomelessness.pdf.

Rabinovitz, S., M. Desai, A. Schneir, and L. Clark. 2010. *No Way Home: Understanding the Needs and Experiences of Homeless Youth in Hollywood.* Hollywood Homeless Youth Partnership. https://5mt2b2.p3cdn1.secureserver.net/wp-content/uploads/2023/05/HHYP -Research-Brief-No-Way-Home-Understanding-the-Needs-and-Experiences-of -Homeless-Youth-in-Hollywood-November-2010.pdf.

Rand, E. J. 2004. "A Disunited Nation and a Legacy of Contradiction: Queer Nation's Construction of Identity." *Journal of Communication Inquiry* 28 (4): 288–306. https://doi .org/10.1177/0196859904267232.

Rapp, C. A., and R. Chamberlain. 1985. "Case Management Services for the Chronically Mentally Ill." *Social Work* 30 (5): 417–22. https://doi.org/10.1093/sw/30.5.417.

Ray, N. 2006. *Lesbian, Gay, Bisexual and Transgender Youth: An Epidemic of Homelessness.* National Gay & Lesbian Task Force. https://www.thetaskforce.org/app/uploads/2007/01 /Lesbian-Gay-Bisexual-and-Transgender-Youth-An-Epidemic-of-Homelessness.pdf.

Ream, G. L., K. F. Barnhart, and K. V. Lotz. 2012. "Decision Processes About Condom Use Among Shelter-Homeless LGBT Youth in Manhattan." *AIDS Research and Treatment* 2012. https://doi.org/10.1155/2012/659853.

Ream, G., and A. Peters. 2021. "Working with Suicidal and Homeless LGBTQ+ Youth in the Context of Family Rejection." *Journal of Health Service Psychology* 47 (1): 41–50. https:// doi.org/10.1007/s42843-021-00029-2.

Reddy-Best, K. L., and E. L. Pedersen. 2015. "The Relationship of Gender Expression, Sexual Identity, Distress, Appearance, and Clothing Choices for Queer Women." *International Journal of Fashion Design, Technology and Education* 8 (1): 54–65. https://doi.org /10.1080/17543266.2014.958576.

Rew, L., N. Slesnick, K. Johnson, R. Aguilar, and A. Cengiz. 2019. "Positive Attributes and Life Satisfaction in Homeless Youth." *Children and Youth Services Review* 100: 1–8. https://doi.org/10.1016/j.childyouth.2019.02.021.

Rew, L., M. Taylor-Seehafer, N. Y. Thomas, and R. D. Yockey. 2001. "Correlates of Resilience in Homeless Adolescents." *Journal of Nursing Scholarship* 33 (1): 33–40. https://doi.org/10.1111/j.1547-5069.2001.00033.x.

Rew, L., T. A. Whittaker, M. A. Taylor-Seehafer, and L. R. Smith. 2005. "Sexual Health Risks and Protective Resources in Gay, Lesbian, Bisexual, and Heterosexual Homeless Youth." *Journal for Specialists in Pediatric Nursing* 10 (1): 11–19. https://doi.org/10.1111/j.1088-145x.2005.00003.x.

Rhoades, H., J. A. Rusow, D. Bond, A. Lanteigne, A. Fulginiti, and J. T. Goldbach. 2018. "Homelessness, Mental Health and Suicidality Among LGBTQ Youth Accessing Crisis Services." *Child Psychiatry & Human Development* 49 (4): 643–51. https://doi.org/10.1007/s10578-018-0780-1.

RI International. n.d. "Services." Accessed May 26, 2025. https://riinternational.com/services/.

Rice, E. 2013. *The TAY Triage Tool: A Tool to Identify Homeless Transition Age Youth Most in Need of Permanent Supportive Housing*. Homeless Hub. https://homelesshub.ca/resource/tay-triage-tool-tool-identify-homeless-transition-age-youth-most-need-permanent-supportive-housing/.

Rice, E., A. Barman-Adhikari, H. Rhoades et al. 2013. "Homelessness Experiences, Sexual Orientation, and Sexual Risk Taking Among High School Students in Los Angeles." *Journal of Adolescent Health* 52 (6): 773–78. https://doi.org/10.1016/j.jadohealth.2012.11.011.

Rice, E. R., G. DiGuiseppi, L. Onasch-Vera, E. Casey, T. Cooper, and M. DiBattiste. 2023. "A Longitudinal Exploration of How Connections to Staff Facilitate Efficacy and Service Use in Drop-In Centers Serving Youth Experiencing Homelessness." *Journal of Prevention* 44 (3): 359–71. https://doi.org/10.1007/s10935-023-00728-0.

Rice, E., R. Petering, H. Rhoades et al. 2015. "Homelessness and Sexual Identity Among Middle School Students." *Journal of School Health* 85 (8): 552–57. https://doi.org//10.1111/josh.12280.

Robbins, A. M. 2021. "Can Scientists Be Good Policy Advocates?" American Society for Microbiology, September 9. https://asm.org/articles/policy/2021/august-21/can-scientists-be-good-policy-advocates.

Robbins, M. S., J. F. Alexander, C. W. Turner, and A. Holliman. 2016. "Evolution of Functional Family Therapy as an Evidence-Based Practice for Adolescents with Disruptive Behavior Problems." *Family Process* 55 (3): 543–57. https://doi.org/10.1111/famp.12230.

Robinson, B. A. 2018a. "Child Welfare Systems and LGBTQ Youth Homelessness: Gender Segregation, Instability, and Intersectionality." *Child Welfare* 96 (2): 29–45.

——. 2018b. "Conditional Families and Lesbian, Gay, Bisexual, Transgender, and Queer Youth Homelessness: Gender, Sexuality, Family Instability, and Rejection." *Journal of Marriage and Family* 80 (2): 383–96. https://doi.org/10.1111/jomf.12466.

——. 2021. "'They Peed on My Shoes': Foregrounding Intersectional Minority Stress in Understanding LGBTQ Youth Homelessness." *Journal of LGBT Youth*. https://doi.org/10.1080/19361653.2021.1925196.

Roe, S. 2017. "'Family Support Would Have Been Like Amazing': LGBTQ Youth Experiences with Parental and Family Support." *Family Journal* 25 (1): 55–62. https://doi.org/10.1177/1066480716679651.

Roeder, K. M., and D. A. Cole. 2019. "Simultaneous Longitudinal Examination of Hopelessness, Thwarted Belongingness, and Perceived Burdensomeness as Predictors of Suicide Ideation." *Suicide & Life-Threatening Behavior* 49 (4): 1058–71. https://doi.org/10.1111/sltb.12508.

Rosario, M., E. W. Scrimshaw, and J. Hunter. 2012a. "Homelessness Among Lesbian, Gay, and Bisexual Youth: Implications for Subsequent Internalizing and Externalizing Symptoms." *Journal of Youth and Adolescence* 41 (5): 544–60. https://doi.org/10.1007/s10964-011-9681-3.

——. 2012b. "Risk Factors for Homelessness Among Lesbian, Gay, and Bisexual Youths: A Developmental Milestone Approach." *Children and Youth Services Review* 34 (1): 186–93. https://doi.org/10.1016/j.childyouth.2011.09.016.

Rosik, C. H., A. L. Beckstead, and G. T. Lefevor. 2023. "Sexual Orientation Change Efforts: Health Associations, Sexual Identity Labeling, and Reports of Change By Engagement Status." *Psychology of Sexual Orientation and Gender Diversity.* Advance online publication. https://doi.org/10.1037/sgd0000631.

Rossman, K., P. Salamanca, and K. Macapagal. 2017. "A Qualitative Study Examining Young Adults' Experiences of Disclosure and Nondisclosure of LGBTQ Identity to Health Care Providers." *Journal of Homosexuality* 64 (10): 1390–1410.

Rotheram-Borus, M. J., C. Koopman, C. Haignere, and M. Davies. 1991. "Reducing HIV Sexual Risk Behavior Among Runaway Adolescents." *Journal of the American Medical Association* 266 (9): 1237–41. https://doi.org/10.1001/jama.1991.03470090071034.

Rothman, E. F., D. Exner, and A. L. Baughman. 2011. "The Prevalence of Sexual Assault Against People Who Identify as Gay, Lesbian, or Bisexual in the United States: A Systematic Review." *Trauma, Violence, & Abuse* 12 (2): 55–66. https://doi.org/10.1177/1524838010390707.

Roy, E., N. Haley, J.-F. Boudreau, P. Leclerc, and J.-F. Boivin. 2010. "The Challenge of Understanding Mortality Changes Among Street Youth." *Journal of Urban Health* 87 (1): 95–101. https://doi.org/10.1007/s11524-009-9397-9.

Rubin, A., and E. R. Babbie. 2017. *Research Methods for Social Work*, 9th ed. Cengage Learning.

RHYA (Runaway and Homeless Youth Act), 42 U.S.C. § 5732a. 1974. https://www.govinfo.gov/content/pkg/USCODE-2010-title42/html/USCODE-2010-title42-chap72.htm.

RHYTPA (Runaway and Homeless Youth and Trafficking Prevention Act), H.R. 6041, 118th Congress. 2023a. https://www.congress.gov/bill/118th-congress/house-bill/6041/all-actions.

——, S. 3125, 118th Congress. 2023b. https://www.congress.gov/bill/118th-congress/senate-bill/3125/related-bills.

RHYTTAC (Runaway and Homeless Youth Training, Technical Assistance, and Capacity Building Center). n.d.a. "Screening Tool." Accessed November 3, 2024. https://resources.rhyttac.org/resources/screening-tool.

——. n.d.b. "What Is RHYTTAC?" Accessed December 28, 2017. https://www.rhyttac.net/what-is-rhyttac.

Russell, S. T., and J. N. Fish. 2016. "Mental Health in Lesbian, Gay, Bisexual, and Transgender (LGBT) Youth." *Annual Review of Clinical Psychology* 12: 465–87. https://doi.org/10.1146/annurev-clinpsy-021815-093153.

Ryan, C. 2010. "Engaging Families to Support Lesbian, Gay, Bisexual, and Transgender Youth: The Family Acceptance Project." *Prevention Researcher* 17 (4): 11–13.

——. 2014. *A Practitioner's Resource Guide: Helping Families to Support Their LGBT Children.* HHS Publication No. PEP14-LGBTKIDS. Substance Abuse and Mental Health Services Administration. https://familyproject.sfsu.edu/sites/default/files/documents /FamilySupportForLGBTChildrenGuidance.pdf.

——. 2019. "41.3 Family Acceptance Project: Culturally Grounded Framework for Supporting LGBTQ Children and Youth." *Journal of the American Academy of Child & Adolescent Psychiatry* 58 (S10): S58–59. https://doi.org/10.1016/j.jaac.2019.07.391.

Ryan, C., D. Huebner, R. M. Diaz, and J. Sanchez. 2009. "Family Rejection as a Predictor of Negative Health Outcomes in White and Latino Lesbian, Gay, and Bisexual Young Adults." *Pediatrics* 123 (1): 346–52. https://doi.org/10.1542/peds.2007-3524.

Ryan, W. S., N. Legate, and N. Weinstein. 2015. "Coming Out as Lesbian, Gay, or Bisexual: The Lasting Impact of Initial Disclosure Experiences." *Self & Identity* 14 (5): 549–69. https://doi.org/10.1080/15298868.2015.1029516.

RYPHA (Reconnecting Youth to Prevent Homelessness Act), S.961, 112th Cong. 2011. https://www.congress.gov/bill/112th-congress/senate-bill/961/text.

Sabia, J. J. 2014. "Sexual Orientation and Wages in Young Adulthood: New Evidence from Add Health." *ILR Review* 67 (1): 239–67. https://doi.org/10.1177/001979391406700109.

Sackett, D. L., S. E. Strauss, W. S. Richardson, W. Rosenberg, and R. B. Haynes. 2000. *Evidence-Based Medicine: How to Practice and Teach EBM.* Churchill-Livingstone.

Saewyc, E. M., C. L. Skay, S. L. Pettingell et al. 2006. "Hazards of Stigma: The Sexual and Physical Abuse of Gay, Lesbian, and Bisexual Adolescents in the United States and Canada." *Child Welfare* 85 (2): 195–213.

Saleebey, D. 2012. *The Strengths Perspective in Social Work Practice*, 6th ed. Pearson.

Salomonsen-Sautel, S., J. M. Van Leeuwen, C. Gilroy, S. Boyle, D. Malberg, and C. Hopfer. 2008. "Correlates of Substance Use Among Homeless Youths in Eight Cities." *American Journal on Addictions* 17 (3): 224–34. https://doi.org/10.1080/10550490802019964.

SAMHSA (Substance Abuse and Mental Health Services Administration). 2014. *SAMHSA's Concept of Trauma and Guidance for a Trauma-Informed Approach.* HHS Publication No. (SMA) 14-4884. https://store.samhsa.gov/sites/default/files/sma14-4884.pdf.

——. 2022a. "Homeless and Housing Resource Center." https://www.samhsa.gov/resource /tta/homeless-housing-resource-center-hhrc.

——. 2022b. "Interagency Task Force on Trauma-Informed Care." https://www.samhsa.gov /mental-health/trauma-violence/trauma-informed-care.

——. 2024. *Key Substance Use and Mental Health Indicators in the United States: Results from the 2023 National Survey on Drug Use and Health.* HHS Publication No. PEP24-07-021, NSDUH Series H-59. https://www.samhsa.gov/data/sites/default/files/reports /rpt47095/National%20Report/National%20Report/2023-nsduh-annual-national .pdf.

Samuels, G. M., C. Cerven, S. R. Curry, and S. R. Robinson. 2018. "'Nothing Is for Free . . .': Youth Attitudes About Engaging Resources While Unstably Housed." *Cityscape* 20 (3): 35–68. https://www.jstor.org/stable/26524871.

Sandfort, T. G. M. 2003. "Studying Sexual Orientation Change: A Methodological Review of the Spitzer Study, 'Can Some Gay Men and Lesbians Change Their Sexual Orientation?'" *Journal of Gay & Lesbian Psychotherapy* 7 (3): 15–29. https://doi.org/10.1300/J236v07n03_02.

Santa Maria, D. M., K. Breeden, S. A. Drake et al. 2020. "Gaps in Sexual Assault Health Care Among Homeless Young Adults." *American Journal of Preventive Medicine* 58 (2): 191–98. https://doi.org/10.1016/j.amepre.2019.09.023.

Santa Maria, D., P. Cuccaro, K. Bender, S. Cron, M. Fine, and E. Sibing. 2020. "Feasibility of a Mindfulness-Based Intervention with Sheltered Youth Experiencing Homelessness." *Journal of Child and Family Studies* 29 (1): 261–72. https://doi.org/10.1007/s10826-019-01583-6.

Santa Maria, D. M., S. C. Narendorf, and M. B. Cross. 2018. "Prevalence and Correlates of Substance Use in Homeless Youth and Young Adults." *Journal of Addictions Nursing* 29 (1): 23–31. https://doi.org/10.1097/jan.0000000000000206.

Santa Maria, D. M., S. C. Narendorf, H. Yoonsook, and N. Bezette-Flores. 2015. "Exploring Contextual Factors of Youth Homelessness and Sexual Risk Behaviors: A Qualitative Study." *Perspectives on Sexual and Reproductive Health* 47 (4): 195–201. https://doi.org/10.1363/47e6715.

Savin-Williams, R. C. 2001. *Mom, Dad. I'm Gay: How Families Negotiate Coming Out.* American Psychological Association. https://doi.org/10.1037/10437-000.

Savin-Williams, R. C., and G. L. Ream. 2003. "Sex Variations in the Disclosure to Parents of Same-Sex Attractions." *Journal of Family Psychology* 17 (3): 429–38. https://doi.org/10.1037/0893-3200.17.3.429.

Sawicki, D. A., B. N. Meffert, K. Read, and A. J. Heinz. 2019. "Culturally Competent Health Care for Sex Workers: An Examination of Myths That Stigmatize Sex-Work and Hinder Access to Care." *Sexual and Relationship Therapy* 34 (3): 355–71. https://doi.org/10.1080/14681994.2019.1574970.

Sax, L. 2002. "How Common Is Intersex? A Response to Anne Fausto-Sterling." *Journal of Sex Research* 39 (3): 174–78. https://doi.org/10.1080/00224490209552139.

Schmitz, R. M., and K. A. Tyler. 2018a. "Contextual Constraints and Choices: Strategic Identity Management Among LGBTQ Youth." *Journal of LGBT Youth* 15 (3): 212–26. https://doi.org/10.1080/19361653.2018.1466754.

——. 2018b. "LGBTQ+ Young Adults on the Street and on Campus: Identity as a Product of Social Context." *Journal of Homosexuality* 65 (2): 197–223. https://doi.org/10.1080/00918369.2017.1314162.

Schneider, R. L., and L. Lester. 2001. *Social Work Advocacy: A New Framework for Action.* Wadsworth/Thomson Learning.

Schueller, S. M., A. C. Glover, A. K. Rufa et al. 2019. "A Mobile Phone-Based Intervention to Improve Mental Health Among Homeless Young Adults: Pilot Feasibility Trial." *Journal of Medical Internet Research* 7 (7): e12347. https://doi.org/10.2196/12347.

Schutt, R. K. 2012. *Investigating the Social World: The Process and Practice of Research*, 7th ed. Sage.

Scott, J. T., J. C. Larson, S. L. Buckingham, K. I. Maton, and M. Crowley. 2019. "Bridging the Research-Policy Divide: Pathways to Engagement and Skill Development." *American Journal of Orthopsychiatry* 89 (4): 434–41. https://doi.org/10.1037/ort0000389.

SCOTUSblog. 2017. "Obergefell v. Hodges." http://www.scotusblog.com/case-files/cases/obergefell-v-hodges/.

Sedgwick, E. K. 1993. *Tendencies*. Duke University Press.

Segal, E. A. 2016. *Social Welfare Policy and Social Programs: A Values Perspective*, 4th ed. Brooks/Cole Cengage Learning.

Semborski, S., A. Srivastava, H. Rhoades, A. Fulginiti, and J. T. Goldbach. 2021. "Burden, Belonging, and Homelessness: Disclosure and Social Network Differences Among LGBTQ Youth Recruited from a Suicide Crisis Service Provider." *Journal of Homosexuality* 69 (5): 894–910. https://doi.org/10.1080/00918369.2021.1898801.

Serovich, J. M., S. M. Craft, P. Toviessi, R. Gangamma, T. McDowell, and E. L. Grafsky. 2008. "A Systematic Review of the Research Base on Sexual Reorientation Therapies." *Journal of Marital & Family Therapy* 34 (2): 227–38. https://doi.org/10.1111/j.1752-0606.2008.00065.x.

Sexton, T. L., and J. F. Alexander. 2000. *Functional Family Therapy*. NCJ 184743. Office of Justice Programs. https://www.ojp.gov/pdffiles1/ojjdp/184743.pdf.

SF LGBT Center. n.d. "Transgender Employment Program." Accessed August 22, 2022. https://www.sfcenter.org/transgender-employment-program-tep/.

Shannon, C. L., E. M. Keizur, A. Fehrenbacher et al. 2019. "Sexually Transmitted Infection Positivity Among Adolescents with or at High-Risk for Human Immunodeficiency Virus Infection in Los Angeles and New Orleans." *Sexually Transmitted Diseases* 46 (11): 737–42. https://doi.org/10.1097/OLQ.0000000000001056.

Shelton, J. 2015. "Transgender Youth Homelessness: Understanding Programmatic Barriers Through the Lens of Cisgenderism." *Children and Youth Services Review* 59: 10–18. https://doi.org/10.1016/j.childyouth.2015.10.006.

——. 2018. "LGBT Youth Homelessness: What Are You Going to Do About It?" *Public Integrity* 20 (6): 542–45. https://doi.org/10.1080/10999922.2018.1441963.

Shelton, J., and L. Bond. 2017. "'It Just Never Worked Out': How Transgender and Gender Expansive Youth Understand Their Pathways Into Homelessness." *Families in Society* 98 (4): 284–91. https://doi.org/10.1606/1044-3894.2017.98.33.

Shelton, J., J. DeChants, K. Bender et al. 2018. "Homelessness and Housing Experiences Among LGBTQ Young Adults in Seven U.S. Cities." *Cityscape* 20 (3): 9–34. https://www.jstor.org/stable/26524870.

Shelton, J., M. A. Wagaman, L. Small, and A. Abramovich. 2018. "I'm More Driven Now: Resilience and Resistance Among Transgender and Gender Expansive Youth and Young Adults Experiencing Homelessness." *International Journal of Transgenderism* 19 (2): 144–57. https://doi.org/10.1080/15532739.2017.1374226.

Sherraden, M. S., B. Slosar, and M. Sherraden. 2002. "Innovation in Social Policy: Collaborative Policy Advocacy." *Social Work* 47 (3): 209–21.

Shidlo, A., and M. Schroeder. 2002. "Changing Sexual Orientation: A Consumers' Report." *Professional Psychology: Research and Practice* 33 (3): 249–59. https://doi.org/10.1037/0735-7028.33.3.249.

Shpiegel, S., and C. Simmel. 2016. "Functional Outcomes Among Sexual Minority Youth Emancipating from the Child Welfare System." *Children and Youth Services Review* 61: 101–8. http://doi.org/10.1016/j.childyouth.2015.12.012.

Siconolfi, D., J. S. Tucker, W. G. Shadel, R. Seelam, and D. Golinelli. 2019. "Health, Homelessness Severity, and Substance Use Among Sexual Minority Youth Experiencing Homelessness: A Comparison of Bisexual Versus Gay and Lesbian Youth." *Journal of Sex Research* 57 (7): 933–42. https://doi.org/10.1080/00224499.2019.1695723.

SIECUS (Sexuality Information and Education Council of the United States). 2018. *Sex Ed & Parental Consent: Opt-In vs. Opt-Out.* https://siecus.org/wp-content/uploads/2018/09/Policy-Brief-Opt-in-v.-Opt-out-Redesign-Draft-09.2018.pdf.

Simons, J. D., M. W. Bahr, and S. M. Ramdas. 2022. "Counselor Competence Gender Identity Scale: Measuring Bias, Knowledge, and Skills Among School Counselors." *Professional School Counseling* 26 (1): 1–15. https://doi.org/10.1177/2156759X221110790.

Singh, A. A., and l. m. dickey. 2017. Introduction to *Affirmative Counseling and Psychological Practice with Transgender and Gender Nonconforming Clients*, ed. A. A. Singh and l. m. dickey. American Psychological Association.

Singh, A. A., S. E. Meng, and A. W. Hansen. 2014. "'I Am My Own Gender': Resilience Strategies of Trans Youth." *Journal of Counseling & Development* 92 (2): 208–18. https://doi.org/10.1002/j.1556-6676.2014.00150.x.

Slesnick, N., G. Erdem, S. Bartle-Haring, and G. S. Brigham. 2013. "Intervention with Substance-Abusing Runaway Adolescents and Their Families: Results of a Randomized Clinical Trial." *Journal of Consulting and Clinical Psychology* 81 (4): 600–614. http://dx.doi.org/10.1037/a0033463.

Slesnick, N., G. Erdem, J. Collins, D. Bantchevska, and H. Katafiasz. 2011. "Predictors of Treatment Attendance Among Adolescent Substance Abusing Runaways: A Comparison of Family and Individual Therapy Modalities." *Journal of Family Therapy* 33: 66–84. https://doi.org/10.1111/j.1467-6427.2010.00530.x.

Slesnick, N., X. Feng, X. Guo et al. 2016. "A Test of Outreach and Drop-In Linkage Versus Shelter Linkage for Connecting Homeless Youth to Services." *Prevention Science* 17 (4): 450–60. https://doi.org/10.1007/s11121-015-0630-3.

Slesnick, N., M. Glassman, R. Garren, P. Toviessi, D. Bantchevska, and P. Dashora. 2008. "How to Open and Sustain a Drop-In Center for Homeless Youth." *Children and Youth Services Review* 30 (7): 727–34. https://doi.org/10.1016/j.childyouth.2007.12.004.

Slesnick, N., X. Guo, B. Brakenhoff, and D. Bantchevska. 2015. "A Comparison of Three Interventions for Homeless Youth Evidencing Substance Use Disorders: Results of a Randomized Clinical Trial." *Journal of Substance Abuse Treatment* 54: 1–13. http://dx.doi.org/10.1016/j.jsat.2015.02.001.

Slesnick, N., and J. L. Prestopnik. 2005. "Ecologically Based Family Therapy Outcome with Substance Abusing Runaway Adolescents." *Journal of Adolescence* 28: 277–98.

——. 2009. "Comparison of Family Therapy Outcome with Alcohol-Abusing, Runaway Adolescents." *Journal of Marital and Family Therapy* 35 (3): 255–77. https://doi.org/10.1111/j.1752-0606.2009.00121.x.

Slesnick, N., J. Zhang, X. Feng, Q. Wu, L. Walsh, and D. H. Granello. 2020. "Cognitive Therapy for Suicide Prevention: A Randomized Pilot with Suicidal Youth Experiencing Homelessness." *Cognitive Therapy and Research* 44: 402–11. https://doi.org/10.1007/s10608-019-10068-1.

SMHAA (Stewart B. McKinney Homeless Assistance Act), H.R.558, 100th Congress. 1987. https://www.congress.gov/bill/100th-congress/house-bill/558.

Social Enterprise Alliance. n.d. "About Us." Accessed January 30, 2022. https://social enterprise.us/about.

Social Security Administration. 1999. "The Foster Care Independence Act of 1999." http://www.ssa.gov/legislation/legis_bulletin_112499.html.

Solari, C. D., A. Shivji, T. de Sousa, R. Watt, and M. Silverbush. 2017. *The 2016 Annual Homeless Assessment Report (AHAR) to Congress: Part 2: Estimates of Homelessness in the United States*. U.S. Department of Housing and Urban Development. https://www.huduser.gov/portal/sites/default/files/pdf/2016-AHAR-Part-2.pdf.

Solorio, M. R., N. G. Milburn, R. E. Weiss, and P. J. Batterham. 2006. "Newly Homeless Youth STD Testing Patterns Over Time." *Journal of Adolescent Health* 39 (3): 443.e9–16. https://doi.org/10.1016/j.jadohealth.2005.12.017.

Souhami, D. 1999. *The Trial of Radclyffe Hall*. Doubleday.

Spicer, S. S. 2010. "Healthcare Needs of the Transgender Homeless Population." *Journal of Gay & Lesbian Mental Health* 14 (4): 320–39. https://doi.org/10.1080/19359705.2010.5 05844.

Spitzer, R. L. 2003. "Can Some Gay Men and Lesbians Change Their Sexual Orientation? 200 Participants Reporting a Change from Homosexual to Heterosexual Orientation." *Archives of Sexual Behavior* 32 (5): 403–17.

——. 2012. "Spitzer Reassesses His 2003 Study of Reparative Therapy of Homosexuality." *Archives of Sexual Behavior* 41: 757. https://doi.org/10.1007/s10508-012-9966-y.

Stack, P. F. 2014. "Longtime Support Group for Gay Mormons Shuts Down." *Salt Lake Tribune*, January 14. https://archive.sltrib.com/article.php?id=57344806&itype=cmsid.

Staller, K. M. 1997. "Homeless and Runaway Youth." In *Child Welfare for the Twenty-First Century: A Handbook of Practices, Policies, and Programs*, ed. G. P. Mallon and P. McCartt Hess. Columbia University Press.

Steinberg, A. M., C. M. Layne, E. C. Briggs et al. 2019. "Benefits of Treatment Completion Over Premature Termination: Findings from the National Child Traumatic Stress Network." *Psychiatry* 82: 113–27. https://doi.org/10.1080/00332747.2018.1560584.

Steinke, J., M. Root-Bowman, S. Estabrook, D. S. Levine, and L. M. Kantor. 2017. "Meeting the Needs of Sexual and Gender Minority Youth: Formative Research on Potential Digital Health Interventions." *Journal of Adolescent Health* 60 (5): 541–48. https://doi.org/10.1016/j.jadohealth.2016.11.023.

Sterzing, P. R., G. A. Ratliff, R. E. Gartner, B. L. McGeough, and K. C. Johnson. 2017. "Social and Ecological Correlates of Polyvictimization Among a National Sample of Transgender, Genderqueer, and Cisgender Sexual Minority Adolescents." *Child Abuse & Neglect* 67: 1–12. https://doi.org/10.1016/j.chiabu.2017.02.017.

Stewart, M., L. Reutter, N. Letourneau, and E. Makwarimba. 2009. "A Support Intervention to Promote Health and Coping Among Homeless Youths." *Canadian Journal of Nursing Research* 41 (2): 55–77.

StopBullying.gov. 2023. "About Us." Accessed June 30, 2023. https://www.stopbullying.gov/about-us.

Storms, M. D. 1980. "Theories of Sexual Orientation." *Journal of Personality and Social Psychology* 38 (5): 783–92. https://doi.org/10.1037//0022-3514.38.5.783.

Sue, D. W. 2010. *Microaggressions in Everyday Life: Race, Gender, and Sexual Orientation.* Wiley.

Sunseri, P. A. 2003. "Predicting Treatment Termination Due to Running Away Among Adolescents in Residential Care." *Residential Treatment for Children & Youth* 21 (2): 43–60.

Tate, C. C., J. N. Ledbetter, and C. P. Youssef. 2013. "A Two-Question Method for Assessing Gender Categories in the Social and Medical Sciences." *Journal of Sex Research* 50 (8): 767–76. https://doi.org/10.1080/00224499.2012.690110.

Teasdale, S. 2012. "Negotiating Tensions: How Do Social Enterprises in the Homelessness Field Balance Social and Commercial Considerations?" *Housing Studies* 27 (4): 514–32. https://doi.org/10.1080/02673037.2012.677015.

Thompson, R. G., C. Aivadyan, M. Stohl, E. Aharonovich, and D. S. Hasin. 2020. "Smartphone Application Plus Brief Motivational Intervention Reduces Substance Use and Sexual Risk Behaviors Among Homeless Young Adults: Results from a Randomized Controlled Trial." *Psychology of Addictive Behaviors* 34 (6): 641–49. https://doi.org/10.1037/adb0000570.

Tobin, R. D. 2015. *Peripheral Desires: The German Discovery of Sex.* University of Pennsylvania Press.

Tompsett, C. J., P. J. Fowler, and P. A. Toro. 2009. "Age Differences Among Homeless Individuals: Adolescence Through Adulthood." *Journal of Prevention & Intervention in the Community* 37 (2): 86–99. https://doi.org/10.1080/10852350902735551.

Toombs, E., C. J. Mushquash, J. Lund et al. 2021. "Adaption and Implementation of the Housing Outreach Program Collaborative (HOP-C) North for Indigenous Youth." *American Journal of Orthopsychiatry* 91 (1): 96–108. https://doi.org/10.1037/ort0000520.

Toomey, R. B., and R. A. Richardson. 2009. "Perceived Sibling Relationships of Sexual Minority Youth." *Journal of Homosexuality* 56 (7): 849–60. https://doi.org/10.1080/00918360903187812.

Tordoff, D. M., J. W. Wanta, A. Collin, C. Stepney, D. J. Inwards-Breland, and K. Ahrens. 2022. "Mental Health Outcomes in Transgender and Nonbinary Youths Receiving Gender-Affirming Care." *JAMA Network Open* 5 (2): e220978. https://doi.org/10.1001/jamanetworkopen.2022.0978.

Toro, P. A., A. Dworsky, and P. J. Fowler. 2007. "Homeless Youth in the United States: Recent Research Findings and Intervention Approaches." Paper presented at the National Symposium on Homelessness Research, Washington, DC, March 1–2. https://aspe.hhs.gov/system/files/pdf/180406/report.pdf.

Tracey, T. J., and A. M. Kokotovic. 1989. "Factor Structure of the Working Alliance Inventory." *Psychological Assessment* 1 (3): 207–10.

Treatment Innovations. n.d. "Seeking Safety." Accessed May 26, 2025. https://www.treatment-innovations.org/seeking-safety.html.

Trevor Project. 2023. *Research Brief: Age of Gender Identity Outness and Suicide Risk.* https://www.thetrevorproject.org/wp-content/uploads/2023/03/March-2023-Research-Brief-Final.pdf.

Trotta, D., and F. Trianna. 2013. "U.S. Group That 'Converted' Gays Closes Its Doors and Apologizes." *Reuters*, June 20. https://www.reuters.com/article/usa-gay-exodus/u-s-group-that-converted-gays-closes-its-doors-and-apologizes-idINDEE95K03520130621.

True Colors United, National Law Center on Homelessness & Poverty. n.d. "LGBTQ Youth: 4 Ways You Can Prepare to Safely Access Housing Services." Accessed January 30, 2022. https://truecolorsunited.org/wp-content/uploads/2020/04/LGBTQ-Youth_-4-Ways-You-Can-Prepare-to-Safely-Access-Housing-Services.pdf.

Tucker, J. S., J. Hu, D. Golinelli, D. P. Kennedy, H. D. Green Jr., and S. L. Wenzel. 2012. "Social Network and Individual Correlates of Sexual Risk Behavior Among Homeless Young Men Who Have Sex with Men." *Journal of Adolescent Health* 51 (4): 386–92. https://doi.org/10.1016/j.jadohealth.2012.01.015.

Tucker, J. S., L. Sebastian, E. R. Pedersen et al. 2021. "Pilot Randomized Clinical Trial of a Text Messaging-Based Intervention for Smoking Cessation Among Young People Experiencing Homelessness." *Nicotine & Tobacco Research* 23 (10): 1691–98. https://doi.org/10.1093/ntr/ntab055.

Tucker, J. S., W. G. Shadel, D. Golinelli, and B. Ewing. 2014. "Alternative Tobacco Product Use and Smoking Cessation Among Homeless Youth in Los Angeles County." *Nicotine & Tobacco Research* 16 (11): 1522–26. https://doi.org/10.1093/ntr/ntu133.

Tyler, K. A. 2008. "A Comparison of Risk Factors for Sexual Victimization Among Gay, Lesbian, Bisexual, and Heterosexual Homeless Young Adults." *Violence and Victims* 23 (5): 586–602. https://doi.org/10.1891/0886-6708.23.5.586.

——. 2013. "Homeless Youths' HIV Risk Behaviors with Strangers: Investigating the Importance of Social Networks." *Archives of Sexual Behavior* 42 (8): 1583–91. https://doi.org/10.1007/s10508-013-0091-3.

Tyler, K. A., S. L. Akinyemi, and L. A. Korty-Butler. 2012. "Correlates of Service Utilization Among Homeless Youth." *Children and Youth Services Review* 34 (7): 1344–50. https://doi.org/10.1016/j.childyouth.2012.03.010.

Tyler, K., L. Melander, and E. Almazan. 2010. "Self Injurious Behavior Among Homeless Young Adults: A Social Stress Analysis." *Social Science & Medicine* 70 (2): 269–76. https://doi.org/10.1016/j.socscimed.2009.10.008.

Tyler, K. A., K. Olson, and C. M. Ray. 2019. "Understanding Daily Depression, Drinking, and Marijuana Use Among Homeless Youth Using Short Messaging Service Surveying." *Journal of Child & Adolescent Substance Abuse* 28 (3): 170–79. https://doi.org/10.1080/1067828X.2019.1667286.

Tyler, K. A., and C. M. Ray. 2019. "Risk and Protective Factors for Substance Use Among Youth Experiencing Homelessness." *Children and Youth Services Review* 107: 1045–48. https://doi.org/10.1016/j.childyouth.2019.104548.

Tyler, K. A., and R. M. Schmitz. 2018a. "Bullying at School and on the Street: Risk Factors and Outcomes Among Homeless Youth." *Journal of Interpersonal Violence* 36 (9/10): NP4768-NP4787. https://doi.org/10.1177/0886260518794024.

——. 2018b. "A Comparison of Risk Factors for Various Forms of Trauma in the Lives of Lesbian, Gay, Bisexual and Heterosexual Homeless Youth." *Journal of Trauma & Dissociation* 19 (4): 431–43. https://doi.org/10.1080/15299732.2018.1451971.

Tyler, K. A., L. B. Whitbeck, D. R. Hoyt, and A. M. Cauce. 2004. "Risk Factors for Sexual Victimization Among Male and Female Homeless and Runaway Youth." *Journal of Interpersonal Violence* 19 (5): 503–20. https://doi.org/10.1177/0886260504262961.

Tyler, K. A., L. B. Whitbeck, D. R. Hoyt, and K. D. Johnson. 2003. "Self-Mutilation and Homeless Youth: The Role of Family Abuse, Street Experiences, and Mental Disorders." *Journal of Research on Adolescence* 13 (4): 457–74. https://doi.org/10.1046/j.1532-7795.2003.01304003.x.

UN (United Nations). 1948. *Universal Declaration of Human Rights.* https://www.un.org/sites/un2.un.org/files/2021/03/udhr.pdf.

——. 2015. *Resolution Adopted by the General Assembly on 25 September 2015: 70/1. Transforming Our World: The 2030 Agenda for Sustainable Development.* https://docs.un.org/en/A/RES/70/1.

Unger, J. B., M. D. Kipke, T. R. Simon, S. B. Montgomery, and C. J. Johnson. 1997. "Homeless Youths and Young Adults in Los Angeles: Prevalence of Mental Health Problems and the Relationship Between Mental Health and Substance Use Disorders." *American Journal of Community Psychology* 25 (3): 371–94. https://doi.org/10.1023/a:1024680727864.

University of Michigan. n.d. "Intergroup Relations: CommonGround." Accessed October 30, 2024. https://igr.umich.edu/commonground.

University of Minnesota. n.d. "Eli Coleman Institute for Sexual and Gender Health." Accessed June 30, 2023. https://med.umn.edu/sexualhealth.

University of Minnesota. n.d. "Trans Advisory & Action Team." Accessed May 26, 2025. https://gsc.umn.edu/programs/trans-advisory-action-team-taat.

U.S. Bureau of Labor Statistics. 2023. "Table 2. Labor Force Status of Persons 16 to 24 Years Old by School Enrollment, Educational Attainment, Sex, Race, and Hispanic or Latino Ethnicity, October 2023." https://www.bls.gov/news.release/hsgec.t02.htm.

U.S. Census Bureau. n.d.a. "Selected Population Profile in the United States—Table S0201: 2023 ACS 1-Year Estimates Selected Population Profiles." Accessed October 16, 2024. https://data.census.gov/table/ACSSPP1Y2023.S0201?q=puerto%20rican&g=160XX00US3651000.

——. n.d.b. "Table DP02: Selected Social Characteristics in the United States: 2020: ACS 5-Year Estimates Data Profiles: New York City, New York." Accessed August 2, 2022. https://data.census.gov/cedsci/table?q=Native%20and%20Foreign%20Born%20new%20york%20city&tid=ACSDP5Y2020.DP02.

——. 2020. "Annual Estimates of the Resident Population by Sex, Age, Race, and Hispanic Origin for the United States: April 1, 2010 to July 1, 2019. https://www2.census.gov/programs-surveys/popest/tables/2010-2019/national/asrh/nc-est2019-asr6h.xlsx.

U.S. Department of Education. 2016. *Education for Homeless Children and Youths Program Non-Regulatory Guidance: Title VII-B of the McKinney–Vento Homeless Assistance Act, as Amended by the Every Student Succeeds Act.* https://www.ed.gov/sites/ed/files/policy/elsec/leg/essa/160240ehcyguidance072716.pdf.

——. 2017. *Education for Homeless Children and Youths Program Non-Regulatory Guidance.* https://www2.ed.gov/policy/elsec/leg/essa/160240ehcyguidance072716updated0317.pdf.

U.S. Department of Justice. 2015. "The Matthew Shepard and James Byrd, Jr., Hate Crimes Prevention Act of 2009." https://www.justice.gov/crt/matthew-shepard-and-james-byrd-jr-hate-crimes-prevention-act-2009-0.

U.S. Department of Labor. 2017. "Executive Order 11246: Regulations Prohibiting Discrimination Based on Sexual Orientation and Gender Identity." Internet Archive. https://web.archive.org/web/20200426194002/https://www.dol.gov/agencies/ofccp/executive-order-11246.

U.S. Office of Civil Rights. 2023. "Executive Orders on Diversity, Equity, Inclusion and Accessibility." Internet Archive. https://web.archive.org/web/20230729190757/https://www.commerce.gov/cr/programs-and-services/executive-orders-diversity-equity-inclusion-and-accessibility.

USD (University of San Diego). 2015. "Jhette Diamond's Emancipation." USD News Center. https://www.sandiego.edu/news/law/detail.php?_focus=52607.

USDHUD (U.S. Department of Housing and Urban Development). 2015. "Determining Homeless Status of Youth." https://www.hudexchange.info/resource/4783/determining-homeless-status-of-youth/.

——. 2017. "Youth Homelessness." https://www.hudexchange.info/homelessness-assistance/resources-for-homeless-youth/.

——. 2022. "Housing Discrimination and Persons Identifying as Lesbian, Gay, Bisexual, Transgender, and/or Queer/Questioning (LGBTQ)." Internet Archive. https://web.archive.org/web/20220804164435/https://www.hud.gov/program_offices/fair_housing_equal_opp/housing_discrimination_and_persons_identifying_lgbtq#_Fair_Housing_Act.

——. 2023a. "During Pride Month, HUD Launches Initiative to Address LGBTQI+ Youth Homelessness." Press release, June 8. Internet Archive. https://web.archive.org/web/20240930060822/https://www.hud.gov/press/press_releases_media_advisories/HUD_No_23_112.

——. 2023b. HUD 2023 Continuum of Care Homeless Assistance Programs Homeless Populations and Subpopulations. https://files.hudexchange.info/reports/published/CoC_PopSub_NatlTerrDC_2023.pdf.

USICH (U.S. Interagency Council on Homelessness). 2015. Preventing and Ending Youth Homelessness: A Coordinated Community Response. https://www.csb.org/cdn/files-YouthHomelessnessCoordinatedResponse.pdf.

——. 2018. Criteria and Benchmarks for Achieving the Goal of Ending Youth Homelessness. https://www.usich.gov/sites/default/files/document/Youth-Criteria-and-Benchmarks-revised-Feb-2018.pdf.

Van Leeuwen, J. M., S. Boyle, S. Salomonsen-Sautel et al. 2006. "Lesbian, Gay, and Bisexual Homeless Youth: An Eight-City Public Health Perspective." Child Welfare 85 (2): 151–70.

Vaughan, R. 2017. "Oversampling in Health Surveys: Why, When, and How?" American Journal of Public Health 107 (8): 1214–15. https://doi.org/10.2105/AJPH.2017.303895.

Vitopoulos, N., L. C. Lielburger, T. J. Frederick, K. McKenzie, and S. A. Kidd. 2017. "Developing a Trauma-Informed Mental Health Group Intervention for Youth Transitioning from Homelessness." Professional Psychology: Research and Practice 48 (6): 499–509. http://dx.doi.org/10.1037/pro0000168.

Wagner, D. 2010. *Nowhere to Go: Issue Brief on Gay and Transgender Youth Homelessness.* Center for American Progress. https://cdn.americanprogress.org/wp-content/uploads/issues/2010/08/pdf/nowhere_to_go.pdf.

Wagner, L. S., L. Carlin, A. M. Cauce, and A. Tenner. 2001. "A Snapshot of Homeless Youth in Seattle: Their Characteristics, Behaviors and Beliefs About HIV." *Journal of Community Health* 26 (3): 219–32. https://doi.org/10.1023/A:1010325329898.

Walls, N. E., and S. Bell. 2011. "Correlates of Engaging in Survival Sex Among Homeless Youth and Young Adults." *Journal of Sex Research* 48 (5): 423–36. https://doi.org/10.1080/00224499.2010.501916.

Walls, N. E., J. Laser, S. J. Nickels, and H. Wisneski. 2010. "Correlates of Cutting Behavior Among Sexual Minority Youths and Young Adults." *Social Work Research* 34 (4): 213–26. https://doi.org/10.1093/swr/34.4.213.

Walls, N. E., C. Potter, and J. Van Leeuwen. 2009. "Where Risks and Protective Factors Operate Differently: Homeless Sexual Minority Youth and Suicide Attempts." *Child & Adolescent Social Work Journal* 26 (3): 235–57. https://doi.org/10.1007/s10560-009-0172-2.

Ward, V., A. House, and S. Hamer. 2009. "Knowledge Brokering: The Missing Link in the Evidence to Action Chain." *Evidence & Policy* 5 (3): 267–79. https://doi.org/10.1332/174426409X463811.

Warf, C., K. Gharabaghi, G. Charles, and K. Ginsburg. 2020. "Interviewing Homeless Adolescents in the Context of Clinical Care: Creating Connections, Building on Strengths, Fostering Resilience, and Improving Outcomes." In *Clinical Care for Homeless, Runaway and Refugee Youth: Intervention Approaches, Education and Research Directions*, ed. C. Warf and G. Charles. Springer.

Weeks, A., D. Altman, A. Stevens, J. Lorthridge, and L. Heaton. 2018. "Strengthening the Workforce to Support Youth in Foster Care Who Identify as LGBTQ+ Through Increasing LGBTQ+ Competency: Trainers' Experience with Bias, a Preliminary Evaluation." *Child Welfare* 96 (2): 125–50.

Weeks, J. 1977. *Coming Out: Homosexual Politics in Britain from the Nineteenth Century to the Present.* Quartet.

Weick, A., C. Rapp, W. P. Sullivan, and W. Kisthardt. 1989. "A Strengths Perspective for Social Work Practice." *Social Work* 34 (4): 350–54.

Weinberg, M. S., C. J. Williams, and D. W. Pryor. 1994. *Dual Attraction: Understanding Bisexuality.* Oxford University Press.

——. 2001. "Bisexuals at Midlife: Commitment, Salience, and Identity." *Journal of Contemporary Ethnography* 30 (2): 180–208. https://doi.org/10.1177/089124101030002002.

Wenzel, A., G. K. Brown, and A. T. Beck. 2009. *Cognitive Therapy for Suicidal Patients: Scientific and Clinical Applications.* American Psychological Association.

Wenzel, A., and S. Jager-Hyman. 2012. "Cognitive Therapy for Suicidal Patients: Current Status." *Behavior Therapist* 35 (7): 121–30.

Wenzel, S. L., J. S. Tucker, D. Golinelli, H. D. Green Jr., and A. Zhou. 2010. "Personal Network Correlates of Alcohol, Cigarette, and Marijuana Use Among Homeless Youth." *Drug and Alcohol Dependence* 112 (1–2): 140–49. https://doi.org/10.1016/j.drugalcdep.2010.06.004.

Wernick, L. J., A. Kulick, and M. R. Woodford. 2014. "How Theater Within a Transformative Organizing Framework Cultivates Individual and Collective Empowerment Among LGBTQQ Youth." *Journal of Community Psychology* 42 (3): 838–54. https://doi.org/10.1002/jcop.21656.

Whitbeck, L. B., X. Chen, D. R. Hoyt, K. A. Tyler, and K. D. Johnson. 2004. "Mental Disorder, Subsistence Strategies, and Victimization Among Gay, Lesbian, and Bisexual Homeless and Runaway Adolescents." *Journal of Sex Research* 41 (4): 329–42. https://doi.org/10.1080/00224490409552240.

Wiessner, D. 2025. "Explainer: Why Trump is Ending Enforcement of Civil Rights Laws That Ban 'Disparate Impact.'" *Reuters.* https://www.reuters.com/world/us/why-trump-is-ending-enforcement-civil-rights-laws-that-ban-disparate-impact-2025-05-05/.

Wilbur, S., C. Ryan, and J. Marksamer. 2006. *Best Practice Guidelines: Serving LGBT Youth in Out-of-Home Care.* National Center for Lesbian Rights. https://www.nclrights.org/wp-content/uploads/2013/07/bestpracticeslgbtyouth.pdf.

Wilder Research. 2005. *Homeless Youth in Minnesota: 2003 Statewide Survey of People Without Permanent Shelter.* https://homelesshub.ca/resource/homeless-youth-minnesota-2003-statewide-survey-people-without-permanent-shelter/.

William Bridges Associates. n.d. "Bridges Transition Model." Accessed May 26, 2025. https://wmbridges.com/about/what-is-transition/.

Wilson, B. D. M., K. Cooper, A. Kastanis, and S. Nezhad. 2014. *Sexual and Gender Minority Youth in Foster Care: Assessing Disproportionality and Disparities in Los Angeles.* Williams Institute. http://williamsinstitute.law.ucla.edu/wp-content/uploads/LAFYS_report_final-aug-2014.pdf.

Wiltz, T. 2015. "Anti-Panhandling Laws Spread, Face Legal Challenges." Pew Trusts. https://www.pewtrusts.org/en/research-and-analysis/blogs/stateline/2015/11/12/anti-panhandling-laws-spread-face-legal-challenges.

Winiarski, D. A., A. K. Rufa, D. T. Bounds, A. C. Glover, K. A. Hill, and N. S. Karnik. 2020. "Assessing and Treating Complex Mental Health Needs Among Homeless Youth in a Shelter-Based Clinic." *BMC Health Services Research* 20 (1). https://doi.org/10.1186/s12913-020-4953-9.

WPATH (World Professional Association for Transgender Health). 2016. *Position Statement on Medical Necessity of Treatment, Sex Reassignment, and Insurance Coverage in the U.S.A.* https://wpath.org/wp-content/uploads/2024/11/WPATH-Position-on-Medical-Necessity-12-21-2016.pdf.

Woronoff, R., R. Estrada, and S. Sommer. 2006. *A Report on Regional Listening Forums Highlighting the Experiences of Lesbian, Gay, Bisexual, Transgender, and Questioning Youth in Care.* Lambda Legal. https://www.lambdalegal.org/sites/default/files/publications/downloads/out-of-the-margins.pdf.

Wright, E. R., B. K. Attell, and E. Ruel. 2017. "Social Support Networks and the Mental Health of Runaway and Homeless Youth." *Social Sciences* 6 (4): 117. https://doi.org/10.3390/socsci6040117.

Wright, J. D., T. L. Allen, and J. A. Devine. 1995. "Tracking Non-Traditional Populations in Longitudinal Studies." *Evaluation and Program Planning* 18 (3): 267–77. https://doi.org/10.1016/S0149-7189(95)00020-8.

Yates, G. L., R. MacKenzie, J. Pennbridge, and E. Cohen. 1988. "A Risk Profile Comparison of Runaway and Non-Runaway Youth." *American Journal of Public Health* 78 (7): 820–21. https://doi.org/10.2105/ajph.78.7.820.

Young, J. F., L. Mufson, and C. M. Schueler. 2016. *Preventing Adolescent Depression: Interpersonal Psychotherapy–Adolescent Skills Training*. Oxford Academic.

Youth.gov. n.d.a. "About Us." Internet Archive. Accessed August 3, 2022. https://web.archive.org/web/20220801184318/https://youth.gov/about-us.

——. n.d.b. "Physical and Reproductive Health." Internet Archive. Accessed January 9, 2020. https://web.archive.org/web/20240522021808/https://youth.gov/youth-topics/homelessness-and-housing-instability/physical-and-reproductive-health.

——. n.d.c. "Positive Youth Development." Internet Archive. Accessed May 18, 2019. https://web.archive.org/web/20190414124300/https://youth.gov/youth-topics/positive-youth-development.

YouthBuild. n.d. "Our Core Elements: Education." Accessed December 28, 2017. https://youthbuild.org/why-youthbuild/core-elements/#education.

Yu, V. 2010. "Shelter and Transitional Housing for Transgender Youth." *Journal of Gay & Lesbian Mental Health* 14 (4): 340–45. https://doi.org/10.1080/19359705.2010.504476

Yule, M. A., L. A. Brotto, and B. B. Gorzalka. 2015. "A Validated Measure of No Sexual Attraction: The Asexuality Identification Scale." *Psychological Assessment* 27 (1): 148–60. https://doi.org/10.1037/a0038196.

Zhang, J., and N. Slesnick. 2018. "Substance Use and Social Stability of Homeless Youth: A Comparison of Three Interventions." *Psychology of Addictive Behaviors* 32 (8): 873–84. http://dx.doi.org/10.1037/adb0000424.

Zook, T. 2017. "Promising Pedagogy: Advancing the Educational Experience of Queer Students Through Transformative Leadership." *Journal of Homosexuality* 64 (13): 1755–77. https://doi.org/10.1080/00918369.2016.1267462.

Zuckerman, M. 2005. *Psychobiology of Personality*, 2nd ed. Cambridge University Press.

Index

GPSR Authorized Representative: Easy Access System Europe, Mustamäe tee
50, 10621 Tallinn, Estonia, gpsr.requests@easproject.com

www.ingramcontent.com/pod-product-compliance
Lightning Source LLC
Chambersburg PA
CBHW021847020426
42334CB00013B/219